The British musical film

MANCHESTER
1824

Manchester University Press

The British musical film

John Mundy

Manchester University Press
Manchester and New York
distributed exclusively in the USA by Palgrave

Published by Manchester University Press
Oxford Road, Manchester M13 9NR, UK
and Room 400, 175 Fifth Avenue, New York, NY 10010, USA
www.manchesteruniversitypress.co.uk

Distributed exclusively in the USA by
Palgrave, 175 Fifth Avenue, New York,
NY 10010, USA

Distributed exclusively in Canada by
UBC Press, University of British Columbia, 2029 West Mall, Vancouver, BC, Canada V6T 1Z2

British Library Cataloguing-in-Publication Data
A catalogue record for this book is available from the British Library

Library of Congress Cataloging-in-Publication Data applied for

ISBN   978 0 7190 6320 6 *hardback*
ISBN   97 80 7190 6321 3 *paperback*

First published 2007

16 15 14 13 12 11 10 09 08 07   10 9 8 7 6 5 4 3 2 1

Typeset
by SNP Best-set Typesetter Ltd., Hong Kong
Printed in Great Britain
by Biddles Ltd, King's Lynn

Contents

Illustrations   *page* vii

Acknowledgements   ix

Introduction   1

1 Reclaiming the silence   11

2 The 1930s: a most musical of decades   33

3 The 1940s: constructing communities   84

4 The 1950s: from tradition to innovation   145

5 The 1960s: youth, home-grown talent and American money   181

6 The 1970s and beyond: signs of success   221

Postscript   255

Bibliography   258

Index   269

Illustrations

1 Kingsway Cinema, Levenshulme, Manchester:
Programme brochure, 1934. *Sleepless Nights* –
A musical starring Stanley Lupino and Polly Walker,
with music by Noel Gay   128

2 Kingsway Cinema, Levenshulme, Manchester:
Programme brochure, 1934. *For the Love of Mike*
and *The Mask of Fu Manchu*   129

3 Broadway, Eccles, Manchester: Programme brochure,
1932. *Happy Ever After*   130

4 From the same: Broadway, Eccles, Manchester: Programme
brochure, 1932. *Happy Ever After* and *The Ghost Train*   131

5 Pavilion Theatre, Liverpool: Programme brochure, 1934.
Radio Week!   132

6 Pavilion Theatre, Liverpool: Programme brochure, 1934.
Alfredo and his Gypsy Band   133

7 Vera Lynn, sheet music cover for 'Be Like The Kettle
And Sing', from the film *We'll Meet Again*   134

8 Vera Lynn, sheet music cover for 'I Love To Sing', from
the film *Rhythm Serenade*   135

9 Arthur Askey, sheet music cover for 'I'm Only Me', from
the film *Miss London Ltd*   136

10 Arthur Askey, sheet music cover for 'Happy Days –
Happy Months – Happy Years', from the stage musical
The Love Racket (music by Noel Gay)   137

11 Flanagan and Allen, sheet music cover for 'We'll Smile
Again', from the film *We'll Smile Again*   138

12 *Popular Music and Dancing Weekly*, Volume 1, Number 1,
October 1934   139

13 *Popular Music and Dancing Weekly*. 'Ooh! That Tiger
Harry!', Gossip column on band-leader Harry Roy   140

14 Jessie Matthews advert for Lux Soap, *Radio Times*,
7 May 1937   141

15 *King's Rhapsody* (from *ABC Film Review* January 1956)   142

16 *Oh . . . Rosalinda!!* (from *ABC Film Review* January 1956)   143

17 *The Duke Wore Jeans* (from *ABC Film Review* April 1958)   144

Acknowledgements

It is commonplace to thank fellow academics and teachers for their part in seeing a book through from conception to fruition. Unfortunately, the neglect of the musical film within British cinema is so total that I have rarely been able to discuss my enthusiasm for the subject with others who share my interest. However, I am grateful to my colleagues in Film and Media within the Department of Humanities at the University of Central Lancashire for listening to me without pronouncing my insanity. I am grateful to the University of Central Lancashire for a period of research leave that enabled me to complete this book, and for colleagues who proved, in my absence, just how dispensable I really am. Invidious as it is to single out individuals, thanks go to Mick Gornall for taking over the many administrative responsibilities that go with teaching in British higher education. I can never thank Professor David Mayer of The University of Manchester enough for his support and continuing belief in me. Thanks, too, to Matthew Frost at Manchester University Press for his by now legendary – but hugely productive – patience and support. Thanks go, above all, to my wife, best friend and partner Karen, to my daughters Ellyn and Alice, and to Simon, who shares the agony and ecstasy involved in supporting Crewe Alexandra F.C.

Introduction

Writing in 1947, the British film music critic John Huntley made it clear that, while he recognised the popularity and commercial success enjoyed by the Hollywood musical, he had little regard for something he regarded as essentially 'vulgar escapism'. Though extolling the virtues of film scores by contemporary British composers such as William Walton, Ralph Vaughan Williams and William Alwyn, and praising the work of British film musical directors such as Muir Mathieson, Louis Levy and Ernest Irving, Huntley showed little regard for the British film musical:

> Britain is backward in the production of musical films in the Hollywood sense. We just do not seem to understand the technique of the big, Technicolored, Betty Grable Super-Musical. Of course, in some cases we have no equipment available to tackle this type of production, but we do have the talent, the orchestras and occasionally the big sound stages necessary for this sort of picture. Many attempts have been made over here, but none have so far been up to Hollywood standards. (Huntley 1947: 10)

With some rare exceptions, Huntley dismissed British film musicals, seeing them as at best insipid imitations of the Hollywood product. Compared to what he regarded as significant films emerging from the British film industry, 'the slick modern musical is our most unsatisfactory product at present' (Huntley 1947: 16).

If anything, the contribution and significance of the British film musical has been subject to greater disdain and neglect since Huntley wrote about the specific situation in the 1940s. With a few notable exceptions, the terms 'British' and 'musical film' have been treated by critics as ineluctably incongruous. True, these exceptions are considered important. The films of Jesse Matthews in the 1930s, particularly *Evergreen* (1934) and *First A Girl* (1935), Powell and Pressburger's *The Red Shoes* (1948) and Carol Reed's *Oliver!* (1968), seem at first glance to stand out like exceptional beacons in an otherwise barren landscape.

Yet, like Francois Truffaut's notorious and unjustified assertion about British cinema, this viewpoint seems wilfully ignorant of the rich history and significance of the British musical film.

This book looks at the British musical film and its relationship with popular entertainment from the 1920s onwards, an area of film and popular culture that suffers from critical neglect. Whilst the musical genre has had some critical attention in recent years, writing on the genre is still comparatively rare and has concentrated on the Hollywood musical. Yet music was always an intrinsic part of the British cinema-going experience, even in the so-called silent era, and the musical film has been important in British film production and exhibition since early experiments with the introduction of synchronised sound in the mid-1920s. Its significance grew in the 1930s when it was both a staple product for domestic consumption and occasionally attempted to compete in the international market. In spite of Huntley's comments, British film studios produced more musicals in 1944, 1945 and 1946 than any other single genre, though the growing dominance of the Hollywood musical from the late 1940s reflected the growing influence of American popular culture in Britain. The influence of American popular music increased from the late 1930s and early 1940s, affecting the market for those British musicals featuring distinctively British musical artists and musical traditions, as British audience tastes were increasingly seduced by Hollywood films and American popular music idioms. Yet production of British musical films continued, influenced by American popular culture, but with formal, aesthetic and thematic qualities that marked them as distinctive. Like their American counterparts, British musicals of the late 1950s and 1960s were forced to confront the emergence of a youth culture centred largely if not exclusively on young people's identification with new and emergent forms of popular music. Like its Hollywood counterpart, from the 1970s onwards the British musical film adopted forms and styles that differed from previous decades, but still promoted the importance of popular music and musical performance on screen.

Discussion of British cinema invariably locates it in its relationship with the American film industry, its films and their meanings. In particular, the conflation of the musical genre and the seductive ideology of 'Americanness' is something that dominates critical discussion of the musical. Writing about Broadway musicals of the 1940s such as *Oklahoma*, *Carousel* and *South Pacific*, all of them to become important Hollywood film musicals in the following decade, Ethan Mordden concludes that '[t]he Musical *is* America: democratic, fast-moving, innovative' (Mordden 1999: 270). Summarising the critical attention paid by scholars to the film musical, Steve Cohan notes that the genre is conventionally regarded as 'the quintessential expression of Americanness' (Cohan 2002: 14). This view, that the film musical is somehow ineluctably and rather exclusively an American cultural form, is reinforced in a recent textbook assertion that the musical is a genre that is irrevocably identified with Hollywood (Pearson and Simpson 2001). The most influential analyses of the musical genre have been based on the Hollywood product and its specific forms and sensibilities. For Dyer, the Hollywood musical constructs its essentially utopian sensibility through categories he labels as energy, abundance, intensity, transparency and community, all of which are related to specific inadequacies in society, and work by drawing attention to the gap between what is and what may be, resolving the gap in a positive and optimistic resolution (Dyer 1992). In this way, for example, the energy expressed in a song and dance number dispels the exhaustion associated with the problems of daily existence, a community is brought together through collective action and resists the threats of fragmentation posed by economic or other pressures. Altman's impeccable analysis of the structure and style of the American musical and his sub-generic categorisations of the Fairy Tale, Show Business and the Folk musical work well for the classical Hollywood product, but are less relevant both to more recent developments within the American genre and the musical film from elsewhere (Altman 1989).

The economic, cultural and critical hegemony exercised by the American musical, in particular the dominance of the so-called 'classical' Hollywood musical, has until recently effaced the significance, even the very existence, of musical film within other national cinemas. While not necessarily conforming to the generic conventions we have come to associate with the Hollywood musical, films that draw upon and valorise cinematic constructions of music, song and dance are important in other national cinemas. Song sequences and dance have been central to commercial Hindi cinema since the introduction of the first Indian 'talkie' in 1931 and continue to be attractive in contemporary 'Bollywood' (Majumdar 2001). Musical films flourished in such unlikely circumstances as Stalin's Soviet Union from the 1930s into the 1950s, Franco's Spain, and in communist East Germany in the 1950s and 1960s. However, the generic conventions we associate with the Hollywood musical remain of limited use in understanding either the form or meaning of these distinctive musical films.

This process of effacement has been particularly damaging to our understanding of British cinema generally and, in particular, the British musical film. Since the 1960s, British cinema has become much more 'known' through a process of critical recuperation that has focussed not just on notions of national cinema and national identity, but on the distinctive aesthetics of a British cinema which is seen to be, when judged by appropriate criteria, rich, diverse and interesting. Though acknowledging the importance of the realist tradition in British cinema, much recent critical work on British cinema is at pains to celebrate its non-realist or anti-realist tradition, articulated through genres such as comedy, horror, melodrama or costume drama (Murphy 1989, Landy 1991, Cook 1996, Cook 1997). Curiously, the scholarly archaeology that has unearthed this rich diversity and helped begin to construct appropriate critical paradigms for both engaging with and celebrating British film has not extended to the British musical film and its distinctive treatment of spectacle, excess and fantasy, constructed through visual and sonic 'impossibilities'.

Though British cinema cannot be understood without referencing its relationship with Hollywood, it remains distinct from the American product. Yet, unlike Hindi musicals or musicals produced in the Soviet bloc in the 1960s with their evident formal, aesthetic and ideological differences from the Hollywood musical, defining the distinctive qualities of the British film musical is much more difficult, not least because of American involvement in British film production, distribution and exhibition, articulated in terms of ownership, finance and a cross-fertilisation of talent. While a comprehensive history of the transatlantic traffic between the two production industries remains to be written, that traffic existed from the early days of both industries. Quite apart from the presence of American studios with a production base in Britain, American directors, actors, songwriters and choreographers came to work in Britain. British companies attempted to assail the American market and British actors, directors and technicians were constantly working in America and often used what they had learnt when working on British productions.

While retaining a distinctive form, aesthetic and ideology, American influence has meant that British musical films have laboured under a double colonisation, firstly through ideological and aesthetic subordination to the Hollywood musical and the dominant critical discourses that surround it and, secondly, through economic subordination, so that for many years British musical films often occupied a supporting role in cinema programmes, either as 'B' features or as short programme fillers. One problem in defining British national cinema, and particularly the British musical film, is that the majority of films watched by British audiences in British cinemas are American. By the 1950s, the musicals that audiences in Britain saw were overwhelmingly American, itself an indication of the growing hegemonic power of American popular culture in that decade (Lacey 1999).

It is tempting to give some weight to the view that a national cinema can be defined by the films that audiences consume (Sorlin 1996), but this does nothing to explain the distinctive qualities of the British film musical and only serves to efface those significant exceptions when British product has been what British audiences wanted to see, and not only at times when there was a shortage of American product in British cinemas. From the 1930s onwards, a number of domestically successful British musical films achieved distribution in America, though broader and recurrent issues around the difficulties associated with the exhibition of British films in the American market meant that very few made a significant impact on American audiences.

In his attempt to account for differences between American film stars and their rather more understated and under-celebrated British counterparts, Bruce Babington locates the distinction deep within cultural differences between Britain and the United States:

> British culture was undoubtedly in the first half of the century more tradition-oriented, more class-bound, and less materially wealthy. It was equally different in the second half of the century as it adapted with difficulty to its shrunken prestige, its loss of Empire but confusing new gaining of a multiculture, its middling economic power status and the apparent dissolution of a middle-class hegemony into an anxious fluidity. (Babington 2001: 19)

Babington's comments suggest that an underlying diffidence characterises not just British cinema, but also the critical discourse that surrounds it. As I argue in this book, an element of self-deprecation, evident in so much of British film culture, plays an important role in both the construction and reception of the British musical film. This lack of confidence in the British product, the tendency to compare British film unfavourably with its American counterpart, clearly has implications for a genre that is supposedly imbued with exuberant optimism and an underlying utopian sensibility. The implications of this sense of cultural difference for British cinema have long been recognised. Looking back in 1951 over a lengthy career, early British film pioneer Cecil Hepworth remained convinced of the need for British cinema to develop its own distinctive qualities, whatever the influence of the American film industry:

> When the Transatlantic films began to get a stranglehold upon the trade over here it came to be generally assumed that the American method and style of production was the reason for their success, and a great majority

of our producers set about to try to imitate them. The Americans have their own idiom in picture making just as they have their own accent in speaking. It is not necessarily better than ours and it cannot successfully be copied. We have our own idiom too which they could not copy if they tried. It is our part to develop along the lines which are our heritage, and only in that way can we be true to ourselves and to those qualities which are ours. (Hepworth 1951: 144)

Having criticised the British film musical for failing to imitate the Hollywood product, John Huntley suggested that to compare the two was actually rather redundant:

> Of course, it is questionable whether we even want to rival Hollywood in this type of production. We have evolved our own strong line and have no need to enter this foreign field. But it is possible that eventually we shall evolve our own special type of musical, as they have done in Russia and France, and that there will be the Hollywood musical and the Denham musical – two entirely different forms of cinema. (Huntley 1947: 98)

While both Hepworth and Huntley accepted the economic grip exercised on British cinema by the American film industry, they argued for British film as a space to articulate specific cultural distinctions. Though 'the Denham musical' never attained the status that Huntley fantasised about, British musical films that are different from the Hollywood product in a number of ways were produced across the decades.

It is possible to recognise something of the British film musical in these analyses by Dyer and Altman. In films as different as *I'll Be Your Sweetheart* (1945), *The Young Ones* (1962) and *The Commitments* (1992) energy, abundance, and the construction of community are clearly evident and all three evince some resemblance to Altman's subgeneric classifications. Yet, for all the illuminating benefits of critical work on the American musical, it has hampered an appreciation of the British film musical and of the specific generic inflections that characterise it. If, for example, a sense of optimism, energy and abundance are said to characterise the classical Hollywood musical, we need to start from an acknowledgement that British musicals are perhaps simply less optimistic, less energetic, less abundant and fulsome. In the British musical, utopia is often, at best, tentative, constrained by an awareness of the realities of class and region. If British musicals are exuberant, they are so in ways that differ from the exuberance associated with the American musical. Moreover, we perhaps need to come to terms with the fact that the British industrial infrastructure was never as supportive of musicals as was Hollywood, that the creative talent in terms of direction, choreography, musical composition, and lyrics lacked depth and breadth when compared with the very best American talent. With a few exceptions, the British film musical did not produce stars with cross-national marketing appeal, and the exceptions often found themselves working in Hollywood. Above all, we need to remind ourselves that British cinema is essentially a low-budget cinema, subject to important economic dictates. This difference is expressed in a number of ways, from overall production values to the clipped pronunciation of song lyrics and restrained orchestration so evident in many British musical films.

Such distinctions, however subtle, are compounded by problems in defining the British musical film, taking into account such issues as finance, of production staff, the personnel working on a film, of where a film was shot. A number of European musical co-productions that emerged in the 1930s are considered to be British films, such as Associated Sound Film Industries' trilingual production *City Of Song* (1931), even though the film was directed by Italian Carmine Gallone, produced by Austrian Arnold Pressberger with a Hungarian cameraman and a Danish editor, and starred the young Polish tenor Jan Kiepura. On the other hand, Herbert Wilcox's *Irene* (1940) clearly a musical judged by conventional generic criteria, starring British actors Anna Neagle and Ray Milland but produced in America, is not considered a British film. A narrow definition of genre that stems from the dominant classical Hollywood model excludes Terence Davies' films *Distant Voices, Still Lives* (1988) and *The Long Day Closes* (1992) as musicals, despite the important presence of music in constructing both films' regimes of meaning, and the director's own admission that musicals were hugely influential in his work (Everett 2004).

This problem of definition is particularly acute for British musical films produced in the 1930s. Films starring Gracie Fields, George Formby or Leslie Henson are critically recuperable when treated as comedies, though to approach them as such usually reveals nothing about the formal, aesthetic or ideological role that music plays in their films (Sutton 2000). With far less justification, Jesse Matthews' films can be treated as comedies (Sutton 2000) or as melodramas (Landy 1991), but only if we wish to ignore the role of music and dance in the construction of meaning, affect and pleasure. Though Gifford defines a number of films such as Formby's *Feather Your Nest* (1937) and the Crazy Gang's *O-Kay For Sound* (1937) as comedies, they contain sufficient musical content for them to be defined as musical comedies, though many of them stray from conventional generic norms (Gifford 1986). This blurring of hard and fast generic boundaries can lead to problems and contentious choices, but one of the central arguments in

this book concerns the centrality of music in British cinema, a centrality that has been ignored in too many critical studies. The 1950s and
1960s Norman Wisdom comedies sit just outside my broad definition,
but this should not mean that we ignore the role of music within those
films, given Wisdom's important, if brief, career as a 'hit parade' record
artist.

The tendency throughout this book to use the term 'musical film'
rather than 'film musical' reflects the broad definition the subject
deserves. Though some of the films examined here adhere to generic
conventions recognisable from the Hollywood musical, many do not
and contest these conventions in important and distinctive ways. British
cinema and the British musical film developed and were implicated in
specific cultural and aesthetic traditions that valued the literary and theatrical, but also recognised the importance of distinctive musical traditions. British musical culture in the early twentieth century was a
composite that ranged from the robust traditions of music hall, variety,
the 'West End' revue and light operetta, to the classical concert hall, via
a number of regional and class-inflected musical traditions such as brass
band and folk music (Pearsall 1975). Like British cinema, British
musical culture increasingly defined itself with reference to the growing
hegemony of American music, at times absorbing and replicating new
influences, at other times contesting and resisting them. This process
became more pronounced with the coming of synchronised sound in the
1930s, and helps to account for the distinctiveness of the British musical
film.

One of the arguments in this book is that British musicals both drew
upon and articulated important and distinctive aspects of British
national identity, including contentious issues of social class, regionalism, attitudes to youth, as well as gender. Like the notion of a national
cinema, the notion of British national identity is both dynamic and problematic. The earliest British musical films also initially reflected the
strong and distinctive traditions of British popular entertainment, since
they linked the British film industry to other important institutions of
popular entertainment. In the 1920s and 1930s, these included music
hall, variety theatre, the BBC and its radio dance orchestras, the sheet
music publishing industry, and the British gramophone industry. The
talent employed in these early musicals was often talent drawn from
those existing arenas of public entertainment. From the late 1950s, the
film industry drew upon and acknowledged the central importance of
television and the rise of pop music based on sales of records. Across
the decades, film musicals offered a product which was distinctive and
popular with British audiences and, occasionally, with overseas audi-

ences. We misread much cultural history by ignoring ways in which audiences were always positioned within multimedia entertainment landscapes, including film, radio, sheet music, live variety, records and television. At the same time, we need to contest any purist notion of a British national identity, suggesting instead the need to understand British cultural production and consumption as responses to a wide range of regional, national and international influences and determinants.

The decision to structure this examination of the British musical film chronologically by decades is clearly not an inspired one, but it does serve to highlight important shifts in production context as well as engage with wider cultural dynamics. There is an argument for beginning and ending each chapter on the seventh or eighth year of each decade, since events and shifts of major import have tended to occur at that point. The opening chapter argues the case that music was a significant element in the British cinema-going experience even before the commercial development of synchronised sound. In this sense, the introduction of sound needs to be understood as a cost-effective industrial solution to embedded expectations that British audiences had about hearing music at the cinema. The British musical film of the 1930s really deserves a book of its own, but Chapter 2 outlines the distinctive forms that emerged within the musical film during the decade, and examines a few of the films in greater detail to illustrate the variety of forms that characterised the British musical film. The 1940s produced some outstanding British musical films during a period of national crisis and Chapter 3 examines ways in which British films harnessed a broad range of musical talent and tradition in ways that were quite exceptional. Though not overt propaganda, 1940s musical films are remarkable in the extent to which they engage with broader social concerns, though this is something that characterises British musical films across all decades. Chapter 4 focuses on some profound shifts in the British film industry during the 1950s and traces some quite remarkable distinctions between different musical films as, towards the end of the decade, they engaged with emergent popular musical forms and the rise of a youth culture. Chapter 5 attempts to capture something of the excitement that marked British society and culture during the 1960s, arguing that the musical film was as significant as 'New Wave' films in charting quite profound structural changes taking place in Britain, even if its position was often one of conservative resistance. Like its Hollywood counterpart, the British musical film experienced a decline in popularity and some expensive commercial failures in the late 1960s, only for the form to reinvent itself in a number of ways. Chapter 6 examines films produced during the 1970s onwards, and suggests that the musical film retained its distinctive relevance during a period in which popular music became as deeply entrenched in everyday life as it was in the 1930s. Throughout each chapter, I have attempted to address ways in which the British musical film has contributed to debates around identity and to examine the ways in which the films delivered their specific pleasures. I also suggest that a number of films are actually, by whatever criteria we might wish to apply, films of real merit and quality. Occasionally, as with *Oliver!* (1968), this has been recognised in Oscar nominations and awards, but I suggest that a number of British musical films deserve much more than the customary neglect with which they have been treated.

Far from being a definitive account, this book attempts to redress what has been the critical dereliction of an important area of British cinema. The choice of films and, more likely, some significant omissions, will infuriate some. There is still a great deal of research that needs to be done, but I hope that the material in here will at least inspire others to take the British musical film with the seriousness it deserves.

1

Reclaiming the silence

However odd it may appear to begin a study of the British musical film with an examination of British cinema in the two decades *before* the coming of synchronised sound in the late 1920s, there is a reason. Towards the end of that decade, two fulcrum 'events' – one broadly technological, the other broadly political – influenced the pattern for British cinema for years to come. Both these events, the coming of synchronised sound and the legislation that rooted much British production in low-budget 'quota quickies', represented a stage in the changing, complex and often difficult relationship the British film industry had experienced with its American rival since the early 1900s. Both were influential in shaping the distinctive mode and aesthetic of the British musical film from the early 1930s. However, neither low-budget film production nor the transformation to synchronised sound film can be said to represent a radical rupture from practices that characterised British cinema prior to 1927–28. Raising sufficient, even if modest, finance for British film production had always been a recurrent problem. Sound, particularly music, had been part of the pleasures of British cinema-going long before 1928, both as accompaniment to the films themselves and as an additional attraction performed by live singers and other variety acts wrapped around the films. Though far from inevitable, the commercial development of sound cinema represented part of that process of industrial standardisation that was as much a feature of British cinema as any other national cinema; what was highly probable, given its importance to the cinema-going experience of so-called 'silent' cinema, was that music would figure prominently in that process and that the musical film, in all its variety, would become an important part of British cinema.

With the notable exception of the war years 1914–18, British cinema from 1906 and throughout most of the 1920s was seen as a cinema in crisis, beset with problems in both production and exhibition, problems intended to be addressed by the Cinematograph Films Act of 1927. Though the mechanism through which it hoped to achieve its aims centred on distribution and exhibition, establishing yearly increasing sliding-scale quotas for renters and exhibitors, the 1927 Act was primarily designed to protect and promote British film production, savaged by American competition to the point where, in 1925, only 5 per cent of films shown in British cinemas were British, a decline from 25 per cent in 1914. In 1926, only 37 British films were given a trade showing, itself never a guarantee of exhibition. Yet if the decrease in the number of British films being seen in cinemas was a cause for concern, so too was the decrease in cinema attendance from 1917 and throughout the early 1920s, in part a result of the government-imposed Entertainment Duty. For the British Cinematograph Exhibitors Association (CEA), this was a greater worry than any concern about the origin of a film's production. When the Entertainment Duty was amended and partially removed in 1924, cinema attendance the following year increased to an estimated twenty million, matching ticket sales at their peak in 1917. Problems of declining attendance and over-capacity, fuelled by concerns over changing patterns of distribution and the development of 'block-booking', preoccupied the CEA throughout the 1920s and into the 1930s (Hiley 1999).

Clearly, such concerns about production and exhibition policy are essential for informing our understanding of British cinema of the 1920s and, indeed, of any period. However, to understand the cultural significance of cinema – including the ways in which films were received, made an impact, or were ignored and forgotten about – we need to know much more about audiences, about the experiences which going to the cinema entailed. In particular, we need to recognise that an important part of those experiences was, and still is, musical. Nowhere is this more important than in the early years of British cinema where, by concentrating our attention on surviving 'silent' prints from that era, we have misread the cinema-going experience. By clinging to those visual remnants which remain from the years 1895 to the late 1920s, we ignore the audible experience and, in particular, the all-important contribution of music to the overall experience during this period. Though much of the later analysis in this book concentrates on films produced from the 1930s onwards, it is important to recognise that the British musical film built upon audience experiences and expectations of music in the cinema in the so-called 'silent' period.

Music and early cinema

As Richard Crangle reminds us, magic-lantern slide shows, precursor to moving pictures, were far from being silent. There is clear evidence that, amongst the variety of genres that constituted a typical show, the use of comic commentary and songs was widespread, even if the factual lecture was accompanied by more sober commentary (Crangle 2001). The important Yorkshire-based firm of James Bamforth was offering photographic slide sets based on popular British songs from the late 1870s. In his memoirs, film pioneer Cecil Hepworth, whose father was one of Britain's most successful lanternists, recalls giving a programme in the early 1900s which consisted of lantern slides and a short 40-foot moving film entitled *The Storm*, rescued, Hepworth claims, from discarded footage in Bert Acres' 'junk basket'. Musical accompaniment was provided by Hepworth's piano-playing sister Effie, playing music by Schumann for the calm scenes of sea and sky and by Jensen for the wild dashing waves and the storm (Hepworth 1951). Watching pictures on a screen in a darkened auditorium or similar space was never a silent activity.

The sounds of early cinema were a fixture in even the most undesirable of exhibition venues. A well-known Heath Robinson cartoon from the early 1920s offers a savage caricature of the shabby state of many British cinemas. A mere three patrons sit scattered amongst the dilapidated assortment of benches, chairs and other seats, as an aging projectionist hand-cranks an apology for a projector which is lit by an old oil-lamp, its pictures projected not onto a screen, but on an old apron strung up on a piece of string at the front of the room. Significantly, the only other person in the room apart from the few paying customers is female, sitting at the piano, though not in a position to see what is happening on the screen, busy playing random accompaniment to the picture (Bamford 1999).

While Heath Robinson's self-deprecating visual humour has a resonance whenever we consider British cinema, we should not misread the importance of music to British cinema during this period. The extent to which musical accompaniment to film had become not just commonplace, but essential to the aesthetics and pleasures of cinema by the mid-1920s, can be gauged by comments made by British pioneer director George Pearson about his 1924 film *Reveille*, a film dealing with the bereavement and loss which was so much a part of the 1914–18 war. Reflecting on how he sought to maximise the dramatic impact of the two minutes' silence to acknowledge the Armistice (the eleventh hour of the eleventh day of the eleventh month), Pearson recounted how, at the trade showing of the film, the conductor Louis Levy was instructed to stop the orchestral accompaniment, put down his baton and keep the musicians silent for two minutes, so that what audiences saw on screen was viewed in total silence. Pearson recounts that the experience of this 'frozen silence' moved him to tears (Pearson 1957: 130). In a later 1968 television interview, he said that was 'the greatest moment in any film I ever made' (Peet 2001: 78). The dramatic impact of this particular conceit was only possible because audiences expected orchestral musical accompaniment. Real silence, if only for these two minutes, was the exception that challenges ingrained assumptions about so-called silent cinema.

Early cinema audiences

Despite some early experiments with sound, it is true that the overwhelming number of films projected lacked any sort of synchronised soundtrack. Before the early nineteen-teens, this very absence of a soundtrack often served to encourage a noisy interaction between the audience and events they were seeing on the screen, as they clapped, shouted encouragement or booed at scenes which variously engaged their patriotic fervour or offended their class, gender or ethnic sensibilities. This matches the situation in American cinemas where contemporary accounts of audience behaviour indicate something of this interaction between the picture being shown and members of the audience. In 1911, Mary Heaton Vorse, visiting a cinema in New York's East Side frequented by a largely Jewish audience, recalled the women behind her exhorting the on-screen characters to 'take care, take care! Those wild and awful people will get you!' (Vorse 2002: 51). Writing about audience reception of the relatively short-lived labour-against-capital films popular in American cinema in the 1910s and early 1920s, Steven J. Ross states:

> Class-conscious movie-goers of all ages reacted passionately and sometimes physically to films that praised or disparaged the efforts of labour and radical movements. A six-year old boy attending a New York showing of *Tim Mahoney, The Scab*, in May 1911, grew so disgusted with its anti-union message that he 'forget himself and cried out: "Gee, I'd hate to have a scab for a father"'. (Ross 1999: 95–6)

Although research on early British film audiences remains undeveloped, there is every reason to believe that audiences in Britain behaved in similar fashion, that they were 'awkward, dirty and unruly' (Hiley 1998: 102). Certainly, in the period up to the First World War, there was a great deal of concern from those in authority to control what was seen as noisy, licentious and unacceptable behaviour, through attempts to regulate standards of behaviour in the cinemas, as well as influencing the actual content of films. There was, Lise Shapiro Sanders argues, an element of cause and effect between the regulation of film content, the development of narrative film form, and the behaviour of audiences, as

> audiences were increasingly encouraged to watch the longer feature films in relative silence and with less interaction between members of the audience in the darkened viewing space of the cinema theatre. (Sanders 2002: 98)

Sanders' comments relate primarily to lower-middle- and working-class audiences attending the relatively smaller exhibition venues which were typical up to the early nineteen-teens, but even the structural drift to larger and more 'respectable' venues of the 1920s were no guarantee of 'improved' behaviour. Much depended on location and clientele. James Blades recalls 'depping' as a cinema musician in Brick Lane, East London, in the late 1920s, just before the coming of the sound film:

> Most of the audience came loaded with two bottles of ale and made a practice of rolling the empty bottles down the sloping gangway into the pit. They also got rid of the beer towards the end of the night by widdling down the slope and presenting the band with wet feet. (de Jonge 1994: 26)

The development of early British cinema was inevitably implicated in the institutional practices of existing entertainment and leisure provision. As a result, early British films were exhibited in a variety of locations, including travelling fairgrounds, skating rinks, small shop-front exhibition spaces known as 'penny gaffs', as well as a variety of private and public lecture halls, often those already being used by magic-lantern entertainers (Barnes 1976). Early cinema audiences brought with them behaviours that had been part of the music-hall and fair-ground experience including, crucially, participatory responses to the entertainment on offer. At many early exhibition venues, audiences were able to sing along with the 'Bouncing Ball', in which the words to a song were projected onto the screen and the audience followed a moving dot of light above the words in time with the music. Music itself, an increasingly important element in the reception experience of early cinema, certainly contributed to the volubility of audience response, particularly in smaller exhibition in venues seating less than 500. Live musical accompaniment to otherwise silent films was an important part of and helped to promote a kind of audience communality central to the cinema experience at this period, particularly for working-class audiences. As Blades' comments suggest, so-called 'silent' films could be rather noisy affairs, the musical accompaniment provoking and sometimes competing with verbal comments from the audience as they engaged with the film. However, this became increasingly uncommon, as music for pre-synchronised sound cinema moved away from the serendipities of solo piano improvisation towards larger-scale, complex orchestration which demanded attention and refused audience participatory activity. Put simply, in the bigger city-centre and suburban cinemas that were opening by the mid-1920s, audiences were increasingly encouraged to listen to the music rather than sing along with it, not least because the music they experienced no longer consisted of simple, familiar, melodies and harmonies. However, such tendencies sometimes sat uneasily with the provision of live musical and variety entertainment that was characteristic of the cinema-going experience, at least in many cinemas, throughout the 1920s. What seems clear is that musical provision, as much as the location, size and general condition of the cinema, reflected important class differences between cinema audiences at this period.

The cinema industry prospers

Confidence in cinema as a viable economic and business proposition had grown sufficiently in Britain by 1907–08 for the first purpose-built cinemas to appear, though often in the face of stated scepticism from those who believed that a permanent location dedicated to the showing of moving pictures was doomed to financial extinction once their novelty value with audiences had been exhausted. In spite of partly justified trepidation fuelled by the commercial failure of a number of permanent venues for film exhibition in London and elsewhere, there was a significant spate of cinema building in Britain between 1908 and 1914. As Hiley shows, much of this was fuelled by speculative investment in construction that outpaced the growth in audience demand for film entertainment. The estimated 2,000 purpose-built cinemas in existence in Britain by 1911 sold some four million tickets each week; in 1914, 5,000 purpose-built cinemas were selling some seven million tickets a week. The conclusion from this is seems clear: 'on the eve of [the 1914] war, most British exhibitors must have been showing to largely empty halls' (Hiley 2002: 122). However, though the economic stimulus may not have been primarily driven by audience demand, cinema exhibition in Britain from 1915 was mainly, if not exclusively, associated with purpose-built or specially converted cinemas (Hepworth 1951).

The years of the First World War showed a remarkable increase in cinema-going, especially amongst the working class. The weekly sales of tickets had leapt from 7 million in 1914 to 20.6 million in 1917, fuelled by relatively cheap seat prices. Though, as we have seen, the imposition by the wartime government of an Entertainment Duty signalled a decline in weekly attendances which continued until 1924, when the duty was abolished for cheaper seats costing less than 6d, weekly attendances rose again. The conventional, if sometimes disputed, view is that from this period onwards, going to the cinema became a seemingly irreversible element of British social life, prompting one local historian of north-west England to the view that, 'by the 1920s, the cinema was truly an obsessional hobby for large numbers of the population' (Roberts, 1976: 54).

Musical accompaniment to 'silent' films becomes professionalised

It is clear that a major attraction of cinema-going throughout this period was live music and the use of mechanical sound effects to accompany the films. As much a part of the 'programme' as the films themselves, music was pervasive, expected and an important element in the commercial competition between cinemas, as important an element of differentiation as the films themselves, the size and location of the building, and the scale and quality of cinema furnishings. Certainly, as Louis Levy, perhaps Britain's most distinguished cinema musical director of the mid-century asserts, by the 1920s 'the degree of ability of the local cinema's musical director to "fit" his pictures played an important part in the box-office receipts' (Levy 1948: 23).

Initially, the most common form of musical accompaniment to the film was initially a single, often poorly paid, pianist. Complaints that what was played often bore little relationship to what audiences were watching on the screen were legion; as late as 1914 the *Illustrated Films Monthly* denounced 'the incongruous tinkling of amateurs on cottage pianofortes at the picture shows' (Hiley 1998: 100). The poor quality of much musical accompaniment was noted and criticised by early commentators such as Vachel Lindsay who, in 1915, criticised the 'fathomless imbecility' of cinema music's 'hoochey koochey strains' (Low 1997: 201). The *Kinematograph Weekly* for 1 January 1920 noted that the change from solitary pianist to small ensembles using strings, woodwind and brass had been significant, but even when the pianist was supplemented by other musicians playing other instruments, this was no guarantee that the appropriateness of the musical accompaniment to the film was improved. Percival Mackey, later to become a very prolific film composer and musical director in the 1930s and 1940s, was part of the 'Royal Irish Animated Picture Company Grand Orchestra', which – consisting of a 72-year old trumpeter, a drunken violin player and the 18-year old Mackey on piano – accompanied silent film screenings in

Ireland (Huntley 1947: 27). On another occasion in the early 1920s, playing at a cinema on the Harrow Road, London, Mackey's neck-ache caused him to abandon his piano, leaving the film to run in silence.

Louis Levy recounts similar experiences from his days as a cinema musician:

> there was no ordered routine to ensure that the music fitted the film. . . . after a while, feeling we had played long enough, the six of us would file out, leaving the audience flat, while we went in search of a beer or a quiet smoke! (Levy 1948: 21)

Levy also recounts the blatant disregard which musicians often had for the watching audience and offers further evidence of the noise which was often part of the cinema experience in the so-called 'silent' era:

> Much music would be put on the stands, the leader of the band would let the picture start in absolute silence, look up to the screen above him to see what the opening scene was about and decide what was the best piece to play! If it was a dramatic film . . . and he had on the stand something like the Romance in F, he shouted at the top of his voice to the orchestra all sitting in the semi-darkness, 'Romance in F'. And if that was not enough, he would also shout the composer's name! (Levy 1948: 23)

Such incidents became increasingly unusual throughout the early 1920s, as cinema owners, particularly in the large cinemas of the big cities, scrambled to attract a better class of clientele with more polished and professional musicians, often recruited from established hotel and restaurant orchestras, whilst also worrying about the cost of hiring those musicians.

As early as 1915, a 300-seater cinema in Leeds employed a string quartet and flute as well as a pianist. Prestige screenings at London venues could involve a very large number of musicians, as with the screening of *The Three Musketeers* at Covent Garden in 1922, when Eugene Goossens conducted the 65-strong London Symphony Orchestra. When Hepworth exhibited the still unfinished *Coming Through The Rye* at the 1923 British Film Week in London, it had specially selected music and an orchestra of 28 musicians. Though such prestige occasions had their place, most cinema managers worried about the salary bill for musicians since, as Ehrlich points out, though increasingly indispensable to the commercial success of cinemas, their services were relatively expensive because they remained a labour-intensive, unmechanised and therefore a relatively inefficient element in what was otherwise a highly efficient technologically based arm of the entertainment industry (Ehrlich 1985: 195). By the 1920s, most cinemas had orchestras of between three and twelve players, depending on their size, location, and the extent to which musicians could 'double' on different instruments. Talented musicians were in demand and, if not everyone achieved the Musicians' Union recommended rate of £3.15s a week for playing twice nightly in 1925, there was also much poaching of musicians, especially in London. Levy claims that earnings for musicians in the 1920s were good, recalling that 'it became Klondyke time for musicians who specialised in this work, and large sums of money were earned' (Levy 1948: 24).

The change from a single pianist to the use of small to medium-sized orchestral outfits was reflected by profound changes in the structure and organisation of the cinema music business and by the growth of professionalism amongst cinema musicians. Levy recalled that

> Music publishers began to notice the new field of development open to them, and some of the more enterprising publishers soon engaged composers to specialise in incidental music for the film, and to compose numbers to fit all cinema moods. (Levy 1948: 23)

The growth in demand for cinema music which was no longer arbitrary or improvised led to the involvement of agencies which provided music catalogues and sheet music specifically for the cinema. Some of these agencies had previously supplied music for the music-halls, but found a new lucrative market in the cinema. Ehrlich cites one music lending-library in Stockton-on-Tees that offered over 4,000 pieces 'selected to suit all films, to give true atmosphere, which is quite essential in the art of playing to pictures' (Ehrlich 1985: 197). Individual cinemas built up their own music libraries or hired sheet music from specialist lending agencies such as the New Century Picture Company, which supplied sheet music to cinemas in the Bradford and Leeds areas, or the Clement Millard Company, which supplied cinemas in Newcastle-upon-Tyne. In London in the early 1920s, Chappell and Company's Band Music Department offered selected lists of 'Suites, Overtures, Entr'actes Etc., most suitable for Picture Houses and Restaurant Work'. The musical score compiled by Albert Cazabon for Maurice Elvey's 1926 film *The Flag Lieutenant* was supplied by the Motion Picture Music Company of Denman Street, London and is one of the few surviving scores from a British feature film of the 1920s (Brand 2002). Though British music publishers never produced specialist catalogues as extensive and exhaustive as Erno Rapee's 1925 *American Encyclopaedia of Music For Pictures*, a number of specialist catalogues were published in the 1920s including Paxton's *Music For All Occasions* and Miss Cynthia Bishop's *Picture Palace Sketches*.

Though by the mid-1920s important American epics such as *Ben Hur* or *King of Kings* arrived with special scores packed in metal boxes along with the film cans, which were then parcelled up and sent on to the next cinema, most films shown at most British cinemas relied heavily on the musical director to arrange appropriate musical sections to accompany the film, a process known as 'fitting the picture'. In addition to arranging the music itself, this process included arranging and 'spotting' sound effects, using a variety of commercially produced instruments to produce a variety of sounds such as tug-boat whistles, horses hooves and bird calls. Although local practice varied a great deal, 'fitting the picture' often took place on a Monday morning for a film that was to be shown during the rest of that week. The importance of music as part of the reception experience gave growing importance to the role of musical director, an importance which carried on over into sound film production.

Though playing the musical accompaniment to the film being screened represented the main work for the cinema musicians, many cinemas used their orchestras to provide additional musical entertainment for cinema-goers. In fact, it was common for cinemas to combine showing films with a range of different live variety and musical acts. In 1915, whilst touring northern England in a revue called *Yes I Think So*, a young Gracie Fields found time to appear on a variety bill at the cinema in West Houghton near Bolton. Christine Gledhill cites a 1926 report in the *Daily Sketch* that students in a university town showed their disapproval of the live entertainment on offer before the screening of the film by sustained stamping of their feet (Gledhill 2003: 13). As late as 1929 and just at a time when cinemas were converting to sound, the *Kine Year Book* noted that what it termed 'Kine-Variety', live variety and musical acts wrapped around the film programme, was now 'definitely established . . . as a regular feature of the houses'. This, it reported, was supported by 'orchestral work . . . of a far higher quality . . . than ever before', along with 'the most wonderful organs in the world . . . installed in all kinemas with any pretensions' (Gledhill 2003: 12–13).

Billy Stean worked as a drummer at numerous cinemas during the 1920s, including the 1,350-seat Theatre Royal cinema in Bradford, and recalled how popular 'musical interludes' were with audiences:

> After the main picture we played musical interludes and on Tuesdays we did a one-hour broadcast at 3pm. We played each day from 2–4 pm and sometimes on Sundays we did a charity concert, 'A Musical Melange'. (de Jonge 1994: 32)

These musical interludes and live prologues were the subject of increasing criticism as the 1920s wore on, a criticism that was itself part of a wider discourse about the cinema-going experience as it moved away from working-class origins towards being a more middle-class activity. Though much of the music provided for accompaniment to the films themselves was designed to be generically adaptable, the increasingly frequent use of and quotations from respected composers such as Delibes, Grieg, Schubert and Wagner lead some commentators to make claims that cinema orchestras provided a degree of 'cultural enlightenment' to audiences who otherwise might have been denied it. Cyril Ehrlich cites the music critic Edwin Evans writing in 1929 that the cinema was

> the sole, or at any rate the chief, venue by which music reaches three-quarters of the potential audience in the population. For about fifty-nine hours weekly, music is being performed in upwards of three thousand cinemas, and for shorter periods in perhaps a thousand isolated halls. (Ehrlich 1985: 199)

The growing respectability of cinema music even attracted attention from composers and conductors who were more usually associated with the classical concert and recital hall: Richard Strauss and Sir Landon Ronald, chief conductor at Covent Garden, conducted cinema orchestras in London in the 1920s.

In this sense, music in cinemas should be seen as making a major contribution to a more disciplined auditorium, to the movement away from the noisy, unruly behaviour which stigmatised working-class audiences towards the growth of what was considered a more respectable middle-class audience. The role of music in attracting a 'better' class of clientele needs to be acknowledged alongside more conventionally recognised influences, such as the growing comfort and sophistication which transformed 'picture houses' into 'picture palaces' with their regulatory agents such as ushers and commissionaires, the concern over the 'uplifting' content of the films themselves (dating from the establishment of the British Board of Film Censors in 1913 and articulated by pressure groups such as the National Council for Public Morals from 1917), and the development of increasingly complex narratives which demanded greater audience attention.

The mechanisation of sound

In addition to its role in this profound cultural shift in reconfiguring the cinema audience and the ways in which these audiences behaved, music in the cinema assumed an important economic role. The importance of live music to British cinemas in the 1920s can be gauged by employment statistics for musicians. Ehrlich cites Musicians' Union estimates that, in 1924, cinemas employed half of its members and that by 1928 they accounted for between 75 and 80 per cent of all paid employment for musicians. In March 1929, just under 4,000 musicians were said to be working in London cinemas and at least 20,000 in cinemas in Britain as a whole (Ehrlich 1985: 199). Whilst this was good news for players, this clearly represented a drain on cinema exhibitor profits and attempts were made to reduce the wages bill for musicians. These included the unsuccessful attempt by the Gaumont-British circuit to undercut union-agreed wage levels, their promotion of the British School of Cinema Organists, designed to train cinema organists who would replace cinema orchestras, as well as active trade promotion of mechanical devices such as the 'J.S. Orchestral Gramophone Electrical Reproducer' which played amplified gramophone records. From early 1927 to the end of 1928, electrical reproducers such as British-Brunswick's 'Panatrope' were installed in over 1,000 British cinemas, initially to provide prologue or interlude music and, later, in an attempt to use gramophone records to 'fit' the picture (Allen 2001: 71–2). The *Kinematograph Weekly* for 20 October 1927 announced the formation of a specialist company who would choose and supply appropriate records to suit particular films (Allen 2001: 73). Though electrical reproducers made some inroads in replacing live musicians, their limitations were evident. The sheer scale and consequent cost of live cinema musicians proved a major factor in the drive towards the installation of a more effective and flexible technological solution to the unquestioned need for musical and sound-effect accompaniment, using the sound systems which British exhibitors knew were being introduced into American cinemas.

Of course, numerous patents for machines designed to synchronise sound and image had been registered since the beginning of the twentieth century, in the United States and, increasingly, in Europe. As early as 1904, Sigmund Lubin had marketed his Cinephone in the United States, using Victor Monarch disc records to deliver image and sound simultaneously. In Britain, Robert W. Paul's turn-of-the-century experiments with British-made copies of Edison's Kinetoscope proved commercially unviable. Eugene Lauste had patented film which had a synchronised soundtrack along its edge as early as 1906, Will Barker patented the Cinephone, and Gaumont's Chronophone, also a disc-based system, had been trialled in Manchester in 1907. Cecil Hepworth patented his Vivaphone system in 1910, an attempt to synchronise film and a gramophone record, and recorded amongst other things short 'talking films' of politicians such as Bonar Law and F.E. Smith (later Lord Birkenhead) (Hepworth 1951: 99–100). Throughout 1912,

Hepworth was producing two Vivaphone shorts a week, some of them using music-hall and stage singers and performers. There is evidence of 'talkie films' being shown in Blackpool in 1914 (de Jonge, 1994: 33).

Problems of inter-operability, of different equipment and different technical standards, made these and other technological innovations commercial unsustainable. However, by the mid- to late 1920s, audience expectations of good-quality musical accompaniment at the cinema – reinforced by the growing availability of music heard on BBC radio and, from 1924, on electrically recorded gramophone records – combined with the cost of paying wages to cinema musicians, were becoming a major commercial consideration for cinema owners and managers. Clearly, any commercially viable technological solution to what was becoming an intractable business dilemma would be welcomed by exhibitors, if not by members of the Musicians' Union.

In an age of the telephone, the radio and the gramophone, an age of 'electrical affinities' (Crafton 1999), it was perhaps not surprising that 'thermionics', the emerging technologies based on the development of the vacuum tube or valve, would be exploited by those with investment interests in the film industry. Given the conversion in the late 1920s to synchronised sound film in America, it was perhaps inevitable that the British film industry and British cinemas would follow, given the growing dominance of American films in Britain. Though in retrospect the commercial conversion to sound film may have seen rapid, this perception disguises not just a much longer period of experimentation, but also some crucial uncertainties about ways in which new technologies would be utilised and exploited, and by whom. The introduction of sound cinema in Britain can only be understood in the context of other developments in the entertainment and communication industries that were taking place throughout the 1920s.

The conversion to sound in cinemas.

Just as the assertion that *The Jazz Singer* (1927) was the first talking picture disguises the complexities of the development of the American sound film, so too in Britain the development of commercially viable synchronised sound film was characterised by a series of experiments, failures and some successes. However, the conversion to sound was given an added dimension in Britain, where attempts to install British technology were countered by the efforts of the big American corporations to ensure that it was their technology that achieved market dominance. These efforts were, of course, helped considerably by the undoubted domination of American product within British distribution and exhibition, as British film producers in the early 1920s struggled to finance their films and show them in British cinemas. As things proved, the growing cultural hegemony enjoyed by American films went hand-in-hand with the industrial hegemony enjoyed by American sound-systems technology, which itself was dominated by AT&T's Western Electric, General Electric and RCA. British firms were to prove much less successful in resisting American technology than Klangfilm-Tobis were in Germany.

Apart from some disparate and isolated experiments alluded to earlier, one of the more successful sustained attempts to produce syn-chronised sound film came from Lee de Forest's Phonofilm company in the United States. The Phonofilm system, using photoelectric cells and electrical amplifiers, had caused some interest in America with the announcement of its development in April 1922. Owing much to the German Tri-Ergon system developed in Berlin, de Forest did not initially see his synchronised sound system as being of interest or benefit to the established Hollywood silent feature film. He saw Phonofilm as being an alternative, short, film form utilising talent from vaudeville and variety theatre, especially musical and comedy acts, closer to radio than to film, a method of 'recording voices . . . that eventually may be broad-cast' (Crafton 1999: 64). Whilst this may be difficult to understand given our knowledge of cinema history, de Forest's concepts were dominated by the established importance of live variety theatre and vaudeville, and by the rapidly emerging importance of radio and the gramophone as domestic technologies. Given the increased sophistica-tion of silent feature films, it should not be surprising that de Forest saw his short sound films as an adjunct to, not a replacement for, an estab-lished and commercially successful cultural form. This itself reflected contemporary uncertainties about the direction in which the new elec-trical technologies would develop, uncertainties which saw, amongst other things, live radio broadcasts being relayed to cinemas and exper-iments with 'radio pictures' or 'television'. It is not without significance that, when we look at British musical films such as *Elstree Calling* (1930), *The Television Follies* (1933), *On The Air* (1934) and *Radio Parade of 1935* (1934), both radio broadcasting and the early attempts to establish television figure prominently within the films' imaginary; both are implicated in what amounts to a meta-discourse about ways in which the new technologies would be used, about notions of public communication and the public sphere, about the very project of moder-nity implicit in the 'electrical revolution' of the 1920s.

In the United States, the inaugural public showing of the Phonofilm system took place on 15 April 1923 in New York and featured a series of Broadway acts, including Weber and Fields, and Eddie Cantor. In the attempt to promote interest amongst exhibitors, it was the prospect of seeing and hearing 'stars from opera, musical comedy and vaudeville' that was emphasised (Crafton 1999: 69). Despite the interest aroused, de Forest and Phonofilm were locked out of the innovations being developed by larger corporate rivals AT&T and RCA, as well as exhibition circuits increasingly owned and dominated by Loews, Paramount and First National, who were taking product from their own associated studios. As a result, De Forest Phonofilm, Inc. was insolvent by 1926. Yet the way in which de Forest and Phonofilm promoted the short film displaying talent from vaudeville and variety was hugely influential on the programming developed by both Fox-Movietone and Vitaphone in their early innovations with synchronised sound film. As Donald Crafton argues

> The realisation of the special value of the speaking and performing star would later prove to be an essential component of the talkies. This conception of sound cinema as virtual Broadway – New York stage material and radio-like delivery – proved to be far longer lasting than the Phonofilm system itself. (Crafton 1999: 70)

Given the increasing dominance of American production and distribution in Britain in the 1920s, these developments in the United States were invariably influential on the British cinema industry. Phonofilm itself proved to be briefly influential in developing the sound film in Britain during the mid-1920s and also did much to establish the musical short as a distinct cultural form within British cinema. One month following a demonstration of the system at the Finsbury Park Cinema in June 1923, the British rights to Phonofilm had been bought by C.F. Elwell and the system was used to make a series of shorts at the small, noisy and airless converted railway arches which served as a studio at Clapham between 1923 and 1926 (Wood, 1937). These early experiments at synchronised sound were technically imperfect and some of those present at the demonstration at the Finsbury Park Cinema were as critical as their American counterparts had been, describing the sound produced as 'throaty' (Low 1997: 202).

Such criticisms did not detract from the wider sense of excitement that the new 'thermionic' technologies were generating. In that same year, 1923, a newly licensed BBC had transmitted its first outside radio broadcast, had moved into premises at Savoy Hill London, had opened stations in Glasgow, Cardiff, Birmingham, Aberdeen and Bournemouth, and had begun publication of the *Radio Times*. By the end of the year, 595,496 wireless receiving licences had been sold and countless thousands of amateur 'constructors' were also building and listening to radio sets. As Briggs shows, concerts and 'musical evenings' played by small ensembles 'became the staple broadcasting fare' on BBC radio by 1923 (Briggs 1961: 74). In the same month that Phonofilm was being demonstrated, John Logie Baird was advertising for someone to assist him in developing his 'seeing by wireless' machine. In 1923 the Gramophone Company had received the royal seal of approval from King George V and was busy selling hundreds of thousands of dance-band records on its HMV label, whilst its rival, the now British-owned Columbia Graphophone Company, manufactured 6.7 million records. The gross output of the British gramophone industry, valued at £74,000 in 1907, had reached an estimated £2,285,000 in 1924, reflecting the rapid growth of this aspect of the entertainment business and its incursion into daily life (Nott 2002: 14).

Whatever its early technical deficiencies, production of Phonofilms continued at the Cranmer Court Studios at Clapham. Though legally and financially separate from the American company, British Phonofilm was influenced by de Forest's concept of the short sound film as something distinct from full-length feature films. Though the company produced a number of non-musical sound shorts, it was their use of music-hall and light-opera singers and musicians that dominated production. Just as American companies saw sound films as the opportunity to deliver 'virtual Broadway' to even the remotest cinemas, so too Phonofilm offered the opportunity to deliver 'virtual West End' as well as the best of 'virtual music hall' and light entertainment to a range of cinema audiences throughout Britain. The attraction of both hearing and seeing well-known music-hall, radio and gramophone artists was clearly a strong one and Phonofilm produced over 100 shorts featuring a huge range of popular artists. This paradoxical ability to deliver 'authentic' comics, singers and musicians through mediated and democratised technological processes represented an important development in the cinema-going experience, one that was to prove attractive to audiences throughout Britain. It also made commercial sense, at least for cinema managers and the exhibition circuits such as Gaumont-British who relished the prospect of replacing live musicians with the 'virtual orchestra' that these synchronised shorts promised.

The enthusiasm for cost-saving technological devices to replicate live music can only be understood by understanding just how important music was to the experience of watching 'silent' films in British cinemas. In 1928, George Pearson was planning a second feature for the Scottish singing star Sir Harry Lauder, *Auld Lang Syne*. Whilst the film included Lauder mouthing six of his most famous songs, including 'I Love A

Lassie', his voice would not, of course be heard; instead, Pearson placed his confidence in the ability of 'film orchestras [who] could play the well-known melodies', an indication of just how well established musical accompaniment was by that time (Pearson 1957: 152). Quite apart from musical accompaniment to the films themselves, a number of British companies produced short films that attempted to exploit and extend the relationship between music, singing and what was shown on screen, a disciplined and orderly replication of the communal experience of the music-hall. For example, in 1925 G.B. Samuelson produced a series called *Milestone Melodies* for Reciprocity Films that involved singers on stage accompanying films that pictorialised appropriate scenes from songs familiar to music-hall audiences such as 'Auld Lang Syne', 'I Do Like To Be Beside The Seaside' and 'Little Dolly Daydream'. In that same year, James A. Fitzpatrick produced a similar series called *Famous Music Melodies* using live singers on stage and short films that illustrated the lyrics. Whilst catering for an obvious demand from cinema audiences for music, these broken-backed experiments using cost-effective industrialised visual technology, coupled to expensive live performers, were rendered unattractive to cinema exhibitors once synchronised shorts became more widely available.

From September 1926, British Phonofilm issued a series of musical shorts, beginning with the first sound-on-film produced in England featuring comedian Billy Merson. In that year, Merson appeared in three Phonofilm shorts, *Billy Merson in Russian Opera*, *Billy Merson Singing Desdemona* and *Billy Merson in his Harry Lauder Burlesque*. In that same year, Phonofilm issued shorts featuring a range of comic, music-hall and light-operetta stars, including Joe Termini the 'somnolent violinist', the Houston Sisters, Marie Lloyd Jr, the singer and cellist Gwen Farrar, and Dick Henderson (who featured in six shorts including *Dick Henderson Singing Tripe* and *Dick Henderson the Great Yorkshire Comedian*, in which he sings 'I've Never Seen A Straight Banana'). Also in late 1926, English pianist, composer and bandleader Billy Mayerl teamed up with Gwen Farrar in 'I've Got A Sweetie On The Radio'. Though British Phonofilm released a number of shorts featuring classical music and other elements of official culture, including Act Two of *Rigoletto* and Edith and Sacheverall Sitwell reading two of their poems, the vast majority of over 100 Phonofilm shorts featured popular music and West End variety artists, including novelty bands such as The Irish Jewzaleers, Kohala Marsh and His Hawaiian Revellers, and Percy Pryde and his Phonofiddle.

In August 1928, British Phonofilms was acquired by British Talking Pictures which set up a subsidiary, British Sound Films, with ambitious plans for synchronised sound production, stimulated in part by the evident success of *The Jazz Singer* both in America and at its London opening. British Sound Films produced a number of shorts in 1928 and into 1929, following the production policy established by Phonofilm and featuring music-hall, variety and light-classical stars such as Albert Whelan, Clapham and Dwyer, Josephine Earle and Teddy Brown. They also produced a number of shorts which made use of established radio acts, including Fred Elizalde and his Orchestra, and John Henry and Blossom reproducing their radio domestic cross-talk in *The Superior Sex* (1928).

By late 1928 and early 1929, British Sound Films was facing competition from a number of other companies producing synchronised shorts, including the Blattner Picture Corporation and British Instructional, both using the British Phototone disc-based recording system. The limitations of this system were evident and the British Instructional studio at Welwyn installed German Klangfilm-Tobis sound-recording equipment to produce the feature film, *A Cottage On Dartmoor*, in 1929. From March 1929, Butchers handled a deluge of Electrocord shorts, 26 short three-minute films that month, a further 27 in May 1929 and a further 19 in June of that year. Directed by Dave Aylott, these featured a range of minor music-hall and variety artists.

The commercial viability of these synchronised films depended on there being exhibition venues for them. On one estimate, 40 cinemas in Britain had been wired to show Phonofilms by 1928. The average cost of installation was £300, with cinemas paying £16.10s a week for the hire and maintenance of the equipment and a weekly 3000-foot programme (Low 1997: 203). According to Louis Levy, the first cinema to be fitted with a sound system, an American-made Movietone system, was the New Gallery in Regent Street, and it showed the American film *Seventh Heaven* in late 1927. The first purpose-built sound cinema was the New Commodore in Hammersmith, which opened in November 1929 (Levy 1948: 30). Conversion to sound was initially slower in Britain than it had been in the USA. Writing in the *New York Times* of 18 November 1928, John McCormack remarked on what he saw as the 'complete apathy evinced by exhibitors in England' towards converting to sound (Crafton 1999: 420). Although Electrical Research Products Inc. (ERPI), a subsidiary of Western Electric, was reported as having 50 installation engineers working in Britain, by January 1929 there were only 11 cinemas in Britain that had bought Western Electric sound systems (Crafton 1999: 419). RCA also actively promoted its Photophone system in Britain. Low claims that by June 1929, 400 UK cinemas had been wired, by the end of that year 685 had been converted, whilst by the end of 1931 3,537 UK cinemas had been wired for sound (Low 1997: 75).

Kine Weekly carried out an analysis of 30 different sound systems which were in operation in October 1930, though most of these failed to survive for any length of time. Initially, British sound systems enjoyed some success in competition with American sound systems. Butcher's Film Service had installed 115 Electrocord systems by late 1929. Oscar Deutsch's Odeon circuit installed the British Thompson-Houston system that, by the end of 1932, had installations in 700 cinemas. British Acoustic also made significant progress and by September 1938 boasted 650 installations, to which it added a further 350 when it acquired British Talking Pictures and their Phonofilm/Klangfilm Tobis system. However, RCA and Western Electric, both initially more expensive to install than some British systems, reduced their installation prices in 1931, at the same time as exercising some muscle by refusing films to exhibitors using what they termed 'bootleg' systems. This, combined with the adoption of RCA and Western Electric recording systems in a growing number of British studios, meant that American technology was to prove increasingly dominant. For example, British International Pictures (BIP) had eight sound studios by the end of 1930, using RCA and Ambiphone, a British system based on RCA technology.

It was not just in studio recording and cinema hardware installation that American interests were able to assert themselves. Music in synchronised sound films was controlled by national and international copyright agreements. In the United States, the American Society of Composers, Authors and Publishers (ASCAP) was demanding royalties for music heard in sound movies. In December 1927, ERPI did a deal with ASCAP whereby, in return for a lump sum paid to ASCAP, it effectively licensed all music rights for sound films. Three years later, 52 British and 97 European music publishers had also reached a similar agreement with ERPI. American interests were further served when, in 1927, Warner Bros bought a controlling interest in the British music publishers Chappell & Co.

The process of wiring cinemas for synchronised sound made little immediate impact on audience attendance, but it reinforced the movement towards larger exhibition venues and concentration of economic power within the hands of the major exhibition circuits, forcing smaller independent venues out of business. The cost of adapting to sound, where they could afford it, made the smaller and more basic cinemas even more unattractive in comparison with the new larger auditoria seating anything between 1,000 and 2,000. As Hiley comments,

The smaller and cheaper venues, mostly ten or more years old, were simply unable to compete, and during 1933 hundreds of them closed for the last time. (Hiley, 1999: 42)

If the move towards sound cinema changed film exhibition in favour of larger city-centre cinemas owned by consolidated circuits at the expense of smaller circuits and venues, reactions to the coming of synchronised sound amongst British film-makers was more varied. Some established British producers and directors such as Victor Saville and Herbert Wilcox were enthusiastic about the coming of synchronised sound film and both went to the USA to learn about and produce early talking films, including Saville's *Kitty* (1929), starring Estelle Brody and John Stuart, which had a synchronised talking final reel. Wilcox claims that was so keen that he produced a film, *Black Waters*, directed by Marshall Neilan in the United States, only to find problems in finding a cinema in Britain wired for sound in which he could show the film:

> only two theatres in London were wired for sound, the Piccadilly and the Tivoli. So under my arm I had a talkie costing £45,000 and nowhere to show it! Ironically I found a cinema in Coventry wired for sound. To produce the fifth talkie ever made and be sent to Coventry! (Wilcox 1967: 84)

George Pearson also embraced the possibilities and managed successfully to add fully synchronised sound to his 1928 Harry Lauder film *Auld Lang Syne*, and showed it at the Plaza Theatre in London as a 'Paramount Synchronised Sound Picture', though only after persuading sceptical RCA engineers that true synchronisation was possible (Pearson 1957: 156–7). Other British directors were less enthusiastic about the changes introduced. Adrian Brunel, admittedly often embroiled in disputes with important figures such as John Maxwell, spoke of his 'horror' at the introduction of the talkies:

> Naturally I resented the threatening business-technique of foisting this new invention on us just after the first Quota Act came into operation and British films were beginning to get on their feet; but more deeply did I resent American electrical interests smashing the art of the silent film. (Brunel 1949: 156)

Whatever his retrospective opinion of the 'talkies' and the growing American domination it represented, Brunel made a short sound film for Gainsborough, *In A Monastery Garden*, in 1929. The experience was not entirely a happy one and he recalls his embarrassment at the first showing at London's Capitol Cinema of what was advertised as a major advance in cinematic realism:

the main titles came on screen – but not a sound came from the loud-speaker. When the picture itself appeared, still without a sound, some of the audience giggled nervously. Suddenly the sound blared out – and it was out of synchronisation, being about five seconds behind the picture. The effect was excruciating, and this was my first adventure into sound films. (Brunel 1949: 158)

There are conflicting claims as to which film was Britain's first all-talking film. Patricia Warren argues that it was British Lion's *The Clue Of The New Pin* in 1929, using the British Phototone system, though Rachel Low argues that the system proved impracticable and the film was shown silent at its trade showing in March 1929 (Low 1997: 177). Frank Launder claimed that Harry Lachmann's 1929 production *Under The Greenwood Tree*, a film with 'wonderful opportunities for sound effects' with its 'medlies of hymns and traditional songs' (Brown 1977: 28) could have been the first British full-length talking film if Hitchcock's *Blackmail* had not got in first. Whatever the merits of these competing claims, it became increasingly clear that, as in Hollywood, conversion to synchronised sound was the way forward. Though this process was slower in Britain than it was in the United States, both BIP and Gainsborough embraced the new technology. Even initially scepti-cal directors such as Adrian Brunel found the tide irresistible, as the potential of synchronised sound film to conflate the technically disparate but increasingly economically and culturally integrated technologies of entertainment – music hall, revue, radio, cinema and early experiments with television – became clear. Brunel's *Elstree Calling*, shot at BIP's Elstree Studios in 1930, featured an array of British music hall, variety and radio talent in a series of sketches which privileged spectacle at the expense of narrative system and introduced what has become an endur-ing fascination with the business of entertainment, a fascination that the self-reflexive strategies of the musical film were able to exploit. From its opening exterior shots of BIP's actual studio, the film's visual and aural regimes are inscribed with the factory-like processes of sound film pro-duction, with the *work* involved in popular cultural production. As I have argued elsewhere, the film not only establishes a hierarchy of popular entertainment, but offers an implicit critique of important dis-tinctions within popular entertainment that draws upon inflections of class, gender and region (Mundy 1999). Whatever its limitations, *Elstree Calling* is in many ways a seminal British film. In exploiting the aes-thetic potential of synchronised sound, particularly through its use of celebrity performers, it paves the way for the development of the musical film in ways that are distinctly British, not least through its ironic and self-deprecating treatment of its celebrity performers, treatment which is in marked contrast with most early American musical films. At another level, the film exploits the potential synergies between extant branches of the entertainment industry, particularly between the popular music and film industries, synergies that would be exploited in increasingly complex and lucrative ways over the coming decades. Significantly, the appeal here is to British audiences, articulated through mostly British artists and performers, though there are some American performers, notably Teddy Brown, who had forged careers in Britain. *Elstree Calling* also confirms an appetite and expectation amongst British cinema audiences that music was part of their cinema-going experience, an appetite and expectation that was evident from the earliest days of cinema.

2

The 1930s: a most musical of decades

The commercial implementation of synchronised sound, together with the effects of the 1927 Cinematograph Films Act, led to an unprecedented increase in British film production in the 1930s. British Film Institute statistics indicate that 81 feature films had been produced in 1929. In 1932, the number of feature-length productions had increased to 110, to 145 in 1934 and to 192 in 1936. Though crime and comedy films were made in abundance, so too were musical films. The new, cost-effective technologies of synchronised sound and wired cinemas were able to fulfil audience expectations of hearing music as part of their cinema-going experience almost to excess. One estimate is that of the 1,500 full-length feature films produced during the 1930s, over 220 can be described as musical films (Guy 1998: 99). Even this seriously under-estimates the importance of the musical film to British film production and its contribution to British cinema programming throughout the 1930s, when the broad range of musical films is taken into account. One commentator claims that by 1933, musical films accounted for 25 per cent of all British production and that, in 1936 they accounted for as much as 36 per cent of total output from the British studios (Nott 2002: 90).

The films of Jesse Matthews, Gracie Fields and George Formby dominate most critical commentaries on 1930s British cinema and, given the importance of music to their films, it is inevitable that they loom large in this chapter. However, it is important to remember that their films represent a prominent, admittedly gilt-edged, tip of a cinematic iceberg that was the British musical film of the 1930s. In fact, such was the importance of music in 1930s British cinema and so prolific was the industry in churning out musical films, that it really merits a complete book to itself. As it is, this chapter looks at some of the films by Matthews, Fields and Formby and offers some explanation for their enormous popularity with British audiences. It also examines a relatively small number of other popular films that, in one way or another, can be seen to represent the diversity of British musical films produced throughout the decade. As an examination of the careers of Matthews, Fields and Formby as well as those of less well-know performers reveals, British cinema was heavily reliant on artists, singers and bands who had already constructed successful careers in other spheres of the British entertainment industry. Most important amongst these were live theatre, music hall, variety and radio, though success as gramophone recording artists and on the live music circuit was also significant. It is impossible to understand the appeal of many of these films to British cinema audiences – and the pleasures they delivered – without recognising that their featured artists were drawn from what was, in effect, a complex multimedia entertainment industry that was developing synergies at various levels. Whilst it may not be possible to share the frisson that 1930s audiences must have experienced on seeing well-known radio or gramophone artists 'in the flesh' for the first time, that desire to *see* singers and performers, what I have called elsewhere the visual economy of popular music, remains central to the enduring contemporary popularity of music on screen (Mundy 1999).

The reliance of newly synchronised sound cinema on performers who were already successful as music hall, variety, radio, record and dance-band stars invariably influenced the structure and format of the films themselves, so that what passed as musical film was remarkably catholic and varied. One major source of material was the West End stage musical and many of these transmuted into film musicals that conformed fairly closely to the generic conventions being established in Hollywood, the Jesse Matthews vehicle *Evergreen* (1934) being a good example. Such films were often produced with an appeal to the American market in mind and often made some use of American talent, whether songwriters, choreographers, performers or technical crew. British musical operettas were almost as popular in the early and mid-1930s as their American counterparts, though British cinema proved unable to sustain the exoticised talents of Richard Tauber or of Jan Kiepura in ways which matched the success of Jeanette MacDonald and Nelson Eddy in Hollywood operettas of the same period. Moreover, whilst the Hollywood musical developed a high degree of generic coherence, characterised by sub-generic classifications styled by Rick Altman as the fairy-tale musical, the show musical and the folk musical (Altman 1989), British musicals resisted such coherence. Though a significant number of British musicals throughout the 1930s and beyond can be said to imitate or adopt generic conventions associated with the Hollywood product, they also proved remarkably resistant to it. Even

films such as the Matthews vehicles, whilst sharing some structural similarities, offer evidence of ideological and aesthetic resistance to the
normative conventions of the Hollywood musical. Though utopian optimism is never entirely absent from these generically 'pure' British musicals, it is rarely as unalloyed as it tends to be in their American
counterpart.

The reliance on comic talent that had been developed elsewhere
within British entertainment meant that musical comedies were particularly important within British cinema. The importance of the combination of music and comedy was evident in early short films such as
The Musical Beauty Shop (1930) and *The New Waiter* (1930) produced
by Pathé Musical Comedies. Many musical comedies were constructed
around the particular talents of individual comics, with often rather
flimsy narratives designed to promote and showcase individual comic
personas. Though the blunt northern earthiness of Gracie Fields and the
inept, gormless blunderings of George Formby are the two most obvious
examples, comedians as diverse as Jack Hulbert, Stanley Lupino and
Leslie Henson, together with comedy duos and ensembles such as
Clapham and Dwyer and the Crazy Gang, featured in musical comedies
in the 1930s. Though Fields and Formby were also recording stars in
their own right, an inability to sing did not preclude other comedians
from appearing in musicals, their comic personas sandwiched between
musical numbers. Even bandleaders such as Henry Hall, Jack Hylton,
Jack Payne and Harry Roy found their talents stitched into musical films
that exploited their music and sometimes, as with Harry Roy, their
rather dubious acting abilities.

Though musical comedies were characterised by a degree of narrative
and plot, no matter how insubstantial or flimsy, the enormous popularity of singers and bands was reflected in a number of what are best
described as revue musicals. Paralleling developments in America, a significant number of early 1930s films were revues, *Elstree Calling* (1930)
being a good example. Strung together by a linking device, in this case
the announcements of Tommy Handley and a series of cameo scenes
around attempts to get a television set working, *Elstree Calling* showcased a series of largely unconnected acts and artists in which performance and spectacle are given clear priority over narrative in what
Rubin, referring to 1930s Hollywood revue films, terms aggregate musicals (Rubin 1993: 14). Built upon performances honed in music hall and
live variety, such films were to have limited appeal as sound cinema,
with its improved microphone technology and actors better equipped to
deliver dialogue, developed the ability to handle increasingly complex
narratives. C.B. Cochran, the leading stage producer and impresario,

planned to produce 'Charles B. Cochran's Revue of 1930', but only a five-minute comedy fragment *The Shaming Of The True* (1930) was actually shot. However, the continuing appetite to see famous acts familiar to audiences from radio, live variety or just by reputation developed in the growing number of fan magazines, meant that the basic revue film transmuted into the 'parade' film. Often using a show-business setting to deliver the pretext of plot and to establish at least a basic narrative enigma, films such as *Radio Parade* (1933) and *Variety Parade* (1935) were still able to present a series of acts, often on the pretext of 'putting on a show'. The fascination with the prospect of television continued in the early 1930s in film curiosities such as *The Television Follies* (1933), a revue musical in which a Lancashire family watch a series of performers on their television set.

Though, as we shall see, some of the British musicals that most closely resembled their American counterparts were designed to appeal to an international audience, the vast majority of musical comedies, musical revues and musical 'parades' were produced for the domestic audience, sometimes as the main feature, though increasingly as a supporting feature. Where such films did get American distribution, often with new titles designed to make them more comprehensible to American audiences, they rarely succeeded outside one or two East Coast cities. The considerable number of musical shorts produced during the 1930s were almost solely designed for domestic consumption as programme fillers. As we have seen, the development of synchronised sound cinema in the late 1920s was very dependent on musical acts and performances, and it is not surprising that the short musical film continued throughout the 1930s. Cheap and quick to produce, they served a function for the industry in meeting production and exhibition quotas, but were also popular with audiences because of their ability to present the latest bands, singers and acts. A number of short-lived production companies produced individual shorts. In addition, musical shorts were produced as part of series such as *Pathétone*, *Pathé Pictorial* and British Lion's *Equity Musical Review* and *Variety*.

These broad categories of British musical film, 'full-blown' musicals, musical comedies, musical revues and musical shorts, relied for much of their appeal on the entertainment value provided by the artists and songs that they featured. Like the American musical, performance and spectacle are as important as narrative and often more important to the pleasures delivered. Like the American musical, many of them used a self-reflexive show-business background to foreground the 'work' involved in cultural production. Yet, even the most generically 'pure' British musicals often retain an element of self-deprecation in which triumph and optimism are tempered with the tendency to deflate and undermine the importance of success. With the exception of most musical shorts, British musical films also engaged with concerns about the structure of the British social fabric, with issues of class, gender, regionalism and, to a lesser extent, with ethnicity. These films were hugely entertaining for British audiences, but they often went beyond the merely entertaining.

The importance of popular music

Whilst popular music occupies a central place in our contemporary cultural landscape, it would be a mistake not to recognise the importance that commercialised popular music had for people in the 1930s, an importance famously reflected in Dennis Potter's BBC television drama series *Pennies From Heaven* (1978). James Nott quotes from an anonymous contributor to a 1935 trade publication pronouncing the importance of music:

> Never probably in the whole course of the world's history has music played so important a part in the life of the community as it plays today. . . . In the home, in the theatre, in the street, in (and on) the air, music now figures so prominently as a means of entertainment that it would be impossible to contemplate a world in which it no longer provided such a constant source of popular enjoyment. (Nott 2002: 1)

The two domestic technologies of the gramophone player and radio, established in the 1920s, made listening to music at home, particularly popular music, an every-day pleasure during the 1930s. Sales of acoustic gramophones rose throughout the late 1920s and by 1930 over half-a-million gramophones were manufactured for the domestic market. Sales inevitably declined during the economic depression in the early years of the decade, though towards the end of the decade sales were stimulated by the availability of the new electric gramophones and radiograms. The manufacture and sales of records was even more significant, with over 25 million records being produced in 1935 (Nott 2002: 18). The consumption of popular music on record was helped considerably by the Decca label's decision to concentrate on developing a catalogue of popular as opposed to classical or 'serious' music, and by the lowering of unit price as a result of competition from smaller companies that sold their records through retailers such as Woolworths and Marks and Spencer. As a result, listening to records by a wide range of popular-music bands and singers became an accepted part of British cultural life during the 1930s.

Time spent listening to records on gramophone players was matched during the 1930s by listening to radio. The BBC, for all its Reithian concern with 'uplift', featured some popular singers, dance bands and even records on both its National and Regional services. For example, in the week covering the Coronation of George VI in May 1937, the *Radio Times* lists *Swing Music Records* presented by James Holloway on Monday 10 May. On Thursday 13 May, *The Coronation Costume Ball* with Ambrose and his Orchestra was followed at 11.00 pm by *The Scottish Empire Coronation Ball* featuring Gracie Fields with Jack Payne and his Band. Both programmes occupied the late-night slot normally given over to music featuring dance bands such as Roy Fox, Geraldo, Joe Loss and Billy Cotton. The day before, the National Programme broadcast *Britain Dances – A Programme of Dance Music from the British Isles* featuring six dance bands linked together by Henry Hall and the BBC Dance Orchestra. Though these dance-band broadcasts were usually also carried by Regional Programmes, they were often supplemented by additional programmes, such as Northern Ireland's *The Chalet Club Dance Orchestra* and *Al Collins and his Dance Orchestra*. Though popular music was at this time given less prominence than classical or 'light' music, some airtime was given to artists such as Gert and Daisy, Cicely Courtneidge, and The Western Brothers, who were also successfully appearing in live variety, music and the cinema. By the mid-1930s, increasing numbers of listeners tuned in to commercial off-shore stations such as Radio Luxembourg, Radio Normandie and Radio Lyons, which concentrated on playing popular music using gramophone records, making good use of close relationships with the record companies. The popularity of such radio stations undoubtedly reflected public disappointment, even hostility, towards the BBC's programming policy under Reith, especially its attitude towards Sunday broadcasting. Their popularity also reflected the appetite for popular music: as James Nott shows, of the 52.5 hours broadcast weekly by Radio Luxembourg, 47.5 – over 90 per cent – were devoted to popular music (Nott 2002: 75).

Popular music on record and on radio was supplemented by live music performed in a variety of venues. The growing popularity of dancing to live dance bands and the commercialisation of dance-halls, dominated by organisations such as the Mecca group, meant that live popular music was a significant element of British popular entertainment throughout the 1930s. Though figures were not always reliable, a 1933 survey found that there were 1,000 dance bands operating in London, employing some 6,000–7,000 musicians (Nott 2002: 129). Some bands made use of semi-professional and amateur musicians, itself an indication of the extent to which live music permeated leisure activities in 1930s Britain. British musical films of the 1930s were able to draw upon music by a number of British songwriters, including Noel Coward, Ivor Novello, Ray Noble, Noel Gay, Harry Woods, Fred E. Cliffe, Harry Gifford, Vivien Ellis and Harry Parr-Davies, as well as leading British dance bands such as those led by Jack Payne, Henry Hall and Harry Roy. Even when they played numbers by American songwriters, these bands developed and perpetuated a distinctly British style of orchestration and playing which, like British musicals films of the decade, served to differentiate them from the American product. As we have seen, there had been considerable transatlantic traffic in the film industries prior to the 1930s with, for example, American directors and actors involved in British production. However, although the growing influence of American songwriters, popular music and American dance bands was increasingly evident as the 1930s progressed, prompting some calls for a protectionist quota system for the British music industry along the lines of that introduced for the film industry, this was a period in which a distinctive British aesthetic in popular musical culture was clearly discernible, in live performance, on record and in musical films.

Film production policy in the 1930s

As a result of the 1927 Act, British film production in the 1930s fell into two distinct camps, quality films that possessed some distinctive merits, and 'quota' films that did little more than fulfil the requirements imposed by legislation:

> Approximately half the enormous number of films turned out by British studios up to 1937 were produced at minimum cost simply to exploit the protected market or, at worst, to comply with the law. (Low 1997: 115)

Though the distinction between quality and quota was one important axis of British production policy, it was not the only one. As Andrew Higson has shown, production policy in the 1930s was also characterised by two parallel but distinct strategies, one targeted primarily at the domestic and still relatively small Empire market, the other intended to appeal both to the domestic market and beyond, particularly the lucrative American market. Significantly, Higson uses two musicals, Basil Dean's Associated Talking Pictures' *Sing As We Go* (1934) and Gaumont-British's *Evergreen* (1934), to illustrate these two production strategies. Whereas the Gracie Fields' vehicle *Sing As We Go* works 'self-consciously with cultural traditions, reference points and performers which are nationally, and in many cases, regionally specific' (Higson 1997: 165), *Evergreen*, starring Jesse Matthews, is a product of Gaumont-British's determinedly internationalist production and distribution policy and, as a consequence, is a film that engages with the generic conventions being established within the Hollywood backstage musical, not least in its privileging of performance, spectacle and excess. However, though this double axis, of quality/quota and national/ international, is important in understanding British film production of the 1930s, it remains problematic. Whatever the very real distinctions between *Evergreen* and *Sing As We Go*, they are both, in their own way, films of quality. Moreover, though Gaumont-British was promoting some of its product on the American market, Gainsborough was also producing films, including musicals and musical comedies, which were resolutely national and domestic in terms of content and appeal.

British film production in the 1930s centred on British International Pictures (BIP) and Gainsborough, both of them part of effectively vertically integrated companies with their own distribution companies and exhibition circuits, BIP with Associated British Picture Corporation (ABPC) and Gainsborough with Gaumont-British (G-B), Together with Herbert Wilcox's British and Dominion Film Corporation (B&D), these companies were largely responsible for those films regarded within the trade as 'quality'. They were joined by Basil Dean's Associated Talking Pictures (ATP) based at Ealing and by Alexander Korda's London Films, which used various studios including Associated Sound Film Industries' Wembley, B&D's Elstree, and the Worton Hall studios at Isleworth, before building the studios at Denham in 1935. Together with smaller production companies including Julius Hagen's Twickenham Film Studios, British Lion Film Corporation at Beaconsfield, and Sound City Films at Shepperton, as well as a host of companies such as Rock Studios at Elstree who concentrated on producing low-budget 'quickies', many of whose existence was often extremely short-lived, these were the companies responsible for the significant increase in British film production in the years up to 1937.

In the early 1930s, a number of British productions involved significant European involvement, whether through formal co-production agreements or through the use of European directors, actors, technicians and other creative personnel, co-operation which survived the relatively short-lived attempts to produce multilingual versions of films in the very early 1930s for a number of years (Higson 1997).Though marketing and promotion usually masked the European connections, the English-language version of such films proved popular with domestic audiences, as in the case of *Happy Ever After* (1932), starring Lilian Harvey, Sonnie Hale, Cecily Courtneidge and Jack Hulbert, which was actually shot at the UFA studios in Germany. In the first half of the decade, certainly until the political threat of fascism in Spain, Italy and Germany became apparent, a number of British musical films made use of European settings (often created in the studio, of course) and European musical inflections, both of which proved popular with British audiences.

More significant was the involvement in the major American companies such as Fox, Paramount, RKO and Warner Bros. Needing to respond to newly imposed quota requirements, the American companies adopted a variety of strategies designed to ensure continuing dominance of American product on British cinema screens. As Ryall points out, these included investment through part-ownership of British companies, commissioning and acquisition of low-cost films from British production companies, as well as the establishment of production units in Britain designed specifically to meet the quota requirements, again through low-budget production (Ryall 2001). In addition to these formal economic and institutional arrangements, there continued to be considerable involvement in British production by American directors and other film personnel, as well as some, more restricted, opportunities for British talent to work in the United States. This dual European and American dimension to British film production of the 1930s is evident, for example, in Jack Buchanan's first British sound film *Man Of Mayfair* (1931), directed by Frenchman Louis Mercanton and produced by Paramount British as a bilingual production.

Both at the time and subsequently, criticism about the detrimental effects of 'quota quickies' centred on the role of the American distributors in either acquiring or in producing poor-quality films designed to meet the rising requirement to screen British product. Understandably not wanting to be responsible for producing, investing in, and distributing films which would challenge the dominance of their own first-feature product in British cinemas, the American companies responded largely by instituting a policy of producing and distributing low-cost British films. In June 1934, *Film Weekly* articulated growing concern about 'quota quickies':

> as long as the present quota regulations remain in force [the British cinema-goer] is in danger of having his (sic) time wasted and his (sic) patience exhausted by inferior British pictures which have been produced, not to stand on their own merits as entertainment, but to enable some American film company to fulfil its legal obligations. (Napper 2001: 47)

A year earlier, in 1933, the findings of a Board of Trade internal report confirmed that the majority of low-cost films were American-sponsored though, as Wood points out, it was also accepted that many of these films produced to meet quota requirements were actually considered to be 'good programme pictures' (Wood 2001: 54).

The reality was, of course, complicated. Though many of the 'quota quickies' were dire and have simply disappeared from film history, many of them had merit, clearly appealed to British audiences, and a significant number of them were musical films. Moreover, the impetus given to production succeeded in creating something like a British film industry, opening up opportunities for a range of personnel, from directors and actors to editors and set designers, to find work making films. Often these were films which 'went under the radar', contributing a supporting role as a second or 'B' feature. An example would be Producers Distributing Corporation's (PDC) *Eve's Fall* (1930), a 34-minute musical directed by then relatively unknown Monty Banks. In addition, cinema programmes usually included one or more short films and a newsreel that acted as a 'buffer state between the second feature and the big picture' (Lynn 1975: 49). Musical shorts were fairly commonplace in 1930s programming and had a role in maintaining British technicians in work. George Pearson, for example, directed nine short films featuring Harry Lauder and his songs, each three minutes long, for Michael Balcon at Gainsborough, a project that, Pearson claimed, proved popular and 'enabled us to keep a footing in the industry' (Pearson 1957: 188). Though most American films proved more popular than most British films during the 1930s, it seems clear that as a result of increased production, British films enjoyed considerable success with British audiences during these years, often as shorts or as supporting 'B' features, and sometimes as top-billing features.

British studios and 1930s musical films

As suggested earlier, the division between quality and quota production was further complicated by the different production strategies adopted by those production companies who saw themselves firmly within the quality camp. Despite the implications of its name, by 1930 British International Pictures, which had become part of the Associated British Picture Corporation in 1933, had largely abandoned its ambitions to produce for an international market. Concentrating on the domestic market proved relatively successful, as the company produced a stream of comedies and crime films, in addition to a significant number of musicals following the interest attracted by *Under The Greenwood Tree* (1929). Determined to exploit the new sound technology, BIP quickly produced over 20 musical shorts including *Jazz Time* (1929) featuring Jack Payne and the BBC Dance Band, and then launched a series of feature-length musicals beginning, as we saw in the previous chapter, with the revue *Elstree Calling* (1930), featuring mainly domestic music-hall, variety and revue talent such as Stanley Lupino, Lupino Lane, Leslie Fuller and, in *Out Of The Blue* (1931), Jesse Matthews.

As well as artists established in variety and music hall, some of the films featured established stars from the silent era such as Betty Balfour in *Raise The Roof* (1930) with a plot centred on the attempt to ruin a stage revue, whilst others, like Thomas Bentley's *Harmony Heaven* (1930), in which a young composer is helped to success by Polly Ward, used experienced directors struggling to make the transition to sound. American Bebe Daniels starred in *The Song You Gave Me* (1933) and *A Southern Maid* (1933). Like a number of other of these early BIP musicals, in these two films the narrative resonates with an imagined European exoticism, in this case Paris and Spain respectively. *The Flame Of Love* (1930), starring Anna May Wong and John Longden, is set in Russia of 1913, *Gipsy Blood* (1931) is based on Georges Bizet's *Carmen*, set in Seville, Gene Gerrard's *Lucky Girl* (1932) employs a Ruritanian setting, and Lupino Lane's *Maid Of The Mountains* (1932) is set in Italy and features Alfredo and his Gypsy Orchestra who, in the previous year, appeared in a Pathétone short playing 'The Blue Danube' and 'You Will Remember Vienna'. Firmly directed towards domestic audiences, these films appeared to capitalise on the implicit romanticism that European settings seemed to hold for British audiences, pleasures reinforced through the vogue for accordion-drenched orchestrations of central European 'gypsy' music. Though it was Herbert Wilcox's B&D which specialised in operetta, BIP produced two lucrative musicals, *Blossom Time* (1934) and *Heart's Desire* (1935), starring the popular Austrian tenor Richard Tauber, before losing him to Max Schach's Capitol and, in the 1940s, British National. Many of these BIP films were featured as the main attraction in cinemas throughout the early and mid-1930s, as the programme for the Kingsway Levenshulme in Manchester for June 1933, advertising Stanley Lupino's musical *Sleepless Nights* and the comedy *Money Talks*, makes clear (Fig. 1).

BIP continued to make musicals until production output was seriously curtailed in 1938. They encouraged the film career of promising musical-hall star Clifford Mollinson in films such as *Give Her A Ring* (1934), *Mr Cinders* (1934) and *Radio Parade of 1935* (1934), though Mollinson was eclipsed in that film by Will Hay. Other BIP musicals included *Let's Make A Night Of It* (1937), a backstage story about putting on a radio show that starred Americans Buddy Rogers and June Clyde and featured six dance bands including Joe Loss, Jack Jackson and Harry Acres, *Glamorous Night* (1937), based on Ivor Novello's Drury Lane Ruritanian musical show, and the Stanley Lupino vehicle

Over She Goes (1937), an adaptation of Lupino's successful stage musical.

Gaumont-British under Michael Balcon moved in the opposite direction to BIP in the 1930s, making a determined attempt to produce films appealing both to the domestic market and to the potentially lucrative American market. Despite his enormous popularity with domestic audiences, the company failed to promote Jack Hulbert's films in America and were disappointed with the commercial returns from the Jesse Matthews' films. Though slower off the mark in making synchronised sound musicals than BIP and Herbert Wilcox's B&D, the Gainsborough studios at Islington had been converted to sound production by mid-1929, where *Armistice* (1929), a short directed by Victor Saville, was shot. Featuring the band of the Coldstream Guards and the Welsh Guards Male Voice Choir, the film was a rather uninspiring trot through some of the songs made famous in World War I. In the following year, 1930, Balcon produced fifteen shorts under the series title *Gainsborough Gems*, featuring amongst others Martini and his Band, Dick Henderson and Lewis Hardcastle's Dusky Syncopaters. That same year, an attempt was made to produce a full-length musical revue, to be called *The Gainsborough Picture Show*, but a decision was made to release the material as a series of shorts of about fifteen minutes each. *Symphony In Two Flats* (1930), based on the stage play by Ivor Novello and starring him, featured an appearance by Jack Payne and the BBC Dance Band. Such was the perceived 'Englishness' of the film that the US distributors insisted that Jacqueline Logan, an American actress, should replace Benita Hume for the American version (Noble 1952: 147).

Following production of two feature-length musicals – *Just For A Song* (1930), which included a colour sequence, and *Greek Street* (1930) – along with *Alf's Button* (1930), a comedy with singing and dancing from the Gotham Quartette, Anton Dolin and Anna Ludmilla, the breakthrough for Gaumont-British and Gainsborough came with *Sunshine Susie* (1931). This had already been filmed in a German version, and the decision was made to team Jack Hulbert with the lead in that German version, Renate Muller. Hulbert was already a well-established and hugely popular revue and musical-comedy star on the British stage, had toured the United States, had his own BBC radio programme *The Hulbert Brothers* and had appeared in Gainsborough's highly successful *The Ghost Train* (1931). Directed by Victor Saville, and featuring the song 'Today I Feel So Happy', which became immensely popular, *Sunshine Susie* provided the evidence that, handled properly, feature-length musical films could be commercially profitable in the domestic market. Hulbert was signed by Balcon 'on excellent terms' to star in *Jack's The Boy* (1932), *Love On Wheels* (1932), *Jack Ahoy* (1934), *The Camels Are Coming* (1934) and *Bulldog Jack* (1935). Though Gifford categorises these films as comedy, singing and dancing were supremely important in their commercial success, something Hulbert recognised at the time he was making *Jack's The Boy*:

> After the success of *Sunshine Susie* the introduction of singing and dancing was inevitable . . . composers and lyric writers were engaged and I worked overtime with Philip Buchel on the dance routines. . . . Everything was going splendidly until some chap called Fred Astaire suddenly appeared on the screen. . . . Philip came up with some splendid stuff, but who could dance like Fred Astaire? (Hulbert 1975: 181)

Hulbert's doubts about the quality of his dancing did not detract from the pleasures British audiences got from the film, nor from its commercial success. His Master's Voice (HMV) were so anxious to release one of the songs from the film, 'The Flies Crawled Up The Window', that they pursued Hulbert to the south of France to record it. Hulbert sang 'The Hat's on The Side Of My Head' in *Jack Ahoy* and 'Sweep All Your Troubles Away' in *Jack Of All Trades* (1936) and these cheerful, humorous songs, together with his dancing, described by Low as 'neither acrobatic or elegant, but casual, floppy and humorous' (Low 1997: 138), clearly appealed to British audiences, aided, no doubt, by promotional interviews on BBC radio (Hulbert 1975: 189–94).

Gaumont-British had entered into formal co-production agreement with UFA in May 1932. Though Balcon was later to disown the arrangement, and performers such as Jack Hulbert and Cecily Courtneidge found working in Germany uncongenial, the deal produced some interesting results, not least in art direction (Bergfelder 1996). However, by 1934 and buoyed by the success in America that Korda had enjoyed with *The Private Life Of Henry VIII* (1933), Balcon had decided that, in order to develop international significance, part of Gaumont-British strategy should be to target the American market through the establishment of a Gaumont-British distribution network in the United States (Sedgwick 2000: 212–3). The success of the Jack Hulbert films in Britain appeared to make these appropriate vehicles for American distribution. Though correct in being wary of the American majors' reluctance to distribute British product and in the attempt to short-circuit it through G-B's own system, the problems in selling *Bulldog Jack* (1935) in America, where it was titled *Alias Bulldog Drummond*, indicated real differences between British and American film product and audience tastes. An internal company memo in New York liked the pace of the film, but seriously objected to Hulbert's performance:

whether or not we should release the picture in America depends entirely on just how much Hulbert can be eliminated . . . Hulbert is never going to be accepted in America in the type of work he is doing . . . They do not like him and do not want him. His comedy is exaggerated to the point where it is pitiful . . . (Sedgwick 2000: 219)

Balcon clearly recognised the need to produce films tailored for the perceived tastes of American audiences if his determined assault on the potentially lucrative American market was to succeed and he clearly placed much business faith in the Jesse Matthews musicals, not least perhaps in his use of American songwriters such as Rodgers and Hart. In this, though he came close, he was ultimately disappointed.

A few other Gainsborough musicals of this period were released in America, including *Aunt Sally* (1933: US title *Along Came Sally*), starring Cicely Courtneidge, with singer and pianist Billy Milton singing 'You Ought To See Sally On Sunday', along with a string of other variety acts and Debroy Somers and his Band. Alfred Hitchcock's rather unremarkable *Waltzes From Vienna* (1934) was released with the US title of *Strauss's Great Waltz*, but the change of title did nothing to improve its box-office takings. However, Gaumont-British and Gainsborough also continued to produce musicals for domestic consumption during the mid-1930s, including *Britannia Of Billingsgate* (1933) with Gordan Harker and John Mills, and *Princess Charming* (1934) and *Evensong* (1934), both starring Evelyn Laye. *Heat Wave* (1935) was set in Ruritania and *Car Of Dreams* (1935) featured John Mills much higher up the credits list. Like BIP, Gainsborough made use of proven British comedy talent in films such as *Oh Daddy* (1935) starring Leslie Henson and Frances Day. Though considerable faith was placed in the Jesse Matthews' musicals, which we examine later, by 1936 a policy of retrenchment was evident, signalled by the departure of Michael Balcon to MGM-British that year. Comedy was proving more lucrative, though there was still room for hybrids such as the Crazy Gang's *O-Kay For Sound* (1937).

Neither BIP nor Gainsborough went unchallenged in producing musical films during the early 1930s. Herbert Wilcox and his British and Dominion Film Corporation had eagerly embraced sound film and adapted his Imperial Studios at Elstree to produce them. *The Blue Danube* (1932), an interesting formal experiment using only music to comment on the action and featuring the gypsy music of Alfred Rode and his Tzigane Band, was not successful, earning Wilcox 'plenty of kicks in the pants' (Wilcox 1967: 139). However, his fortunes and reputation were reversed with the signing of Jack Buchanan and a young Anna Neagle in *Good Night, Vienna* (1932). The film cost £23,000 and recouped £150,000 in Australia alone; it played for 13 consecutive weeks at the Capitol in the Haymarket and, according to Wilcox, 'broke records throughout the country' (Wilcox 1967: 91), though John Sedgwick ranks it in sixth place in the most popular films of 1932 (Sedgwick 2000). Wilcox enjoyed another success in 1932 with *Say It With Music*, featuring Jack Payne and the BBC Dance Band. The professional and personal partnership between Wilcox and Neagle was to continue into the 1940s and beyond, but Wilcox also worked with Jack Buchanan on musicals including *Yes Mr Brown* (1933) and *That's A Good Girl*, the latter directed by Buchanan. Buchanan took a cameo role in the Anna Neagle vehicle *Limelight* (1936) and starred in *This'll Make You Whistle* (1936), an ambitious musical that made good use of American songwriters and the services of American choreographer Buddy Bradley, and that reflected Wilcox's continuing determination to make films that appealed to the American market. Buchanan also appeared in Capitol's *When Knights Were Bold* (1936) and later formed his own production company before departing to work in Hollywood. Though British and Dominion ceased trading in 1936, Wilcox secured a series of deals that enabled him to continue production in the late 1930s, often to considerable success with films such as the non-musicals *Victoria The Great* (1937) and *Sixty Glorious Years* (1938). His interest in musical film remained and resurfaced in the 1940s.

The other significant production company to make a mark with successful musical films was Basil Dean's Associated Talking Pictures (ATP). Dean was a successful stage producer but, like Wilcox, had been impressed by the developments in sound cinema he had seen in America. Dean secured a distribution deal for ATP films through RKO, though they were essentially using him to fulfil their quota requirements. Ironically, given his cultural ambitions for sound film and the numerous contacts he had with 'legitimate' theatre, Dean found success with a series of films built around music-hall stars Gracie Fields and George Formby. Though ATP produced a number of films drenched with middlebrow cultural cachet, such as *Lorna Doone* (1935) and *Midshipman Easy* (1935), the latter starring Hughie Green and Margaret Lockwood, these were paid for by the increasing lucrative returns from the films starring his two music-hall comedy discoveries.

Though these production companies were responsible for meeting much of the demand for musical films in the 1930s, a number of small, independent companies, many of them short-lived, were busy producing musical films which exploited British music hall, variety, radio, record and dance-band talent, almost exclusively for the domestic market. George Pearson, attempting to survive in the sound era, formed

British Screen Productions that produced one musical film, *London Melody* (1930), before folding in 1932. A young Michael Powell had a share in Westminster Films that produced two musicals directed by him, *His Lordship* (1932) and *Born Lucky* (1932). Many of these short-lived production companies were used by American majors as part of their attempt to fulfil quota requirements. One such company was Nettlefold Productions, who produced the Ruritanian musical *Prince Of Arcadia* (1932) featuring Ida Lupino and *Two Hearts In Waltztime* (1934) starring Carl Brisson, Frances Day and a young Valerie Hobson. Sound City and Rock Studios produced a number of musicals, the latter being responsible for the Harry Roy vehicle *Everything Is Rhythm* (1936). Other companies such as Julius Hagen's Twickenham Films (also known as Real Art) were more successful and enduring. Hagen produced a number of musicals beginning with *Lily Of Killarney* and *Say It With Flowers* (both 1934) and achieved considerable success with *Music Hall* (1934) directed by John Baxter. British Lion, the company founded by Edgar Wallace in 1927 and with a series of financial transmutations yet to come, produced series of musical shorts from 1933 onwards, featuring British dance bands and singers, before venturing into musical features such as the revue *Calling All Stars* (1937). Taken together, the musical film output from these and other companies such as Butchers was significant, and serves to confirm just how important the musical film was both to British production and to British cinema audiences.

By 1938, British film production was in crisis, as the number of long films registered fell from 228 in 1937 to 103 in 1938. Before that, and despite all the criticisms of quota films, a stream of important – and not-so-important – musical films had been produced. Whilst those featuring Gracie Fields, George Formby and Jesse Matthews enjoyed sustained success at the British box-office, a variety of other musical films also proved popular with audiences. What they shared in common was a reliance on artists, performers, singers and bands who were already deeply implicated in the wider British entertainment industry, people with an existing reputation for giving pleasure. Together, they provided a complex articulation of British culture that recognised, but was still resisting, American influences, a culture in which identities were recognisably dependent on and defined by class, gender and region.

Gracie Fields and George Formby

Though they are far from representative of the variety of British musical film produced during the 1930s, the films of Gracie Fields and George

Formby have received much critical attention, not least because they were undoubtedly popular with British audiences. As Peter Stead remarks,

> These music hall stars had been put into films to make money but the evidence suggests that even the producers were surprised at how much money was made and at how popular the stars themselves became. (Stead 1989: 108)

The importance of Gracie Fields within the British entertainment business and her influence on British society and culture in the 1930s has been widely acknowledged, not least by Jeffrey Richards, who argues that 'Gracie Fields was more than just a film star. She was a phenomenon. . . . Gracie became a symbol for the nation as a whole in the Thirties' (Richards 1984: 169–72). Though the coming of synchronised sound film was able to privilege Fields' voice and songs, her appeal and her attraction went far beyond this. In fact, whilst she had recorded her first gramophone record for HMV in 1919, this was never released and it was not until 1928 that her first commercially available record, 'Because I Love You' coupled with 'My Blue Heaven' was released on HMV. Fields' reputation prior to her first film appearance in 1931 was built largely upon her live variety and revue appearances, initially in revues such as *Yes I Think So!* and *It's A Bargain* which toured northern England. These appearances were themselves built upon an apprenticeship in variety in the north with companies such as Clara Coverdale's Boys and Girls and Cousin Freddy's Pierrot Concert Party. Billed alternatively as 'Rochdale's Own Girl Vocalist' and as a 'versatile comedian', Fields established a reputation for sharp comedic performances and a range of vocal abilities securely grounded in her northern working-class roots, though arguably it was not until the London run of the revue *Mr Tower of London* that she attracted the interest of major entertainment business impresarios:

> *Mr Tower of London* went on and on. At the end of six and a half years the little show had grossed something over a quarter of a million pounds I believe and Sir Oswald Stoll booked it for a week at the Alhambra Theatre, bang in the middle of London's West End. (Fields 1960: 47)

Fields stumbled in to film-making. Without her knowing it, husband Archie Pitt and manager Bert Aza had signed a deal with Basil Dean's Associated Radio Pictures (ARP, from 1931 Associated Talking Pictures ATP) for her first film *Sally In Our Alley* (1931), directed by Maurice Elvey. As ARP's newly acquired Ealing Studios was still being equipped with the RCA Photophone system, the film was shot at the newly converted British Lion sound studios at Beaconsfield. Claiming that 'none of us knew anything about film making', Fields found this and her subsequent films an exhausting, frustrating and tedious process (Fields 1960: 81). Bret claims that she 'hated every minute of this new enterprise' and records that during shooting for the film undertook a series of music-hall appearances, much to the annoyance of Basil Dean (Bret 1995: 37). In spite of Fields' dislike of film-making and of Basil Dean's inherent distaste for such 'low-brow' musical-comedy pictures, *Sally In Our Alley* proved a significant financial success and Fields went on to make a total of seven films with Dean, four of which he directed. As Low argues, these and other similar films including, of course, the George Formby films from 1935, were to become the mainstay of what became Associated Talking Pictures (ATP) profits in the 1930s (Low 1997: 153). In the process, some of the distinctive aesthetic qualities of one important strand of the British musical film, its ability to harness musical numbers with broad comedy in the tradition of the music hall, was firmly established. Though *Sally In Our Alley* wears some of its technical deficiencies on its surface and suffers from some excesses in performance, not least from Florence Desmond, it is a remarkably effective, at moments even a poignant, film. Based on Charles McEvoy's play *The Likes Of Her*, with a screenplay by Miles Malleson and Alma Reville, the film is centred on the relationship between sweethearts Sally Winch (Gracie Fields) and George Miles (Ian Hunter) at the time of the First World War. However, George's absence from much of the film provides space for an important sub-plot based around Florrie Small (Florence Desmond), a frail victim of an oafish, bullying and criminal father who physically abuses her. Having declared their intention of marrying once the war is over, George is wounded in action and decides to release Sally from her commitment. He does this by persuading his army buddy Alf to declare back home that George is dead. Despite attentions from other men, Sally, by this time an orphan, remains in love with George, faithfully keeping his framed photograph on her bedroom shelf. Though she is tempted by the economic security offered her by Sam Bilson, owner of the café where she works as a waitress, her dedication to George proves resolute. She does this even when she is told that George is not only alive, but is married to a woman he met 'out east'. In the meantime, Sally takes responsibility for the abused Florrie, who finds psychological refuge in reading film magazines and survives her father's abuse by lying and cheating. This, combined with Florrie's aversion to work, rebounds on Sally's effort to rehabilitate her. Having taken Florrie in, Sally is betrayed by her when George, having recovered from his wounds, returns to the alley. Florrie persuades

George that Sally is no longer interested in him. She also relieves George of his money by stealing his wallet. Though bewildered by George's rejection of her and believing that he is already married, Sally manages to rescue Florrie from her anti-social ways, forcing her to address her problems by encouraging her to smash Sally's prized possessions until she breaks down and overcomes 'the devil inside her'. A victim of social and economic circumstances, Florrie makes amends and repays Sally's kindness by being instrumental in bringing Sally and George together again. He enters the café where she is performing 'Sally' in time for her to sing, looking directly at him, 'you're more than the whole world to me'.

Though much of the film seems imbued with an almost Victorian sensibility, epitomised by the plaque hanging on Sally's wall proclaiming 'Patience Is A Virtue', trading upon an aesthetic reliant on melodrama and coincidence, it is deeply interesting as an example of the distinctive qualities of British musical film. At one level, of course, the film is a vehicle for Fields' songs and 'Sally', the song written by Harry Leon, Leo Towers and Bill Haines, occupies a central place both in the film and in Gracie Fields' career, to the point where she was reputedly sick of it (Bret 1995: 38). At another level, and deploying the working-class and northern imaginary woven around Fields, the film promotes the implied virtues of working-class community and its solid values, contrasting these with the superficial and uncaring hostilities Sally experiences when she is in upper-class company.

Arguably, these class contrasts are represented through the geographies of carefully delineated spaces. The title of the film itself emphasises the importance of place, the ambivalently liberating yet restrictive 'alley' that serves as the locus for much of the narrative action. Beyond this space, whether it is high-society parties or the horrors of the battlefield, indifference, hostility and chaos reign. By contrast, the alley, whilst not without its conflicts and problems, offers a space in which communal resolution overcomes individual misunderstanding, a place where identity is reaffirmed and endorsed, often through song and its power to bind people together. The film begins with its opening titles against documentary-style footage of children playing in a confined urban working-class location, with music from a barrel organ in the background. It then cuts to George and Sally pledging their love for each other, riding in a pony and trap through a rural setting not seen again in the film, a rural England normally denied to the working class, an idyll blasted away by the trumpets of war. Documentary footage of the battlefields gives way to the hospital ward where George declares that, crippled as he is, he is not good enough for Sally. The emblematic power of the River Thames and London's Tower Bridge carries us to the Green Man public house, the alley, the café where Sally works and to the community that lives in these spaces. Incongruously, in this London café, Sally sings the 'Lancashire Blues', declaring her preference for her northern roots, as she sings 'give me some clogs and you can keep your shoes', rejecting 'corn on the cob and waffles' for 'Lancashire hot-pot'. This is no song of diasporic alienation, however, as the assembled customers join in the coda of 'eeh by goom' and demand another song – 'Sally' – from her. Equally incongruously, this working-class communal experience is shared by an upper-class couple who declare that 'she is quite too marvellous'. This leads to an invitation, later in the film, for Sally to sing for 'ten guineas' at a high-society party hosted by the Duchess of Wexford.

Sally's caution in accepting this invitation is justified by the treatment she receives at the party. The coded contrast between Sally's 'alley' clothes and the silk party dresses worn by the upper-class women is evident and the Duchess greets Sally with suspicion and disdain. However, Sally is quickly made over and remodelled, given a bath and a backless black dress to wear, which only serves to increase her discomfort. Asked to sing a song like the ones she sings in the café, she doubts that the band will know 'Fred Fanackapan', but they do and she does. Her rendition of this comic novelty song, replete with heavy Lancastrian intonations, is a source of great amusement to the socialites. However, whereas the working-class audience in Sam's café join in spontaneously with her performances in a show of communal solidarity, Sally has to prompt a choral response from the party-goers, and the Duchess struggles to pronounce the words to the song.

Having performed her song and offered the party the pleasures which stem from 'slumming it', Sally is ignored as the party-goers begin to dance. Unable to understand why she is being excluded, Sally grabs a young man to dance with, only to discover that he is one of the waiters. A fellow Lancastrian, the young man is sacked on the spot and Sally leaves the party, ignored by guests and servants alike. Forced to engineer her exit from upper-class space, whistling for her own taxi, Sally returns to the alley and Sam's café where an expectant crowd are waiting for her to perform. The raucous but warm-hearted reception she gets is in stark contrast to the cold civilities of the society party. Still wearing her borrowed party dress, a signifier of Fields own real-life trajectory into fame and fortune, she lampoons upper-class ways and pronunciation in her performance, bringing gales of laughter from her alley audience. Performed on a raised stage at one end of the café, framed by a banner that says 'Welcome To Our Sally', the number is both narratively motivated and a privileged performance space for Fields' evident talents, and ends in the reconciliation of Sally and George, to the delight of the communal 'audience'.

Contrasting ways in which American cinematic melodrama displaces class conflict into other more acceptably egalitarian conflicts that are resolved through the temporal biographical trajectory of the hero or heroine, such that 'biography conquers geography', Christine Gledhill argues that

> British culture, and its cinema, requires a geographic mapping of social-class-defined spaces that inhibits the individual's progressive trajectory through time, working to reinstate the boundaries that divide protagonists. Geography rules. (Gledhill 2003: 20)

In *Sally In Our Alley*, the heroine's brief, uncomfortable journey into a social space different from her own only serves to reinforce her identity with the working-class community of which she is a part. Interestingly, in this 'other' space, her identity is altered and becomes false, her songs serving only as amusement to an audience who are indifferent to her and to the expressive powers of song and performance. These powers, the capacity of song to move, change, resolve and unite, only become possible within those working-class spaces around the 'alley'. Far from being the figure of 'national consensus' which she became, here Fields is identified squarely with the working class. Much of the humour in the film springs from her acerbic mockery of upper-class manners and assumptions, or from the clear and often amused acceptance of working-class strategies for survival in an otherwise hostile world.

If in *Sally In Our Alley* she seems unequivocally the champion of a section of the English nation, the transformation of Fields into a figure embodying national consensus was in part achieved through the important changes in her subsequent films. Florrie's obsession with 'the pictures', her imitations of Garbo in front of Sally's dressing-table mirror, and her desire to 'be in the pictures', offers an element of self-reflexivity in a film which at every other level rejects interest in the world of entertainment, apart from a brief scene in the alley where a Punch and Judy show and a barrel organ compete to entertain the children and provide an opportunity for Grace to lead them in 'Fall In And Follow The Band'. In fact, Florrie's fixation with the glamorous world of cinema is presented as part of the reason why she is work-shy. In *Sally In Our Alley*, though much of the social activity is centred on consumption, in the café and at the Green Man public house, the business of entertainment has nothing to do with the world of work.

However, her next two films, *Looking On The Bright Side* (1932) and *Love, Life and Laughter* (1934) relied much more on a 'show-biz' setting, reflecting perhaps the influence of the 'backstage' American film musical. Though in the earlier film, she refuses the opportunity to become the star that her talents obviously merit, in *Love, Life and Laughter* she undergoes a transformation from bar maid to film star. This growing concern with entertainment and with the view that success in entertainment can be as legitimate as success in every other endeavour mirrors Fields' real-life trajectory, which simultaneously brought her very great wealth and yet kept her in touch with concerns experienced by ordinary people. Much of this wealth came from record sales based on songs in her film, such as 'Looking On The Bright Side Of Life' issued on EMI's HMV label. In February 1933 Fields made a much-publicised visit to the EMI production plant at Hayes to press her four millionth record (Martland 1997: 217–18). The cultural significance that Fields increasingly had for the nation is constructed through fictional representations that help legitimise success in the world of entertainment, in part through the suppression of some of the material consequences of that success.

Apart from the fact that many believe it to be her best film, *Sing As We Go* (1934) is a key text in this process. With a script by J.B. Priestley, the film connects with some of the structural changes taking place in Britain. The most obvious of these was unemployment in industrial northern England. Gracie, along with the rest of Greybeck Mill, is thrown out of work when the factory closes. At the end of the film, thanks to an unlikely chance encounter at Blackpool Pleasure Beach with Sir William Upton, inventor of an artificial silk, the Mill reopens thanks to the new 'miracle' process and Gracie returns to work, promoted to the role of Welfare Officer. Just as she had led the factory closure with it, so the return to work is led by Gracie's singing the film's title song. Yet, this narrative framing device is largely redundant to the central core of the film, as peripheral as Gracie's thwarted desire for the mill-owner's son Hugh Phillips (John Loder). The central attraction and the pleasures of the film reside in the episodic narrative stitched around Gracie's experiences in Blackpool as she moves from one job to another, as a 'human spider', a song plugger and 'Crunchy Wunchy' salesgirl. The film's centre of gravity and its attractions for audiences relate to the carnivalesque pleasures of leisure, consumption and entertainment, pleasures driven and delivered by the vocal and comedic talents of Fields. The film's insistence on privileging performance space, of providing opportunities to exploit Gracie Fields, over and above any concern to construct the character 'Gracie' within narrative space, is compounded by the extensive use of narratively inconsequential comedy, much of it based on music-hall and variety tradition.

This can lead to what in other modes of film-making would be considered serious flaws. For example, the early comic business built around Uncle Murgatroyd and 'clumsy and gormless' Ezekiah Crowther as they return home drunk to what they hope will be an empty house and their subsequent exploits with the Staghunters in Blackpool do nothing to prepare us for Ezekiah's role in the moving rendition of 'Love Wonderful Love', where his beautiful baritone voice mingles with Fields' introspective delivery of her poignant declaration of thwarted love for Hugh Phillips. Sung in Madame Osiris' ironically named 'Mon Desir' boarding house, the duet – underscored by a sweeping string, wind and harp orchestration – plays over scenes of other lovers united, or dreaming of love, over the dimming lights of the Pleasure Beach, of night descending on Blackpool, before brass chords cue the segue into the film's narrative conclusion, the return to work at Greybeck Mill.

Contrasting *Sing As We Go* with *Evergreen*, Andrew Higson draws upon Gunning's concept of the cinema of attractions in arguing that

> *Sing As We Go* is an impressive instance of the emergence of the cinema of attractions within the field of narrative cinema. Indeed, it makes more sense to see *Sing As We Go* not as a narrative film in which music and comic gags feature as interruptions or inserts, but as a film which is organised around its various attractions ... The attractions are the point of the film, not its flaws; the pleasures of this film are less the drama of narrative integration, and more the attraction of potential disintegration. (Higson 1995: 145–6)

Higson is particularly interested in the role of comic gags here, but arguably it is Fields herself, particularly her musical performance, which sits at the heart of the film. Her ability to deliver comic songs drawing on her northern working-class roots, as well as her ability to undertake serious singing of ballads, even light opera, is fully exploited in her screen appearances. Significantly, as she sings the title song at both the opening and closing of *Sing As We Go*, Fields addresses the camera directly, a clear if transgressive crossing over from narrative space into performative space, announcing the extent to which music and its performance are central to the film. After all, apart from the concern that the mill is closing just as it has got a good football team together, Gracie's main worry is whether it is worth continuing rehearsals for the factory show. Rejecting any notion that the mill closure has 'knocked the song and dance out of her', she leads the workers in a display of communal solidarity and resistance in the face of financial disaster by singing 'Sing As We Go', albeit to the sparse accompaniment of a solitary harmonica. This resistance to the whims of economic power are further evident when she does her mock music-hall routine, with bowler hat and false moustache. Her decision to find work in Blackpool and the bicycle ride there is underscored by the title song, by way of references to policeman Stanley Holloway's comedy song 'Sam Pick Up Thee Musket' (and, later, at the Zoo, to his 'Albert And The Lion') and a brass band playing on the street corner. The organised chaos that is Mrs Clotty's boarding house in Blackpool is underscored by singing and piano music. Amongst the jobs she undertakes, one is singing 'Just A Catchy Little Tune' over and over again for music publishers Ritz and Finglestein. Her performance attracts a large audience who sing and whistle along with her in a show of communal togetherness. In Blackpool, music is the backdrop to life, whether it is the Staghunters marching brass band, the band that accompanies the circus acts, or the dance orchestra at the Tower Ballroom, where Gracie extricates herself from embarrassment and hostility by singing the comedy number 'In My Little Bottom Drawer'. Following 'Love Wonderful Love', the film's triumphal title song plays over newspaper headlines announcing the return to work, this time with full orchestral accompaniment as Fields, singing directly to camera, hits her trademark top C.

Fields consolidated her already highly successful variety career through her film appearances and became hugely popular with British audiences. Using evidence based upon popular newspapers and trade papers, Richards argues for the popularity that Fields, like George Formby, enjoyed with the British cinema-going public. In November 1933 she was voted the most popular female film star in a reader's poll for the *Daily Express*; by 1936 she had retained her position as the most popular British star and was third in a list of most popular international stars, ahead of Jesse Matthews (Richards 1984: 160–1). This evidence is challenged to an extent by the work of John Sedgwick, who claims that Gracie Fields' seven films released between 1932 and 1937 were popular but not particularly amongst the highest ranking in their respective years. Using a measure of individual film popularity based on exhibition exposure which he terms POPSTAT, Sedgwick argues, for example, that *Looking On The Bright Side* can only be ranked 63rd in popularity for 1932; *Sing As We Go* was ranked as 37th in 1934 (Sedgwick 2000: 176). This apparent disparity can be explained to some extent by important differences in regional tastes, exhibition structures and cinema-going patterns which were important in the 1930s; the manager of the Imperial Cinema in Bolton in 1937 was in no doubt that, at his cinema, Gracie Fields and George Formby were the main attractions (Richards 1994: 157). However, it is also important to recognise that perceptions of popularity were based on the range of entertainment activities a performer engaged in. As we have seen, it is a mistake to divorce Fields' film work from her success as a live hall and variety artist and as an enormously prolific and popular recording artist.

Fields' popularity with British audiences was certainly enough to attract the attention of American producers. In 1935 MGM had expressed interest, but regarded her as 'too national'. However, with the momentum built by *Look Up And Laugh* (1935), *Queen Of Hearts* (1936) and *The Show Goes On* (1937), all with narratives set within the world of show business, developing what Richards calls 'the deliberate glamourisation of Gracie' (Richards 1984: 185), and following the financial success of *We're Going To Be Rich* (1937), her second film to be directed by Monty Banks, Fields was offered and accepted a four-picture deal with Twentieth Century Fox for 'the highest salary ever paid to a human being' (Fields 1960: 110). However, even if one Bolton cinema fan reported to the Mass-Observation team in 1937 that he was eagerly awaiting the result of the combination of Hollywood and 'Our Gracie', Fields' film career was losing momentum (Richards and Sheridan 1987: 83). *Shipyard Sally* (1939), reputedly her favourite film, does however mark an energetic return to some of the concerns of earlier films, based around the threat of unemployment in the Clydebank shipyards.

As in *Sing As We Go*, the key to economic power resides with the upper classes, in this case with Lord Randall. A minor, struggling, variety artiste specialising in 'Songs, Dances and Funny Sayings', Sally Fitzgerald (Gracie Fields) takes over The Bonnie Brig, a Glasgow pub, with her father Pop (Sydney Howard). Her generosity leads to her being deputed to go to London, armed with a signed petition, and fight the case for the shipyards when they are closed. Cheered by the workers at the station, she sings 'Wish Me Luck As You Wave Me Goodbye'. Needless to say, after a series of setbacks and humiliations, she manages to persuade Lord Randall, Head of the Commission examining the resumption of shipbuilding, to reopen work on Clydebank.

Given Fields' own career trajectory and the growing problems faced by the British film industry after 1938, not least because of American competition, one of the most interesting preoccupations in the film centres on notions of identity. Sally buys the Bonnie Brig from an Irishwoman who puts on an act of poverty, only to throw off her widow clothes once the sale goes through, having sold the pub for 'three times its value'. Sally, a Lancastrian amongst Scots, gets the men in the pub on her side by singing a comedy song 'Grandfather's Bagpipes' and the lyrical ballad 'Annie Laurie' in a Scottish accent. Later, in an attempt to meet Lord Randall at the men-only Argyle Club, Sally rents some men's clothes from a theatrical costumier and poses, in a wonderfully comic sequence, as 'Sir Richard Aldershot', whose Swahili 'does twenty miles to the gallon', and whose suit delivers a series of magic tricks before falling off and revealing the woman beneath. Outside Lord Randall's London home, Linda Marsh, an American singing star, mistakes Pop for the peer, giving Sally the idea of taking Linda's place in order to get in to see Lord Randall at the society party that evening. Posing as Americans, they gain entrance to the house and Sally sings the up-tempo swing number 'I Got The Jitterbugs', clearing registering the American influence on British popular music which had gained momentum as the 1930s progressed. To placate Lord Randall and his dislike of 'jazz' and all things 'loud and artificial', Sally sings a straight version of 'Danny Boy' with a mixed Irish/Scottish brogue. Later, at Lord Randall's country estate, another case of mistaken identity leads to the rumba number 'In Pernambuco'. Believing that the shipyard has not been reprieved, Sally and Pop return to Glasgow, only to discover that Lord Randall has been influenced by the workers' petition and they are greeted by the jubilant community. Superimposed against a montage of industrial activity, Gracie Fields sings 'Land Of Hope And Glory'. She becomes, for Jeffrey Richards, 'Britannia', a symbol for the nation as a whole.

However, in writing about the 'extraordinary ordinariness' of Gracie Fields, Marcia Landy makes the point that whilst

> descriptions of Gracie as a national icon are intrinsic to her success as a star and connect the milieu of the early 1930s to British cinema . . . they do not sufficiently account for the theatrical character of her acting, her musical performing style, and the meta-cinematic dimension of her films. (Landy 2001: 56)

Arguably, the popularity of her films in Britain and their struggle to make an impact in America has much to do with the distinctive qualities of British musical comedy and the local reference points on which it invariably drew. Though they get drawn towards some of the changing cultural practices explicit in Hollywood narrative cinema, the films of Gracie Fields represent the attempt to reproduce in cinematic form British performative traditions found in music hall, live variety and on record, traditions which enjoyed a distinctive resonance with British audiences, both because of, and despite, the class and regional inflections which marked her public persona.

If the musical comedies of Gracie Fields point to the inadequacies of generic classifications when discussing British cinema, the films starring

George Formby during the 1930s and into the early 1940s reinforce these inadequacies. The son of a well-known music-hall star, Formby rejected attempts to employ him as a horse-racing jockey and finally drifted into the entertainment business. His first film appearance was in 1915 as a jockey in Will Barker's *By The Shortest Of Heads* and he made his music-hall debut at Harrison's Picture House in Earlestown Lancashire in April 1921. His success in music hall and his three-year record deal with Decca in 1932 led to a contract for two films produced by John Blakeley's Mancunian Films, *Boots, Boots* (1934) and *Off The Dole* (1936). Both low-budget affairs, they nonetheless did well in cinemas in the North and Midlands, reawakening the interest of Basil Dean's ATP at Ealing who had earlier turned down the chance to use Formby.

Michael Balcon later wrote of the difficulties of incorporating Formby's songs into his films, though he recognised the centrality of their appeal to audiences. Formby had built a reputation for songs many of which relied on sexual innuendo. The 1933 Decca version of 'With My Little Ukulele In My Hand' was withdrawn after advance copies had been sent to trade papers for review and in 1936 the Regal Zonophone version of 'When I'm Cleaning Windows' was officially banned by the BBC, though it did receive some airtime. Director Anthony Kimmins decided against using 'I Wonder Who's Under Her Balcony Now' in *Trouble Brewing* (1939), feeling that the lyrics were too risqué. In these and many other recordings, Formby's songs betray what Richards refers to as a juvenile attitude to sex, but one that appealed to many in a society which repressed open discussion of sexual relationships. In the films, Formby confronts adversity, gets the girl despite having, as a character says in *It's In The Air* (1938), a 'face like a horse and teeth like a graveyard', and usually succeeds in his ambition in a formula which Richards describes as 'a simple story-line fleshed out with cheerful songs, plenty of slapstick and comic chases' (Richards 1984: 199).

What this formula also delivered, of course, was the opportunity for musical set pieces, often in ways that acknowledged the risqué reputation that Formby's songs enjoyed. This can be seen in his first film at Ealing, *No Limit* (1935), directed by Monty Banks and co-starring Florence Desmond. Based on a story by best-selling author Walter Greenwood, Formby plays the gormless but well-intentioned George Shuttleworth whose ambition is to win the Isle of Man TT Races. After a series of setbacks, George succeeds both in winning the race and in getting the girl. Along the way, the songs are positioned in ways that are either narratively motivated or at least naturalised within the

narrative space. On his way to the Isle of Man by train, George entertains the packed, boozy carriage with 'Riding In The TT Races', one of
the many songs written for Formby by Harry Gifford and Fred Cliffe.
We have already learnt from the letters that George writes to Rainbow
Motorcycles begging for sponsorship that he plays the ukulele, so it is
no surprise when George emerges from behind his fellow passengers and
offers to sing, accompanying himself on the ukulele. This bacchanalian
scene, with men women and children guzzling drink and gulping sand-
wiches, not only serves to endorse the collective excitement of working-
class holidays and gives expression to George's aspirations through
lyrics which see him 'coming down the hill at breakneck speed', it also
foregrounds the 'dirty tricks' we later witness and the promise of anticipated comedy as he invites his friends to 'pop along and see me riding
in the TT races'. Referring to his anticipated riding exploits with 'all his
spare parts sticking out', George's ukulele playing is augmented after
16 bars with the muted orchestration from Ord Hamilton and his
Twentieth Century Band, and the diegetic singing of the chorus line by
his fellow revellers, in a visual and sonic endorsement of his role of
working-class 'everyman'.

The power of singing and music to elide distinctions and construct a
sense of community is evident in the number sung in the ship's bar on
the way to the Isle of Man. Following some effective comic business
involving George's attempts to order drinks, Florrie sings, 'I'm Riding
Around On A Rainbow'. In a self-reflexive acknowledgement of the cen-
sorial attitudes which often surrounded Formby's songs, George proposes singing 'The Old Woman From Gloucester' only to be told that
'you can't sing that here', even though, as he says, 'they do in Wigan'.
This is an interesting meta-cinematic moment, which like similar
moments in Gracie Fields' films, emphasises the complex relationship
that the film shares with an audience possessing unusual extra-textual
knowledge about its leading performer. The song, of course, refers to
the literal riding around that George will undertake on his Rainbow
motorcycle, but also draws upon the symbolic significance of the
rainbow, with all its connotations of happiness and eventual success 'at
the end of the rainbow', a clear reference to the TT race prize money
at stake. This up-tempo number – neatly underscored by the Hamilton
dance band, snickety trumpets and smooth saxophones curtailed by
controlled high-hat snatches – is shot with tilted and low-angle camerawork which serves to emphasise the sheer enjoyment of the ship's passengers, most of whom have made good use of the ship's bar. Though
Desmond leads the song, it is taken up not only by Formby, but by the
barman, singing of drinks that 'will lift you sky-high', the ship's captain

and the other passengers, including a loving couple, a father and his ten children and a couple playing darts. With lines such as 'life is a long holiday', 'sailing away from the blues' and 'bringing the sunshine to you', along with references to betting and gambling, it is easy to understand the pleasures that working-class audiences in particular would gain from this number. It is an exquisitely shot, wonderfully orchestrated and exuberant number which benefits from performances which look genuinely as if the experience is being enjoyed on set.

Following a series of comic mishaps, mainly involving George's lack of money, with Florrie's help he tries to raise enough to pay for his hotel room by performing a blackface act on the beach. 'In A Little Wigan Garden' undertakes a number of functions. Narratively motivated by his need to get some money, the sequence not only serves to compound George's problems, as his landlady discovers him and he is forced to turn over the money he has earned to a charity collecting for the 'birds of the frozen north', it also deepens the distinction between George's good nature and the arrogant bullying of his main rival Bert Tyldesley, making Florrie's rejection of Bert and love for George increasingly believable. The blackface act also serves as a marker of an important tradition in and reminder of Formby's roots in music hall, as well as offering a self-deprecating comment on George's self-consciousness and feelings of inadequacy, not just amongst the professional TT riders such as Tyldesley, but in the world at large, inadequacies marked by the faltering rendition of the song when George spots his landlady in the crowd. The regional, northern working-class dimension to this self-consciousness is evident in the lyrics to the song; deriding the 'meadows farms and fields so grand' and the 'gardens at Kew', the song praises a 'spot that can beat all the lot', a garden in Wigan where 'crocuses croak with the frog and the smoke, From the gas works near', where every thing 'grows upside down'. All this sits alongside the evident ability that George has to attract and amuse a large crowd on the beach, a crowd that reacts with hostility to the landlady's racist attitudes. Again, his popularity here foregrounds his success and resulting popularity in the TT races themselves.

A potential improbability in this and his other films is that Formby gets the girl, in this case metropolitan middle-class Florrie. Their relationship is naturalised through the duet that they sing in the company of other loving couples, amongst them the elderly couple we saw earlier on the ship with their ten children. On the Manx hills, lit by the intermittent sweep of the lighthouse beam, George, despite feeling 'daft talking like this', expresses his desire for Florrie and they break into the sweetly melodic 'Your Way Is My Way'. It seems entirely appropriate that Desmond holds the harmonic line with greater surety than Formby does, given his lack of confidence and inability to seize the moment. He wants to talk about the weather, she is prepared to 'walk all night and day', he feels that 'when it's late at night, you should be home in bed like me'. It is Florrie who questions whether the couple need to do 'these things as they are supposed to be'. In may ways a conventional lilting love song with a strong melodic line, it nonetheless manages to make reference to the Formby persona and his conventional stage and screen catchphrases, including his cry 'Mother!': she sings 'You're so sweet / I'd like to go and meet / Your folks in Wigan by the sea' and he responds, 'You're so nice / I'll ask me Ma's advice / If you can come to our house to tea'. George is interrupted by the rival Sprocket Company boss, who has bribed him not to take part in the races, but his panic and apparent cowardice are coded through his discordant delivery of the final lines of the song, as he hustles Florrie away, much to her confusion.

At the film's climax, George acknowledges to Florrie that he is a coward, though it is important that his reluctance to ride in the race is based on the fact that earlier in the trials he narrowly missed killing a child, an experience that has unnerved him. After a fight with Tyldesley, he decides to ride and, in a carefully shot and edited race sequence, George proves triumphant. Importantly, though the coded differences between them are clear, George and Florrie declare their love for each other over the race Tannoy, a very public declaration of his success in love and career. This is the double-helix narrative evident in American musicals, but presented and structured in a distinctly different manner.

In total, Formby made eleven films for Dean's Associated Talking Pictures at Ealing. The two films following *No Limit*, *Keep Your Seats Please* (1936) and *Feather Your Nest* (1937) have George as an unsuccessful concert-party artist and a clumsy technician working for a record company respectively. The former film has a stronger plot to it, as George hunts for some jewels hidden in a chair that rightfully belong to him. Florence Desmond co-stars playing another unemployed variety artist and duets 'Standing On The Tip Of My Toes' with Fiona (Binkie) Stuart and 'Goodnight Binkie' with Formby, who sings 'When I'm Cleaning Windows' which, written by Cliffe and Gifford, caused some offence but sold huge numbers when released as a record by Regal Zonophone. In *Feather Your Nest*, it is the accidental breaking of 'I'm Leaning On A Lamp Post' by crooner Rex Randall that prompts him to record the song himself. It becomes a huge hit and Willie Piper (Formby) is able to realise his middle-class suburban dreams and settle down with Mary (Polly Ward).Though subsequent films followed the tried and tested Formby formula, there appeared to be a growing self-importance attached to the music in them. This did not always mean that the motivation for the songs was necessarily stronger. For example, in *It's In The Air* (1938), as George Brown, Formby has wandered into the air-raid exercise control room and, only four minutes into the film, launches into 'They Can't Fool Me' in response to the open-topped bi-plane pilot's request for a 'hot gramophone record' to warm him up. With no gramophone records to hand, Formby gives a 'live', apparently impromptu, rendition over the aircraft two-way radio system, at the end of which the airman remarks, 'Swell record, I must get it. What's its number?' Actually, it was MR 2891 on Regal Zonophone, when the song was released that year. However, the number was shot in a way designed to emphasise Formby's musical talents, with several close-ups of his banjo playing. In the title song from *Keep Fit* (1937), the number is introduced through a close shot of a record on a record player, as George undertakes his training for the boxing match, only for him to pick up the words of the song as he goes through his exercises, but without directly addressing the camera.

However, in these Formby films of the later 1930s, music is given a much greater presence than in the earlier films. In *Keep Fit*, dance band music is featured at the Regal Stores staff dance, where there is an extended sequence around the 'Paul Jones' dance, with numbers such as 'Red Sails In The Sunset' and 'Oh What A Beautiful Girl' played on the score. In *It's In The Air*, apart from the Sergeant-Major's long-running concern to learn to play the ukulele, music is foregrounded in the aerodrome canteen as Formby goes into the title song. In the number, Formby is accompanied by a harmony trio before the whole canteen joins in, accompanied by a swing orchestration featuring jazz clarinet, the number serving to code George's acceptance by the airmen. The film ends with George achieving his ambition to join the Royal Air Force, even if his role is confined to the on-stage RAF revue where he reprises the title song. In these later films, the scoring behind the opening titles is more extended and more complexly orchestrated, clear evidence of the influence of Ernest Irving (in *It's In The Air* and *Trouble Brewing* 1939) and Louis Levy (*Spare A Copper* 1940) as musical director. In the latter film's title sequence, for example, Levy provides a rich over-ture of songs featured in the film, very much in the manner of the Hollywood musical.

Like the films starring Gracie Fields, much of the appeal of George Formby's films for audiences relied on musical performance, even though these films fail to fit the normative generic patterns that marked American film musicals of the period. Of course, American cinema did have its equivalent musical comedies, not least the series of films featuring the Marx Brothers. However, it is importance to recognise that the appeal of these British films derived primarily from the music and from the complex interplay between the various elements of the entertainment industry, itself heavily dependent on traditions practised in music and variety. Though the films do have plots and undertake narrative development, these are largely incidental in their overall appeal. What mattered were the ideological constructions built upon the Fields and Formby personas, the recognition of distinctions which both mattered and could be overcome for the greater good, especially at a time of national crisis in the late 1930s. Equally important was the music, which served to elide differences, to articulate a range of feelings to which ordinary people could relate and to provide an uplifting sense of restrained optimism, of community, of 'seeing things through'.

Of course it is right to emphasise the reasons for the popularity of both Fields and Formby, reasons that went beyond the films themselves. However, even at the time these films were being produced, not everyone accepted that such an emphatically domestic product was in the best interests of the British film industry. Writing in 1938, the journalist Aubrey Flanagan noted their popularity, but argued that such 'vaudevillean melanges' were 'not the way forward for the British industry' (Stead 1989: 109). However, as the films of Jesse Matthews were to prove, even deliberate attempts to construct products designed to appeal to the American market were not always as successful as producers hoped they would be.

Jesse Matthews

Like Gracie Fields, Jesse Matthews experienced the deprivations of a, in this case London, working-class upbringing. In her own opinion, 'dancing came to me naturally' (Matthews 1975: 32) and her abilities as a dancer were soon recognised. After specialist dance training, she appeared in revues such as C.B. Cochran's *Music Box Revue* and then joined Andre Charlot's troupe, sailing to America where she eventually became understudy for Gertrude Lawrence. Even before this she had minor parts in three British films, *Beloved Vagabond* (1923), *This England* (1923) and *Straws In The Wind* (1924). Success in *Charlot's Revue of 1926* in the West End led to a new contract to appear in the Rodgers and Hart revue *One Damn Thing After Another* for Cochran, where she met her future husband and co-star Sonnie Hale. Matthews enjoyed considerable success on stage in the United States, not least in *Wake Up And Dream* co-starring with Jack Buchanan in 1929. Her success led to screen tests with Paramount and interest from Metro-

Goldwyn-Mayer and Warner Bros, though her commitment to her Cochran stage contract meant that this chance to work in Hollywood went unheeded. Back in England, she made her first 'talkie', *Out Of The Blue* in 1931 for BIP at Elstree. Based on a stage musical and using a plot that revolves around the growing contemporary obsession with radio, the film's technical limitations ensured that the numbers were rather leaden and, despite Sonnie Hale's conviction that 'the future was in the film industry', both he and Matthews were disappointed with what they saw when the film was released in March 1932. However, despite his initial reaction that Matthews 'was a dead loss as far as films are concerned' (Thornton 1974: 95), Michael Balcon signed her to a two-year contract with Gainsborough and she appeared in *There Goes The Bride* (1932), *The Man From Toronto* (1933) and *The Midshipman* (1933) before being cast in *The Good Companions*, directed by Victor Saville in 1933.

Though Matthews resented the hard work involved in film-making and expressed a preference for working with Victor Saville rather than the demanding Albert de Courville, *There Goes The Bride* remains an interesting film. Though not conforming to the American musical conventions that characterised her later films, the musical numbers, particularly 'I'll Stay With You', are executed effectively by Matthews and the underscoring by Louis Levy, whilst often 'mickey-mousing' in a very literal manner, offers perfect support for the comic farce on offer. Capitalising on the growing popularity of dance-band music, the film makes extensive use of Carroll Gibbons and The Savoy Orpheans, both on the soundtrack and at the society party where his music is privileged. Thrown together when she runs away from her arranged marriage, Annette Marquand (Jesse Matthews) and Max (Owen Nares) agree to spend time together until Annette's intended husband (Basil Radford) has left for South America. In the process, and after a series of comic misunderstandings and mistaken identities, Max loses his own fiancée and falls in love with Annette. Matthews' screen innocence makes a perfect foil for the risqué comedy and the sexual innuendo that punctuates the narrative. Max's fiancée, Cora, having taken off her wet dress and then discovered Annette in the flat, leaves his apartment in anger and asks a man in the street to get her a car; the way she is dressed and the situation clearly intimates prostitution. Back in the apartment, Max comments that 'they'll think she's everybody's – fiancée'. When Annette coyly says to Max, 'I hope I shan't be ruined', the implication is clearly sexual. At the society party, though she flirts with several men, Annette declares her emotions and seals the relationship with Max in the song 'I'm Looking For You'. Although there are further comic complications and a climactic rush to reach Annette at the railway station before she is hauled back to her arranged marriage, the two finally declare their love for each other, perched on the luggage at the railway station.

There Goes The Bride persuaded Balcon to offer Matthews a lucrative two-year contract with Gaumont-British, but working with Victor Saville, first on *The Good Companions* and then *Evergreen* (1934), transformed Matthews into an international star. *The Good Companions*, regarded by Charles Barr as a 'prototype for the wartime national epic' (Barr 1997: 58), is based on the novel by J.B. Priestley. Matthews plays Susie Dean, a character born to be a success in the entertainment world, rising from concert-party performer to become a star in London's West End. A role in Hitchcock's *Waltzes From Vienna* (1934), a less than satisfactory attempt at the fashionable Viennese subgenre and based on the life and music of the Strauss family, did little to impress although, as we have seen, the film did obtain a release in America with the title *Strauss's Great Waltz*. If this and another run-of-the-mill film *Friday The Thirteenth* (1934) failed to exploit Matthews' talents as a singer and dancer, then *Evergreen* more than compensated.

Based on her appearance in the stage musical *Ever Green*, with a score by Richard Rodgers and Lorenz Hart and with the addition of the Harry Woods songs 'Over My Shoulder Goes One Care' and 'When You've Got a Little Springtime In Your Heart', the film represented a conscious attempt by Balcon at Gaumont-British to appeal not just to the British and Empire market, but to the potentially lucrative American market. In addition to the relatively lavish budget of £60,000, what distinguished the film was the involvement of a number of Americans in the production. Apart from Rodgers, Hart and Woods, cameraman Glen MacWilliams and choreographer Buddy Bradley were American, director Victor Saville had already spent time working in America, and Michael Balcon was determined to achieve what he termed 'the high technical perfection of the Hollywood film'. There had been, and would be again, talk of pairing Matthews with Fred Astaire, though this never materialised. It was no surprise given these personnel involved in the production that, as Higson argues, '*Evergreen* takes on board the iconographic, thematic, discursive and structural conventions of contemporary Warner Bros. Backstage musicals' (Higson 1997: 135). The film succeeds as a fine British example of what Martin Rubin calls the 'integrated musical', its numbers perfectly woven into the linear narrative, with its show-business setting (Rubin 1993: 11). Perhaps the best known of her films, *Evergreen* was successful in the domestic market, ranking as the fourteenth most popular film of 1934, but arguably failed to make quite the impact on the American box-office that had been hoped for, especially outside New York and other east coast cities, though Jesse Matthews herself attracted positive critical attention.

Whatever the deliberate intention to emulate the Hollywood model, there are elements of the film which betray some differences from its American counterparts, most importantly in the early scenes set in the Edwardian music hall, which serve to delay narrative action. In the same way, the complicated processes of impersonation and masquerade which involve Matthews playing both Harriet Green and Harriet Hawkes, mother and daughter, but with the daughter forced into 'acting' the mother, present complications in the handling of desire in more complex ways than is usual in many Hollywood musicals of this period. Though, unlike Fields, Matthews does end up with the man she desires, this process is delayed considerably in her films through often quite complex layers of impersonation and (mis)identification. The ways in which desire is delayed were compounded by the very real failure to find a male dancing partner for Matthews who could carry sufficient dramatic and romantic weight in the narrative, as proved by *First A Girl* (1935) and *It's Love Again* (1936), both directed by Victor Saville. Gaumont-British's confidence in Matthews' appeal to American audiences was sufficient for them to premiere both films in New York before their London openings.Based on a stage play, *Viktor und Viktoria* by Reinhold Schunzel, and following earlier 1933 French and German versions of the film, *First A Girl* concerns Elizabeth's (Jesse Matthews) attempts to escape from the drudgery of working behind the scenes at a fashion house and to become a theatrical entertainer. She succeeds in this, but only after adopting a public persona involving considerable gender-bending masquerade and intimations of homoerotic desire. In an opening sequence referencing Warner Bros' *Fashions Of 1934*, Saville establishes the geographic and class divide that separates Madame Serafina's upper-class clientele from the seamstresses who watch proceedings from an upper balcony window. Two opening numbers, the crooning 'Little Silkworm' and an orchestral version of the rumba 'I Can Do Everything But Nothing With You', inscribe the importance of music and Elizabeth's desire to perform; as she is rushing to deliver some expensive dresses, even the clocks in the street chime these two melodies. A meeting with Victor (Sonnie Hale), a female impersonator, leads to success as a revue artist, Elizabeth playing a man playing a woman. Rooted in the rumbustious vulgarities of British music hall, the film rapidly rejects this milieu in favour of the cosmopolitan cabaret scene across Europe, providing the opportunity to stage big production numbers such as 'Half And Half', as well as offering metatextual comment on G-B's production strategy at this time. The attraction for audiences of the travelogue-like European scenes needs no explanation at a time when continental Europe resonated with a degree of exoticism for both domestic and American audiences. Along the way, the film makes effective use of the songs by another set of American songwriters who also wrote the songs for *When Knights Were Bold* (1936) starring Jack Buchanan, Sigler, Goodhart and Hoffman. These numbers, 'I Can Do Everything But Nothing With You', 'Close Your Eyes' and 'Everything In Rhythm (With My Heart)' are treated with staging, choreography and orchestration of the very highest order, more than matched by Glen MacWilliams' cinematography.

First A Girl betrays some echoes of the co-production strategies that underpinned the 'Film Europe' movement of the mid- and late 1920s, not least in sets designed by Oscar Werndorff. However, it is significant that the film makes more than a nod towards the specifically British comic cultural tradition despite its internationalist intent, not least in the comic musical underscoring in the scene where a drunken Victor attempts to put an even more drunk Elizabeth to bed, and in the knockabout finale where Victor takes on the role of 'Victoria' with the gusto of a pantomime dame. Much of the comic interplay centres on the gendered identities which Victor and Elizabeth construct, a narrative ploy which renders declaration of desire both comic and problematic, successfully delaying the romance between Elizabeth and Robert until the film's climax.

It's Love Again has music and lyrics by Sam Coslow and Harry Woods, with a musical score by Louis Levy and Bretton Byrd. Matthews plays Elaine Bradford, an aspiring singer and dancer who is having problems breaking into show-business. Failing to impress bored, soporific impresario Mr Raymond with her song and solo dance 'It's Love Again', performed in his luxurious art-deco apartment, she confides that to get into showbiz 'all you need is a big name, you don't need anything else'. This central concern with identity, with *who* rather than *what* you are, is presaged by the way in which disgraced journalist Freddie (Sonnie Hales) ghosts newspaper articles for Peter Carlton, played by American Robert Young. Eager to get an 'angle' and thus a jump ahead of their rival newspaper, Freddie and Peter decide to 'invent a celebrity of our own' and create the fictitious Mrs Smythe-Smythe, the literally fabulous multi-talented consort of the equally fictitious Maharajah of Myrashar. Their plan becomes complicated when, unknown to them, Elaine decides to adopt the persona of Mrs Smythe-Smythe in the attempt to further her career. At the Imperial Palace Hotel, she literally stops proceedings, then takes centre stage on a carefully lit podium with dance partner Cyril Wells in an exotic rumba. Dance, music and lyrics emphasise 'eastern' exoticism, announcing 'like the thump of a drum / you awaken something / from the deep and mysterious past', though also commenting ironically 'the moment we met I knew who you were'.

Having recognised the mutual benefit in perpetuating the deception, Elaine and Peter signal their growing romantic attraction for each other in a reprise of 'It's Love Again', with close-ups of their dancing feet. At a society party with an 'Indian theme', held in Mrs Smythe-Smythe's honour, and following a harmony trio singing a swinging 'Tony's In Town', an exotically costumed Elaine has to muddle her way through a supposedly ethnic dance, accompanied by four Indian musicians. However, the number rapidly acquires a swing orchestration, cuing a more conventional tap dance from Elaine. Further comic business is provided by yet another impersonation, when Freddie tries to pass himself off as Colonel Edgerton, the real Colonel having threatened to expose Peter and Elaine's deception.

Convinced of her talent, Peter and Freddie arrange for impresario Raymond to see Elaine perform in a local park, Peter's 'country seat', though Raymond only agrees to come because Freddie tells him the girl has a 'name'. In an impressive solo number, 'Dance My Way To Heaven', Matthews uses a grassy area for a romantic high-kicking ballet, the sandy path to dance a soft-shoe shuffle and then a paved area to dance tap accompanied by stride piano. The song's lyrics reflect the film's concerns with deception and impersonation, as Elaine sings in the opening verse, 'I wear a cloak of mystery / but darling in reality / there's not one thing to conceal. / Beneath my outward attitude / you'll find I'm really in a mood / restless, romantic and real'. Although this is a solo number, it attracts a growing number of onlookers, from the early-morning milkman to the large crowd, including a fine bass policeman, who join in the chorus. This joint affirmation of evident star attraction and the power of music to construct utopian community provokes Raymond to declare that she has it all, 'looks, talent and a name'. Elaine's declared intention to Peter that she is determined to succeed as herself is undermined by Raymond's perception that she is a 'name' and his determination to put her name in lights – as Mrs Smythe-Smythe.

This preoccupation with masquerade, perception and identity climaxes in the staging of Raymond's show 'Safari', where the nemesis of exposure threatens Elaine with disgrace and failure. Making good use of the huge complex proscenium staging and dressed in a sparkling sequinned cat-suit, Matthews/Elaine/Mrs Smythe-Smythe performs 'I Nearly Let Love Slip Through My Fingers'. Again, though he has no other function within the film, Cyril Wells dances with Matthews, before the number segues into a big-production finale. Blackmailed by Montague, a journalist from a rival newspaper, Elaine walks out of the show, telling Peter that she can't 'spend the whole of her life at a fancy-dress party'. Peter's reply is interesting: 'there's a girl for you. She wants to be, she is, and then she doesn't want to be'. Only when the audience has left and she returns to the empty auditorium and Raymond overhears her singing 'I Nearly Let Love Slip Through My Fingers' and witnesses the theatrically impossible but cinematically impressive reprise of 'Dance My Way To Heaven', with superimposed images from all the previous routines in the film and an exceptionally clever orchestral accompaniment accommodating the music from the different numbers, does Raymond decide to re-engage her as herself. Even then there is a twist. Asked for her name, Peter tells Raymond that she is Elaine Bradford, spelt C-A-R-L-T-O-N, her future married name.

Like *Evergreen*, *First A Girl* and her other later films, *It's Love Again* has many characteristics associated with the Hollywood musical of the 1930s, not least the central thematic preoccupation with success in the world of entertainment. The numbers, scoring and orchestrations match those heard from Hollywood and, certainly with Matthews herself, the choreography comes close. However, there remains a residue of Englishness centred firmly in Matthews singing style, with its emphatic pronunciation rejecting contemporary American singing idioms. Though these musicals represent an important strand of British musical film production, they are far from typical.

In late February 1937, Gaumont-British announced that it was closing down its Shepherd's Bush studios. Matthews' last two musicals, *Gangway* (1938) and *Sailing Along* (1938), both with lacklustre direction from Sonnie Hale, were shot at Pinewood following a deal which saw C.M. Woolf's General Film Distributors taking responsibility for distributing Gaumont-British product. The closure of Shepherd's Bush, temporary as it was to prove, was part of the larger crisis which hit British film production in 1937; as Thornton argues:

> Although nobody chose to recognise it at that time, the writing was already on the wall so far as the British film musical was concerned. (Thornton 1974: 139)

Certainly, whilst in 1934 British musical films had accounted for eight of the top 50 most popular films in Britain, by 1937 not one British musical film made the top 50, with Matthews' *Head Over Heels* ranking at 57th and *Gangway* at 70th (Sedgwick 2000: 157).

What was intended as the final picture under her existing Gaumont-British contract, a musical slated as *Asking For Trouble*, never went into production, though this may have been due to G-B's concerns over Sonnie Hale as director. A version of the film was made in 1938, without the five musical numbers, as *Climbing High*, directed by Carol Reed, with Matthews opposite Michael Redgrave. Personal problems, combined with another of the recurrent crises in British film production, effectively ended Matthews' film career, but her contribution to the British musical film was significant.

Despite the dominance that Fields, Formby and Matthews invariably command in critical writing about British cinema of the 1930s, it is important to recognise the scale and variety of the musical film during the decade, and to acknowledge the significant contribution made by a host of other artists to this most important element of British film production and exhibition at this period. Though it is impossible to do justice to all these artists and the many films they appeared in, the following comments do something to exemplify British musical film production and the pleasures they delivered in the 1930s.

British musical operetta and Ruritania: *Heart's Desire* (1935)

British cinema's institutional, economic and aesthetic flirtation with European film production in the early 1930s found expression in musical operetta and musical films that employed the exotic romanticism of southern-central Europe, particularly of Vienna and the imagined 'Ruritania'. Though the appropriation of this latter exoticised, imaginary central European realm – where time, space and social relations appeared to have been frozen – continued into the late 1950s with Tommy Steele's *The Duke Wore Jeans* (1957), it was particularly significant in the British musical film of the early and mid-1930s, a period before it became clear that European social and political relations were changing profoundly and in ways that threatened national interests. Films such as *Prince Of Arcadia* (1933), Herbert Wilcox's *The Queen's Affair* (1934) and Gainsborough's *Princess Charming* (1934) are interesting in their use of displaced geography as a means to explore, as their titles imply, aspects of class and social relationships. It was also a period in which European musical traditions, particularly the orchestral Viennese waltz, Hungarian gypsy music and light opera were as popular as newly emerging American popular music, evident in part by the huge popularity of massed accordion bands, their musicians draped in bandanas and billowing silk 'gypsy' trousers and blouses. Though the aesthetic use of this ill-defined European imaginary informs both nineteenth-century operas such as Bizet's *Carmen* as well as silent cinema, the ability to exploit the music blossomed in sound cinema. One of the earliest examples was BIP's *Gypsy Blood* (1931) based on *Carmen*. The same studio's *The Maid Of The Mountains* (1932), featuring music from Alfredo and his Gypsy Orchestra, proved popular, but the fascination with a highly romanticised central Europe was boosted by the enormous success of *Good Night, Vienna* (1932).

The vogue for male tenors who were capable of crossover from classical opera to stage and film was exploited in several films in which neither historical accuracy nor musical authenticity was at a premium. The Polish tenor Jan Kiepura had appeared in Polish and German films in the late 1920s and early 1930s before starring in *City Of Song* (1931) set in Naples and *Tell Me Tonight* (1932) set amongst the Swiss Alps, both films casting Kiepura as an Italian tenor. Kiepura went on to make two further films for British-Gaumont, *My Song For You* (1934) and *My Heart Is Calling* (1934). Kiepura was popular, but was eclipsed by the Austrian tenor Richard Tauber. Having appeared in two Pathétone shorts, Tauber starred in BIP's *Blossom Time* (1934) as Franz Schubert who, disappointed in love, pours his energies into his work and music after a display of romantic self-sacrifice. The studio capitalised on the success of the film with *Heart's Desire* (1935) another vehicle concerned primarily to display Tauber's considerable talent.

In their search for a tenor to appear in his latest London musical show, composer Oliver Desmond (Carl Harbord) and upper-class socialite Frances Wilson (Leonora Corbett) stumble across Karl August Franz Ludwig Josef Steidler (Tauber) singing in a Vienna café. They overcome his reluctance and persuade him to come to London, where he scores a major success with London's social elite and in Desmond's stage musical production *Venetian Moon*. However, Steidler has fallen in love with Frances and, disappointed when she announces her engagement to Desmond, he decides to return to his Viennese roots after only one performance. This theme of unrequited love, the slender plot which turns around the attempts to lure Steidler to London and the comic business that surrounds it, serve merely as an excuse to motivate and showcase Tauber's impressive vocal qualities and to exploit his existing popularity on radio and records. Whether singing in German at the Vienna café, accompanied by a small four-piece Viennese band, in the train carriage on the way to London, at the socialites' welcome party in London, or on stage in Desmond's new production, Tauber's outstanding singing retains its impact some 70 years later. The two numbers sung to the privileged socialite audience, Schumann's 'Devotion' and Tauber's own

'Let Me Awaken Your Heart' are delivered with impeccable vocal purity and make some contribution to plot development as the camera makes clear the growing romantic attachment Steidler feels for Frances, as well as her rather coy encouragement of his feelings. This linking of plot development with musical numbers is most evident in Steidler's stage performance; having overheard that Frances is engaged to marry Desmond, Steidler performs his on-stage role of a character whose love is unrequited in the number 'All Hope Is Ended'. Having been told that this finale will have to reach 'unprecedented heights' because 'it is in his contract', Steidler does just that, both his stage role and his screen character expressing the bitter disappointment of unrequited love, art imitating 'life'. Tauber's performance and director Paul Stein's effective use of soft-focus cut-aways of Frances as she listens to the song create a genuinely moving cinematic experience, resistant even to the underlying sentimental pathos expressed when Steidler declares 'I am just a voice, but who asks for me?' His return to his Viennese roots is sealed in the triumphal final number 'Vienna City Of My Dreams'.

Though primarily concerned to showcase Tauber's singing, *Heart's Desire* offers a glimpse of ambivalent British attitudes to European 'otherness', on the one hand intrigued by the imagined exotic romanticism implicit in songs and scenery, on the other asserting the supposed centrality of British culture, as when Frances declares that 'All the world comes to London'. The film is not devoid of an element of self-deprecation. Steidler's attempts to improve his English revolve around the eccentricities of British social etiquette, the authenticity of his Viennese home and friends is in sharp contrast with the ignorant affectations of English upper-class aristocracy in the shape of Lady Bennington, and their obsession with how Steidler will *look* rather than how he will sound indicates a certain shallowness. However, it is Tauber and the pleasures of his voice that sit at the heart of the film, as in the number 'As Sweet As Roses' where he conveys a profound sense of melancholic regret for his homeland and the woman he has left behind. The vogue for operatic tenors and the European imaginary was to fade rapidly in the second half of the decade as the political situation in Europe changed and the policy of European co-production and co-operation stuttered to a halt. Both Tauber and Vienna-born director Paul Stein settled in England, working together again on *Lisbon Story* in 1946. The popularity of 'gypsy' music, the Viennese waltz and male tenors was perpetuated for a while by the Moldavian-born, US-based tenor Arthur Tracy in films such as *Limelight* (1936) and *Command Performance* (1937), but their heyday had largely passed by the late 1930s.

Show-business and the Parade film: *Radio Parade of 1935*

From the early experiments with synchronised shorts, revue films such as *Elstree Calling*, Gainsborough's *Just For A Song* (1930), Mancunian's *Love-Mirth-Melody* (1934), Butcher's *Stars On Parade* (1936) and British Lion's *Calling All Stars* (1937), to those films that utilised a basic narrative to display show-business talents, the British musical film culled performers from music hall, variety, West-End productions, records and radio. Though revue musicals were an excuse to string a series of acts together, most made at least some use of a linking device, no matter how inconsequential, so that the revue evolved into a parade of acts. Like the American musical, many of these films developed an element of self-reflexivity through backstage narratives that offered versions of the work involved in cultural production. Using characters who were singers, dancers, composers and impresarios in scenarios set in cabaret, night-clubs, music halls, opera, ballet, dance bands, record companies, even film studios and television broadcasts, a string of films worked through love affairs, solved crimes, and celebrated success. Given the popularity of radio, it is not surprising that a number of these back-stage musicals, including *Radio Parade* (1933), *On The Air* (1934), *Death At Broadcasting House* (1934), *Street Song* (1935), *Radio Pirates* (1935), *Radio Lover* (1936) and *Variety Hour* (1937), featured radio stations and characters playing radio stars. Whilst the appeal of many of these were centred on performance rather than narrative suspense or complexity, they were rarely devoid of social or cultural comment and relevance, as a look at *Radio Parade of 1935* (1934) reveals.

Released in December 1934, *Radio Parade of 1935* starred an accomplished music-hall and film comedian, Clifford Mollinson, though he was eclipsed in the film by Will Hay, himself a product of British music hall. Hay made an appearance in *Eve's Film Review 356* in 1928 and another sound short, *Know Your Apples* in 1933. *Radio Parade of 1935* was the second of Hay's three films for BIP before he signed for Gainsborough in 1935, the studio where he went on to make his best-known comedy films including *Oh Mr Porter!* (1937) and *Convict 99* (1938). *Radio Parade Of 1935* is a sophisticated example of the parade musical, combining a series of revue acts within a narrative that makes some acerbic criticisms of the BBC and its programming policies. Using BIP's own – and soon to be redundant – Ambiphone Sound System, the film also included colour sequences using the Dufaycolor system.

Playing the incompetent, lazy Director General (DG) Garlon of the National Broadcasting Group or NBG (audiences would have shared the joke, NBG standing for 'no bloody good'), Hay is content to let his army of bureaucratic underlings run the radio station like a military operation, even though the dull, highbrow programmes put out by the station are disliked by the listeners. Young Jimmy Clare (Mollinson) is in charge of the Complaints Department and is a 'very busy man'. Not recognising the DG, he tells him the programmes are awful, and then shows him just how unappealing they are by giving him a tour of the studios, something the DG has never done before. As a result, Jimmy Clare is given the temporary job of Programmes Director, with the remit to bring fresh and exciting programmes to the station. Joan Garlon, the DG's daughter, is assigned as Clare's secretary, 'Miss Remington', though Jimmy is unaware that the woman he enjoys a developing romantic relationship with is Garlon's daughter. Jimmy is initially successful in bringing a fresh 'vaudeville broadcast, a galaxy of world famous theatrical and variety stars' (including Ted Ray and Ronald Frankau), but runs into opposition from Carl Graham (Alfred Drayton), Director of the Theatre Trust who, faced with the prospect of empty variety theatres, orders a complete ban on contracted artists working for the NBG.

Initially downhearted, Jimmy and Joan recruit talent they find in-house, including two singing cleaners (Lily Morris and Nellie Wallace) and a singing window-cleaner (Gerald Fitzgerald). The film also features other well-known contemporary acts such as Stanelli and his Hornchestra, Claude Dampier, Fred Coyningham, and Teddy Joyce and his Band. With the help of an inventor, A. Bird, who has invented a thing called 'television' and who has spent the entire film trying to tell someone in authority at the NBG about his invention, Jimmy and Joan are able to stage 'a first in the history of radio, an outdoor television broadcast in colour', relayed to the eager crowds gathered in public parks by a whole gamut of outside-broadcast television vans. The two colour sequences are a huge success, putting the entertainment back into NBG, and Jimmy and Joan decide to get married.

The film clearly delivers many of the conventional pleasures we associate with popular cinema. Whilst the pleasures of narrative are not particularly strong in this, as in other musicals, there is a certain frisson associated with mistaken identities, with those dramatic ironies that the audience could share. Much of the pleasure must have come from seeing a succession of talent drawn from variety and music hall, from the songs and other performative aspects paraded before them, such as the comedy card tricks from Havers and Lee and the vocal impressions of Beryl Orde. Audiences would have enjoyed the thinly disguised attack on the BBC and its programming policy, particularly its reluctance to extend the hours devoted to popular dance music beyond those already broadcast. The DG is exposed to some pretty awful highbrow music before he comes to discover the joys of 'hot' dance-band music and the song style that 'the Americans call crooning'.

Though these games played around the film's historical referents were clearly important and are still interesting, contemporary interest remains in the film's meta-discourse around the very notion of broadcasting and, in particular, the coming of television. The sustained running gag about the inventor trying to get past bureaucratic disinterest and inefficiency in the shape of the NBG commissionaire (comedian Billy Bennett) offers implicit criticism of the BBC's inability to welcome innovation, but of greater interest is the film's comment on the coming of television and the form it would take. Here, on the cusp of a new technological development, the social formation is revealed as being deeply unsure of what form this cultural innovation will take. In *Radio Parade of 1935*, television is seen as essentially a public and community medium, something to be seen by large, collective audiences on very large screens within public spaces such as parks. This is a truly Habermasian vision of publicly utilised rhetoric, truly television as public sphere. This meta-discourse of a public use of television is reinforced by actuality footage of crowds gathering and by the spectacle afforded by the use of Dufaycolor for the two closing colour sequences. Both of these are revealing. Alberta Hunter singing 'Black Shadows' opens up a deeply problematic take on racial attitudes and narratives of the exotic, whilst the second number 'There's No Excusin' Susan' raises questions about gender relations. Whilst *Radio Parade of 1935* reflects British musical film's introspective reliance on existing entertainment talent, it also serves as a reminder that the musical film is capable of substance that goes beyond a concern just to entertain, able to engage as much as any other genre with recurrent social and cultural preoccupations.

Popular dance bands and the musical: *Music Hath Charms* (1935) and *Everything Is Rhythm* (1936)

British dance bands figure prominently in musical films throughout the 1930s. Often they appear in a supporting role when events take place at night-clubs or society parties, but bands are frequently given privileged performance space in their own right. The popularity of certain bands, based upon their radio broadcasts, record and sheet music sales, was reflected in films in which they occupy a central role. Two such films were *Music Hath Charms* (1935) featuring BBC bandleader Henry Hall and *Everything Is Rhythm* (1936) featuring Harry Roy and his Band.

British International Pictures' *Music Hath Charms*, directed by Thomas Bentley, offers further evidence of the importance of BBC radio and the power of popular music in the 1930s. After having been accused by a passing motorist of 'ruining his daughter', Henry Hall and the BBC Dance Band question the influence of their radio broadcasts. Though they receive loads of fan mail, they remain unconvinced that they 'do anybody any good'. Through a series of scenes that interlace the band and their music with scenes of British radio listeners across the world, the conclusion is positive; wherever they are, whatever they are doing, people have 'got a lot to thank Henry Hall for'. Hall's contemplations are fleshed out in four basic narrative strands, in English suburbia and a farcical court hearing, on board an ocean liner, in the African jungle, and up a remote Highland mountain. These spaces, ranging from the most domesticated English habitat to the far reaches of Empire, are brought together through the power of music on BBC radio and on gramophone record.

This construction of Home and Empire as community is peppered with comic self-deprecation, often at the expense of Henry Hall and his musicians. When Hall is mistaken for an escapee from a 'mental asylum', a policeman urges him to be more ambitious in his delusions as he protests that he really is Henry Hall. Secure in their actual popularity, the film constantly teases the band, not least in the sequences in which their attempts to provide a day out for local schoolchildren ends in chaos. Disregarding the moments of sexual innuendo which ripple through the film, *Music Hath Charms* foretells something of 1940s Ealing whimsy, as the evident self-assuredness of British culture is gently mocked by a recognition of its eccentricities and limitations, not least the inability to openly articulate feelings and emotions, evident in the shocked embarrassment when the love letters between the young suburban middle-class couple Jack and 'ruined' Marjorie, their love affair compounded by Hall's radio broadcasts of 'Honey Coloured Moon', are almost made public property in the courtroom.

Central to the film, of course, is the music of Henry Hall and the BBC Dance Band. The film opens and closes with a close-up of Hall looking directly at camera and, in between, we see and hear the band playing in rehearsal, during broadcasts, being listened to on the radio and on gramophone records. Their music is everywhere, diegetically and non-diegetically, as numbers such as 'Honey Coloured Moon', the 'jungle' number 'Ju-Ju', 'There's No Time Like The Present' and 'Here's To The Next Time' are heard several times. In this quintessentially English film – though there are references to American music, to 'hot jazz' and songs such as 'Alabama Sugar Daddy' – spoken dialogue, vocal delivery, instrumental playing and band orchestrations resist American idioms; verbal phrases such as 'beastly mist' and musical phrasing in numbers such as 'Honey Coloured Moon' resonate with a distinctly English accent. The film offers an optimistic affirmation of British cultural and political power, enshrined in the BBC, which is shown as operating a global reach. This affirmation, based as it is on the concept of Empire and the dominance of southern suburban middle-class culture, was already under threat. Challenges to the supposed stability of class, gender and regional identities, as well as the growing encroachment of American popular culture, were already making films such *Music Hath Charms* quaintly old-fashioned. The very title of the film and its quotation from William Congreve's *The Mourning Bride* does little to presage the changes to British culture, let alone the changes to the BBC, which were epitomised by the departure of Reith as Director General in 1938.

Everything Is Rhythm (1936), produced by Rock Studios and directed by Alf Goulding, an Australian who had directed in America in the silent era, was one of two films starring British bandleader Harry Roy. Whereas Henry Hall's acting ability was non-existent, *Everything Is Rhythm* manages to harness Roy's more extrovert personality in a more substantial narrative that centres on romance and mistaken identity. Roy plays Harry Wade, leader of a struggling dance band determined to succeed. Along the way he infiltrates high society and, masquerading as a waiter, falls in love with the Ruritanian Princess Pearl who is visiting London. She is equally enchanted by him and, after a series of misunderstandings, of obstacles thrown in their way and some fortuitous coincidences, the couple escape the clutches of Prince Rudolf, the princess's oafish fiancé, though not before the band has demonstrated its international appeal as they undertake a world tour. The closing sequence, structured around the number 'Sky High Honeymoon', has the lovers escaping on an impossibly un-airworthy aeroplane, even more rickety than Astaire's in *Flying Down To Rio* (1933), the entire band 'playing' perched on top of the plane's wings. Like Roy's other film *Rhythm Racketeer* (1937), *Everything Is Rhythm* was popular enough to merit a reissue under the title *Floor Show* in the early 1940s.

For contemporary audiences, the pleasures of seeing and hearing one of Britain's most popular dance bands in numbers such as 'I'm Naturally Happy', 'Black Minnie's Got The Blues' and 'The Internationale' was compounded by the added in-joke afforded by their extra-textual knowledge that the part of Princess Pearl was played by Elizabeth Brooke, who happened both to be married to Harry Roy and to be a real princess, the daughter of the Rajah of Sarawak. Such knowledge was circulated through a number of sources, including articles in magazines such as *Popular Music and Dancing Weekly*. Goulding manages to direct the numbers with zest and an over-riding sense of good humour, aided by some extremely competent choreography, as Roy's band, on their world tour, plays music plundered from a range of popular musical idioms, not least American-inspired blues, swing and fashionable Latin-American dance numbers. Audiences would have enjoyed the way in which one of Britain's most successful dance bands is humbled on screen by constant demands that they do something different and novel, demands which lead to some extreme comic costuming for some of the numbers. Excellent use is made of available special effects in 'comic novelty' numbers such as 'Make Some Music' where a diminutive Roy plays, sings and dances on top of a piano and along its keys, a number which matches anything Hollywood was then producing. Unlike *Music Hath Charms*, *Everything Is Rhythm* draws upon generic elements being established by the Hollywood musical, with its double helix narrative interweaving professional success with romantic success, the increasing integration between narrative and spectacle, gender stabilities structured around the chaser and the chased, though with an assertion that modern woman will not be bossed around by chauvinist autocrats such as Prince Rudolf, and the element of self-reflexivity attached to the 'work' involved in becoming successful in show-business.

Musical comedies: *Oh Daddy* (1935) and *O-Kay For Sound* (1937)

Though the films of Gracie Fields and George Formby dominate the 1930s, a host of other British comedians and variety artists appeared in a string of musical comedies. One such minor talent was Leslie Henson, who appeared in Gainsborough's *Oh Daddy* (1935). London-born Henson spent most of his career as a stage comedian, though he had appeared in a string of British silent films since 1916, including a version of *Alf's Button* (1920). *Oh Daddy*'s comedy relies on an exposure of British upper-class hypocrisy, centred on the descent of Lord Pye (Henson), leading light of Dumhampton's Purity League and its crusade against 'demon alcohol and his confederates frivolity and worldliness', into the temptations offered by the world of show-business in the shape of cabaret singer Benita de Lys (Frances Day) who, it transpires, is actually his step-daughter. Though the audience are made aware of this, Lord Pye is not, so that having missed the train to the Purity Conference in Birmingham, that city of 'lights, music and frivolity', his seduction into the delights of London social life resonates with the comic frisson stemming from his shallow hypocrisy. At the Hotel Milano, Pye encounters Bonita singing 'Now I Understand', a song that clearly relates to Pye's journey from puritanical hypocrisy to an acceptance of the normative demands of romance, pleasure and familial love.

Exploiting mistaken identities and Pye's discomfort when confronted with his own double standards, Bonita manages to transform the Purity League into the League of Happiness, banishing puritanical Uncle Samson (Alfred Drayton) from the family home and Dumhampton, where the villagers enjoy a party in the company of Bonita, the girls and the band from the cabaret. *Oh Daddy* is primarily a vehicle for Henson and his comic talents, but benefits from a sharp script written by Michael Powell, sharp direction from Graham Cutts and Austin Melford and effective numbers that amplify and reinforce the film's themes. With one exception, these numbers are motivated within the film by the hotel cabaret setting, where Bonita performs 'Now I Understand' and 'The Savage In Me', with its exotic off-beat orchestration and choreography. At the film's climax, Pye promises 'never to be good again' and, finding the savage in himself, finds the courage to get rid of Uncle Samson. At the closing village party, the cry is 'down with doom and gloom, up with joy and jollity', a transformation presaged in the dream-like number 'Hang On To Happiness' in which Pye, in a state of drunken excess, is transformed from an objectionable formally dressed prig to a satyr mingling with the dancing girls, a convert to the pleasures that the world can offer.

Oh Daddy reveals the extent to which British cinema of the 1930s felt impelled to reflect the importance of popular music in its product. Though owing little formally to generic conventions being developed within the Hollywood musical, *Oh Daddy* is a fine example of British musical comedy, a component of British film production that continued throughout the rest of the decade in films such as *O-Kay For Sound* (1937) starring the Crazy Gang, an energetic hybrid that combines comic gags, slapstick and songs with a series of revue acts in a flimsy self-reflexive backstage narrative traversing the entertainment landscape of film and live variety theatre.

Themselves the victims of economic depression and hard times, the six members of the Crazy Gang, including Bud Flanagan and Chesney Allen, are propelled from busking in a London street into the film industry when, hired as film extras, they are mistaken for a wealthy Bradford woollen industrialist who invests in film production (a clear reference to J. Arthur Rank) and his entourage. As a result of this mistaken identity, the Gang are set loose upon the in-debt, crisis-ridden Goldberger Film Studios, initially creating havoc, but finally saving the company through their cobbled-together *Sensational Screen Revue*, also called *O-Kay For Sound*, which premieres at the London Palladium to great acclaim. Along the way, the film harnesses a number of revue acts such as the impressive novelty dance duo Lucienne and Ashour, singers The Radio Three, and Peter Dawson, whose baritone voice had first been heard as early as 1907 in a Chronophone sound short *Bedouin's Love Song*, all wrapped around lengthier sequences in which the Crazy Gang reprise sketches based on their live London Palladium shows. These sketches offer some acerbic comments on aspects of contemporary popular culture, from the references to film titles suggested by the Gang's trademark gags and slapstick to the more strident comment on British and American cultural differences, made evident in the differences between a BBC style commentary on a wrestling match and its American counterpart. Though both are pilloried, the key difference is that, whereas the American script is 'written in advance' and is punctuated with commercial references, the BBC commentary, although enacted incompetently by 'Lord Baden-Baden', at least has the merit that it 'tells the truth' even if the match is bad. This acknowledgement of increasing American cultural influence is reinforced in Bud Flanagan's blackface number 'There's A Big Day Coming', which makes for uneasy viewing today, as does the faded comic conceit behind the malicious cross-dressing in the sketch, which parodies a costume ballet we see being filmed at the studio.

Self-deprecating as much of the film is, not least in the savage though endearing lampoon of the British film industry and its problems centred on the chaos that is the Goldberger Studios, the film's climax offers an assertion of British national pride and military might, reflecting awareness of the changing political situation in Europe and threats of war. Slipping effortlessly between screen and stage, the final number, combining 'Ta-Ta! Ta-Ta!' and Noel Gay's 'The Fleet's Not In Port Very Long' has the Crazy Gang joined by the Band of the Royal Marines, as shots of Royal Navy ships, their guns firing, are superimposed over the rousing finale. This intimation of British military resolution is followed by a return to self-deprecating normality, as the Crazy Gang find themselves back on the street, busking for their living, despite the apparent triumph of Goldberger's film. This film within the film, the result, as Bud Flanagan says, of putting some 'bits of film together and calling it a revue' describes, of course, the film that we have just watched, *O-Kay For Sound*. Built upon the popularity of the Crazy Gang and their hugely popular shows at the London Palladium, the specific vocal appeal of Flanagan and Allen which is highlighted in the performance of the Michael Carr and Jimmy Kennedy number 'Free', the revue acts and the five songs featured in the film, *O-Kay For Sound* offers an interesting meta-textual commentary on the pressures on British popular culture, not least in the recurrent crisis in British film production and the pressures on culture and identity stemming from the spread of American popular cultural idioms, especially in the field of popular music.

The musical short: British Lion (1933–36)

Musical shorts, so important in the transition from 'silent' film to synchronised sound film at the end of the 1920s, continued to be important for British film production under the quota system in the 1930s. They remained a presence in British cinema until the advent of single-feature programming and the introduction of music video on cable and satellite television. In addition to their economic importance to British production in the 1930s, musical shorts enabled audiences to see bands and singers whilst their popularity was at its height and whilst numbers were current. Invariably musical shorts were unpretentious affairs, concerned to showcase the talent with little aspiration to cinematic innovation or, on some occasions, competence. In addition to individually produced musical shorts from minor and often short-lived companies, series such as *Ideal Cinemagazine*, *Pathétone* and *Pathé Pictorial* showcased a host of now-forgotten British talent such as baritone Tom Kinniburgh, singer Beryl Davis and pianist Patricia Rossborough, as well as artists such as the Crazy Gang, Stanelli and Richard Tauber and bands led by Billy Cotton, Maurice Winnick and Carroll Gibbons. Many are no longer accessible, but some have survived, including those produced by British Lion from 1933 onwards, firstly in their *Musical Film Revue* series, in the 1935 *Equity Musical Revue* series, and in the *British Lion Varieties* series from 1936 onwards. These shorts were sufficiently popular to be re-issued on 9.5mm film format by Pathéscope for home consumption, a forerunner of home video.

British Lion musical shorts maintained a format that invariably included three numbers from artists who appeared in more than one film. One prominent band featured was that led by Joe Loss, playing numbers such as 'The Wheel Of The Wagon Is Broken' in *British Lion Varieties Number One* (1936) and, with Vera Lynn as vocalist on 'Love Is Like A Cigarette', 'My Heart Wouldn't Beat Again' and 'The General's Fast Asleep' on *Varieties* from 1936. Though bands such as those led by Terence McGovern, Reggie Bristow and Roy Fox appeared frequently, the *Varieties* also regularly featured musical and novelty acts such as The Three Accordion Kings playing an extract from Gounoud's *Faust*, singing impressionists The Three Radio Rogues and tap-dancing group The Petite Ascots, as well as more occasional appearances by novelty musical acts such as The Modernique Quartette playing 'Tiger Rag'.

Varieties directors such as Herbert Smith were usually content to frame artists such as The Petite Ascots with a static camera, though in numbers featuring big bands, there was some attempt at visual variety as the camera cut to different instrumental sections, individual players and singers. These low-budget, hastily produced shorts offer some insight into British popular music of the mid-1930s, including the taste for novelty musical acts, instruments long out of favour such as the accordion, the insistent British pronunciation of lyrics by singers such as Eve Becke, Bob Lively, Betty Astell and Phyllis Stanley, even when singing numbers such as 'I've Got The World On A String' and 'Minnie The Moocher's Wedding Day', and the clipped, rather rigid, British orchestration and instrumental playing by bands such as Roy Fox in numbers such as 'Hunting The Fox'. The limitations of bands such as Terence McGovern's in numbers such as 'The London Fire Brigade', or the increasingly old-fashioned qualities of the Albert Sandler Trio playing what are best described as the 'light classics', perhaps help to explain the extent to which American popular music and American bands increased in popularity both during and after the Second World War, a period which also witnessed some profound changes in British film production and cinema attendance.

3

The 1940s: constructing communities

The crisis that hit British film finance in the late 1930s saw a drastic reduction in the number of films produced. British Film Institute statistics suggest that the 176 feature films produced in 1937 reduced to 134 in 1938, and then shrank to 84 in 1939. Even taking into account short films, Rachel Low suggests that the number of productions declined from 228 in 1938 to 103 in 1939 (Low 1997: 198). Gifford lists 195 productions for 1938, 112 for 1939 (Gifford 1986). Whatever the disparities in the statistics, the overall trend is clear: although cinema admissions continued to rise in the late 1930s, fewer British films were being made and seen in the cinemas. Although there was a degree of uncertainty around the new quota system being considered by the 1936 Moyne Committee and due to be introduced through the Cinematograph Films Act of 1938, the production crisis was in large part the result of over-optimistic, often injudicious, investment in British film production. Michael Balcon described how the 'City of London was pouring money into film production' at this period:

> So-called producers, whose reputations and talents were, to anybody with a knowledge of the industry, more than questionable, were able to obtain backing, often for several films, as it was quite plausible to ask for the finance for a second before the box-office results of the first were known. (Balcon 1969: 96)

When the banks and insurance companies who had lent money realised that they were not going to get a return, a much-publicised court case, centred on the activities of Max Schach and the investment trust known as the Aldgate Trustees, destroyed confidence in British film production.

The outbreak of the Second World War on 3 September 1939 compounded the crisis, as the Government's initial reaction was to close all cinemas and other entertainment venues. Mindful of both public and commercial pressure, this decision was rapidly reversed and throughout

September and October that year, cinemas were allowed to reopen with certain restrictions. Vera Lynn, a key figure in popular entertainment during this period, recalled that

> When [the war] started, there was a general dither and *everything*, except radio, shut down completely. . . . When it was realised that it wasn't going to be like that, and that ordinary people were going to need entertainment more than they'd ever done in their lives, the industry pulled itself together, the theatres gradually re-opened, the hotels re-started their dances, and there was a boom in the whole cheer-up business. (Lynn 1975: 85)

By early November 1939, it was very much business as usual and cinemas experienced a significant increase in admissions, from 990,000 in 1939 to 1,494,000 in 1942 and 1,585,000 in 1945. This increase in admissions was happening at a time when British studio capacity was severely curtailed. Whereas, in 1939, 22 studios were providing 65 sound stages, in 1942 there were only 9 studios with 30 sound stages, as facilities such as Rank's newly acquired Amalgamated studios at Elstree were requisitioned by the Government. Yet despite this shrinkage in available studio space and the effects on technical and creative personnel that troop mobilisation entailed, the industry in the 1940s 'displayed a competence and maturity hitherto lacking in British cinema' (Murphy 1983: 165).

After the war, admissions continued to increase, reaching a peak in 1947. However, the 1940s saw some radical changes in the industry, most notably the rapid dominance of Rank that began in 1941 and which had a profound influence on production strategy and exhibition. Inevitably, given the circumstances of war, most British film production was aimed predominantly at domestic and Empire audiences in the first half of the 1940s, though with the ending of war some attempts were made to appeal to the American market, driven by Rank's initially promising alliances with American companies such as Universal (Murphy 1983: 167–9). In all this, the British musical film played a part, not just during the war years, but in the latter half of the decade when musicals such as *London Town* (1946: released in the US as *My Heart Goes Crazy*) and Herbert Wilcox's *The Courtneys Of Curzon Street* (1947: US title *The Courtney Affair*) attempted to compete with American product. Throughout the 1940s, the musical film featured in the production schedules of Gainsborough, Ealing, Columbia-British, Mancunian/Butchers, Rank and its associated independent production companies, as well as smaller independent companies.

A significant number of these 1940s musical films drew upon, and were often set in, the world of entertainment, both by using contemporary radio, record and live variety stars and by more nostalgic reference to music hall, and were aimed primarily at the domestic market, especially during the war years. Others attempted to replicate generic conventions more usually associated with the American musical film, often making use of American talent in order to find a foothold in the US market. Other films addressed issues of national identity by dealing with systemic issues of class and with aspects of what were conventionally regarded as 'elite' culture. Along the way, some important developments in film scoring occurred which significantly enriched British film culture, constructing a British national cinema which was not just in touch with popular generic material, but equally aware of what Merz characterises as 'the contribution of the avant-garde' (Merz 1994: 126).

The effects of war on British musical film production

Given the legacy of the financial crisis affecting the industry in 1937–38 and the restrictions placed upon both production capacity and film content during the early years of the war, it was inevitable that the number of musical films being made declined. In particular, there was a severe decline in the production of musical shorts, though the on-going *Pathé Pictorial* and *Pathé Gazette* series often featured musical artists and bands. Inspiration Films, a small independent production company distributing through Paramount, made three shorts in 1939, the longest lasting 17 minutes: *Tunes Of The Times*, *Radio Nights* and *Eddie Carroll And His Boys*, all produced and directed by bandleader Horace Shepherd. In the same year, Pathé produced the 39-minute *Pathétone Parade of 1939* and the slightly longer *Pathétone Parade of 1940*. One other short produced in 1939 and distributed by Columbia-British, *A Tramp In Killarney*, represented the totality of short films produced that year, a drastic reduction in the significance that the musical short previously enjoyed during the decade. In 1940, there were no musical shorts apart from two revue films, *Hullo Fame!* introducing 'new faces' such as Peter Ustinov, and *At The Havana* with Jack Davis and the Havana Club Band. For the rest of the war years until 1945 – with the odd exception of shorts which were mobilised to directly help aspects of the war effort such as *The Savings Song* (1941), featuring the Jack Hylton Band, four more shorts from Horace Shepherd at Inspiration, the *Pathé Pictorial* series and short revues including *Pathétone Revue of 1941* and *Pathétone Revue of 1942*, all of them very much part of the 'cheer-up business' – the short musical film and revue lost the importance it had held for 1930s cinema programming.

This curtailment of the musical short resulted from both wartime restrictions in film materials and facilities, as well as the influence of government, articulated through the Ministry of Information (MOI). At the beginning of the war, whilst some influential voices recognised the potential of film in the war of ideas that all such conflicts entail, the MOI had little grasp of what propaganda was, no real propaganda policy, and was confused about the relationship between feature films that provided 'entertainment' and documentary film with its evident 'propaganda' potential (Chapman 1998: 46).

As wartime film policy evolved, the value of the feature film to provide effective propaganda through entertainment was recognised. As with documentary films such as *London Can Take It* (1940), feature films helped construct a notion of 'the people's war', an ideological position that emphasised

> national unity and social cohesion: [in which] class differences have all but disappeared and have been replaced instead by a democratic sense of community and comradeship. (Chapman 1998: 161)

What makes the 1940s such an interesting decade for the British musical film is the range and diversity of musical talent that was harnessed for film production. In addition to calling upon established and up-and-coming stars from the world of popular culture – whether radio, records or live stage and variety entertainment – the studios also make effective use of what had been conventionally regarded as 'elite' cultural traditions, notably classical music and, in the case of at least one important film towards the end of the decade, ballet. Occasionally, as in Strand Films *Battle For Music* (1943), in which Jack Hylton appeared alongside Sir Adrian Boult and Sir Malcolm Sargeant with the London Philhamonic Orchestra, popular cultural traditions were combined with more elitist musical culture. This exploitation of distinctive and previously mutually exclusive cultural traditions was itself a reflection of uncertainties in government policy and attitudes, a reflection of the continuing debate about the respective values and roles of 'entertainment' and 'information', about the class structure and its associated values and tastes, as well as an articulation of the desire for national unity and social cohesion. Whilst these diverse cultural traditions were evident in the documentary films of Humphrey Jennings such as *Listen To Britain* (1942), they are equally evident in the cycle of feature-length musical films made during the war and in the years immediately following.

Despite the profound shifts that all this represented and an absolute decline in the number of films produced, the early war years proved to be significant for the British musical film. Although, as we have seen, the relative commercial failure of the later Jesse Matthews films raised doubts about the future of British musical film production, the early 1940s and beyond saw a number of interesting productions. Gracie Fields had departed for America, where she made an appearance in Frank Borzage's *Hollywood Canteen* (1943), but her career as a British musical film star was over. George Formby continued to make films during the war years. The last three films he made for ATP at Ealing, *Let George Do It* (1940), *Spare A Copper* (1940) and *Turned Out Nice Again* (1941), largely continued with the tried and tested formula, a mixture of slapstick comedy and songs, amongst them 'Grandad's Flannelette Nightshirt', 'I Wish I Was Back On The Farm', 'The Emperor Of Lancashire' and 'Auntie Maggie's Remedy'. Aspirations to have his acting taken more seriously led Formby to sign with Columbia in November 1941. Though the films he made for Columbia, including *South American George* (1941), *Much Too Shy* (1942), *Get Cracking* (1943) and *Bell-Bottom George* (1944) are not without merit, there was some resentment that he had signed for the American company and, though they remained popular with his fan base, the films were treated with increasing critical hostility. Flanagan and Allen had enjoyed moderate success in the 1930s with a number of films including ATP's *The Dreamers* (1933), *A Fire Has Been Arranged* (1935), *Underneath The Arches* (1937) and *O-Kay For Sound* (1937), and they continued their formulaic combination of comedy and songs in Gainsborough's *Gasbags* (1940), British National's *We'll Smile Again* (1942), and three films for John Baxter, *Theatre Royal* (1943), *Dreaming* (1944) and *Here Comes The Sun* (1945), this last film featuring five of their songs.

In addition to stars who had been popular in the 1930s, a number of artists familiar to British audiences through radio, records, sheet music and live variety appeared in musical films in the early 1940s, including Tommy Trinder, Arthur Askey, Vera Lynn, as well as less well-known talent such as Canadian Hughie Green, later to become a major television performer, who appeared with his 'Gang' in Butcher's *Music Hall Parade* (1939), featuring Billy Cotton and His Band, and British Screen Service's *Down Our Alley* (1939) (Green 1965: 26). Again, though many of the films in which they appeared defy strict generic categorisation, the central importance of music and its performance, often within a show-business setting, is something they all share. In the first year of the war, with conscription, domestic disruption and absence now a reality, even if most British troops were largely stationed in Britain, a number of musical films – including *Garrison Follies* (1940), featuring Betty Lupino and Percival Mackey's Band, *Laugh It Off* (1940) featuring Tommy Trinder with Geraldo and his Orchestra, and Mancunian's

Somewhere In England (1940) with Frank Randle – used plots based on attempts to run successful shows and concerts for the troops. Another plot fixation was the need to thwart spies and the 'enemy within' from disrupting the war effort. Though the best known of these were Formby's *Let George Do It* and *Spare A Copper* (both 1940), Gainsborough's *Band Waggon* (1940) with Arthur Askey and Richard Murdoch, Grand National/British Lion's *Under Your Hat* (1940) with Jack Hulbert and Cecily Courtneidge, Butcher's *Facing The Music* (1941) with Percival Mackey's band, and New Realm's *The Balloon Goes Up* (1942) featuring three songs from Donald Peers, all invoked the need to be alert, a message reinforced effectively in Ealing's dramatic feature *Went The Day Well?* (1942) directed by Cavalcanti.

With important exceptions, an increasingly pronounced element of these films was their emphasis on the, often London-based, working class, apparent most readily in *The Lambeth Walk* (1939), directed by Albert de Courville, based on Noel Gay's stage play 'Me And My Girl', with Lupino Lane starring in both the West End production and the film. A fantasy about the apparent unimportance of the class structure in the face of romance, the film exploited the 'Lambeth Walk' dance craze which had been heavily promoted by the Mecca group in 1938, and which was enjoyed by all sections of the British public, 'in Mayfair ball-rooms, suburban dance-halls, cockney parties and village hops' (Nott 2002: 164).

Though *The Lambeth Walk* proved a useful vehicle to construct images of social cohesion, other films were able to do this more effectively in ways that were more cinematically satisfying. War and crime films – crimes often involving foreign spies or agents – dominated production in the early years of the war, reflecting a public appetite for what was considered more escapist entertainment, an appetite which tended to increase as the war effort turned in favour of the Allied powers. Indeed, there was evidence by 1942 of public boredom and hostility towards what were increasingly regarded as propaganda films (Aldgate and Richards 1986: 12). Chapman concedes that, in addition to realist genres that drew much from the documentary aesthetic of the 1930s, comedies also played their role in the attempt to create national cohesion, but ignores other genres which were a significant part of British production during the first part of the 1940s. Genres such as melodrama, historical costume dramas and the musical were popular at the box-office and the reason is perhaps not hard to fathom. Such films were enjoyed by British audiences as part of what has been called a 'discourse of escapism'. For example, a cinema owner in Plymouth offered the opinion in the *Kinematograph Weekly* of 11 January 1940 that 'people do not want films dealing with war and its horrors or propaganda films which preach at patrons who pay to be entertained' (Harper 1994: 97).

Towards the end of the war, Gainsborough's Maurice Ostrer, writing in the *Kinematograph Weekly* of 20 December 1945 noted that 'costume dramas pack the box-office. I suggest that this is an escape from the drabness of this present day world of clothes coupons and austerity' (Harper 1994: 122). Certainly Gainsborough's melodramas, historical and costume dramas were more successful at the box office than the historical films produced by Ealing with their realist aesthetic. Despite the decline in the absolute number of musical films being produced, they too were popular with audiences, as is evident in the films starring both Arthur Askey and Tommy Trinder, two of the most successful comedians of the period.

Arthur Askey: *Miss London Ltd* (1943) and the American alliance

Liverpool-born Arthur Askey carved out a career in concert parties and variety halls in the 1920s before becoming a household name in the BBC radio programme *Bandwaggon* in 1938. An often surreal mixture of sketches, corny old jokes, some invitations for listener participation through letter writing, as well as music from The Bandwaggoners, The Jackdaus, and Reginald Foort or Charles Smart at the BBC Theatre Organ, it attained cult status in 1939. Capitalising on the success of the radio show, Askey signed an eight-picture deal with Gaumont-British (Askey 1975: 98). Gainsborough took the basic format, but had Askey and partner Richard Murdoch running a pirate television station from a castle apparently haunted by ghosts. With music from Jack Hylton's Band, Bruce Trent and Freddie Schwietzer, together with some appearances from BBC staff Jasmine Bligh and Jonah Barrington, the plot revolved around the discovery and capture of a gang of spies, a theme which, as we have seen, occupied numerous British films during the early stages of the war. A combination of simplistic plot and opportunities for revue numbers, *Band Waggon* (1940) harnessed both the need for cheery entertainment and more subtle propagandistic messages about possible infiltration by the enemy.

Following the success of *Band Waggon*, Askey's contract with Gainsborough films produced *Charley's (Big-Hearted) Aunt* (1940), *The Ghost Train* (1941), *I Thank You* (1941) and *King Arthur Was A Gentleman* (1942). All these films included at least one song and exploited Askey's comic persona, itself built upon his short insubstantial frame, quick-witted repartee, his catch-phrases and comic novelty songs, and slightly anarchic anti-authoritarian behaviour, a persona capable of expressing 'popular values of resistance to authoritarianism through the exercise of collective action' (Stokes 2000: 133). *Miss London Ltd* (1943) – directed by Val Guest, who, with Manning Sherwin, wrote the music and lyrics under the musical direction of Louis Levy – exploits all these aspects of Askey's popularity and is the most satisfying of all his films. It also reflects important changes in the war effort and a more relaxed mood within the nation at a period when the United States had entered the war. In fact, the growing influence of American popular culture is very evident, both in the musical numbers and in the casting of Evelyn Dall as Terry Arden. American born, Dall had actually carved a career in Britain with Ambrose and his Orchestra, appearing in a number of 1930s musical shorts, in the revue *Soft Lights And Sweet Music* (1936) and in musical features such as *Calling All Stars* (1937), *Sing As You Swing* (1937), *Kicking The Moon Around* (1938) and *He Found A Star* (1941), all of them using a show-business setting of one kind or another.

Dall plays the newly arrived American business partner of Arthur Bowden (Arthur Askey), who runs a failing escort agency supplying dates for 'gentlemen soldiers on leave'. She breezes in, blows the cobwebs off, literally and metaphorically, and manages to turn the agency into a thriving concern. Along the way, there is ample opportunity for some bracing dialogue celebrating the differences between British and American ways of doing things (not least between Dall and Peter Graves, playing Captain Rory O'More) whilst recognising the strength of their combination, a display of expensively costumed female glamour, a plethora of comic business (some of it rather dated and cloying), as well as some fine songs, all of which manage to comment with ironic self-deprecation on the strictures of wartime Britain. This intimation of American zest and energy is reinforced by the constant references to elements of American popular culture, not least through Jack Train's impersonations of American screen characters such as W.C. Fields and Rochester. In his number 'I'm Only Me', Askey regrets not being Clark Gable or Fred Astaire. Having acknowledged a debt to Abbott and Costello, Dall, Askey and Train undertake a passable imitation of the Marx Brothers. With restrictions on wartime clothing coupons an ever-present reality, some of the film's pleasures must have come from the costumes worn by the girls who agree to work for the agency, doing 'for the English girl what Ziegfeld did for the American girl' and, in the process, donating profits to the Prisoners of War Fund.

The film starts brilliantly with Anne Shelton singing 'The 8.50 Choo Choo To Waterloo-Choo', managing to capture the resilience with which Londoners put up with deprivations, mocking the 'pleasures' of crowded wartime train travel but knowing that it's all in a good cause, introducing the leading characters through the lyrics, as well as managing to scan English place names such as Fareham and Wareham without making them ridiculous. Wooden as her acting performance is, Shelton brings real vocal quality to the film in this and her other numbers, 'If You Could Only Cook' and 'You Too Can Have A Lovely Romance'. Inevitably, much of the film's comic business is rooted in contemporary concerns, not least running gags on wartime shortages, as when the one remaining sugar cube is dipped in the tea on the end of a piece of string. Askey gives a warmly acerbic performance, starting with his masquerade as 'Miss London', a 'technical nom-de-thing', blundering through his attempts to recruit girls for the agency. The Anglo-American alliance is sealed in the breezy up-tempo swing number (instrumentally reprised several times on the soundtrack) 'A Fine How Do You Do', which starts with Askey careering across the office furniture, cleaning as he goes, the lyrics declaring his romantic affection for Terry, something which, given Askey's screen persona, will remain narratively unrequited. Dall, Train and even the telephone engineer and switchboard girl join in, forging a number that seals the impression that the alliance will get things moving, if not romantically, then at least for the business and, by implication, for the war effort.

One of the more remarkable elements of *Miss London Ltd* is its clear acknowledgement of the increase in sexual promiscuity during the war. Though constant reassurances are given in the dialogue that the escort agency is strictly 'above board', the frisson of implied sexual promiscuity runs throughout the film.

In an early sequence, Arthur wanders around Waterloo Station where, watched with suspicion by a policeman, he attempts to recruit girls to the agency, making 'propositions' and 'suggestions' that, whilst played for comic effect, clearly carry overtones of promiscuity. His proposition to one attractive young woman (Jean Kent) is matched by her 'proposition' to him, eliciting a jaw-dropping response from Arthur. In this case, far from any sexual liaison, what results is an unwanted set of encyclopaedias, a tactic to both raise and disarm the spectre of illicit sexual activity. The policeman intervenes as Arthur tries persuade Gail Martin (Shelton) to join the agency, but Arthur reassures her that far from 'annoying young ladies' he was 'just propositioning' them for 'business', that he 'wants them to work for me'. As Arthur has just stroked and commented on Gail's lingerie in her open suitcase, the sexual intimations are meant to be evident. He manages to reassure her by explaining the agency's purpose, though she confesses that she expected ' a needle in the arm any minute' and to 'wake up in South America'.

This implication of sexual promiscuity ripples throughout the film, often centred on comments from the elegantly attired glamorous escort girls such as 'I hope I don't disappoint him'. It takes on an element of 'gold-digging' when Evelyn Dall sings 'Keep Cool Calm And Collected', with its rather cynical advice on how to turn a date into marriage, but is countered by Askey's asexual comic persona, his short stature and unconventional facial features undermining masculine sexual prowess, and by the way in which other numbers manage to elide any suggestions of promiscuous relationships with romance. This is most evident in Anne Shelton's lush string-orchestrated ballad number 'You Too Can Have A Lovely Romance', with its assertion that, rather than be lonely, 'you can enjoy / all of the urge that happens / when girl meets boy' a refrain picked up other guests and waiters at the hotel, a number which serves, within the film's narrative space, to naturalise the liaison between a serviceman and a young woman at the hotel and, by implication, extend understanding towards the wider issue of sexual activity during wartime.

At the film's climax, Arthur is drafted into the navy, but not before one of the film's many self-reflexive moments allows him to perform one of his comic novelty numbers, 'The Moth'. Askey, playing Arthur Bowden (Bowden was actually his mother's maiden surname), 'impersonates' Arthur Askey, even though he declares 'I can't stand that silly little man – he stinks'. This pleasing confusion between character and 'real life' persona sits, of course, at the heart of many musical films, with its clear rejection of naturalism and realist identification through constructed 'believable' characters. What lends it charm here is the element of self-deprecation involved, the ability not to be seen to be taking 'stardom' too seriously, an ability which is perhaps a defining quality of British cinema, and one which was reinforced by Askey's own comments on the verdict of *Daily Sketch* critic Elspeth Grant that, in *Miss London Ltd*, Val Guest had succeeded in lifting an Arthur Askey vehicle out of the 'films to be suffered' category:

> Nice work! I thought this was a bit of a back-handed compliment, but she had spelt my name correctly and that's really all that matters. (Askey 1975: 129)

Though Askey continued to be popular in the post-war years, particularly in television, the poor critical reception of *Bees In Paradise* (1944) marked the end of his contract with Gainsborough and, with the exception of comedies such as *Ramsbottom Rides Again* (1956) and Lance Comfort's *Make Mine A Million* (1959), of his career in film.

Tommy Trinder and *Champagne Charlie* (1944):
English traditions re-examined

The other comedian to make a significant impact during the early 1940s, and who made at least one significant musical film, was Tommy Trinder. London-born, Trinder made his first appearance at Collins Music Hall in 1921 and built a career in variety and on radio before his first film appearance in 1938. Though primarily a comedian and character actor, Trinder's vocal talents were strong enough to be harnessed in his film appearances, most notably in *Champagne Charlie* (1944).

Trinder had earlier starred in *Laugh It Off* (1940), a musical directed by John Baxter for British National in which his army character gets promoted by organising a successful concert, an opportunity for the film to parade a number of contemporary acts including Geraldo and his Orchestra. Trinder's appeal to wartime audiences, based on his chirpy good-natured cockney humour, was confirmed in the three films he made at Ealing before *Champagne Charlie*, *Sailors Three* (1940) which featured two numbers, 'All Over The Place' and 'A Happy Go Lucky Song', *The Foreman Went To France* (1941) in which Trinder sings 'The Smoke Goes Up The Chimney' in an attempt to reassure French refugee children traumatised by the savage attacks from enemy aeroplanes, and *The Bells Go Down* (1942), the story of a fire-fighting unit who remain cheerful despite all the hardship.

Produced by Michael Balcon and directed by Cavalcanti, *Champagne Charlie*, based on the lives of real-life music-hall performers George Leybourne (1842–84) and Alfred Vance (1838–88), both 'major stars of [the music-hall] at this period' (Bailey 1986: x), offers a rather fanciful account of their careers and the rivalry between them. With the intention of getting into a boxing career, Fred Saunders and his brother Joe (Tommy Trinder) arrive in London in 1860 from Leybourne, their provincial mining village. However, it is Joe who impresses when he sings 'Arf Of Arf And Arf' at the Elephant and Castle public house. Though he initially fails to impress with the over-maudlin 'Don't Bring Shame On The Old Folks', he eventually is contracted by Bessie Bellwood (1857–96) to appear at the Mogador Music Hall using the name George Leybourne. His growing success attracts the attention of the Great Vance (Stanley Holloway), star attraction at the Oxford, a rivalry expressed through a hierarchical succession of songs about drink, starting with ale and culminating with champagne, by way of port, claret, sherry wine, gin and rum, each of them giving ample opportunity for both Holloway and Trinder to perform. Their rivalry is more professional than personal and both are dismayed by the other's acceptance of a challenge to a pistol duel, played with a comic bravura under-pinned by our knowledge that there are no bullets in the pistols. In the end, the music-hall stars unite against the threat from legitimate theatre interests who attempt to close the halls by paying for hooligans to disrupt performances and create havoc. The attempt to discredit the halls fails to convince the committee looking into the regulation of licensed entertainment, not least because of the past romantic relation-ship between Bessie Bellwood and 'His Grace' the Duke (Austin Trevor), the committee chairman.

Though Andy Medhurst is right in pointing to the weaknesses in the film's narrative (Medhurst 1986: 181), this is to miss the point. The film succeeds for a number of reasons, not least the ebullient performances from Trinder and Holloway, with solid support from Betty Warren and Jean Kent. It has a sharp script by Austin Melford, John Dighton and Angus MacPhail, with some telling comic detail and an interesting romantic sub-plot raising issues around class distinction, as Lord Petersfield falls in love with Dolly, Betty's dancing daughter. The film benefits from Michael Relph's set designs, which are reasonably faith-ful to existing prints of music halls such as the Oxford in the 1860s. Authentic touches such as the supper tables near the stage, common practice in music halls at this period, together with placing the Mogador's chairman with his back to the stage, viewing performances in a dressing mirror, give the film a certain authority (Earl 1986: 5). Given his work in documentary film, this attention to detail must have also come from the director; Cavalcanti actually privileges this latter detail with a close shot of the mirror reflecting the performance on stage, one example of his evocative direction and insistence on some refresh-ing camera set-ups and use of depth-of-field which pervade the film. It is against this convincing visual backcloth that the ideological work of the film takes place.

Perhaps the biggest factor in the film's success and for its continuing appeal, are the songs and incidental music. The combination of origi-nal songs associated with the actual music hall artists, notably 'Champagne Charlie', the 1866 song associated with Leybourne and based on the drunken spendthrift fourth Marquess of Hastings (Kilgarriff 1998: 16), together with additional songs in music-hall style by musical notables including Noel Gay, Una Bart, Lord Berners and Billy Mayerl under the musical direction of Ernest Irving, provide not just a nostalgic acknowledgement of the power of music-hall entertain-ment, but a reassertion of the contemporary importance of community and collectivity. The emphasis on the pleasures of song, of drink, of entertainment and conviviality that permeates the film must have suggested to contemporary audiences that, after the hardships of the war, it was becoming acceptable again to expect pleasure as part of life's experiences. Specially written songs, such as Vance's opening number 'Strolling In The Park', with its formal music-hall verse/chorus pattern and strong if simplified melody line, erect a sense of continuity with tradition, whilst as the same time allowing lyrics which reflect more contemporary mores, including overt criticism of the upper classes.

The most interesting number, especially written, comes towards the end of the film. It is not unreasonable to read 'By And By' as an overtly political number, rooted not in the 1860s but in the mid-1940s with the tide of the war having turned. Against an opening brass section, six working men march across the stage, 'armed' with the tools of their trade in place of rifles, a hint perhaps that the strength of men in the forces can be mobilised in the peace to come. This is reinforced by the opening lyrics to the verse, in which Leybourne/Trinder expresses his disillusionment with the status quo, the government promising much but doing nothing, and considers going into politics himself. The lyrics of the chorus express the sense of disillusion with the present state of thing succinctly, declaring that 'everything will be lovely / when the pigs begin to fly'. As if to intimate the battles ahead, paid thugs interrupt the performance, but are defeated with the help of Vance and staff from Gatti's music hall. The allies triumphant, the number resumes, the lyrics expressing the desire for the sort of political change which was delivered at the end of the war with the landslide Labour victory.

Vera Lynn: war, democratic ordinariness and unpretentious sentiment

Askey and Trinder were predominantly comedians and variety artists who also had a degree of singing talent. Vera Lynn, on the other hand, was a singer with sufficient ability to appear in films that exploited her public persona. Born in London in 1917 in the midst of the First World War, Vera Lynn enjoyed enormous popularity and achieved almost iconic status during the Second World War, becoming known as the 'Forces' Sweetheart'. Her popularity in the early 1940s was largely built on her records and her appearances on BBC radio, particularly her programme *Sincerely Yours* that began in November 1941, serving as a link between Britain and its forces fighting abroad. She was a gifted child singer and was launched on an entertainment career at an early age, appearing in local working-men's clubs from the age of seven and later joining Madame Harris's Kracker Kabaret Kids dance troupe, often appearing on the stages of bigger London cinemas. However, it was her talents as a singer which were noted and, before she was twenty, she was featured singing with bandleaders Howard Baker, Charlie Kunz, Joe Loss and Ambrose. Her first BBC radio broadcast was with Loss in 1935 and she made a string of recordings on Crown both as featured singer with these bands and as a solo artist on the Rex label until 1937, when Rex was taken over by Decca. Her special status was sealed during the war years with her Decca recordings such as 'It's A Lovely Day Tomorrow' (1940), '(There'll Be Bluebirds Over) The White Cliffs Of Dover' (1940), 'Smilin' Through', 'When They Sound The Last All Clear', 'Yours' (all 1941), and 'We'll Meet Again' (1942). The wistful but hopeful sentimentality which characterised these songs, together with the melodic purity of her voice, clearly struck a chord at a time when absence, loss and uncertainty featured in so many lives. Lynn herself referred to 'We'll Meet Again' as a 'greetings card song', whose 'unpretentious off-the-peg sentiments' represented 'a very basic human message of the sort that people want to say to each other but find embarrassing actually to put into words' (Lynn 1975: 81).

Given her significance as a wartime entertainer whose persona was constructed around her very ordinariness, together with the sheer scale of her successful recordings and radio broadcasts and her evident ability to connect the home front with the forces fighting abroad, it must have seemed expedient to mobilise her appeal within the broader project of British wartime cinema which, whilst eschewing propaganda, nonetheless emphasised the 'positive virtues of British national characteristics and the democratic way of life' (Aldgate and Richards 1986: 12). The problem was that, whatever the appeal of her singular vocal style and her down-to-earth democratic ordinariness, Lynn was neither a conventional screen beauty nor an actor. Indeed, though Gracie Fields acknowledged Lynn as 'probably the best singer in Britain', she also noted her performative limitations, remarking that she would usually just 'stand there like a slab of cold mutton' (Bret 1995: 137).

Her first screen appearance was an extra in the 1935 Flanagan and Allen film *A Fire Has Been Arranged*, and in 1936 she was featured singing with the Joe Loss Orchestra as part of the series of musical shorts produced by British Lion and distributed by MGM, *British Lion Varieties*. One of these shorts featured Lynn singing 'Love Is Like A Cigarette'. Though the simile fails to appeal today, the lyrics of the song, describing the similarities between the twin addictions of love and smoking, must have seemed clever to an audience who would have been puffing away in the cinema auditorium, with lyrics referring to 'the thrill of touching your lips' and 'fading away' leaving 'ashes of regret'. If not exactly mutton, Lynn's brief visual appearance is rather wooden and inanimate, as she enters frame left and delivers the vocal refrain to a static camera. However, the quality of her voice and ability to deliver tonal purity and clear-cut articulation do much to explain her continuing popularity on record and radio throughout the late 1930s, 1940s and well into the 1950s.

These brief 1936 shorts were Lynn's only named screen appearances until she starred in three wartime features, all produced by Columbia-British and shot at their Riverside Studios. All three films – *We'll Meet Again*, directed by Phil Brandon in 1942, *Rhythm Serenade* directed by Gordon Wellesley in 1943, and *One Exciting Night* (released in the USA as *You Can't Do Without Love*) directed by an aging Walter Forde in 1944 – manage Lynn's evident lack of screen charisma by emphasising those qualities of democratic ordinariness and resigned selflessness in the service of others which resonated with contemporary wishes and desires. This lack of screen charisma, combined with the sheer popularity she enjoyed as a record and radio personality, was both the strength and weakness of her three feature films, as Lynn herself was perceptive enough to realise:

> One of the problems was that I was just Vera Lynn; it was difficult for them to take me out of that established character and get the public to accept me as another person. I was so *me*, it was hard for anyone to write a different kind of part. (Lynn 1975: 103–4)

All three films position Lynn firmly on the home front, supporting the war effort through running evacuation schools or working in munitions factories, acting as a link between the home front and the troops doing the fighting. With its show-business setting, *We'll Meet Again* relies much more than the other two films upon conventional generic self-reflexivity, much of its pleasure stemming from that blurring of demarcation between fictive construct and 'reality'. Lynn plays Peggy Brown, a dancer who accidentally becomes a well-known radio singer on the BBC, eventually fronting a show which mirrors in every respect her actual radio show *Sincerely Yours*. Similarly, real-life band-leader Geraldo plays Gerry, an orchestra pit and dance band conductor. As with Lynn herself, the film offers considerable space for Geraldo and his Orchestra to perform as 'themselves', whilst also serving as a functional narrative device. By using the BBC as a mechanism by which Peggy Brown is propelled to admittedly self-effacing stardom, the film also reflects the importance of BBC radio during the war years.

Columbia British clearly saw Vera Lynn's songs as the film's primary selling point, its promotional poster proclaiming 'The Wonder Voice of the Air – Now triumphant on the screen!' and boasting of '7 Song Hits'.

Music sits at the centre of the film, not just in terms of the pleasures of performance delivered in the five numbers (more if we count the ways in which the same numbers are reprised, together with a non-vocal dance band number), but also in the film's assertion of the importance of music to the war effort. Though he has aspirations as a 'highbrow' composer, Frank is persuaded by Peggy's conviction about the power of popular music and its ability 'to cheer people up'. Music, particularly song, has this ability to construct community, a form of resistance when most other forms are denied. This is evident at the beginning of the film where the audience at the 'Piccadilly Belles' – the only musical running in London – are trapped inside the Orpheus Theatre by an air raid. Initially reluctant, the audience are persuaded to join in when Peggy sings 'Be Like The Kettle And Sing', a bouncy, optimistic number which enjoins people to see the opportunities that even danger can bring, the chorus demanding that 'when you are up to your necks in hot water, be like the kettle and sing'. This opening sequence has a narrative function in demonstrating that Peggy has a voice deserving success, whilst at the same serving a clear ideological purpose in constructing community in the face of adversity.

The pleasures and purpose of popular music are reiterated through the film's narrative development. Following an air-raid attack which damages the museum, leaving Professor Drake despairing at the barbaric attack on culture, Frank is persuaded to write a popular song which can be shared with 'ordinary people on the ground', music which can ' keep people going', music which is 'sunshine which blows away the cobwebs' and which is 'psychologically invaluable in these days'. When a contracted singer fails to appear, Peggy sings the vocals on the demonstration disc for Frank's song 'After The Rain' which, through the comic but benign ineptitude of the BBC secretary, gets played over the radio by accident. Following an initially fruitless search to find her, Peggy is eventually handed a contract with the BBC, but only after she sings the number again in an extended sequence at the 'Pack Of Cards' nightclub where Geraldo and his band play a non-vocal dance number and 'You Never Knew' featuring crooner Len Camber and Geraldo's vocal sextet. 'After The Rain', like so many of the simile-driven songs sung by Vera Lynn, offers a vision of a bright, happy future once present troubles have been overcome, sunshine following the rain, a lyrical acknowledgement both of pain and suffering and the resolution that they will be overcome. The song's melodic poignancy is interrupted by a minor-key phrase in which Lynn asserts that 'thunder and falling rain / are driving us insane', before returning to the overall optimism of the lyrics and the sweeping melodic harmonies from Geraldo's orchestra.

Peggy's work at the BBC in this film clearly reflects Vera Lynn's actual career on radio, the distinction between fiction and fact blurred with the introduction of actual BBC personnel Alvar Liddell, John Watt and John Sharman. In this way, the role of the BBC in general and Lynn in particular is acknowledged, reinforced through a montage of superimposed images of Peggy broadcasting to an array of civilians and uniformed forces. Her star rising, Peggy and the BBC prepare for a special St Andrew's Day broadcast. Rejecting ideas that the broadcast should be 'epic, historic and gigantic', Peggy insists that it should be 'simple and true, for Scotland's sake', Peggy delivers a programme which is clearly based on Lynn's own *Sincerely Yours*, linking people at home with men and women fighting abroad with letters she reads out on air. At the film's climax, Peggy/Lynn delivers a concert broadcast in front of a live audience of RAF personnel, where she sings 'Sincerely Yours' and then leads them in singing 'We'll Meet Again', a fictional reprise of Lynn's actual radio and live performances to British troops.

Though at one level the 'backstage' narrative inscribes Peggy's rise to fame, this is more than offset by the film's romantic sub-plot, the effect of which is essentially to reinforce and exploit Lynn's self-effacing, self-sacrificing persona. Significantly, though Peggy lives in comfortable middle-class surroundings, they resemble a commune rather than any normative family structure. Frank Forster, the composer, acts like a brother, but like Professor Drake and Mrs Crump, doesn't share Peggy's name. At a time when conventional family life had been so disrupted, the film's depiction of collective life characterised by mutual sharing and support clearly served a purpose. Lynn's public persona as someone who consistently put others first is fully exploited in the romantic sub-plot. Though in love herself with Scots soldier Bruce McIntosh, Peggy stands aside when she learns that he is in love with her best friend Ruth (played by Patricia Roc), even singing a highly reverberated 'Ave Maria' at their wedding, her face framed by a huge hat reminiscent of the Madonna's halo in pre-Renaissance paintings. Peggy/Lynn remains ambivalently virginal yet somehow accessible to all men, a composite sister, wife and mother.

Even holding Ruth's baby in the maternity ward, Peggy puts aside her own feelings and sings 'All The World Sings A Lullaby', the lyrics promising 'just how lovely tomorrow will be'.

This assertion that there is a future, not just for these babies but, by implication, for Britain and its fight for decency and democracy, is reinforced with the news that Bruce, feared killed in action, is alive and well. Whatever personal disappointments Frank and Peggy may have experienced are outweighed by the sense that both have contributed to the greater good, he by writing popular songs that people enjoy, she by serving the public through her singing. At the end of the film and before her concert for the airmen, when Frank asks her if she is happy, Peggy replies that she is, remarking that 'it's fun being together, working, making other people happy'. Their happiness is dependent on their working as a team, albeit a celibate team, devoid of any hint of romance. As Peggy, singing 'Yours Sincerely', tells the troops, 'I'm yours sincerely / I want you to know / I'm really, forever, sincerely yours'. She is, after all, the 'Forces' Sweetheart'.

Rhythm Serenade, released in 1943, reveals some important shifts from the earlier film. Here, the romance between Ann Martin (Lynn) and John Drover (Peter Murray Hill) sits at the core of the narrative. He is an apparently work-shy, anti-social and irascible 'conshie' who turns out to be a traumatised naval hero, she is determined to see active service with the WRENs but is led to recognise the value of the work she undertakes in helping factory production. All this takes place against the background of family life which Ann shares with her disabled ex-soldier father and two brothers, both soldiers. True, Lynn still plays a character who, as one of her brothers says, 'as usual, is doing something for somebody' and is given the nickname 'Sunshine'. As in *We'll Meet Again*, there are moments of dialogue which serve an openly propagandistic purpose, as when factory owner Mr Jimson harangues her on the importance of the 'army behind the limelight' and the daytime nursery she runs, allowing more women to work in the factory and thereby increasing production. Such moments are less intrusive, however, and are more than counterbalanced by significant elements of comedy in the film, centred mainly on variety and radio comedy duo Jimmy Jewell and Ben Warris, the antics of the young boy Joey (Jimmy Clitheroe) and, to a lesser extent, Mrs Crumbling (Irene Handl). All this arguably reflects a growing sense that, though there is much to do and increased munitions production remains essential, the war is being won. This is much more a nation at ease with itself, able to make numerous jokes about the fighting forces as when uniformed soldier Jimmy Jewel is able to say that 'we're in the army now, time's our own'.

There is also an important shift in the way Lynn's numbers are handled in the film. Whereas in *We'll Meet Again* the numbers, whilst motivated by the show-business setting, were given privileged performance space, here many of the numbers arise out of, and are integrated more closely with, narrative business undertaken by Lynn's character Ann Martin. In some cases, we only get snatches of a song, rather than the full number. This is exemplified at the film's opening, where Ann, a teacher at the evacuation centre, shares 'I Love To Sing' with the children. Later, posing as a uniformed member of the Women's Legion tending wounded commandos, Ann joins in their singing of 'Home Sweet Home Again' before leading them in singing 'Bye And Bye' as she offers tea and cigarettes to the men. As her widower father gazes with nostalgic longing at a photograph of her mother, commenting on the likeness between them, the camera tracks in as Ann plays and sings one verse and chorus of 'The Sunshine Of Your Smile', a song dating from 1913. Having succeeded in getting Drover to take her to a dinner-dance, Ann sings two choruses of the lush, romantic string-orchestrated 'It Doesn't Cost A Dime' as she gets herself dressed. The exception is the factory concert towards the film's close, where Lynn is given formal performance space, though even here her anxieties about Drover's reaction to hearing her voice yoke performance to narrative development.

The concert is Ann's big moment, not in the sense that stardom beckons as in *We'll Meet Again*, but because it represents her chance of marriage to Drover. It's significant that her first number at the concert, 'With All My Heart' with its 'impossible orchestration', declares love for just one man, this in the presence of Drover. Equally telling, as she launches into the up-beat optimistic 'I Love To Sing', switching the focus of her lyrics and leading the audience in community singing, Drover leaves her to take up a position on a merchant navy ship.

The film's improbably compressed dénouement occurs when Drover, aboard his sinking ship, picks up a BBC radio broadcast of Ann singing 'Rhythm Serenade' from a munitions factory. This sequence serves an important meta-textual function as powerful propaganda, as we see Lynn singing – and talking – against images, some superimposed over her, of munitions being produced in the pursuit of 'the one glorious end, freedom'. This return to the film's exploitation of Lynn's iconic status and the acknowledgement of her actual value to wartime morale is interesting in the light of an earlier revelatory conversation between Drover and Ann and the shift that we can see between *We'll Meet Again* and *Rhythm Serenade*. It turns out that the wounded commando nursed by Ann in the film's early sequence was Drover. Not knowing it was her, Drover is besotted by the voice of what he regards as an ideal woman, declaring that if he ever met her, he would 'shun her like the plague' knowing it is impossible to 'make love to an ideal, unless you drag it down to your level'. Later, at the dinner-dance, Drover suddenly proposes marriage to Ann. Remarking that she thought he was in love with a voice, he promises to turn a deaf ear to the voice, but she wonders if she is second-best, 'the grim reality' who cannot match his ideal woman. This itself offers self-reflexive commentary on the move away from that idealised mediated voice, the idealised feminine support for a nation-at-war, which sits at the centre of *We'll Meet Again*, to a more individualised woman who, whilst fully involved in supporting the war effort, is seen as desiring and deserving individual romance, a romance which forms the narrative core of *Rhythm Serenade*. This tension and the dynamic it involves is continued in Lynn's last film, *One Exciting Night* (1944) where, though she remains connected to and responsible for the nation by working in a munitions factory, the narrative focuses on romance and individuated needs, expressed in numbers such as 'One Love' and 'There's A New World'. It was a film which, as Lynn herself put it, 'moved me farther still from reality on getting me mixed up in a kidnap plot' (Lynn 1975: 103). In this sense, Lynn's three films chart some important changes within wartime Britain and its changing fortunes in the war effort.

John Huntley noted that Lynn made two (sic) films, 'both extremely bad' (Huntley 1947: 93). This is an unjustified conclusion, as I have argued above. Though Vera Lynn's limitations as an actor are evident, the skill of three competent journeyman directors goes a long way in overcoming them. In particular, Phil Brandon's direction and the fluid, sweeping camera work in *We'll Meet Again* ensures that the film remains consistently visually interesting, and both Wellesley and Forde make judicious use of close-ups when appropriate. All three films benefit from solid support from character actors such as Ronald Ward, Betty Jardine and Charles Victor and, even if *Rhythm Serenade* and *One Exciting Night* begin to stretch plausibility, the scripts retain an effective economy.

The films skilfully exploit Vera Lynn's unique appeal in support of the war effort and, under the musical direction of Harry Bidgood, deliver the sort of poignant, wistful but essentially optimistic musical numbers associated with Lynn. They are very much films for their time, but the quality of Lynn's singing voice retains its appeal, even if the songs appear impossibly dated now.

Post-war reconstruction: *I'll Be Your Sweetheart* (1945)

Champagne Charlie was not the only film of the mid-1940s to exploit the ideological potential implicit in the reversion to the Edwardian music hall. Gainsborough's *I'll Be Your Sweetheart* (1945) also harnesses the power of the historical imaginary and popular cultural tradition to comment on the here and now. Directed by Val Guest, the film uses a combination of original music hall numbers and those penned for the film by Manning Sherwin and Val Guest, all under the overall musical direction of Louis Levy, who is also given credit as Associate

Producer. The film's choreography was by Wendy Toye, a former ballet dancer who went on to direct a number of films in the 1950s and early 1960s (Merz 1994: 127). Ostensibly a nostalgic backstage musical centred on the battle for copyright protection for songwriters at the beginning of the twentieth century, the film actually has much to say about the social and cultural reconstruction of a post-war Britain, as the legitimate music publishers outwit and defeat the black-market profiteers. Although class and regional differences are acknowledged and are at the forefront of this film, these structural disparities are overcome in an expression of community that perfectly expresses the political moment which gave birth to a reforming Labour Government. The film does this, in part, by suggesting the power of music to construct community, not least by eradicating distinctions, not just between stage performer and audience as they all join in the song, but between class and region as well. This is clear from the very opening music-hall number, delivered to an audience which mixes the respectable upper class as well as the more boisterous, if equally respectable, working class, the camera sweeping from stage-side box to circle, as the soundtrack cleverly mixes in the more raucous and rumbustious contribution to the song's chorus from the latter.

The corrupting influence of black marketeers within the wartime economy and the need to defeat them had been acknowledged earlier in Elsie and Doris Waters' *Gert and Daisy Clean Up* (1942). In its different way, *I'll Be Your Sweetheart* articulates the same concern for a radical restructuring of British society evident in the closing sequences of *Champagne Charlie*, through its coded concern with the political fight for copyright protection for songwriters in Edwardian England and the elimination of the black economy of underworld and illicit music publishing. The judgement that *I'll Be Your Sweetheart* 'is too wordy to be a proper musical, not funny enough to be a comedy, and not dramatic enough to be a melodrama' (Murphy 1989: 202) is too harsh for a film which has intrinsic merit and which also has a wider significance, not least in the film's assertion of the powerful role of British vernacular popular music in constructing a sense of community and, by implication, of nationhood.

Like *Variety Jubilee* (1943), *Down Melody Lane* (1943) and *Champagne Charlie*, *I'll Be Your Sweetheart* uses its music-hall setting as an affirmation of the strength of a popular culture, seen here as something which can transcend structural barriers such as class and region. Its careful use of authentic music-hall songs and original numbers written in the same style also suggests a continuity between 'then' and 'now'. The film opens with a performance of 'Oh Mr Porter' sung by

Edie Story (Margaret Lockwood) and introduces Bob Fielding (Michael Rennie) whose Mancunian origins are coded by his old-fashioned dress sense if not by Rennie's impeccable Oxbridge accent. Fielding's intentions are to revolutionise the popular music industry by publishing music at prices everyone can afford, whilst at the same time recognising the rights of composers such as George Le Brunn.

Despite the huge popularity of Le Brunn's song and the evident capacity to unite community / nation, the problems are soon made evident . Le Brunn receives no money from legitimate publishers Francis Day and Hunters, who are being undercut by pirated sheet music copies of his song that are sold more cheaply by street traders. Though Le Brunn's songwriter colleagues berate the street seller, it is clear that this will not be enough to eradicate the activities of the black market.

Bob Fielding continues his crusade and with the help of Edie Story, with whom of course, in accordance with the conventions of the genre, he is destined to fall in love, he manages to get the song 'I'll Be Your Sweetheart' published by his own music publishing company. It is successful and the press take notice. Fielding is able to declare his reforming principles and desire to publish 'honest melody at an honest price, honestly paid for and honestly printed'. Importantly, such songs are 'the life-blood of the people'. Significantly, his reforming zeal and desire for a structured, legal and regulated music industry that rewards talent and at the same time makes the music universally available, attracts the attention of the politicians. The battle is on for the kind of public access to the 'life-blood' of music that mirrors the political fight for universal public access to health, welfare and education that was under way in British political culture.

Following a physical attack led by Bob Fielding on the pirate street sellers, Wallace, the pirate publisher responsible for the illegal publishing empire, determines to strike back. Wallace is shown operating from seedy premises that encapsulate the shady nature of the black economy. Played by Garry Marshall, Wallace is as much 1940s spiv as Edwardian pirate. The connections are clear. Wallace's self-interest is in sharp contrast to Bob Fielding's collectivist principles, and his willingness to use physical violence is a clear threat to the regulatory, controlled and legal provision which Fielding wishes to establish.

In a key episode in the film, the battle between Bob Fielding and the rakish Jim Knight, his other rival in the legitimate music publishing business and for Edie Story's romantic attentions, moves to Blackpool. Since the 1870s, Blackpool has been a major holiday town which attracted predominantly though not exclusively working-class holiday-makers released from the cotton towns of central Lancashire and the greater

Manchester area. By the 1930s, Blackpool was attracting unprecedented numbers of holiday-makers from a wide geographical area, lured by its reputation for the range of popular entertainments, including the Tower and the Winter Gardens, which were on offer at a relatively cheap price. The film draws upon the iconic significance of Blackpool as a populist pleasure centre that survived and indeed boomed during the overall deprivations of the war period. It serves as a locus which erodes structural distinctions of class, region and gender and which celebrates the capacity for community and national survival. From the top of the Tower, Edie and Bob reaffirm their determination to continue the fight against the pirates and, by implication, the determination of the nation-as-one to overcome the darkest days of the war. As they look down on the lights below them and notice where some have been extinguished, there is a clear reference to the blackout, the bombing raids, death and the survival of national spirit. Within this affirmation of community and national resilience, they clarify their romantic position and achieve the professional success in the battle of the music business. In all this, the role of the internal audience who join in the chorus singing is important, not least because it implicates ordinary people in the project of social reconstruction.

The premises of the pirate publishers are attacked and destroyed. In Parliament, the battle is taken up by the politicians. Those who oppose T.P. O'Connor's copyright bill are treated ironically; their condemnation of the song 'Boiled Beef And Carrots' indicates their inability to understand the power of popular song in constructing national consensus. The bill becomes law and the film concludes with a triumphal street scene in which the song 'I'll Be Your Sweetheart' gels together former rivals. The message is clear. Collectivist action produces the goods, as the protagonists declare 'one for all and all for one'. Though the film offers an aesthetic suffused with nostalgia, in looking back *I'll Be Your Sweetheart* also looks forward and makes a contribution to important ideological, political and cultural shifts which were underway in Britain in the mid-1940s. It certainly benefits from Guest's assured direction, strong performances from Lockwood, Rennie, Peter Graves and Vic Oliver, some elaborate staging of numbers such as 'The Honeysuckle And The Bee', and a narrative drive which carries conviction and usefully provides space for effectively performed numbers.

Developments in the British film score

Though these and later musicals drew upon popular cultural traditions, the late 1930s and 1940s was an important period in musical composition for British film production generally. As early as 1931 Gustav Holst, composer of the *Planets Suite*, wrote the music for a short multilingual co-production film *The Bells*, shot at British Sound Film Productions studio at Wembley, and showed real interest in film music before his death in 1934. Building on the important work undertaken by musical directors such as Muir Mathieson, Ernest Irving and Louis Levy in establishing studio music departments and raising the profile of film music, a number of contemporary 'serious' composers were persuaded to write for the cinema. Mathieson was instrumental in cajoling Arthur Bliss to score the music for *Things To Come* (1935), a film based on the novel by H.G. Wells. Bliss recorded the tensions he felt in writing music for the screen, but the end result, alongside the sixteen scores that Benjamin Britten wrote for the GPO Film Unit in the mid-1930s, helped create a climate in which it was respectable for serious composers to write for film. Ernest Irving noted the difference at Ealing between Basil Dean's rather penny-pinching approach to music in the films he produced and the attitude of Michael Balcon, who encouraged Walton and others to compose for Ealing films and provided the budgets to pay for more expansive recording and musical production, recognising that 'spending a little more money is often the best way to avoid waste' (Irving 1959: 146). Respected composers who wrote for British cinema during the 1940s included Ralph Vaughan Williams (*49th Parallel* (1941), *The Loves of Joanna Godden* (1947), *Scott Of The Antartic* (1948)), William Walton (*Escape Me Never* (1935), *As You Like It* (1936), *The Foreman Went To France* (1942), *Went The Day Well?* (1942), *First Of The Few* (1942), *Henry V* (1945)) and William Alwyn (*They Flew Alone* (1942), *The Way Ahead* (1944), *The Rake's Progress* (1945), *Odd Man Out* (1947)). Of these composers, Alwyn was the most prolific, though his output was nearly matched by other important film composers such as Richard Addinsell, who wrote the Rachmaninov-inspired 'Warsaw Concerto' for *Dangerous Moonlight* (1941) and Hubert Bath who scored the music for Victor Saville's *Kitty* (1929), Hitchcock's *Blackmail* (1929), *Waltzes From Vienna* (1934) and *Thirty Nine Steps* (1935), as well as the equally Rachmaninov-inspired 'Cornish Rhapsody' for *Love Story* (1944).

Though not as well known and perhaps as revered as Walton and Vaughan Williams, Addinsell and Bath are perhaps more typical of the cultural landscape from which British film music emerged at this period. As well as attempts at classical composition, Addinsell wrote music for Andre Charlot and Noel Coward revues, for BBC radio plays, as well as for the theatre. He also composed a number of popular songs including 'I'm Going To See You Today' and 'Turn Back The Clock' in collaboration with comedienne Joyce Grenfell. He was contracted to write music in Hollywood for RKO for six months in 1933, and in 1936 collaborated with Muir Mathieson in work for Korda's London Films. In the late 1930s and early 1940s he wrote the scores for a number of documentary and feature films including *Goodbye Mr Chips* (1939), *The Lion Has Wings* (1939), *Blithe Spirit* (1945) and *Diary For Timothy* (1946). Hubert Bath wrote symphonic and choral works, but he was also musical adviser to London County Council in the 1920s, responsible for the organisation of public recreation park bands. Before joining Louis Levy at Gaumont-British's music department permanently in 1933, Bath had employed his wide-ranging musical talents for the first talkies in Britain, including BIP's *Under The Greenwood Tree* (1929), the music performed by the British International Symphony Orchestra. Before his death in 1945, he wrote the music for Gainsborough's *They Were Sisters* (1945), directed by Arthur Crabtree and starring Phyllis Calvert and James Mason, and was working on the music for *The Wicked Lady* (1945) starring Margaret Lockwood.

Though none of these composers was writing for films that we might recognise as 'musicals', they represented an aspect of cultural production that was decidedly influential at this period. The awareness and increased use of classical or 'serious' music in British cinema became pronounced during feature-film production in the 1940s. For example, in *Love Story* (1944) Margaret Lockwood plays a concert pianist who believes she only has one year left to live. She writes a piano concerto, the 'Cornish Rhapsody', as an expression of her love for Kit (Stewart Grainger), which is later performed in the Royal Albert Hall, though with concert pianist Harriet Cohen playing the piano on the soundtrack. In similar fashion in *The Seventh Veil* (1945), Ann Todd plays a pianist whose hands have been badly burned and who becomes depressed, convinced she will never play again. Again, the film features a concert with full on-screen orchestra, with concert pianist Eileen Joyce dubbing on the soundtrack. With music by Chopin, Mozart, Grieg, Rachmaninov and Beethoven, the film prompted one American review to pronounce that 'the use of classical music beautifully cued in and performed, adds further distinction to a dignified and distinguished production' (Huntley 1947: 79).

The extent to which classical music was co-opted for British cinema during this period can be judged by the unlikely appearance of concert pianists Rawicz and Landauer, alongside comedy acrobats Donovan and Byl, and dancers Arnley and Gloria in Mancunian Films' Frank Randle vehicle *Home Sweet Home* (1945). Though released the year after the war in Europe ended, Gainsborough's *The Magic Bow* (1946), a biopic of violinist Paganini starring Stewart Granger with violinist Yehudi Menuhin playing on the soundtrack, perpetuated both the interest in and success of films with classical music at their centre; as Donnelly notes,

> *The Magic Bow* did not equate classical music with the middle classes; rather, it attempted to win back such music for the masses. *The Magic Bow* demonstrates the interest in class mobility that had been articulated by previous [Gainsborough] costume dramas, but doubles this by offering art music to everyone. (Donnelly 1997: 167)

In attempting to understand the use, function and significance of classical music in British cinema from the late 1930s and into the 1940s, either as non-diegetic score or woven into the narrative fabric of films such as *The Seventh Veil* and *The Magic Bow*, it is not possible to ignore the influence of the BBC. Though John Reith had resigned as Director General of the BBC in 1938, his influence upon radio broadcasting policy remained significant, not least in attitudes towards music. As we have seen, popular dance bands had been an important part of BBC radio programming throughout the 1920s and 1930s, and many dance bands heard on radio had also featured in British films. However, 'serious' music was much more highly valued within the BBC. Looking back on radio broadcasting in 1942, it noted that 'serious' music broadcasting was 'advanced rather than retarded':

> In the Home and Forces programmes there was a considerable increase in the time devoted to serious music. Two-hour periods were regularly allotted to symphony concert broadcasts, and a full studio opera was presented every month . . . The fortnightly public symphony and lunch-hour concerts were continued on the usual lines. (BBC 1943: 42)

In April 1942 Arthur Bliss had succeeded Sir Adrian Boult as the BBC's Director of Music, though Boult remained as Chief Conductor to the BBC Symphony Orchestra. Considerable merit was attached to the radio broadcasts of new British and American classical works by composers such as Benjamin Britten and Aaron Copland, as well as to the first broadcast performance of Shostakovich's Seventh Symphony, the Leningrad Symphony. All this contributed to what Swynnoe describes as the atmosphere of 'benevolent paternalism which permeated entertainment in Britain' at this time (Swynnoe 2002: 7).

Arguably, however, rather than being seen as a continuation of an elitist cultural tradition, the BBC's determination in the 1940s to provide 'serious' music to its audiences can be seen as a self-appointed policy of democratising culture, of making what were seen as the lasting, civilising values of high culture available to all, at a time when such civilised values appeared to be under threat. There are parallels in the documentary films of Humphrey Jennings from this period, with their message of an inclusive seamless British culture which stretched from the popular to the serious; in evocative films such as *Listen To Britain* (1942) Jennings marries a whole range of different music to suggest a totality of shared cultural experience. Here, as in other films, classical music is seen as part of web of culture and entertainment which reaches across the classes and binds them together. Though in *Love Story* and *The Seventh Veil* the protagonists are middle class and the concert halls are attended by the middle class, the melodramatic, romantic storylines render these people, the places they inhabit and the music they play or listen to, universally accessible. In much the same way, though Laura (Celia Johnson) and Alec (Leslie Howard) in David Lean's *Brief Encounter* (1945) are resolutely middle class, their intense romance, played out against a background of iconic ordinariness, renders the use of Rachmaninov's Piano Concerto No. 2 democratically available to audiences.

As we have seen, although early synchronised sound films had made extensive use of a wide range of popular music hall, variety, gramophone and radio acts, some production companies saw a market for 'high culture' in shorts such as Phonofilms *Rigoletto Act Two* (1926) and British Sound Film Production's *Tannhauser Act Three* (1928). Films based on the lives of famous musicians, composers, artists or writers were not uncommon from the start. Herbert Wilcox's British and Dominions Film Corporation produced the feature *The Loves Of Robert Burns* in 1930 and films about composers in Vienna were legion in the early and mid-1930s. Anthony Asquith's *Dance, Pretty Lady* (1932) had featured Marie Rambert's ballet *corps* with choreography by Frederick Ashton, disliked by BIP chairman John Maxwell because it was 'for the intelligentsia' (Low 1997: 121). Similar objections had been made, despite Walton's contribution to the score and editing by David Lean, to *Dreaming Lips* (1936) a film starring Elisabeth Bergner which included an extended segment featuring the London Philharmonic Orchestra. However, the experience of being at war from 1939 onwards gave an impetus to films which, at their centre, offered some sort of vision of what might be regarded as life's enduring qualities, not least the durability and relevance of the art of serious music, its composers and practitioners. If, as Aldgate and Richards have argued, 'it is clear that the cinema played a positive and purposeful role in its own right in generating adherence to the new found consensus of the war years' (Aldgate and Richards 1986: 13), it is as important to consider the role of music within this reconstructive British cinema, a cinema which could harness talents as wide-ranging and diverse as Tommy Trinder, Paganini, Vera Lynn, Beethoven, Arthur Askey and Handel, in cultural products which variously prompted appreciation and enjoyment through instruction and entertainment.

J. Arthur Rank and the British film musical

Within this specific historical and cultural context, the rise of J. Arthur Rank as a force in British film production and, later, distribution and exhibition, proved deeply significant. As is well known, Rank's growing prominence within the British film industry was driven by his wealth, derived from his family milling interests, and his religious convictions which led him to believe in the potential of cinema to enrich cultural understanding, promote family values, and celebrate what he saw as British values. After financing a series of religious films which, on his own admission, were not really very good, Rank had built new studios at Pinewood in 1936, acquired Denham from Korda in 1938 and bought the Amalgamated Studios at Elstree. The acquisition of Gaumont-British with its chain of cinemas and the Gainsborough production unit at Shepherd's Bush in 1941, together with his control of Odeon Cinema Holdings the same year, gave Rank a prominent position in the British film industry. Rank combined business acumen with his religious views, leading him to a view that cinema had a social role to play, offering 'healthy entertainment . . . for all members of the family' (Porter 2001: 87). Along with the editor of the *Methodist Times*, the Reverend Benjamin Gregory, and director Norman Walker, Rank had set up GHW Productions in 1937, specifically to finance productions with a religious message. One of the most intriguing, making good use of the vogue for classical music, was *The Great Mr Handel* (1942), a film which at one level operates as a biopic of the eighteenth-century composer, but which also attempts to accommodate, through extensive use of Handel's music, Rank's intention that cinema should provide 'uplifting entertainment'.

The film's director, Norman Walker, had begun working under John Maxwell at Elstree in the 1920s and directed *Widecombe Fair* and *Tommy Atkins*, both with screenplays by Eliot Stannard, in 1928. He was keen to explore the technical boundaries available to film-makers, directing *A Romance Of Seville* (1929) in colour and adding a soundtrack in July 1930. He directed a number of talkies, including *Loose Ends* (1930) starring Edna Best, Owen Nares and Donald Calthrop. Walker grew close to J.Arthur Rank, directing Rank's first feature film *The Turn Of The Tide* (1935) as well as a number of films that reflected their shared religious interests. *The Great Mr Handel* certainly includes overtly religious scenes, but Walker claimed the credit for persuading Rank that a film based on Handel and using his music would also have significant commercial appeal, given the number of amateur choirs and musical societies which regularly performed *The Messiah*. Based on a radio play by L. Du Garde Peach, the film was a prestigious Technicolor production, shot by Claude Friese-Green and a young Jack Cardiff, with Ernest Irving as the musical director and with music performed by the London Philharmonic Orchestra.

Though the film functions at one level to detail the struggles experienced by Handel, it also makes pointed reference to the undemocratic and arbitrarily unjust system of patronage on which artists and composers relied in the eighteenth century. Though Handel's music has enjoyed popularity, Frederick Prince of Wales (Max Kirby), at odds with his father the King, dislikes Handel (Wilfred Lawson) and refuses him royal patronage, despite impassioned pleas from John Heidegger, the owner of the King's Theatre in Haymarket. The Prince of Wales' entourage is seen as vicious, trivial and morally bankrupt, with Lord Chesterfield (Malcolm Keen) declaring that, though he personally prefers Handel's music and sees him as the greater composer, fashion, prudence and politics dictate his public preference for the less-talented Buononcini. The moral centre of gravity in the film resides with Handel, who not only despairs at the fashions of musical taste, but treats his creditors with respect and takes pity on the two orphaned children of a starved musician, placing them in the care of Captain Corum, 'an old sailor' who is building the Foundling Hospital. The contrast between Handel's carefully delineated virtue and the foppish venom of royalty is clear when, at the Vauxhall Gardens, the popular pleasure grounds enjoyed by Londoners in the eighteenth century, the Prince of Wales demands that the orchestra stop playing Handel's music, an intimation of the fascist tyranny being fought against two hundred years later. Framed within an orchestra pit which barely seems big enough to contain him, Handel's courage in halting a performance because of the Prince of Wales's loud, disruptive and misogynistic comments about Mrs Cibber offers a stark contrast with later scenes of noisy, organised mobs disrupting concerts and throwing mud at opera play-bills, a comment perhaps on the organised mayhem caused by fascist mobs in Hitler's Germany.

With the continuing support from opera singer Mrs Cibber (Elizabeth Allan) and servant Phineas (Hay Petrie), buoyed by evident love for his music by ordinary people such as the woman serving in a tobacconist's shop, Handel manages to survive royal disfavour, material deprivation and serious ill-health until Charles Jennens persuades him to write the music to his oratorio *The Messiah*. The process of composition is tortuous, as Handel experiences a series of religious visions, framed through his window, and undergoes the ecstasy of intense creative and religious experience, with the clear implication that the two are intertwined. The work completed, it is given its first performance in Dublin in April 1742, and then performed before the King at the Royal Opera House Covent Garden in 1743.

Within this linear narrative framework, every opportunity is taken to make effective use of Handel's music, either in Ernest Irving's skilful manipulation in the score, or in set pieces in theatres and Handel's home. Irving also effectively employs traditional street cries from the period, such as 'Cherry Ripe', 'Who'll Buy My Primroses' and 'Mackerel, New Mackerel' both to mark the passages of narrative time between 1727 to 1743, and to locate and authenticate Handel's place in Georgian England. Rehearsals and concerts pepper the film; Handel's credentials as someone who has chosen to be an Englishman is reinforced at one rehearsal where he dismisses a temperamental Italian singer and declares that he needs to 'engage Englishmen'. Mrs Cibber is given several opportunities to sing arias from both *Xerses* ('Ombra mai fu' and 'Non so sesia la speme') and the *Messiah* ('He was Despised'). Irving's underscoring gives way to diegetic use of Handel's 'Water' music at Vauxhall Gardens and, most powerfully, in the 'He was Despised' aria sung in Handel's home. Mrs Cibber expresses her reluctance, as an actress, to sing sacred music and is concerned what people might think. Handel, in a reply that naturalises the connection between art and religion, tells her that people would think 'that an actress believed in God. Is that so strange?', a connection reinforced when, as Mrs Cibber sings of Christ's rejection and despair in the words of the aria, the camera tracks in on Handel, the man who himself has suffered so much of the same fate. Shot in soft focus close-up, Mrs Cibber's performance of the aria resonates beyond the spatial confines of Handel's house, spilling out onto the street, transfixing people. An impromptu 'audience' of ordinary working people stop what they are doing and listen in awe, a community linked through the music. As Handel declares his faith and belief that 'my redeemer liveth', a street cry goes up that 'all's well, all's well', and people go about their business. Triumphant at the end, Handel conducts at the Royal Opera House, as a rare fluid camera movement ranges across from the audience, which includes the King, to the orchestra and chorus playing and singing 'Hallelujah'.

Whilst the combination of potential commercial appeal and religious message seduced Rank into financing the film, it was not a success in

either business or critical terms. Huntley quotes from an unacknowl-
edged contemporary American review from 1944, which praised ways
in which music is used as 'an integral part in the development of the
story', the 'exceedingly capable cast' the authentic feel of costumes and
sets, and the 'emotional uplift' in the *Messiah* composition sequence
(Huntley 1947: 67). However, despite some success in Australia and
Canada, the film was poor box-office in Britain, running only one week
at its London opening. Huntley, whilst praising the intent behind the
film, makes his own criticisms:

> As a music-lover's film, as a film connoisseur's classic, *The Great Mr.
> Handel* was an outstanding film event of the year, but in all the welter of
> music, period atmosphere, costumes and uplift, the director made one fatal
> mistake. The film was slow. A motion picture must move, and for long
> periods this one did not move. (Huntley 1947: 66)

Even for a cinema founded, in Gledhill's terms, in pictorialism and
theatricalised space and performance (Gledhill 2003: 32) Walker's film
dwells excessively on static compositions, not least in the crucial but,
to contemporary eyes, excruciating sequence where Handel composes
the music to *Messiah*. However, the film remains intriguing, not least
because of its resonance with wider contemporary political concerns, its
comment on identity and implicit polemic against the tyranny of cultural fashion and authoritarian politics. Through celebrating the bicen-
tenary of the *Messiah*, the film makes implicit reference to contemporary
events, positioning audiences to read the film through events they are
currently living through. German-born, Handel chooses to be English,
promoting values and a morality which is, by implication, in stark
contrast to the absence of such values in his ex-homeland. His commitment to a wider 'truth', admittedly ultimately a 'truth' founded in
Christianity, offers a contrast with characters such as Lord Chesterfield
who recognise 'truth' coded through artistic worth, but lack the courage
to act on this perception. As in Jenning's *Diary For Timothy* (1946),
where we hear Beethoven's music and are asked to admire, enjoy and
respect it despite its Germanic origins, so here Handel's music is requisitioned for common humanity, currently seen to be residing in wartime
Britain.

The post-war musical film:
London Town (1946) and *Trottie True* (1949)

The end of war involved major social dislocations, not least the return
of service-men and -women to peace-time occupations, a shift antici-

pated in Butcher's *Demobbed* (1944) with Nat Jackley and Norman Evans, and reflected in their *Under New Management* (1946) featuring 'resident' band Percival Mackey, this time with Jackley and Evans staffing a hotel with ex-army pals, and Columbia-British's *George In Civvy Street* (1946) with George Formby. British National produced a number of musical films in the mid-1940s including *Heaven Is Round The Corner* (1944), *Waltz Time* (1945) and *Lisbon Story* (1946), both featuring Richard Tauber and Peter Graves, who also appeared in *Spring Song* (1946: US title *Springtime*) and *The Laughing Lady* (1946). *Meet The Navy* (1946), with a Technicolor sequence, followed the staging of the Royal Canadian Navy show. In addition to films from Butchers and British National and some programme fillers produced by short-lived independents – such as Tempean Films' *A Date With A Dream* (1948) starring Terry-Thomas and featuring Vic Lewis and his Orchestra, a film about a group of ex-concert party soldiers who reunite to forge a post-war career in cabaret – Herbert Wilcox continued his flirtation with the musical in *The Courtneys Of Curzon Street* (1947) and *Maytime In Mayfair* (1949).

The mid-1940s saw Rank in a position of growing ascendancy within the British film industry, able to capitalise on a series of exhibition deals forged not just in America, but also in Canada, Australia, New Zealand and South Africa. Though group profits came predominantly from exhibition, Rank continued with ambitious production plans throughout the late 1940s by financing independent productions. Rank's assault on the American market was regarded by Michael Balcon as 'the most ambitious yet attempted in this country and also the most thoroughly planned and organised' (Balcon 1946: 73).

Amongst these Rank-financed productions were Wesley Ruggles' *London Town* (1946), The Archers' *The Red Shoes* (1948) and Two Cities' *Trottie True* (1949). Shot in Technicolor at a time when the average British production was in black and white, all three films attempted to emulate production values audiences associated with musicals coming from MGM, Fox and Columbia. Despite this, and in their different ways, the three films met with very mixed receptions, both domestically and in the American market.

London Town is essentially a show-business story about Joe Sanford (Sid Fields), a northern comic from Wigan moving to London with his young daughter (Petula Clark) and eventually getting his big break in the West End show also called 'London Town'. Despite disparaging comments about the differences between the provincial entertainers and their audiences and the sophistication of London shows, Joe finds success. Unlike his fictional triumph, however, the film *London Town* was an all-round box-office disaster. The concept of combining loved and respected British comedian Fields and glamorous starlet Kay Kendall with American directorial and songwriting talent must have appeared alluring, but the end result was an uneven hybrid which satisfied neither the domestic nor the American market.

The increased influence exercised by American popular music idioms during the latter years of the war is evident in some of the numbers written by the Americans, composer Jimmy Van Heusen and lyricist Johnny Burke. 'So Would I', for example, is a lavishly staged swing number delivered by a vocal octet with decidedly neat American phrasing. In the same way, Kay Kendall seems almost at home with 'My Heart Goes Crazy' which segues, by way of a giant eleven-player white piano, into a crooning ballad, and finally into a jazz-inflected version of 'Ampstead Way'. The problem is that these American influences, effectively staged as they are in 'classical' Hollywood musical style, including some lavish sets and splendid shock-red costumes, sit uncomfortably alongside other numbers which can only be described as mock-cockney, as in the painfully embarrassing 'Ampstead Way' number delivered by Pearly Kings and Queens, a number anticipating some of the worst moments in *Mary Poppins* (1964). Though the numerous tourist shots such as the crowded River Thames and Windsor Castle are there to appeal to the American market, they represent a rosy, chocolate-box vision of Britain which had nothing to do with the realities of post-war austerity and recovery.

Worse, the comedy sequences for which Fields was renowned in his live variety acts totally fail to convince. As I have written elsewhere,

> These comic routines, shot without the benefit of any cut-aways to the theatre audience or even soundtrack laughter, are bounded by precisely the sense of provincial music hall and variety comedy which the film purports to leave behind. (Mundy 1999: 159)

American director Wesley Ruggles is effective in directing the elaborate numbers of the show-within-the-film, but is completely unsympathetic to the comedy variety style of Fields and his straight man Jerry Desmond. Their earlier scene, played with camp gusto by the pair of them, remains an interesting retrospective curiosity, but lacks any conviction within the context of the film. This is the film's problem. If earlier production policy had been divided between producing musical and musical comedies for the domestic market on the one hand, and more generically undeviating products for the international, essentially American, market, *London Town* attempts to combine the two within the one feature. This is compounded by the complete absence of romantic engagement between the protagonists, with Joe's affections centred entirely on his young daughter. The result is an uneven, ruptured film that fails to cohere and which remains resolutely uncertain in its tone and address.

Yet, whatever its aesthetic and economic failings, *London Town* does reflect some significant changes in the perception of national identity. The narrative first raises and then is unable to sustain an underlying discourse of regionalism, a clear indication that cultural power is increasing metropolitan. Charlie (Sonnie Hale), the comic Joe replaces, ends up working in Newcastle, the purgatorial fringe of a show-business increasingly dominated by the sophistication of London. This nod towards identities bounded by regionalism, so important for British films in the 1930s, simply gets lost as the film then concentrates on the lavishness of the West End London show. As an image of an emergent London open for business after the deprivations of war, a melting pot, not just for show-business talent but, by implication, of the nation as a whole, it is briefly seductive, especially in the lavish spectacle of the staged numbers. Ultimately though, the attempt to emulate the classless appeal of 'The Lambeth Walk' fails to convince. If the war constructed some sense of national unity, then the post-war period was to witness a resurfacing of social attitudes bound by class divisions, albeit articulated in different ways from the 1930s. However spectacularly staged, the 'Ampstead Way', promoted here as something which will once again elide class distinction, is simply unable to carry the ideological weight imposed on it.

If the romantic sub-plot in *Champagne Charlie*, where the impossibility of marriage between show-girls and the aristocracy occupies a subservient place to the business of music hall, in the Two Cities Technicolor production *Trottie True* (1949: US title *Gay Lady*) this hierarchy is reversed. The film was directed by Brian Desmond Hurst, whose previous films included ABPC's Ruritanian musical *Glamorous Nights* (1937).

Despite being shot at Denham at a time of increasing financial pressure for Rank and the organisation's evident dissatisfaction with Powell and Pressberger's *The Red Shoes*, the film's production values and narrative ebullience show little sign of either constraint or fear. Here, romance and sexual politics sit at the centre of the film, enlivened with production numbers tracing the rise of the eponymous heroine from music hall to marriage into the aristocracy. Set in Edwardian England, its narrative hinges around the social fashion for sexual liaison between gold-digging Gaiety girls and the young male aristocracy. In the film, Trottie True (Jean Kent) is determined from an early age to be a success in music hall. She achieves this, rising from youthful appearances at the foot of the bill as Little Trottie True to headlining at the Bedford Music Hall, then on to 'legitimate' musical comedy, finally becoming one of the famous 'Gaiety' girls in London. Though not unaware of the lure of her sexuality, parading it before audiences to 'make the pits and the gods obey', Trottie has a strong sense of personal sexual morality. Despite her successful career, what she wants is to marry and settle down with Sid Skinner (Andrew Crawford), a 'pioneer' and frequently absent balloonist. She is unprepared for the different morality that operates amongst Gaiety girls such as Bouncie Bonnington (Lana Morris) and their sexual liaisons with members of the male aristocracy. Drawn into this world, though remaining resistant to it, apparently abandoned by Sid whose absences become more and more prolonged, Trottie eventually marries Lord Digby Landon (James Donald). Her determination to remain – and be seen to remain – faithful to her new husband is severely tested, surrounded as she is by a world running on sexual promiscuity. At stake in all this, structured around the fashions and conventions that differentiate social class and gender, is the issue of happiness, the possibility of its achievement and the often ambivalent distinction between 'true' happiness and its merely conventional appearance.

Trottie grows up in a comfortable, conventional and respectable middle-class family environment. Though her mother is initially against her pursuit of a stage career, hoping that she will get a respectable job until 'Mr Right' comes along, her father is always supportive. Though he is referred to as 'the best toucher-upper', this refers not to his sexual proclivities, but to his job in the tinsel postcard business. As his daughter has increasing contact with the promiscuous young male aristocracy, he remains a source of advice, balance and reason. Frustrated in her love for Sid the balloonist, he tells her that love is most important, even if it is with a man who values a 'laundry basket hung on four bits of string'. This is important, given how sexually attractive Trottie is for most of the men she comes into contact with, her life mirroring the lyrics of one of her songs, 'they're all potty over Trottie True / the kid from Camden Town'. She resists the constant marriage proposals from fellow entertainer Joe Juggs (Bill Owen), but is happy to work with him. Her strength of character has already been established during her first childhood appearance on the music-hall stage, where she gets the better of a heckler in the gods and succeeds in leading the audience in the chorus of 'Camden Town', and this strength serves her well amidst the moral and sexual hypocrisy she later encounters.

Trottie's professional success leads her away from music hall to a leading role in the 'legitimate' theatre in George Edwardes' musical comedy *The Belle and the Buoy*. However, Trottie remains true to her music-hall roots when, against all the rules, she invites the audience at the Theatre Royal Bradford to join in the chorus of one of her songs, dismaying fellow performers Joe and Daisy (Hattie Jacques), who feel that she has broken the conventions of legitimate theatre. Impatient with convention, Trottie remains connected to the people, asking 'who wants classy stuff when the pit and gallery love to sing'. Rather than sacking her, Edwardes says if she is 'sensible', a step up to The Gaiety Theatre beckons. This intimation that sexual favours will get her somewhere, that she should 'always be nice to the backers', leads her to have supper with Arthur Briggs, the richest man in Bradford, but Trottie's love for Sid makes her tell him firmly that she is 'a good girl'.

Her loyalty to Sid is apparently misplaced as they argue about marriage, security and having a family and she is forced into a position where she tells him, not really believing it, that she never wants to see him again. Sid is committed to his job as a test balloonist and tells her at the end of the argument 'see you next week, wind permitting'. Complications in her private life do nothing to prevent Trottie's growing professional success, and she lands a job at the Gaiety Theatre in London. Here, in the company of Bouncie Bonnington, she learns what being a Gaiety Girl seems to entail; when Trottie complains about the quality of the number she has sung, Bouncie remarks that 'we're here to be looked at, not to be listened to'. Gaiety girls are, she asserts, 'walking jewellery counters'. These expectations about gendered experiences in this social world are reinforced by the attitudes and comments of the young male aristrocrats who hang around The Gaiety stage door. Fearful that the appropriately named young and inexperienced Lord Maidenhead (Michael Medwin) is in danger of ignoring the rules of the game and of becoming emotionally involved, Lord Digby Landon reminds him that, in this world of promiscuous relationships where the girls are there to adorn and be showered with expensive gifts, but remain strictly dispensable, 'any departure from the formula is dangerous'. In contrast with the world of genuine love and emotion, Trottie now inhabits a sexually ambivalent, insincere world, rigidly structured by differences in class and gender power. As Landon sneeringly reminds Maidenhead, 'art' – by which he means beautiful, non-aristocratic, available, women from the theatre whose sexual favours can be bought and then discarded – 'is inspiration, but life is a fact. They should be kept each in their clearly defined watertight compartments'. This promiscuous approach is in marked contrast with Trottie's reiteration that she likes 'chaps who are serious', that 'there's no sense in messing about'.

Ironically, Lord Digby Landon is unable to take his own advice and on a picnic trip with the Gaeity girls and their aristocratic admirers, without, as Trottie puts it, 'a balloon in sight to spoil things', he expresses his genuine love for her. The importance of social class is evident through his wish, as he tells Trottie, that he could be an 'ordinary chap and not have to worry about the family name'. If respectability counts in Camden Town, what matters in Mayfair are 'appearances'. Confronted with Trottie's assertion that men are all the same, that they talk about love but won't give up anything for it, 'not even a balloon', Landon proposes. Significantly, Trottie rips up a postcard from Sid that asks 'are we drifting apart?' (they are, of course, literally and metaphorically) and she marries Landon. Despite his willingness to make sacrifices, Landon has no need to as, overcoming their initial hostility, Trottie is accepted by Landon's parents, the Duke and Duchess of Wellwater. Significantly, it is Trottie's 'performance' at the Christmas Ball given by the Duke and Duchess that quells their hostility. An immediate hit with Sainsbury the head butler, who confesses to having seen her many times at the Bedford Music Hall and joining in the chorus to her songs, Trottie also dances with the footmen whilst singing 'My Heart Flies To You'. Her infectious singing of a song from the halls, 'When I Take My Morning Promenade' a novelty number about fashion and its role in sexual attraction, has the effect of eradicating class distinction as everybody joins in the chorus, only to fall into silence as an aghast Duchess enters the ballroom. As with the heckler in the music-hall gods, Trottie is unperturbed by this and launches into 'Over The Mountains And Over The Sea', a tender and beautifully romantic ballad with lush orchestration. Just as she won over the heckler and the music-hall audience, Trottie wins over the Duchess, who pronounces 'she'll do'.

The power of music and performance to eradicate class difference and to construct community does not prevent Trottie and Landon drifting apart, as a series of well-intentioned accidents, coincidences and misunderstandings constructs a rift between them. Ironically, though Landon is faithful to Trottie, appearances suggest otherwise and bitter arguments ensue. Running into a disillusioned Bouncie, unhappily married to Lord Maidenhead but consoled by thoughts that 'that was never the idea; I've got my emeralds', Trottie is unable to accept a situation where she has not only a husband who cheats, but has 'to pretend I don't know he is cheating'. However, after listening to advice from her mother-in-law the Duchess about how to handle men and then meeting up again with Sid who declares that he is giving up ballooning to marry another woman, Trottie decides to stay with Landon, even if the price of this decision appears to be her unhappiness.

The significance of the narrative framing device becomes evident when, in the opening sequence as Trottie rides past in a carriage, a character we now know is Joe Juggs, comments that she looks a little sad. As she makes her way towards the camera and the wedding trousseau tea of a friend, a chorus of whispered innuendos on the soundtrack announce that 'marriages like that never work', that it 'is all pretence' and ask 'will it last, should it last?' Now the Duchess of Wellwater, she advises Honour to marry wealth rather than the impecunious young man she actually loves. Before gazing wistfully out of the window and remembering all the good times, she declares that she always knew *how* to get what she wanted, but that it took a long time to know *what* it was she wanted. Trottie's story unfolds in the flashback that forms the bulk of the narrative before, in the ambivalent closing sequence, she appears reunited with her husband. Perhaps Trottie accepts that, in the words of the matronly character who presides over the trousseau tea, he is 'just a man' and that the two of them will learn to 'take each other for granted'. What seems to be acknowledged in both her and Joe Juggs' knowing half-smiles is a recognition of the power that a woman can exercise in a world where most power lies elsewhere. Though far from being a feminist tract, the film betrays considerable sympathy for women who overcome the restrictions of patriarchy articulated through marriage conventions and 'supports class mobility and the right of a lower class to bring its attitudes and values along with it' (McIlroy 1994: 38).

Though perhaps not in the same class as *Gigi* (1958) and *My Fair Lady* (1964), *Trottie True* comes close. Jean Kent's strong performance is supported by James Donald's quietly understated role as Landon, a man who learns that conventional male and class privileges carry a price and warms to a more democratised and gender-equal society. The colour photography remains consistently vibrant, the realisation of music-hall and variety settings is convincing and the numbers are staged with firm authority. Desmond Hurst's direction is both assured and, at times, bold, as in the wonderful sequence where the young Digby Landon arrives at the magnificent Wellwater family home to announce his intention to marry Trottie. Rather than shoot the conversation, the camera remains outside the room, relying on the reactions of Sainsbury the butler and other staff to indicate how things are going, aided by meticulous use of an orchestration which charts the progress of the conversation from frustration to triumph and agreement. Though Desmond Hurst's earlier attempt at a musical, BIP's *Glamorous Nights* (1937), was something of a disaster and was savagely cut after the trade show (Low 1997: 232), a victim in part of the uncertainties surrounding production that year, *Trottie True* indicates what could be achieved with conviction backed by the right budget.

Herbert Wilcox and Anna Neagle

The issue of class in post-war Britain sits at the centre of the Herbert Wilcox/Anna Neagle production *The Courtneys Of Curzon Street* (1947: US title *The Courtney Affair*). Like their earlier *I Live In Grosvenor Square* (1945: US title *A Yank In London*), featuring Carroll Gibbons and his Orchestra, and the subsequent *Spring In Park Lane* (1948) and *Maytime In Mayfair* (1949), the film exploits its title's fashionable London society address in its appeal to the American market, something that Wilcox was adept at. In its epic, melodramatic sweep from Lady Courtney's Servant's Ball on New Year's Eve 1899 to the cosy, domestic, democratic New Year's Eve in 1945, the film charts the fortunes of Irish serving maid Kathie O'Halloran (Anna Neagle) and Sir Edward Courtney (Michael Wilding) as they face high society's snobbish opposition to their marriage across the class divide, opposition which forces them apart for a number of years. Alongside melodramatic sentiment centering on death and loss, the film makes effective use of musical numbers, not just to help ground-sweeping temporal shifts and climactic events – 'Soldiers Of The Queen' during the Boer War, Tchaikovsky's 'Pathétique' Symphony performed before an aging Queen Victoria, 'Whispering' from the early 1920s, 'Lily Marlene' at a World War Two factory concert – but to act as markers of emotionally significant moments and help motivate narrative events.

At the opening Servant's Ball, Kathie's identity as both Irish and serving maid is reinforced in her comic number 'A Place Of My Own', its lyrics announcing her desire for love and domesticity. Though the Ball brings the upper classes and their servants into close social contact for one evening in the year, the boundaries are meant to stay intact. The love between Kathie and Sir Edward breaks those boundaries, much to the concern of Lady Courtney who, whilst not 'wishing to be narrow and bigoted' reminds Edward, despite his protestations that 'this is a new century', that 'family and background are very strong'. Forced away by gossip and hostility from the upper-class women who share Courtney's social world, Kathie becomes May Linton, a music-hall star, a move which marks her self-reliance and strong-willed independence and, when singing 'Roses Of Picardy' to First World War British soldiers fighting in France, leads to a reunion with her estranged husband. Through vicissitudes involving the death in action of their soldier son and the death of his young wife in childbirth, as well as the financial disaster that nearly destroys the family at the time of the Wall Street Crash, their love for each other proves stronger than the class differences that they transcend through marriage. At the film's conclusion, they are able to support their grandson's marriage to working-class Pam, expressing gratitude that in 1945 'there's none of that stupid class prejudice now' which so bedevilled their marriage. Ironically, it is Pam's parents who object to the marriage, worrying that the gap between the future baronet and their working-class daughter will be too big to sustain their marriage, arguing that 'it's what you've done and not what you are born which matters these days'. It is not just this assertion of social modernity, but the success of the Courtneys' marriage through all the vicissitudes of class bigotry that suggest that class divisions are irrelevant in post-war Britain. Such an assertion clearly found resonance with the post-war policies of a reforming Labour government and with the audiences who had voted them to power, even if the film ultimately endorses the ability of class privilege to hang on to what it has got. The Courtneys come close to having to sell the family home, but retain it with the money that Kathie generates through her brief valedictory return to show-business.

Critics have not always been kind about Anna Neagle, regarding her performances as mannered, with their 'infrequent blink rate, the measured uninflected tones', such that the female type she plays 'is presented as outside historical and social forces' (Harper 2000: 149). Certainly, in *The Courtneys Of Curzon Street* the very real limitations of Neagle's singing and, to a lesser extent, her dancing threaten at times to undermine the credibility of Kathie's music-hall and entertainment career. However, her numbers are carefully shot, the restless camera movements, high-contrast lighting and judicious edits steering attention away from any inadequacies in performance. Unlike more generically conventional musicals though, it somehow doesn't seem to matter whether her career is successful; there is nothing here of the struggles and determination that triumph in show-business usually demands. The film benefits from Anthony Collins' rich scoring, especially in the dances that feature in the frequent social events and balls, and the way in which music is used to delineate the passage of time and the significance of the historical moment. The Wilcox talent for melodrama is much in evidence and, combined with adroit use of music, makes for a competent film that resonates with wider cultural and ideological shifts in late-1940s Britain.

The Courtneys Of Curzon Street was the biggest-grossing British film at the box-office in 1948, winning both the *Daily Mail* National Film Award and the *Picturegoer* Annual Award, a triple achievement emulated by the same ensemble cast in *Spring In Park Lane* the following year. With fewer diegetic numbers than *Courtneys*, the film is more romantic comedy than musical, though its hybridity does include some lush scoring from Robert Farnon and one original song by Harold Purcell and Manning Sherwin, 'The Moment I Saw You'. Neagle's singing and dancing limitations are cleverly masked by Wilcox's direction, such as her slow-motion romantic dance with Richard (Michael Wilding), framed and therefore motivated by his apparent day-dreaming. Choreographed by Philip and Betty Buchel, the sequence works to express the convention-defying tender romance between a socialite and her apparently social inferior. Yet in this film, class divisions are a matter of masquerade since Richard, with whom society belle Judy Howard (Neagle) falls in love, though posing as a footman in her house-hold, is actually Lord Brent, a member of the aristocratic Borechesters. Again, what characterises the use of musical numbers in the film is the way in which Wilcox integrates them into the narrative as when Richard, polishing the floor, admires Judy's legs as she sings and plays the piano. Any potential for fetishisation is rapidly countered by the dialogue between them, centring on distinctions between Tchaikovsky and Debussy, a conversation that, along with his piano-playing prowess at classical and jazz numbers, only deepens the enigma surrounding Richard.

Though the film centres its pleasures on its images of privileged if easy-going London society, moments of self-reflexivity break through, not least through the character of Basil Maitland (Peter Graves), the pompous and opinionated British film star who, encountering Richard for the first time, informs him that he looks 'not unlike Michael Wilding', telling Judy that she is looking lovely and 'beautifully lit'. Maitland's constant anecdotes about film-making and his inability to separate fantasy from reality – wandering through the house he remarks that it really is a 'lovely set' – introduce a tone of self-deprecation that is used to good comic effect throughout the film. When Maitland speaks of his feelings for her, Judy has to remind him that 'those are the lines from your last film', whilst Richard plays air-cello to match the non-diegetic sound-track. If Maitland's romantic attention is not wanted by Judy, nor is that of the ineffectual Marquis of Borechester. The enigma resolved, Judy is able to express her love for Richard, her social transgressions having been proved ill-founded. The film ends wonderfully, with the out-manoeuvred Marquis of Borechester left narratively stranded after the end titles, announcing 'we must have been forgotten, mother'.

Though both *The Courtneys Of Curzon Street* and *Spring In Park Lane* benefited from the temporary shortage of American product in British cinemas, a situation that had changed by the time *Maytime In*

Mayfair was released, their appeal to British audiences is undeniable. As an article in the *Picturegoer Annual for 1949* noted, Neagle was the leading film actress at the time; though perhaps devoid of serious content, the Wilcox/Neagle films appealed because they were 'simple tales, simply told, dealing in the main with nice people doing nice things' (Macnab 2000a: 174). This is to ignore the solid quality of the acting, not least from Michael Wilding, the sharpness and wit of Nicholas Phipp's screenplays, Wilcox's skilled direction, the carefully designed sets and the equally careful integration of the orchestral score and numbers, much of which was recognised by peers in the industry as well as by British cinemagoers, not least when huge crowds turned out to greet Neagle and Wilding when they made personal appearances (Wilcox 1967: 145).

The *Red Shoes* (1948) and the crisis for the British film musical

If the Wilcox/Neagle films were popular with British audiences and, along with *Champagne Charlie, London Town* and *Trottie True*, can be said to relate to important ideological shifts in British culture during this period, delivering pleasures which are partly rooted in the musical and performative articulation of popular cultural change and its relation to tradition, we perhaps need a different paradigm to make sense of Powell and Pressburger's *The Red Shoes* (1948). At a variety of levels, the film presented, and continues to present, a number of challenges to expectations of mainstream British cinema. Powell had directed two musical films as early as 1932, both of them very much in the tradition of British musical comedy. *His Lordship*, featuring comedian Jerry Verno, was described by *Picturegoer* as a 'queer mixture of musical comedy, burlesque and satire', and *Born Lucky*, shot on a sound stage at Wembley shared by Alexander Korda, charted 'a humble girl's rise to stage fame' (Christie 1978: 12). Powell and Pressburger were, of course, no strangers to controversy or to critical and establishment hostility. Famously, their *The Life And Death of Colonel Blimp* (1943) had attracted the attention of Prime Minister Churchill who first tried to stop the film whilst in production and then opposed its exhibition abroad (Christie 1978: 105–10). However, the distinctive qualities of Powell and Pressburger's films such as *A Matter Of Life And Death* (1946) and *Black Narcissus* made them difficult to ignore. In the vacuum of an American embargo on film exports to Britain, itself a response to a Government-imposed tax on film imports, Rank was encouraged to expand production to fill the gap and *The Red Shoes* was part of this expansion.

The critical regard that *The Red Shoes* now enjoys is in inverse proportion to its contemporary reception in British cinemas. Rank and John Davis left the first private screening of the finished film in silence:

> They thought they had lost their shirts, collective and individual. . . . Next day we got a curt, official letter . . . asking us when we would be able to deliver the film to the distribution arm, and reminding us that we were already nearly £50,000 over budget. (Powell 1986: 653–4)

Rank's general anxieties about the organisation's debts and production losses and his specific anxieties about The Archers' production, perceived as an 'art' film and therefore unlikely to make money, meant that *The Red Shoes* was denied a premiere and decent distribution in Britain, despite the fact that music composer Brian Easdale and production designer Hein Heckroth both won Oscars. Rank's timidity in distributing and exhibiting the film was symptomatic of the edgy lack of confidence which so often characterises the British film industry, a factor as important as Government tax policy and American embargos, according to a 1949 Board of Trade report (Macnab 1994: 204). Interest in the film in the American art-house circuits and its subsequent 'discovery' by critics resulted in the recognition of *The Red Shoes* as one of the most influential of British films and, eventually, a resounding commercial success for Rank.

Though much is rightly made of the film's mythic dimensions, based as it is on Hans Christian Anderson's late-nineteenth-century romantic tale, it is important to remember that the film is, amongst other things, a backstage musical concerned with the tension between love and professional career. Though films about ballet were not unknown, they were rare and films such as Carmine Gallone's *Going Gay* (1933), Anthony Kimmins' *How's Chances* (1934) and *Invitation To The Waltz* (1935) only used ballet for plot contrivance. By using ballet dancers such as Moira Shearer, Leonide Massine, Robert Helpmann and Ludmilla Tcherina, Powell and Pressburger propelled ballet performance on screen into a new dimension, paving the way for short ballet films including *The Black Swan* (1952) and *Giselle* (1952), longer films such as *The Bolshoi Ballet* (1957) and *An Evening With The Royal Ballet* (1963) and influencing Gene Kelly's *An American In Paris* (1951) and MGM-British's *Invitation To The Dance* (1956).

Unsurprisingly, interpretations of *The Red Shoes*, what Powell called his 'Freudian film-ballet', are both legion and various, ranging from Raymond Durgnat's rather dismissive view of the film as 'bland' and 'schematic' (Christie 1978: 69) to Cynthia Young's psychoanalytic reading of an aesthetically dense, discursively multi-layered text. (Young 1994: 107–19) Though the struggle between life and art, between the love of Vicky Page (Moira Shearer) for composer Julian Craster (Marius Goring) and her love of dancing, together with the central if sinister role exerted by Lermontov (Anton Walbrook), has sufficient melodramatic potential for popular appeal, the film's mythic resonance works against this, as do the complex aesthetic shifts from the realism of the 'back-stage' sequences to the dream-like 'Red Shoes' ballet sequence, suffused with an aesthetic which flows over into the narrative denoument, such that

> When [Vicky Page] flees the impossible conflict between Life and Art, sym-bolized by Julian and Lermontov in her dressing room, the sequence of shots that carry her to the final plunge have a dream-like clarity and inevitability that makes the closing tribute to her in the theatre seem like the awakening from a nightmare. (Christie 1985: 85)

This dystopian view of the conflict between love and career is some-thing that marks a central distinction between the American classical musical and its British counterpart. In contrast to the triumphant optimism that saturates the Hollywood musical, where both career and romance (invariably heterosexual) are mutually dependent and inter-twined, here the impossibility of choice leads to tragic conse-quences involving profound loss. It's difficult to imagine either Julian Craster or Lermontov celebrating the reconciliations extolled in 'That's Entertainment' from MGM's *The Band Wagon* (1953).

In 1949, any imagined future critical status for *The Red Shoes* was irrelevant. What mattered was the serious financial crisis Rank – and therefore British film production – was in. Rank's exhortations to film-makers through the *Kinematograph Weekly* to 'realise that their creative freedom must be related to the economic side' (Macnab 1994: 110) stemmed directly from the crisis experienced by his organisation in the late 1940s, an experience which had a deleterious effect on many aspects of British film production in the early 1950s. If the 1940s had produced some significant musical films and seen a creative surge in quality film scoring, things were going to get harder for musical films in the 1950s, as confidence and finance drained away and structural changes to the industry took their effect.

1 British musicals were capable of occupying headline billing in the cinema programme, especially towards the end of their exhibition run. British International Pictures' *Sleepless Nights* (1932) starring Stanley Lupino with music by Noel Gay was still drawing audiences at The Kingsway Levenshulme, a suburban Manchester cinema, nearly two years after its initial release.

KINGSWAY ::: LEVENSHULME

THURSDAY, JUNE 15th.   FOR THREE DAYS.

BOBBY HOWES

in a picture packed with laughs

"FOR THE LOVE OF MIKE"

— with —

ARTHUR RISCOE and CONSTANCE SHOTTER

Directed by Monty Banks, one of the finest directors of action comedy in the entire film world, says " The Daily Mail."

— ALSO —

A lion hunting picture quite different.

" GET THAT LION "

Adventure ! Thrills ! Suspense ! But they get it in the end !

— ALSO —

The First of the new MICKIE MOUSE CARTOONS

"MICKEY'S NIGHTMARE"

Page Eight

KINGSWAY ::: LEVENSHULME

MONDAY, JUNE 19th.   FOR THREE DAYS ONLY.

BORIS KARLOFF

LEWIS STONE   **MYRNA LOY**

KAREN MORLEY   **JEAN HERSHOLT**

DAVID TORRENCE

in an adaptation of Sax Rohmer's thriller

"THE MASK
OF
FU MANCHU"

A mad dream of power . . . a great brain warped into that of a fiend . . . in the thrill of a lifetime !

PARENTS KINDLY NOTE !

Children under 16 years of age cannot be admitted under ANY circumstances.

Page Nine

---

2 British films such as BIP's *For The Love Of Mike* (1932), directed by Monty Banks, competed for exhibition space alongside American product such as *The Mask Of Fu Manchu* (1932) starring Boris Karloff, as the 1934 programme for The Kingsway, Levenshulme shows.

Manager: LES. S. BENTLEY   'Phone: ECCles 3265
Monday to Friday - Continuous from 6-20. Saturday 6-20 and 8-40.
Matinees Monday, Wednesday, Thursday, 2-30.

THREE DAYS   Week commencing MONDAY, May 22nd.   THREE DAYS
MONDAY, TUESDAY, WEDNESDAY.

LILIAN HARVEY in 'HAPPY EVER AFTER'

3 London-born Lilian Harvey enjoyed a successful silent film career in Germany. This front cover for a 1932 programme for the Broadway cinema in Eccles, Manchester, features her in the bilingual co-production *Happy Ever After* (1932) shot in Germany's UFA studios.

4 Cicely Courtneidge and Jack Hulbert were immensely popular with British
audiences in the 1930s. The Broadway cinema programme promotes the
musical *Happy Ever After* (1932) as well as Gainsborough's hugely popular
comedy *The Ghost Train* (1931).

5 The synergies between different branches of the British entertainment in the 1930s are clear in this programme for the Pavilion Theatre, Liverpool, advertising its Radio Week, a chance for audiences to see radio broadcasting in action live on stage.

"Alfredo and his Gipsy comrades have a personality in themselves and their music such as few, if any, possess. . . . Alfredo knows what the public wants and he gives it to them delightfully."
Edinburgh, THE SCOTSMAN.

"By way of a change band-fans should make a bee-line for whatever theatre Alfredo and his Gipsy Orchestra are adorning. Spirited and infectious playing with a skill that is worthy of high praise."
—THE TATLER.segment

ALFREDO AND. HIS GIPSY BAND

BETTY WHEATLEY
The B.B.C. Soprano

LADD WEST
The Talkative Aerial Puzzle

TOMMY WALKER
Lancashire's Character Comedian

MURPHY & MACK
In "The Major's Reflection."

SUSAN & PAT
Essentially 1934

BRANDON & EMERSON
In "Negrology."

6 Alfredo and his Gypsy Band, live on stage at the Pavilion Theatre, Liverpool, appeared in two *Pathétone* musical shorts in 1932 and 1934, as well as BIP's feature musical *The Maid of the Mountains* (1932), directed by Lupino Lane.

7 Sheet music featuring songs from films was commonplace throughout the 1930s, into the 1940s and 1950s. 'Be Like The Kettle And Sing' was sung by Vera Lynn in Columbia British's musical *We'll Meet Again* (1942), directed by Phil Brandon and produced by George Formby.

8 The sheet music cover for 'I Love To Sing', the opening number sung by Vera Lynn in another Columbia British musical *Rhythm Serenade* (1943), directed by Gordon Wellesley.

9 The sheet music cover for 'I'm Only Me', sung by Arthur Askey in *Miss London Ltd* (1943), the musical directed by Val Guest and featuring Evelyn Dall and Anne Shelton alongside Askey, all three being featured on this cover. Other songs for the film are clearly also available as sheet music to be played at home.

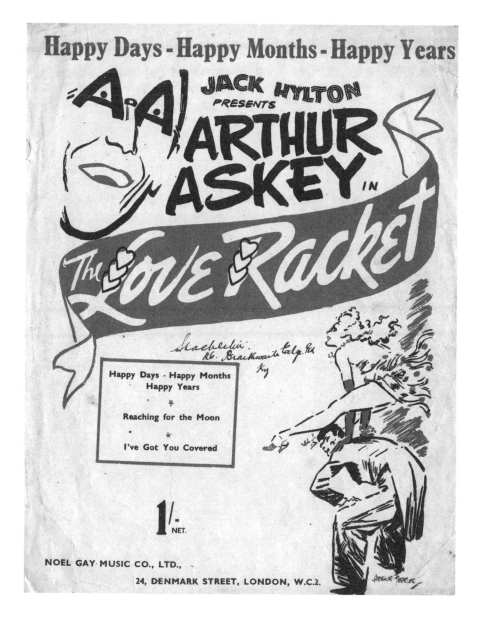

10 Like many other performers in the 1940s, Askey's career spread across radio and the live stage as well as film. This sheet music cover is for 'Happy Days – Happy Months – Happy Years', a number written by Noel Gay for the stage musical *The Love Racket*.

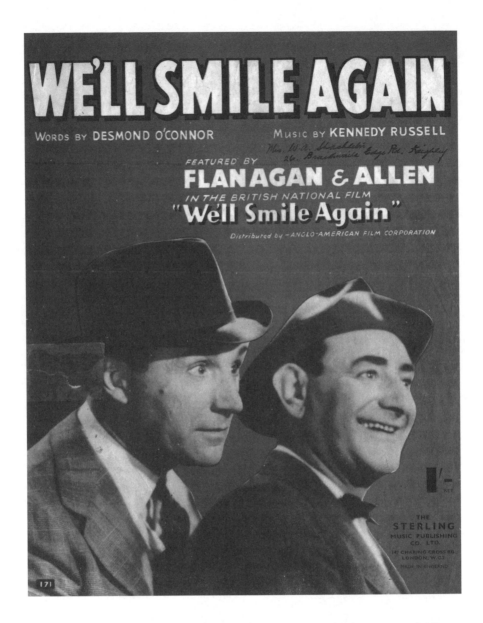

11 Equally at home on stage, on radio and on record, Flanagan and Allen made a number of musical short films and musical comedies between 1932 and 1958. This sheet-music cover features the title song from John Baxter's British National Picture *We'll Smile Again* (1943), which also featured soprano Gwen Catley and pianist Billy Mayerl. Mayerl himself featured in a number of short musical films and features between 1925 and 1951.

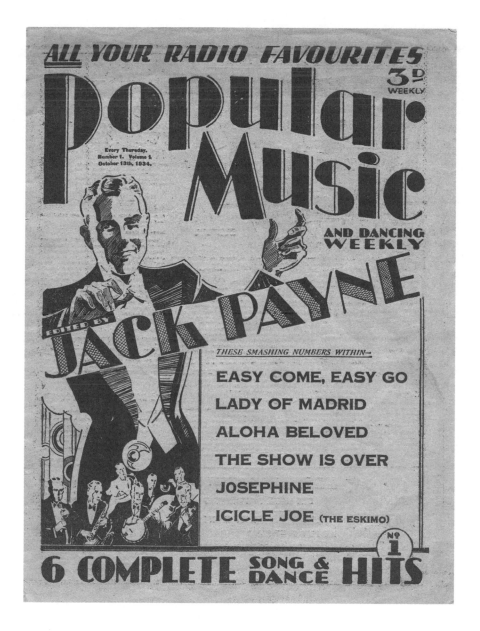

12 The popularity of dance bands and dance halls in the 1930s was reflected in the launch of the weekly magazine *Popular Music and Dancing Weekly*. Edited by band-leader Jack Payne, it featured sheet music for popular songs, articles, 'how-to' instructions for latest dance crazes such as 'The Continental' and gossip columns about British popular-music stars. This cover is from the very first issue in October 1934.

THURSDAY 1ˢᵗ MELODY DAY

OOH! THAT TIGER HARRY!

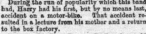

A BRIEF PEN PICTURE OF POPULAR HARRY ROY:

The "Ayes" Have "It" With Harry Roy!

When I say that Harry Roy is enthusiastic, I don't do him justice. Enthusiasm, as the Americans have it, is certainly his middle name.

He has always to be enthusiastic over something. Even as a boy he was enthusiastic. Only, at that time, it was fighting he liked. He only got tired when there were no more boys left in the school willing to fight him.

When he left school he threw up the chance of going into his father's box-making business and went out to find a job for himself. He found it all right. In fact, he got five jobs in the course of five days. I should think this is something of a record. Temporarily tired of making his own way in the world, he went back to his father and making cardboard boxes.

War was declared soon after, and with it came Harry's new craze. He decided that he had the right build for riding a motor-cycle. He managed to go through the next four years without a single serious accident, so that Harry owes a vote of thanks to his guardian angel!

In 1919, his brother, Syd, having left the Army, formed a small dance band, and also gave Harry a clarinet for his birthday. These twin events gave Harry his enthusiasm for dance music, and that enthusiasm is as strong to-day as it was fifteen years ago!

During the run of popularity which this band had, Harry had his first, but by no means last, accident on a motor-bike. That accident resulted in a lecture from his mother and a return to the box factory.

But was this Tiger Ragamuffin downhearted? Within a few weeks, in conjunction with brother Syd, he had collected together another band, and, and, with American collars, and *pseudo*-American accents, they were again making themselves known to the dance-going public. After a short time of working in the factory during the day and in a night-club at night, Harry decided that burning a candle at both ends wasn't too bad, but to burn it in the middle as well was asking for trouble. So once more we find him feeding cardboard to a machine.

But once the music fever had entered his veins, he found it impossible to work it out of his system. On went the American collar once more, and back to a night-club went our Harry.

A Nasty Spill!

After four years, any idea of going back to a factory was forgotten, and the band started playing at the Café de Paris. Then came Harry's last ride on a motor-cycle. He merely argued with a lamp-post while travelling at sixty miles an hour, and lost! That little dust-up gave him a headache for two years and crutches for three months, as well as a life-long dislike of 'bikes. From that time Harry has contented himself with a car.

To-day he is as enthusiastic over three big things: his band, his public, and cricket, of which he is no mean exponent.

One of his greatest fans is the Rani of Sarawak, and it is in her honour that he has composed a new number called "Sarawaki Blues." He and the band have recorded the number, and the Rani took the record back with her when she left England.

Harry is not temperamental, nor has he any eccentricities. He has only one idiosyncrasy. If he feels in need of a rest, he goes to a cinema and sleeps the programme round. I'm afraid I do the same thing, but not for the same reason.

And now, slim, vital and a bundle of nervous energy, Harry stands high in dance-band circles as the Panjandrum of Hot Music. He has almost made "Tiger Rag" a folk song in this country!

Yes, the future looks good for Harry Roy.

HOWARD CORDELL

13 A gossip column in *Popular Music and Dancing Weekly* featuring band-leader Harry Roy. It was through such popular journalism that cinema-goers learned to enjoy the textual in-joke that sits at the heart of Roy's 1936 musical, *Everything Is Rhythm*, in which Roy's wife in real life plays the object of his romantic attentions.

14 Popular stars of the 1930s were no less reluctant to be involved in advertising that they are today. Jessie Matthews' endorsement of Lux soap in the *Radio Times* for 7 May 1937 makes direct reference to her career in front of the camera and to songs featured in her musicals.

15 In the 1950s trade papers were eager to promote new product from the studios and were available free in cinemas. Here, the *ABC Film Review* for January 1956 promotes Herbert Wilcox's rather lame musical vehicle *King's Rhapsody*, a 'Ruritanian' affair starring Errol Flynn.

16 Powell and Pressburger's neglected musical feature *Oh . . . Rosalinda!!* (1955), featured Michael Redgrave, Anton Walbrook, Dennis Price and Mel Ferrer, though this back-cover promotion of the film in the *ABC Film Review* for January 1956 misleadingly teases with Ludmilla Tcherina, who played Rosalinda in this version of *Die Fledermaus*.

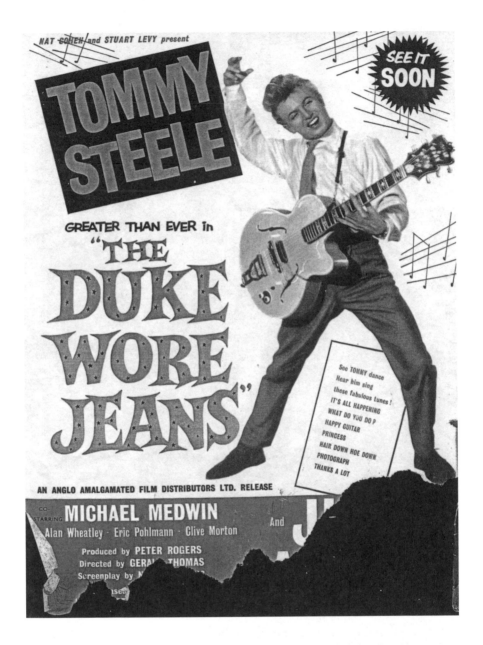

17 No mention is made of the 'Ruritanian' element of *The Duke Wore Jeans* (1958), a musical directed by Gerald Thomas, produced by Peter Rogers and based on a script by Lionel Bart and Mike Pratt, Steele's former colleagues in their band The Cavemen. Instead, the *ABC Film Review* for April 1958 promotes Steele's apparent youthful rebelliousness.

4

The 1950s: from tradition to innovation

If it is possible to make distinctions between British musical films produced during the war years in the 1940s and those produced in the latter
half of the decade, in the 1950s distinctions take on the appearance of
rupture. A decade that could start by producing musicals such as *The
Dancing Years* (1950), set in Vienna in 1910 and involving complicated
if old-fashioned romance, or *Come Dance With Me* (1950) in which
aristocratic class masquerade looms large, yet end with films such as
Serious Charge (1959), dealing with accusations of homosexuality, and
Expresso Bongo (1959) and its celebration of the rise of a teenage pop
star, is clearly a decade in which complex social and cultural dynamics
are under way. Such changes reflected some profound shifts in the perception of national identity, as the quintessential 'Britishness' epitomised
in films such as those starring Kenneth More and Jack Hawkins begins
to accommodate fresh transatlantic influences and the rise of a new
youth culture. However, what makes British cinema of the 1950s interesting is the *process* by which this accommodation occurs, such that the
masculine world of 'immaculately polished brogues, perfectly pressed
flannels and neatly tailored tweed jackets' (Macnab 1994: 215) co-exists
with leather jackets, jeans, loud music and women who are becoming
less afraid to express their sexual identity and explore their sexuality.

This process and the uncertainties that surrounded it were articulated
in wider discourses around British cinema during the 1950s, including
debates about film censorship and analyses from within the industry
about what British cinema could do, what it was good at. Attitudes to
film censorship reveal the 1950s as a period of transition, away from
the apparently unquestioned moral certitudes characteristic of the 1940s
(though, as we have seen, levels of wartime sexual promiscuity posed
challenges to hegemonic attitudes which were only spasmodically
acknowledged) to the so-called permissiveness of the 1960s and those
'New Wave' films which openly questioned a range of social attitudes
and assumptions about class and gender, issues fundamentally about

identity, power and control. Similar transitions can be seen in attitudes towards financing production, not least within the National Film Finance Corporation (NFFC), established in 1948. Under the chairmanship of Lord Reith, the NFFC initially expressed concern with the intellectual and ethical quality of productions in ways that mirrored Reith's previous tenure as Director General of the BBC. By 1955 and with Reith no longer chairman, the NFFC had adopted a more straightforward commercial stance, as the level of investment by American companies in British film production and distribution began to increase, causing renewed concern about exactly what constituted a 'British film'. By the end of the decade, in recognition of the extent of American investment in Britain's film industry, it was accepted that 'any film made in the UK or Commonwealth by an American company would therefore continue to be registered as British' (Harper and Porter 2003: 32).

Conventionally, the 1950s has been seen as perhaps the least interesting decade in British cinema:

> It is commonly characterised as the era in which the national cinema retreated into quaintly comic evocations of community or into nostalgic recollections of the war. . . . Coming after the golden period of the immediate post-war years . . . British cinema of the 1950s has commonly been stigmatised as conservative and dull. (Mackillop and Sinyard 2003: 2)

Other writers have characterised British film production of the 1950s as 'dull', 'anodyne', 'timid' and 'complacent'. Such critical attitudes are changing, not least because British cinema of the 1950s is increasingly regarded as a cinema in transition, reflecting profound cultural shifts through films that both drew upon existing social and aesthetic paradigms and engaged with newly emerging attitudes and forms. Harper and Porter have recently characterised these co-existent strains as 'residual' and 'emergent' film types, 'old and new ways of presenting the world and pleasing audiences' (Harper and Porter 2003: 1). This is clearly in evidence when we examine the British musical film of the 1950s.

The level of British film production remained significant throughout the 1950s, averaging just over 100 features each year, somewhere between 1,000 and 1,200 between 1950 and 1959. At the same time, cinema admissions in Britain fell back from their immediate post-war peak of 1.6 billion to 1.4 billion in 1950, remaining fairly stable until 1955, but then declining rapidly to 515 million in 1959. From 1955, rivalry from other newly emergent leisure and entertainment interests, particularly television and the portable record player, eroded the cinema-going habit in a decade which saw the growth of an increasingly comfortable domesticity fuelled by the rise in home ownership and consumption of labour-saving domestic technologies. The biggest erosion was amongst women, so that by the middle of the 1950s the audience demographic was becoming perceptibly male and young. This, along with the persistence of exhibition practices that met audience expectations for a 'double bill' in an overwhelming majority of British cinemas, inevitably influenced production strategies and meant that there was room for 'B' feature productions and shorts as well as attempts to produce main features (Manvell 1951: 182). Though American influence gained momentum during the decade, whether in terms of increased American investment in British film production; of Hollywood films being shown in British cinemas; of the presence of American stars, directors, and technical or creative staff working on British films; or in terms of broader cultural influence, the 1950s was a decade in which British films remained attractive to British cinema audiences. As Roy Stafford has argued, the 1950s British film industry can be characterised as a

> relatively stable period of genre production with a range of British companies releasing comedies and war films that were well-supported by audiences. (Stafford 2001: 108)

Though there is evidence to support this view about the stability of British film production in the 1950s, it fails to reflect the significant challenges to the cinema-going habit that were in play. As I suggested above, one of the most important of these was the growing popularity of television, particularly after the introduction of commercial television in 1955. What followed was a period of difficult, uneasy accommodation between cinema and television that began with clear hostility towards the new medium, expressed in films such as *Meet Mr Lucifer* (1953). Television was not the only reason for the decline in cinema audiences, of course, but the decline irrevocably changed the social significance of cinema:

> At the beginning of the [1950s], cinema could still be considered as entertainment for all, a prime example of the modern, mass media and one that situated itself within the day-to-day experience of popular culture more generally. . . . By the end of the 1950s, that centrality was no longer the case. Cinema was being thought of and presented itself as a medium that was old-fashioned, uncomfortable and associated with past pleasures. (Geraghty 2000: 20)

In a decade in which war, comedy and crime films dominated, the proportion of musical films produced declined to something less than 10 per cent; Gifford (1986) lists about 78 such films including some less than 60 minutes in length. In part, this reflected the growing success of the musicals coming out from the Hollywood studios – MGM, Warner Bros and Twentieth Century Fox in particular – which were very popular with British audiences in the first half of the 1950s. By 1955, British audience surveys revealed that the musical was by far the most popular genre, seen by 43 per cent of cinema-goers, more than double for any other American genre. As Joanne Lacey in her study of cinema-going in Liverpool in the 1950s shows, the seductive appeal of American musicals and their construction of a version of a utopian 'American Dream' impressed audiences in post-war austerity Britain in the early 1950s. As one woman recalled:

> The Americans gave the impression that if they struggled there was something at the end of it. That's the feeling I got – I got the feeling off Americans that if you did work hard, there was something at the end of it. But here you could work hard and struggle and everything, but then they never wanted you to be happy, or to dance. (Lacey 1999: 60)

Discussion of British cinema invariably locates it in its relationship with the American film industry, its films and their meanings, but this is particularly important in the case of the musical film during the 1950s. As we have seen, the generic conventions that had characterised the development of the Hollywood musical were influential in some British musicals, but the majority drew energy from hybrid influences and traditions that were deeply rooted in British popular culture. Arguably, these influences were becoming less relevant and therefore less sustainable as perceptions of national identity were increasingly influenced by American popular culture. At a period in which audiences were declining, American 'A' films were once again dominating British screens (though there was a shortage of *new* American films from 1954, and 1959 was an exceptionally good year for the British product) and British film production was becoming increasingly dependent on American finance – the pressures to imitate and conform to Hollywood-inspired formal paradigms were evident, even if the inclination was often to resist them.

Crisis and American influences:
Dance Hall (1950) and *Happy-Go-Lovely* (1951)

The result of these shifts and pressures meant that, despite the absolute decline in the number of musical films produced in the 1950s, their sheer variety reflects uncertainties not just about production strategies and the changing audience for British film, but also about changes in national identity, about what it meant to be 'British'. One strategy was to employ American talent in the attempt to emulate the Hollywood musical as in *Happy-Go-Lovely* (1951) and *Let's Be Happy* (1957), both starring Vera-Ellen. Another was to harness proven and popular British comedic talent such as Norman Wisdom in hybrid vehicles that included at least some songs, such as *Trouble In Store* (1953) and *Follow A Star* (1959). Others looked to successful icons of established British culture for inspiration, such as in *The Beggar's Opera* (1953), *The Story of Gilbert and Sullivan* (1953) and *The Good Companions* (1957). Herbert Wilcox persevered with Anna Neagle in *Lilacs In The Spring* (1954), in which she plays a wounded wartime ENSA star who dreams of living as characters from the past, an opportunity to reuse roles from her earlier films, the woeful Ruritanian *King's Rhapsody* (1955), Neagle playing alongside Errol Flynn, as well as *The Lady Is A Square* (1959) which saw Neagle appearing with in-vogue British singer Frankie Vaughn and the modish Anthony Newley. Powell and Pressburger continued in their idiosyncratic but compelling vein with *The Tales Of Hoffman* (1951) and *Oh . . . Rosalinda!!* (1955). There were some continuing attempts to engage with the traditions of show-business as in the Donald Peers vehicle *Sing Along With Me* (1952), in which a composer outwits a crooked music publisher, and *Charley Moon* (1956), in which Max Bygraves finds that stage stardom is shallow and returns to his roots in circus. In between, a number of shorts featuring increasingly dated British bands and singers were served up as programme fillers. Finally, towards the end of the decade, the impact of rock'n'roll found its way into musicals which energetically and often engagingly exploited teenage interest in popular music in television spin-offs such as *6.5 Special* (1958), Tommy Steele's *The Duke Wore Jeans* (1958), which offers a new twist on the Ruritanian tradition, and the two films featuring Cliff Richard referred to earlier. Along the way, there were some memorable scores for films which made no pretence of being in any sense musicals, such as the harmonica-driven theme tune for *Genevieve* (1953) and the jazz-inspired soundtracks of early 'New Wave' films such as *Saturday Night and Sunday Morning* (1960). In the end, it is the variety and, it has to be said, in some cases the infirmities of British musical films of the 1950s that make them so interesting.

British musical film production in the 1950s was not helped by the discourse of self-deprecation that, consistently present in British film culture, was very much in evidence in the 1950s. Faced with the stream of musicals coming out from Hollywood, confidence within the industry in the ability to produce worthwhile vehicles appeared to reach an unprecedentedly low level. At the beginning of the 1950s, the British trade paper *ABC Film Review* lamented what it saw as the continuing decline of the British musical, expressing the view that

> Apart from one or two honourable exceptions like *The Dancing Years* and *Happy-Go-Lovely*, Britain has left practically a clear field to Hollywood in the production of movie musicals. We just never seem to make them these days; yet there was a time when British musical films rivalled the best that America could send us. (Leader 1951: 10)

In a similar vein, Earl St John, head of production at Rank in the mid-1950s, commented that the musical was a genre with which British film-makers struggled, despite the continuing popularity of the Hollywood musical with British audiences at this period; in his view, 'we haven't the talent for choreography, the high-powered dancers or the knack with a popular tune' (Chibnall 2000: 128). Such views reflect the growing hegemonic influence of Hollywood's generic formulae, uncertainties about British production and its ability to compete, as well as less tangible cultural shifts that were redefining perceptions of national identity.

Produced in the same year as *The Dancing Years*, a vehicle based on Ivor Novello's 1939 but already-dated stage musical, which neither Technicolor nor the much-vaunted dancing from Patricia Dainton could really enliven, Ealing's *Dance Hall* (1950), directed by Charles Crichton, foretells many of the changes which British social and cultural life underwent during the decade, not least in its ambivalent but mainly suspicious attitude towards mass culture and its pleasures. Whilst ignoring the film's music, Christine Geraghty writes convincingly about *Dance Hall* as essentially a woman's film, but the film also reveals tensions other than those around sexual politics that were to become evident during the 1950s (Geraghty 2000: 82–4). The story of four young women factory workers who find their pleasures and identities centred on the Palais dance hall, the film evokes a sense of communal public space which was an inherent part of the 1930s and 1940s, but which was to give way to smaller more intimate sub-cultural spaces such as the jazz club, milk bar and coffee bar by the end of the 1950s. The tension between their lives spent working in the factory and the pleasures associated with dancing and dating foretells the shift from a production-based economy to one based increasingly on consumption. The choice that Eve (Natasha Parry) has to make between her marriage to reliable, British but choreographically challenged Phil (Donald Houston) and the flash, well-dressed American Alec (Bonar Colleano), who is involved in the black market, reflects growing tensions between what was increasingly seen as staid Britishness and the lure of a brasher and superficially more attractive American culture even if, as here, British qualities are seen as more reliable, both economically and morally. All this takes place against a musical backcloth supplied by Geraldo and his Orchestra, a fixture in British films since the late 1930s, who play numbers associated with the 1940s including 'There Is A Tavern In The Town', 'Goodnight Sweetheart' and 'Knees Up Mother Brown', and Ted Heath and his Music who play 'Saturday Nite Drag', 'Palais Jive' and 'Post Horn Boogie', numbers more resonant of a 1950s modernity heavily inscribed with American popular culture.

If Alec represents a rather malign American influence in *Dance Hall*, then that influence is wholly benign in Associated-British's *Happy-Go-Lovely* (1951). If the former offered an intriguing mix of realism and melodrama of the sort that Ealing came to be associated with, then the American influence on the latter film ensured that it operates within the rather more anodyne generic envelope of the Hollywood musical. That influence extended through Warner Bros' part-ownership of ABPC: American director Bruce 'Lucky' Humberstone leads Vera-Ellen and Cesar Romero, and a backstage narrative centred on the efforts of director John Frost (Romero) to stage his musical 'Frolics To You' against an array of financial stringencies. The British contribution is, however, considerable, from David Niven's performance as B.G. Bruno the greetings cards millionaire, a sparkling screenplay from Val Guest, musical direction from Louis Levy, and some very good dancing from British male dancers such as Jack Billings, David Lober, Jonathan Lucas, and Douglas Scott and his Debonair Boys.

Happy-Go-Lovely opens by first setting up and then deflating British – in this case, specifically Scottish – cultural pretensions. A sweeping panoramic camera shows off the tourist glories of Edinburgh as the stentorian voice-over extols the wonders of 'the historical city of commerce and tradition' and the Edinburgh Festival, 'dedicated to the highest and purest ideals in art', before cutting to a gaudy poster promoting the stage show 'Frolics To You', an innuendo probably only available to British audiences. The voice-over slips into a more informal register, announcing that occasionally 'something like this slips in' as we segue into the up-tempo number 'MacIntosh's Wedding'. A curious, energetic hybrid with mock-Scottish costume, musical sampling of traditional Scottish refrains mixed with swinging brass and saxophone, this turns out to be a number in rehearsal in front of the show's parsimonious creditors. Not for the first time, Frost successfully begs the creditors for more time, though the star of the show walks out. Amidst this classic 'the show must go on even if the artists are not being paid' scenario, Janet Jones (Vera-Ellen) gets the starring role, Frost mistakenly believing that she is romantically attached to millionaire Bruno (David Niven), 'the richest man in Scotland', who might be persuaded to finance the show.

The central trope of mistaken identity is extended and compounded as Janet falls in love with Bruno, believing him to be local journalist Paul Tracey (Gordon Jackson). Val Guest's intelligent script both accommodates and sustains this central improbability, squeezing some engagingly comic moments from the situation as deception piles upon deception. Bruno's puritanical insistence on 'certain standards of decorum' at his ultra-bureaucratic suite of offices evaporates as his contact with Janet deepens; concerned about her uninformed assumption that he is a 'paunchy' stuffshirt, he undergoes a softening transformation in his identity. As Bruno pretending to be Paul Tracey pretending to be Bruno, he displays a growing sense of humour and humanity; having to berate Bates, his chauffeur, he ends up doubling his salary. Bruno takes to the pleasures of masquerade, rejoicing in his ironic assumption of the trappings of being rich which he normally decries, evident in his preference for a plain omelette over caviar during the genuinely funny dinner-date scene. The deceptions and misunderstanding unravel, as Bruno declares that he wants to 'dance and sing and climb trees', his transformation complete apart from some temporary indignities when his cheque for ten thousand pounds to finance the show is briefly thought to be fraudulent. The farce that this involves is competently handled and leads to the police inspector's authoritative confirmation of Bruno's real identity. A neat touch in Guest's script occurs when Frost finally listens to a chorus girl who has been trying to speak to him throughout the film; she tells him that her father wishes to invest his 'excess profits' in the show.

Though many of the film's pleasures are delivered by the romantic comedy provided by Guest's witty sustained script and by the acting of Vera-Ellen and Niven, the numbers in the film make their considerable contribution. 'MacIntosh's Wedding' involves, as we have seen, a heady blend of American and British musical and cultural styles, celebrating their coming together. Vera-Ellen's rehearsal number 'One, Two, Three' combines the garishly costumed look of Renaissance Italy with a lilting and occasionally syncopated waltz tune, though the dancing never quite reaches the heights of the show-within-the-film number 'Piccadilly Circus Ballet'. Though this number is contained within the diegetic space of the theatre stage, it contains some spectacular dancing. The sequence starts with a busy, bustling brass orchestration for the street scene, on to which a naïve Vera-Ellen enters alone, encountering some hostility from a purple clad street-walker before dancing with two city gents dressed as Bruno was when we first encounter him, bowler hats and umbrellas, in a light, polite tap dance with plucked and shimmering violin accompaniment. A pronounced brass discord leads to a frenzied urban orchestration with boogie-woogie, jive and be-bop intonations, as she dances with a 'sharp-suited', gum-chewing, sexually threatening (all coded as 'American') young man, his sexual advances stopped only by the musically and choreographically dramatic intervention by another young man, who with swirling strings, dances in romantic harmony with her. It is hard not to see this casually attired attractive young man as a vibrant but friendly transatlantic compromise between the over-formality of the two British gents and the aggressive sexuality of the spiv, and the number as a celebration of the Anglo-American alliance which surrounds the film and its production. Vera-Ellen's final solo number is the on-stage 'Would You, Could You', a sweet, romantic ballad she directs at Bruno sitting in his theatre box before launching into her joyful solo dance against a brilliant backcloth of the rising sun.

For audiences still experiencing the effects of post-war austerity *Happy-Go-Lovely*, shot effectively in Technicolor, offered seductive images of plenty, epitomised by the flowers that Bruno fills his office with and those he gives to Janet Jones; Mae (Diane Hart) exclaims that she's 'never seen so many flowers. What did you do, snitch [steal] them?' Other images, such as Bruno's Bentley, the 'chic' dresses and furs that Madame Amanda showers upon Janet, merge with the general sense of affluence that things American convey, offering a sharp contrast with the hesitant, parsimonious attitudes of the show's Scottish suppliers, led by Jonskill (John Laurie). Of course, Bruno's status as a multi-millionaire, the success of the business-owning father of the chorus-girl and his 'excess profits', together with the implied success of 'Frolics To You', all point towards a social and economic utopianism which audiences would have found pleasing.

Happy-Go-Lovely was successful, though Vera-Ellen did not make another film for Associated-British until *Let's Be Happy* (1957), another musical very much within the Hollywood generic mould. Set partly again in Edinburgh, the theme of mistaken identity is reprised, as impoverished Lord James McNairn (Robert Flemyng) chases Jeannie McLean (Vera-Ellen), an American girl he assumes is wealthy. Handled less surely by director Henry Levin, the film includes an energetic central dance sequence based on the theme of cards, Vera-Ellen variously as the four Queens, each with their own distinct music and choreography, such as the Queen of Spades' seductive dance to a 5/4 blues tune, the Queen of Hearts dancing in waltz time. Less successful than *Happy-Go-Lovely*, the film perhaps failed to connect with Britons who were being told by Prime Minister Harold Macmillan that they 'had never had it so good', with those shifts in audience composition and taste which we detailed earlier.

If the lavish budget and high production values for *Happy-Go-Lovely* represent one end of the British musical film production spectrum in the 1950s, then the short films that experienced something of a revival during the decade represent the other. These programme fillers kept artists and technicians in employment and provided an echo of the 'uplifters and entertainers' provision which had characterised 1940s production and which was sustained in the early and mid-1950s before the impact of rock'n'roll on British cinema in the final years of the decade. 'Uplifting' entertainment was provided by shorts such as *The Glasgow Orpheus Choir* (1951), *The Black Swan* (1952), *Giselle* (1952) and *The Nutcracker* (1953), the latter of these produced by John Grierson and directed by Cyril Frankel. Other shorts featured specific artists and bands, such as *Billy Mayerl Entertains* (1951), Stéphane Grappelli in *Mirth and Melody* (1951) directed by Horace Shepherd, *Out Of The Bandbox* (1953) a 30-minute revue featuring Billy Ternant and his Orchestra, Horace Shepherd's series of shorts featuring *Winston Lee and his Orchestra* (1954), and the *Eric Winstone Band Show* (1955), part-financed by the NFFC and shot in CinemaScope. Reliant as they were on exhibition practices that were beginning to be questioned if not actually changed, such productions were an endangered species. Butchers, the distributors of Harold Baim's *Variety Half Hour* (1954) that featured amongst others a certain Windy Blow, a balloon act, must surely have seen which way the British cinema industry wind was blowing.

Powell and Pressburger: *The Tales of Hoffmann* (1951) and *Oh . . . Rosalinda!!* (1955)

Somewhere along this spectrum were Powell and Pressburger's *The Tales Of Hoffmann* (1951) and *Oh . . . Rosalinda!!* (1955). With a running time of 127 minutes, *The Tales Of Hoffmann* presented its own challenges to conventional exhibition patterns, as well as a number of other formal, aesthetic and critical challenges. A leader column in *Picturegoer* asked

> What are we picturegoers going to think about 'The Tales of Hoffmann' by the time that sprawling, colourful mixture of ballet and opera has got well into its local cinema tour . . . there is much that is good in this rather

unusual and rather top-heavy picture . . . [but] will picturegoers turn from
the noise and glamour and sigh for a quiet little film that doesn't try to be
all things to all people? . . . Is 'Hoffmann' entertainment as millions today
understand that word? (*Picturegoer*, 24 November 1951, p. 5)

Based on Offenbach's opera, the film wraps a framing prologue and epilogue around three tales in which the fictional poet Hoffmann (Robert
Rounseville) tells of his disappointments in love, disappointments that
echo his doomed love for the ballerina Stella (Moira Shearer) in the
prologue and epilogue. In each of the tales, Hoffmann's ardour for
the automaton doll Olympia (Shearer), the Venetian courtesan Guiletta
(Ludmilla Tchérina) and the consumptive singer Antonia (Ann Ayars),
is thwarted by magical, sinister figures (all danced by Robert
Helpmann). With the same dancers they had used for *The Red Shoes*
but with the addition of Frederick Ashton as choreographer, the film
relates its narrative in a dialogue-free mixture of opera and ballet, most
of the characters played by two people, a singer and a dancer. Sir
Thomas Beecham took responsibility for the music and the casting of
the singers; Hein Heckroth was once again the designer.

The film was shot quickly, on a tight budget and entirely on a silent
stage at Shepperton, dispensing with normal props and relying instead
on Heckroth's gossamer drapes and paintings within the 'huge cyclo-
rama' that formed the central acting and dancing area. The end result,
characterised as 'the absolute antithesis of realism' (Christie 1985: 86),
was a text rich with hermeneutic possibilities. Despite criticisms that
the film 'is seriously flawed, over-ambitious and uneven', with a plot
that is 'most confusing and at times quite impenetrable', at least
one critic saw *The Tales Of Hoffmann* as an important critique of the
'ideological insidiousness of [mainstream cinema's] commercial aes-
theticism' (Elsaesser 1978: 62). Other commentaries have seen the film
as a critique of the cinematic apparatus and its reception, noting the
obsession with ocularity, with illusion and reality. Still others find evidence not only that the film represents 'the power of art to transcend
loss and death', but also that it represents a more personal tribute by
Powell to his former lover Pamela Brown, claiming that he united 'a
deep and intolerable personal meaning with the healing power of aesthetic form' to compose and endow it with 'universality'(Greenfield
1995: 31).

Clearly not a film with immediate mass appeal, *The Tales Of
Hoffmann* actually did quite good business in British cinemas. Though
attempts to radically shorten the film by removing the third tale failed,
the film was cut slightly before release. It enjoyed a long run in London,
did better in provincial cities than some expected, but met with greater

incomprehension at smaller venues. Raymond Leader, writing in the *ABC Film Review* for March 1955, accepted that, despite 'some fine singing and some exquisite ballet dancing [the film] wasn't every film-goer's cup of tea' (Leader 1955: 10).

Mindful that the films of Powell and Pressburger 'have always figured among the handful of British films that have achieved long runs in America, France and other countries', *Oh . . . Rosalinda!!* (1955) was said to have 'all the polish, wit and spectacle of their other successes' (Jenkins 1955: 16). However, *Oh . . . Rosalinda!!* was regarded by Powell as 'the one failure in this interesting triptych', the others being *The Red Shoes* and *The Tales Of Hoffmann* (Powell 1993: 272). A modern version of the Johann Strauss operetta *Die Fledermaus*, the film transposes the scene to a contemporary Vienna still overseen by the four post-war occupying powers. Though the plot revolves around the sexual peccadillos of individual characters, the film has a streak of underlying political commentary, most evident towards the climax of the film when Dr Falke (Anton Walbrook), who orchestrates his whimsical revenge for the practical joke played on him by French Colonel Eisenstein (Michael Redgrave), pleads with the British, French, Russian and American occupying powers to 'go home. . . . Come back, as our guests. But please, go home.' Given the privileged space granted to Anton Walbrook as he delivers this speech, together with the fact that Powell quotes it in full in the second volume of his autobiography, this was a sentiment felt strongly by Powell and (perhaps more strongly) by Pressburger. Yet, the speech sits strangely at odds with the rest of the film, which has all the depth of bedroom farce, the wafer-thin plot revolving around Falke's revenge on Eisenstein for placing him in a drunken state on the Russian agricultural statue. Though the film opens with a biting parody of the dullest of Soviet newsreels, complete with voice-over replete with the hurt caused to the proletariat by the sleeping figure of the Bat, and takes a rather hostile stance towards General Orlofsky (Anthony Quayle) and most things Russian, this tone is not maintained, but lapses into the whirling waltz rhythms of more conventional operetta.

Given that Powell believed that, in *The Red Shoes*, he had tried and, in *The Tales Of Hoffmann*, had succeeded in producing his vision of the 'composed film', it is hard to explain *Oh . . . Rosalinda!!*'s relative failure simply as 'another isolated prototype for a future British cinema' (Christie 1985: 90). The music works, of course, though the new lyrics by Dennis Arundell have a tendency towards the banal, as when Alfred encourages his former lover Rosalinda to 'drink my darling, drink away / drink till eyes are bright as day' or again, 'why not drop that haughty air / that façade I know it all / have a drink let down your hair / no-one's in the hall'. Michael Redgrave, Anthony Quinn and Anneliese Rothenberger (playing Rosalinda's maid Adele) all sing their own parts, but Rosalinda (Ludmilla Tchérina), Alfred (Mel Ferrer), Major Frank (Denis Price) and Falke are effectively dubbed by professional singers. However, the film suffers from uncertainty of tone, being neither ironic parody nor convincing modernity based on well-known music and plot. The limitations of the lyrics and the choreography by Alfred Rodrigues are matched by the limitations imposed on Heckroth's designs. Whereas his flimsy gossamers in *Hoffmann* made no pretence at realism, here the overtly painted, stage-bound settings only serve to confuse and do nothing to match the enterprise of updating Strauss's original that the notion of the occupying powers suggests. In this confused vehicle, the performances of such as Walbrook and Redgrave seem equally confused.

There are moments where the film succeeds, not least the comedy around the part of Orlofsky, as when he asks his aide Lermontov to give the Russian equivalent of various English words, suggesting that there is no Russian word for 'reason'. Equally, the performance from Tchérina sparkles; she carries the scene at the masked ball well, despite its intrinsic silliness, and outplays Redgrave when his attempted infidelities are exposed. Major Frank's drunken return to the jail-house gives rise to some amusing visual and sonic innovations as he sees and hears 'double'. In the same way, the scene in the jail-house between Ferrer (who is wrongly locked in) and Redgrave (who should be locked in, but isn't), works because of the split set device, used earlier at the Hotel Quadrille. Despite Harper and Porter's assertions that British film-makers 'experienced acute difficulties in the 1950s when coming to terms with American technical innovations such as Eastmancolor, Cinemascope and VistaVision' (Harper and Porter 2003: 2), *Oh . . . Rosalinda!!* makes very good use of CinemaScope, from the opening arc followed by The Archers' arrow in the opening titles to the dancing at the masked ball. A contemporary review in *Films and Filming* for January 1956 accepted that the film had 'none of the vitality of the Hollywood musical', but asserted that it possessed a much-needed gaiety, 'so rare in present-day cinema', concluding that '*Oh . . . Rosalinda!!* proves that Britain can make good musical films.'

Despite attempts to sell the film on the 'saucy goings-on' of the central character Rosalinda, including stories in fan magazines that concentrated on the 'behind-the-scenes' gossip about shooting Tchérina's bath scene, the film failed to appeal to British cinema audiences and failed to achieve an American distribution deal.

Clutching at middlebrow straws: *The Story of Gilbert and Sullivan* (1953) and *The Beggar's Opera* (1953)

Whatever the optimism of *Films and Filming*, the failure of *Oh . . . Rosalinda!!* at the British box-office compounded concerns about the ability to compete with musicals from Hollywood, concerns which began with the disappointing box-office takings for *The Story of Gilbert and Sullivan* and the failure of *The Beggar's Opera* (both 1953). Despite the pedigrees behind the films, both epitomised the uncertainties that characterised much British film production in the 1950s, itself a reflection of growing uncertainties about national identity and what could be regarded as quintessentially British culture. In looking back at an accepted Victorian success story and an innovative, popular eighteenth-century opera which drew upon a plethora of British folk tunes, the two films attempted to anchor national identity in past glories, whatever the present uncertainties. Though neither film wallows in nostalgia, what makes them more interesting is their implication that these past cultural glories ought still to have some direct relevance to the cultural landscape of the 1950s, though even this assertion is rendered problematic by the treatment and tone of both films. Whatever the merits of the assertion, they seem not to have been shared by British cinema audiences of the mid-1950s, with *The Story of Gilbert and Sullivan* grossing a mere £98,139, only marginally more than *Oh . . . Rosalinda!!* (Harper and Porter 2003: 318).

In fact, whilst the appeal of Johann Strauss might have been considered limited, the music of Gilbert and Sullivan and its productions by the D'Oyly Carte company occupied a considerable importance within middlebrow British culture, not just through D'Oyly Carte's own productions and numerous recordings, but also through the multitude of amateur groups dedicated to staging Gilbert and Sullivan operas. Frank Launder and Sidney Gilliat had been involved in the British film industry since the late 1920s, had worked in one capacity or another on musicals such as *My Heart Is Calling* (1934) and *O-Kay For Sound* (1937), and had been particularly successful in their various ways during the 1940s through their own independent production companies with films such as *Millions Like Us* (1943) and *Waterloo Road* (1944), which clearly captured the contemporary spirit. In the 1950s, *The Happiest Days Of Your Life* (1950) and *The Belles Of St Trinians* (1954) were further evidence of their capacity to make films relevant to audiences' emotional needs. If the former resembled something of the whimsical comedy associated with Ealing productions such as *Passport To Pimlico* (1949) which were proving so popular with British audiences, and the latter looked forward to a rather more scatological treatment of British institutional life which surfaced in the later 1950s and 1960s, then it is much more difficult to place *The Story of Gilbert and Sullivan* in a similar contextual frame. True, an earlier Technicolor production of *The Mikado* (1939) had gained an Oscar for best colour photography, but with the exception of a later version of *The Mikado* (1967) and Mike Leigh's Academy-Award-winning *Topsy-Turvy* (1999), Gilbert and Sullivan have not proved popular material for British film production.

Some of the doubts expressed by Launder at the scripting stage were carried over into the actual production of *The Story of Gilbert and Sullivan*. Directed by Sidney Gilliat for British Lion and shot in Technicolor, the film was based on a script by Leslie Bailie, whose primary allegiance was to historical accuracy rather than drama. The end result of this initial treatment 'was an absolutely factual, chronologically accurate story treatment that would have gladdened the hearts of musical historians, but which would have been of minor interest to the public at large' (Brown 1977: 131). Gilliat managed to inject more drama into the script, not least the quarrels between Gilbert (Robert Morley) and Sullivan (Maurice Evans), and then direct some highly effective scenes such as when Gilbert (Robert Morley) conceives *The Mikado*, a model of cinematic purism when compared with the scene in *The Great Mr Handel* where Handel struggles with the conception of *The Messiah*. Though the film necessarily and dutifully contains scenes from a wide range of Gilbert and Sullivan operas, including *The Mikado, Iolanthe, H.M.S. Pinafore, Ruddigore, The Gondoliers* and *Trial By Jury*, these are handled in ways which comment upon and elucidate the dialogue scenes, showing real sensitivity to the often complex relationship which exists between narrative and performed numbers. At the same time Gilliat manages, through an effective montage sequence, to convey the implication that Gilbert and Sullivan's work appeals across all classes, from the privileged upper classes to the working classes in the public houses by way of the whistling middle classes indulging in the new-found leisure activity of cycling. Some credence is given to Sullivan's aspirations as a serious composer, but the film comes down on the side of endorsing his popular output as the thing that matters, though in so doing the text exhibits something of that self-deprecating tone which so often attaches to British films. Though Gilbert and Sullivan were both knighted and their work acknowledged as something of a national institution, it is hard to resist the sense that Gilliat imputes a certain irony to their triumph, such that the climax of the film 'signals an interesting sceptical edge to its own celebrations' (Babington 2002: 31).

Though hardly a backstage musical in the conventional sense, considerable attention is paid to the entrepreneurial role played by Richard D'Oyly Carte (Peter Finch) in getting composer and lyricist together and supporting their work through the company's productions. Though Bruce Babington's temptation to read this as an acknowledgement by Launder and Gilliat of the importance of the Rank Organisation to their own and British film production generally seems tentative (Babington 2002: 32), the scenes in which Gilbert and Sullivan's success in the United States is constrained by American pirated productions of their work does intimate the considerable, long-standing, frustration felt by British film producers in securing American distribution deals in the face of discrete protectionist policies. Though it proved rather unappealing to British audiences, *The Story of Gilbert and Sullivan* remains a film of considerable merit, with some solid singing of familiar numbers, competent use of Technicolor doing more than justice to the costume designs by Elizabeth Haffenden and Hein Heckroth, and Gilliat's firm direction. Its influence on Mike Leigh's *Topsy-Turvy* (1999) is evident testimony to the regard with which the film has come to be held.

No such retrospective regard has been applied to Herbert Wilcox's *The Beggar's Opera*, produced that same year and directed by Peter Brook, his first film assignment following a meteoric rise in reputation as a bold and innovative theatre director. Based on John Gay's innovative, groundbreaking 1728 'ballad opera', the film starred Laurence Olivier, whose earlier screen appearances in *Henry V* (1945) and *Hamlet* (1948) had achieved enormous critical success, including Academy-Award recognition. Featuring a host of rising and established film and stage actors including Stanley Holloway, Dorothy Tutin and Hugh Griffiths, the film promised a great deal. With a screenplay by Christopher Fry and Dennis Cannan, a musical score by Sir Arthur Bliss under the musical direction of Muir Mathieson, 'the cream of the technical cinema world' and a budget of £500,000 to shoot in Technicolor, Wilcox and those around him believed that the film was bound to become 'the outstanding British musical film of all time' (Wilcox 1967: 163).

They were to be disappointed. Despite a premiere at the Royal Festival Hall and a pre-premiere private showing to the British and other European royal families, the film did miserable business when it opened on the ABC circuit. Wilcox, in his rather unreliable memoirs, acknowledged the problems which bedevilled the production, and recalled that the film was taken off after the first night of the circuit booking over here in England, and compensation was paid by the circuit not to show it. As one manager said, 'They didn't even come in on Monday to tell their friends not to come in on Tuesday'. (Wilcox 1967: 167)

Wilcox does rather shake off the catastrophic reception of the film in Britain by crowing about his US distribution deal with Jack Warner whom, he claims, paid $700,000 for the western hemisphere rights despite not having seen the film. He omits to mention that the film plunged British Lion even further into financial crisis and that the NFFC repaid a £100,000 loan to the Bank of America, who had invested in the film, in an attempt to maintain their financial goodwill for future British productions.

Wilcox retrospectively placed much of the blame for the failure of *The Beggar's Opera* on the overt theatricality of Peter Brook's direction, his inexperience and arrogant personality. In truth, the film's problems go deeper than that. It perhaps did not help that Olivier decided to sing his own vocals. This in itself was not too great a problem, since he gives a reasonable singing performance, not least in duets such as 'Over The Hills And Far Away', where his voice is carried by the quality of the dubbed singing voices used for Polly Peachum (Dorothy Tutin) and all the other parts except those played by Stanley Holloway and Olivier himself. In fact, this scene where Macheath meets up with his recently married wife Polly in the stable hay-loft is directed with a firm efficiency and is deeply touching; before we are fully aware of his misogynistic philandering habits, his declaration of love for Polly and her reciprocal allegiance are convincing, made all the more so by the sweet lilting melody of a tune which pre-dates Gay's opera (being first published in Thomas D'Urfey's 1706 *Pills To Purge Melancholy*) and was popular in Colonial and Revolutionary America.

Gay's original stage 'ballad opera' used a total of 69 songs, 41 of them based on popular broadside ballads, most of them pre-dating the opera and many of them remaining popular within British musical culture over the decades; the tune to 'Lilli Burlero' for example first surfaced around 1640 in Ulster, and was the BBC's signature theme during the Second World War. Though having fewer songs than Gay's original, the film makes good use of many of these popular lilting ballads, either to enable characters to express their feelings as when Polly relates her romantic love for Macheath, or when elderly Mrs Trapes reminisces her youthful follies in 'Days Of My Youth', or the raucous choral songs in the tavern where Macheath meets up with his women lovers, all of them prostitutes or thieves. Whilst some of the songs are relatively inconsequential, as when Holloway sings the broadside ballad 'Joan Of

Paddington Green', others attain real poignancy as when Polly and Lucy duet to a recaptured Macheath and the trio sing their farewells as Macheath is about to be hanged. Brook consistently managed to relate the songs to the narrative as in the tavern scene where, having announced to the pot-boy Jack (an early screen appearance for Kenneth Williams) that women will be his downfall, he is unable to resist their charms as he spies on them, finally bursting open a doorway as he sings 'Let's Be Gay'. Macheath cavorts with the tavern whores as they dance and sing 'Love Is Our Duty', a tribute to the pleasures of sex and drink, but the song culminates in his betrayal and arrest.

If the quality of Bliss's score, Mathieson's musical direction and the vocal delivery of the songs deserved better than the oblivion into which the film was plunged, then so did Brook's direction. Though there are moments when the film threatens to lose coherence, Brook shows a number of deft touches, as when a horse chews away at some hay to reveal the diminutive Filtch spying on Polly and Macheath. Brook uses a number of point-of-view shots such as the blindfold at Macheath's hanging and operates a neatly mobile, choreographic camera in scenes such as the initial confrontation between Polly, Lucy and Macheath in the prison. At times, the lighting does excellent justice to the colour of the costumes, the scene with the tavern whores resonant of eighteenth-century genre paintings. Films of far poorer cinematic quality have proved much more popular with audiences. *The Beggar's Opera* deserves some critical reappraisal and a more detailed consideration of the reasons for its commercial failure than can be given here.

In part, the film was a victim of the perennial problem of British film production; designed as an international film, it was produced at a time of severe financial retrenchment at British Lion that was swinging production policy back towards domestic consumption and adding to distribution difficulties. The problem with *The Beggar's Opera* in part resides in its form, although, as we shall see later when we look at Ken Russell's rock opera *Tommy* (1975), there is nothing inevitably unappealing about popular opera on screen. However, this musical is radically different from the generic paradigm established by the Hollywood musical and clearly enjoyed by British audiences. It was also the case that the eighteenth-century imaginary was not – during this period of increasing security, affluence and social complacency (at least on the surface) – one that inspired the British public. Certainly, the implication of unbridled sexual promiscuity would seem to sit uneasily with the growing domesticity that characterised much of 1950s sexual politics, with its emphasis on the role of the housewife and family, on what were to be regarded as 'correct gender identifications' (Geraghty 2000: 187).

Moreover, the gap between the poor and deprived, rotting away their lives in Newgate, and the rich, debauched London aristocracy gambling away huge fortunes and buying sexual pleasure seems very much out of tune with a decade that was characterised by the 'rise of meritocracy'. In aspirational 1950s Britain, criticism of professions such as lawyers was as unwelcome as, in Coronation year, sniping at the titled great and good.

Unable to reassert the radicalism of John Gay's original opera, the film nonetheless deals with issues deeply uncongenial to 1950s Britain, not least the hypocrisy which sits at the centre of British institutions such as the law. Macheath is betrayed by Peachum who has previously been quite happy to act as a fence for the highwayman; 'the dignity of the law' demands, as Lockitt (Stanley Holloway) puts it, that he and Peachum split the reward, before proceeding to forge an arrest warrant. About to be hanged, Macheath makes some swingeing social criticism of social hypocrisies. The 'real' Macheath, imprisoned in Newgate prison and imagining the beggar's poetic fancies which have led him to the gallows, declares in the framing epilogue that he has had enough of the play, that it is too much to expect him to be hanged 'on the same day in game and in earnest', telling the composer beggar (Hugh Griffith) that 'this is no opera for a man of sensibility; you should have written it wiser'. His pleas for a reprieve are taken up by the Newgate inmates and Macheath effects an escape, singing that he has been freed by 'an opera made by a beggar'. In 1953, against a background of growing public antipathy to capital punishment, Britain witnessed thirteen hangings, one of them the hugely controversial execution of Derek Bentley following a trial that was finally adjudged 'unsafe' in 1998. Though connections between cultural products and social events are never transparent, it may be that a film that raised issues around law and justice sat too uncomfortably with contemporary social debates and effectively repressed whatever potential pleasures *The Beggar's Opera* had to offer.

A Ruritanian nadir: *King's Rhapsody* (1955)

If proof were needed for the persistence of what Harper and Porter term 'residual' film types in the 1950s, we need look no further than *King's Rhapsody* (1955). If it is hard to believe that Ivor Novello's stage musical on which the film was based was a commercial success in the West End theatre, it is harder to understand what attracted Herbert Wilcox to it. Described by the drama critic of *Punch* as a 'vast insipid musical' which 'pulled out most of the stops in the organ of easy sentiment' (Staveacre 1980: 115), the play and the film draw upon the

Ruritanian operetta tradition which had gone stale in the late 1930s. The film has nothing of Wilcox's directorial sparkle that made his 1940s musicals so popular, and both Anna Neagle and Errol Flynn give laboured performances based on a creaking script. The simple plot, revolving around exiled prince Richard's (Errol Flynn) return to Laurentia to become king and then face exile once again, is given some tension by his love for his mistress Marta Karillos (Anna Neagle) and his politically expedient arranged marriage to Princess Christiane (Patrice Wymore). Some nod is made towards political modernity when King Richard forms the Forward Party to bring democracy to the kingdom, but the weight of tradition and nepotism turn the people against him. It is tempting to think that Wilcox may have seen implications of democratic America teaching some lessons to a post-war Europe, but if this is the case then the implications remain undeveloped. In any case, it may be that Flynn's performance as the frequently drunk prince and equally drunken king was not a matter of acting; certainly nothing we see on screen motivates or explains why he is in this state for much of the film.

Quite apart from the ponderous direction, the film's numbers lack any real musical, vocal and choreographic quality. Neagle's voice, never strong, is here extremely reedy when she sings the regretful 'Our Forgotten Years' as Richard obeys the summons to return to Laurentia without her or, when supported by peasant serenaders outside the window, she expresses in flashback her delight in the early days of their romance in 'Paradise'. Clearly musical performance was meant to be enhanced by American Patrice Wymore, though her opening number in the embarrassingly artificial studio mountain snow setting, 'Somewhere My Heart', is far from convincing, even though the number is used to express her emotional state and is reprised throughout appropriate moments in the film. Some genuine vocal quality is supplied by Edmund Hockridge, who appears briefly amongst the gypsy serenaders, but his contribution is both limited and modishly outdated. The film does have one number of real intrigue, as Christiane dreams her way into a fantasy ballet, racked by anxiety about her 'contract proxy' marriage, surrounded by male dancers wearing Janus-like face masks of the men who have made arrangements which decide her destiny. Again, the number 'If This Were Love' is used to express her emotional torment, though it is melodically deficient and the choreography (by Jon Gregory) fails to match standards audiences were seeing in Hollywood musicals. In the end, whatever dramatic potential the plot has fails to be realised or to be lifted by the numbers. There is some implicit tension between scenes of modernity, where Richard and Marta seem to occupy a Grace-Kelly-like existence sited in the mid-1950s, and the stuffy costumed Ruritanian world of the Laurentian court. Even the potential pleasures which CinemaScope offers are mishandled in over-long, static or slow pan shots of what are clearly meant to be breath-taking landscape and lush interiors, all too typical of the film's ponderous direction. That Wilcox fails to mention the film in his autobiography is perhaps not surprising and it is hard not to agree with Harper and Porter's view that, with this film, the industry was 'scraping the bottom of the barrel' (Harper and Porter 2003: 100).

Popular music and the revival of the British musical film

What is particularly striking about many of British musical films made during the early and mid-1950s is their neglect of contemporary popular music. When the *New Musical Express* published the first 'Hit Parade' in Britain in November 1952, American singers such as Al Martino, Frankie Laine, Mario Lanza and Guy Mitchell dominated, though some novelty numbers by British artists such as Winifred Atwell's 'Britannia Rag' and 'Coronation Rag', Max Bygraves' 'Cowpuncher's Cantata' and Ted Heath vocalist Lita Roza's '(How Much Is) That Doggie In The Window' did find a place in the charts. This situation resulted from the strong commercial links between British and American song publishers, together with licensing deals that made it easier – and more profitable – for British music publishing and record companies to distribute American songs and records rather than promote British popular music. However, there were some within the British music industry who were increasingly critical of American domination. An internal memorandum written in 1951 by Norman Newell at EMI mirrored many of the concerns that afflicted the British film industry, whilst asserting the potential of British popular music culture:

> Many publishers seem to be of the opinion that the only worthwhile British songs are the type commonly known as the 'corny' variety. Were they to use a little more imagination in their choice of British material, we could bring about a great change in the business. We have the artists, the arrangers, people with ideas, and the promise of support from the BBC. A little more support from publishers and less dollars would leave the country and British artists and material would undoubtedly be on top. (Martland 1997: 227)

By the beginning of 1954, British musical talent was proving more successful. Eddie Calvert's instrumental 'Oh Mein Papa' occupied the number one spot for nine weeks and British singers including David Whitfield, Alma Cogan, Dickie Valentine, Joan Regan, Dennis Lotus and

Ruby Murray enjoyed growing chart success, though often with cover versions of American hits. British bands such as Ted Heath, Billy Cotton, Frank Chacksfield and Mantovani also enjoyed chart popularity. However, the British film industry failed to exploit British popular music artists and was slow to see the potential marketing crossover between popular music and film in the way that Hollywood did when it exploited (admittedly superior) American talent such as Mario Lanza, Doris Day and Frank Sinatra in films such as *The Great Caruso* (1951), *The Student Prince* (1954), *Calamity Jane* (1953) and *Young At Heart* (1955). There were some minor exceptions, most notably Norman Wisdom whose number 'Don't Laugh At Me' from Rank's *Trouble In Store* (1953) was in the charts for fifteen weeks from February to May 1954. Ruby Murray sang the opening title song in *It's Great To Be Young* (1956) and made an appearance in the comedy *A Touch Of The Sun* (1956), Dennis Lotus appeared in *The Extra Day* (1956) and *It's A Wonderful World* (1956) with Ted Heath and his Music, and Winifred Atwell dubbed John Mills' piano playing in *It's Great To Be Young*. Given the extent to which musical films on the 1930s and 1940s had exploited the cross-fertilisation between popular music stars such as Fields, Formby and Vera Lynn and the importance of popular music in British cinema of the late 1950s and into the 1960s and beyond, this hiatus in the early and mid-1950s is striking.

Norman Newell's faith in British popular music talent appeared at least partly justified by the late 1950s. Though American artists such as Bill Haley and Elvis Presley were hugely influential in the emergence of rock'n'roll from the mid-1950s, British artists such as Tommy Steele, Terry Dene and Cliff Richard enjoyed enormous success and were involved in a series of films that spoke to the new, young cinema audience at the end of the decade. A key film in the transition between those 1950s 'residual' musicals we have already looked at and the 'emergent' musicals that both acknowledged and exploited 'new' popular music was ABPC's *It's Great To Be Young* (1956), not least because it is one of several films which keyed into contemporary discourse around important changes in British social structure and attitudes that were taking place in debates about the organisation and social purpose of schooling and its role in establishing what was increasing described as a social 'meritocracy'.

It's Great To Be Young (1956)

Like *The Blackboard Jungle*, released in Britain the previous year, the Associated British-Marble Arch film *It's Great To Be Young* (1956) directed by Cyril Frankel, is concerned with teenage school rebellion. Yet if the American film is basically a narrative of social control, a rather staid discourse on 'the youth problem', then *It's Great To Be Young*, scripted by Ted Willis and based on his own original idea, offers a refreshing commentary on the potential of the young generation and the follies not just of their elders, but of the social and institutional rigidities from which mid-1950s Britain was beginning to emerge.

Like Glenn Ford's character Didier in *The Blackboard Jungle*, Dingle (John Mills) has a natural empathy for young people. For Dingle, however, that empathy is expressed through music and the school orchestra at Angel Hill Grammar School. In many respects, Dingle is as much, if not more, rebellious than his pupils in the sixth form, his rebellion driven by his commitment to music as an essential part of a creative education which wants more than the stuffy academic formalities insisted upon by new Headmaster Frome (Cecil Parker). Even though the classically oriented school orchestra promises to bolster the prestige of Angel Hill by entering the National Festival of School Orchestras, Frome puts every obstacle in the way of rehearsals, refusing to fund much-needed additional instruments and going so far as to lock up what instruments they do have. Through a combination of rebellious activities including some inspired busking and the 'unofficial' removal of the instruments from locked cupboards, together with the blessings of hire-purchase finance paid for by Dingle, who earns the money needed by playing piano at night in a local pub, the orchestra manages to continue its practice and rehearsals.

Architecturally, the school resembles an elite British public school, with some fine dreaming spires and acres of verdant grass where the young people lounge in warm summer sun watching cricket practice. As the film's pre-credit opening sequences imply, these youngsters are in touch with 'natural' feelings and behaviours. Against the soundtrack of contemporary pop sensation Ruby Murray singing 'You Are My First Love', a boy and girl stroll hand in hand through the woods, run alongside a canal and stop to look at where they have carved their names into the trunk of an ancient oak tree. If this pastoral idyll is disrupted by the rush through the imposing gated entrance to Angel Hill School, the children being drawn in as if by some giant hidden magnetic force, neither the romantic sub-plot nor a concern with 'natural' behaviour and a prevailing sense of what is right, proper and just, are locked out of the film. In fact, it is precisely the tensions between, on the one hand, the institutional demands of school with its emphasis on rationality and discipline and, on the other, the desire for what can be seen as a Rousseau-esque desire for liberty, justice and expression of the emotional self. Importantly, this desire is coded through music and the power struggles which take place around the school orchestra, as the film sets out the tension between the formal and rigid demands of conventional power enshrined in the institution and the exuberant demands of the young people, and concludes with the protagonists on both sides recognising the importance of tolerance and compromise.

Having learnt of the Headmaster's deep suspicion of anything that departs from the rigours of a disciplined academic education – Frome has already severely curtailed football practice – Dingle persuades Frome to listen to the young people playing in the attempt to win his support for music. On their way to listen to lunch-time rehearsal, Dingle assures Frome that the school orchestra plays classical music, though is not adverse to including some jazz in their repertoire. Frome's response sets out the boundaries: 'I detest jazz. Personally, I think it ruins character.' No sooner does Frome express his dislike of jazz, than we hear the orchestra (actually the Humphrey Lyttleton Band) in a full swing 'jam session', belting out precisely the music the Headteacher detests so much. Though Dingle initially endorses Frome's authoritarian criticism of the music and its players, he also takes the trumpet to show young Nicky Puttnam (Jeremy Spencer) how to play 'properly' and ends up full of praise for Puttnam's playing.

It is the orchestra's interest in and ability to play 'jazz' which lands them into further trouble. Desperate to raise the money for much-needed additional instruments, Puttnam and the others decide to try and raise some money by busking outside a local boxing hall. Their version of a classical symphony played on limited range of instruments proves unpopular with the queuing public, but they have more success with the up-tempo 'Rhythm Is Our Business', a swing number complete with carefully choreographed dancing. They raise just enough to enable Forest, whose father runs a music business, to put a deposit on some new instruments.

Back in the staff room, Dingle's defence of the importance of music continues, telling stuffed-shirt fellow teacher Routledge that, had he taken music, he would not have been so at odds with the world. What is wrong with the world, asserts Dingle is that there is 'no harmony, rhythm or proportion'; as he says, 'We spend too much time stuffing the head and neglect the heart and soul'.

When the new instruments arrive, Dingle's rational objections to paying for the instruments on 'the never-never' are overcome as Paulette plays one of the new clarinets; Dingle's heart and soul over-rule his head. The orchestra (actually the London Schools Symphony Orchestra) plays John Addison's 'Scherzo' and the music reveals its ability to transcend the mundane monetary problems. The new instruments also reveal little Lawson's (Richard O'Sullivan) ability to play the French horn; his father happens to be a player with the London Philharmonic. Dingle enthuses about the improvements and decides – 'naturally' – to keep the instruments.

However, newspaper reportage of the busking episode gets Dingle and the orchestra in trouble with Frome, who asserts that 'scraping away at a violin will not win scholarships' and demands that the instruments are locked away, unaware that Dingle has agreed to buy them through hire purchase and that they are not, strictly speaking, school property. Faced with Frome's stern authoritarianism, transgression becomes the order of the day, as the pupils take to 'liberating' the locked instruments to continue in clandestine after-school rehearsals and Dingle takes a spare-time job for 'four pounds a week and free beer' playing piano in a local public house to pay for them. Here, as with the earlier sequence, the performance of the London Schools Symphony Orchestra is lovingly privileged, leaving little doubt as to the central importance of the music and Dingle's assertion of its place within education.

The transgressive behaviour of both Dingle and the pupils is doomed to discovery. A visit from a salesman from Mellotone Instruments (played by Bryan Forbes with an unfortunate pronounced Jewish accent) leads to the realisation that Dingle is paying for the instruments and he is dismissed, though not before the pupils, scenting victory over Frome, indulge in a rendition of the 'Marching Strings', signature tune of the BBC's *Top Of The Form* quiz, played on improvised comb and paper, rulers and waste-bins. Dingle's dismissal leads to mounting protestations and rebelliousness. 'I didn't get near them' says Frome after seeing pupils about Dingle's dismissal. 'There's such a thing as justice you know' says Puttnam, initiating a campaign of disobedience, beginning with a refusal to sing at morning assembly and continuing with disruption of a visit by school inspectors. The rebellion soon involves other schools as the youthful community calls for justice and the reinstatement of Dingle. Like their instruments, the pupils end up locked away, though this time it is their decision to barricade themselves in the school buildings.

'These children happen to be standing up for something – someone – they believe in' says Frome recognising his own failures and deficiencies compared with the responses inspired by Dingle. This recognition leads to a meeting between Frome and Dingle, who jointly confront the rebels. In an admittedly very pale imitation of the denouement of Fritz Lang's *Metropolis*, Dingle and Frome recognise fault on both sides, the importance of both rationality and emotion, of head and heart. Faced with adult reconciliation and the reinstatement of Dingle and – by implication – the importance of music within the school, the rebellion comes to an end, though not before Paulette, aware of her feelings for Puttnam, reprises the opening song 'You Are My First Love' in a re-emphasis of the 'naturalness' of young people. Both Frome and Dingle are carried out shoulder high to the tune of 'Marching Strings', this time benefiting from a lavish orchestration.

Significantly, and despite providing the apparent motivation for the new instruments and the need for rehearsal practice, the National Festival of School Orchestras is forgotten about. Though success remains important, it is not the sort of competitive success that the film is concerned with. Rather, what matters are the lessons learnt about the importance of tolerance and compromise. Music is shown to be the vehicle that constructs community, which can even cause that community to rebel and transgress when the cause of natural justice appears to be overthrown. Music and its emotional power are finally inscribed with the same importance as the Headmaster's concern with academic study. Along the way, we are shown the power of classical music and of orchestral ensemble playing to unite and soothe, to overcome trials and tribulations associated with Gradgrindery and formal institutions. Though it remains unsaid, we assume that Frome has changed his mind about the place of music within the school, since his conversion and recognition of his limitations are every bit as significant as Dingle's acceptance that his method was not entirely justified by the worthy ends for which he was striving. Liberty, justice and expression of the emotional self, including, of course, those emotions centred on burgeoning heterosexual attraction, are shown as triumphant.

And the film itself represents something of a small triumph. The performances from John Mills and Cecil Parker are outstanding, even if Parker was reprising a role similar to countless others he had played. Though some of the juvenile performances tend towards the gauche, Jeremy Spenser as Puttnam gives a sense of solidity to the cause the young people find themselves fighting. Musically, the film offers much of interest, much of it seamlessly integrated within the narrative. The appeal ranged from chart-topping Ruby Murray, traditional jazz played by Humphrey Lyttleton's Band of the kind that was to be hugely popular in Britain in the late 1950s and early 1960s, the stride piano tunes, including 'Don't Dilly Dally', 'I've Got Sixpence' and 'Hungarian March' played by Dingle in the local public house, the 'big production number' 'Rhythm Is Our Business', with its genuflection towards the Hollywood musical, through to the classical music played by the Angel Hill Orchestra. This melange of the traditional and the modern reflects the drive towards a modernist Britain contained within the narrative, where the social rigidities of established institutions are challenged by the liberating forces of following the Festival of Britain, including the wonder of hire-purchase.

Though it is now difficult to swallow some of the enthusiasm of contemporary reviews – the *Daily Herald* was of the opinion that 'You will burst your belt with laughter!' – it is easier to understand the tone of welcome relief given to the film as proof that the British film industry was still capable of producing film musicals, not least one that appealed to a younger audience. As the trade paper *The ABC Film Review* put it in its promotional review for August 1956,

> Sounds rather like a musical, doesn't it? Can they make musicals in Britain? We've had our doubts, but we haven't any more doubts at the moment. Here it is, from the Associated British Studios at Elstree, and it's a musical plus, for it tells a truly original story with more glee and gusto than we've seen for years. (Henry 1956: 6)

To an extent, this trade puff expresses a rather tentative reassertion that the British film musical was far from dead, a view that appeared to be confirmed with ABPC's decision to remake a version of *The Good Companions* (1957), directed by J. Lee Thompson. As a director, Thompson had some previous, if not altogether convincing, experience of musical comedies including *As Long As They're Happy* (1955) and *An Alligator Named Daisy* (1955), both with songs firmly rooted in the Tin Pan Alley tradition. *The Good Companions* partly succeeds on its own terms. Shot in Technicolor and Cinemascope, the production values are high, the choreography from Paddy Stone and Irving Davies is effective and Thompson's direction is assured, even if the songs are lacklustre. However, in trying to update the original concept and centring it on Susie Dean's (Janette Scott) attempts to escape from the outmoded variety circuit towards more contemporary stardom and affluence, the film mixes its messages. The result was 'more rocking chair than rock and roll' (Chibnall 2000: 130), a film which even its director considered 'too old-fashioned'.

Though Andy Medhurst concedes the 'consensual charm' which *It's Great To Be Young* exudes, he argues that 'in the light of the rock'n'roll revolution breaking out all around, [the film] is irritatingly coy, indelibly conformist, irretrievably English' (Medhurst 1995: 62). With hindsight, much the same could be said of *The Good Companions*, released at a time when new cultural trends were emerging, not least the shifts in youth adherence to new types of popular music and the 'rumbles of discontent' beginning to be articulated in British theatre and film (Marowitz, Milne and Hale 1965: 39). Arguably, however, this is a rather harsh judgement and one that fails to reflect what was happening within popular music in Britain at the time. It is perhaps worth remembering that Norrie Paramor, whose involvement with British pop musicals was considerable, had scored music for Jack Buchanan, Ivor Novello and Mantovani. Whilst this is not the place to begin a revisionist history of 1950s British popular music, it is important to remember that, whilst the impact of rock'n'roll was significant in terms of the cultural changes it signalled, as a popular music genre it was only one of many, including skiffle, traditional jazz and calypso which, for a time at least, were equally influential. Then, and subsequently, the term rock-'n'roll was used indiscriminately to describe the range of musical genres that attained popularity as an emergent cultural form during the 1950s. Drawing upon distinctive American musical styles as different as white country music and New Orleans jazz, as well as music from the Caribbean, these British generic inflections were a significant element in the development of a new youth-orientated popular-music taste culture. Of course, these new genres co-existed alongside more conventional pop balladry and ever-recurring novelty numbers and, within a relatively short space of time, even ardent rock'n'roll performers were incorporated within the more conventional traditions of popular music. This is not to deny the sense of excitement that surrounded the development of a new youth-orientated popular music, merely a reminder that commercial determinants, eager to respond to market needs, remained important. That the two co-existed is evident in a number of films, including *The Golden Disc* (1958), which purports to chart Terry Dene's rise to fame by way of coffee-bar, record shop and recording contract, combining an admittedly unrealistic representation of the *processes* of economic success with the actual excitement of the music, delivered in this case by talents as diverse as rocker Dene himself, crooner Dennis Lotus, Phil Seamon's Jazz Group, Sheila Buxton (singing 'The In Between Age', used as the title for the film's US distribution) and Sonny Stewart's Skiffle Kings.

The British film musical and the youth audience

Using the broad term rock'n'roll, the British popular music industry promoted and exploited this catholic array of musical genres, as can be seen in *The Tommy Steele Story* (1957). Produced by Nat Cohen and Stuart Levy's Anglo-Amalgamated, the film was intentionally designed to appeal to the British teen market which had already responded well to imported US films such as *Rock Around The Clock* (1955) as were the later *6.5 Special* (1958) and *The Duke Wore Jeans* (1958). As Porter and Harper remind us, this teenage market was now economically significant:

> Britain's teenagers were a booming market, however, and film producers could not afford to ignore the new rhythm. There were over 5 million single people in the 15–24 age group and they were earning about £1.48 billion annually or roughly 8.5 per cent of personal income. What is more, they had plenty of money to spend on themselves. They accounted for over a quarter of all cinema admissions and some 44 per cent of the money spent on records and record players. Moreover, 60 per cent of them regularly went to the cinema every week, and another 27 per cent went at least once a month. (Harper and Porter, 2003: 261)

This awareness of the enormous commercial potential of the youth leisure market, burgeoning as post-war Britain began its inexorable shift from a production economy to a consumption economy, co-existed with powerful, entrenched cultural attitudes that stigmatised youth as a social problem. Though only one amongst many new popular music genres, 'rock'n'roll' seemed to epitomise the challenges posed to residual concepts of British identity, challenges which revolved around perceptions held by some of (yet more) 'Americanisation' and associated issues of juvenile delinquency, increasing sexual permissiveness and general moral laxity. These and indeed other social and cultural tensions were intended to be contained cinematically through the complex process exercised by the British Board of Film Censors (BBFC), which introduced the 'X' certificate in 1951, designed to exclude those under 16 years of age. Though the 'X' certificate often came to imply sordid sensationalism in the public mind, it was intended, in the words of the BBFC Secretary Arthur Watkins, for 'good adult entertainment and films which appeal to an intelligent public' (Aldgate 2000: 59). Watkins clearly had in mind films such as Jack Clayton's *Room At The Top* (1958) which was given an 'X' certificate, a fact which was slyly subverted in the cinema trailer for the film when it announced in sensationalist terms that 'because all trailers must carry a 'U' certificate, we are unable to show you scenes which the censor has passed for adult audiences only'.

This posed particular problems for those films that, through their exploitation of the new music and its performers, were designed to appeal to the teenage market. It is not perhaps surprising that such films eschewed the potential oppositional politics of social challenge in favour of the sounds and images of social inclusiveness. What emerged were sounds and images of reassuring wholesomeness, often suffused with a tone of reluctant self-deprecation about the process of success and stardom. Less affluent than their American counterparts, British youth with musical aspirations found refuge in skiffle, forming groups using low-tech instruments such as a washboard and tea-chest bass. Together with Lionel Bart and Mike Pratt, Tommy Steele had formed The Cavemen, and their number 'Rock With The Cavemen' made a dent in the Top 30 chart in October 1956. Steele had reprised this song together with 'Rebel Rock' in his first screen appearance, *Kill Me Tomorrow* (1957), a thriller directed by Terence Fisher.

The Tommy Steele Story (1957)

Based on Steele's own relatively sudden rise to fame and using songs written by him, Lionel Bart and Mike Pratt, *The Tommy Steele Story* reprises his journey to popular acclaim through narrative flashback after the opening rock'n'roll number, 'Take Me Back Baby' performed at the 'exclusive' Café de Paris Dining and Dancing Cabaret, suggesting that his appeal runs across class, gender and generation. Besieged by journalists who fire a string of questions at him without ever really listening to his answers, he is given the chance to tell his story 'in his own words' in cinematic flashback. A judo injury in Bermondsey leads to a prolonged period of hospitalisation during which, with support and encouragement from a nurse, Steele learns to play the guitar. Pressured by anxious parents to 'get a proper job', Steele joins the Merchant Navy, but his incandescent desire to play and perform is at odds with a career as a seaman. Back in London, a lucky break leads to success singing at a milk bar and, following the conventional show-business paradigm, to record and live performance success. Determined to allay accusations of rebelliousness or of star-struck alienation from his roots, Tommy tells the journalists at the Café de Paris that he wants to thank 'the kids like himself' and organises a concert at Bermondsey Town Hall that forms the film's climax.

Though the film's marketing appeal was firmly based on Steele's reputation as Britain's leading 'rock'n'roller', its musical content is actually much more diverse and reflects the range of music which enjoyed contemporary popularity. The film makes clever use of diegetic space in enabling Steele to perform a series of numbers, such as 'Cannibal Pot', which Steele sings directly to camera while working in the ship's galley, and the wistful blues number 'Will It Be You', sung as a kind of private audition at the request of the milk-bar owner. His earlier progress in learning the guitar in hospital is carefully grounded, his musical progress charted literally alongside his medical progress, and leads to a performance of 'Butterfingers' – a number that featured in the NME charts from May to September 1957 – in front of a cross-generational group of patients in the hospital ward. Further evidence of his wide-ranging appeal is apparent in the numbers he performs when aboard ship in the Merchant Navy, such as the up-beat rock number 'You Gotta Go', which, with its 'impossible orchestration' from a non-diegetic rhythm section and tenor saxophone, has even septuagenarian couples dancing a jive. The scenes detailing Steele's experiences in the Merchant Navy serve not just the purposes of pop-biography, but express his desire to 'pick up a song in every country', articulated musically in the successful chart number 'Handful Of Songs' and enables the film to make reference to the British colonial legacy at a time when it was transmuting into Commonwealth. Docked in the Caribbean, Steele's performance of the calypso-inflected 'Water Water' inscribes his inter-racial appeal, an appeal which is underpinned throughout the film by Chris O'Brien's Caribbeans' all-important 'Narrative Calypso', detailing, explaining and commentating on Steele's rise to stardom from the opening titles to end credits, recounting how 'this lad from Bermondsey, in show-business he made history, with his heart and soul, he sang his ballads and rock'n'roll'. The implicit cultural pluralism of late 1950s Britain is encoded in the climactic concert when traditional jazz performed by Humphrey Lyttleton's band, a calypso sung by Tommy Eytle and His Calypso Band, and 'Freight Train', a chart hit for Chas McDevitt Skiffle Group with Nancy Whiskey, are performed alongside Tommy Steele and the Steelmen's 'Teenage Party'. Interestingly, the film achieved US distribution under the title *Rock Around The World*, an attempt to market the musical and cultural pluralism represented within the film.

Using Norman Hudis's emphatically realist script, director Gerard Bryant manages to convey the sense of down-to-earth ordinariness that permeates this very British story of show-business success. Though there are moments of inspired excess, as in the scene where Steele buys his second-hand guitar from the dusty down-at-heel pawnbrokers, his singing of 'I Like' underpinned by shots of 'ghostly' instruments that are heard on the soundtrack even though no one is playing them, Bryant grounds performance within the diegesis in ways which consistently make Steele's success both believable and accessible, something which is reinforced through Steele's self-deprecating tone at his press conference at the Café de Paris. As a result, *The Tommy Steele Story* manages to exploit the appeal of Steele and 'rock'n'roll' for a youth audience and simultaneously offer reassurance to an older generation, not least through the performance of a number of songs that relate more to conventional pop traditions than the oppositional potential of 'rock'n'roll'.

Curiously, and in stark contrast to the norms of Hollywood pop bio-pics, *The Tommy Steele Story* is devoid of any romantic interest. By focussing single-mindedly on the career trajectory of its eponymous hero, the film rejects many of the generic norms associated with other-wise similar American pop bio-pics and refuses any engagement with the contemporary debates around sexual identity and wider gender pol-itics that are so central to British 'new wave' cinema of the late 1950s and early 1960s.

Steele's rapid absorption into what might be described as mainstream show business was evident in successive films and sustained by his rela-tionship with songwriter Lionel Bart. In *The Duke Wore Jeans* (1958), based on a story by Bart and Mike Pratt with a screenplay by Norman Hudis, produced by Peter Rogers and directed by Gerald Thomas (both beginning to achieve simultaneous prominence with Anglo Amalgamated's *Carry On* series), Steele's multilayered appeal is rein-forced in the double identities he assumes in the film as both an aristo-cratic son and his cockney double. Set in a world of outmoded Ruritanian fantasy with kings, duchesses and princesses, described by Medhurst as 'part Ivor Novello operetta and part Danny Kaye musical comedy' (Medhurst 1995: 64), the film's nine songs, including a version of 'Knees Up Mother Brown', represent a lurch further toward con-ventional show-business traditions. This trajectory was compounded in Steele's subsequent films, including *Tommy The Toreador* (1959) with its novelty chart hit 'Little White Bull', and completed by the time of *Half A Sixpence* (1967).

Whatever limited sub-cultural oppositional potential British 'rock'n'roll' might have offered, as in America it was rapidly absorbed into the commercial mainstream, made safe for consumption, rapidly transmuting into pop. I have argued elsewhere in connection with Elvis Presley's early Hollywood films such as *Jailhouse Rock* and *Loving You* (both 1957) that, far from representing a radical break, these films continued

> the stylistic and narrative conventions of the classical Hollywood musical, and perpetuated dominant ideologies, not least through the discourse of show-business and entertainment. (Mundy 1999: 122)

Though, as we have seen, British cinema's musical films were stylisti-cally much more diverse and less generically coherent, this emphasis on the processes or mechanics of professional success, so evident in films such as *The Golden Disc* and *The Tommy Steele Story*, is visible in *Expresso Bongo* (1959), a story structured around the rising career of young rocker Bongo Herbert, played by Cliff Richard.

Performative excess and narratives of reassurance:
Expresso Bongo (1959)

Like Tommy Steele, Richard was heralded as one of Britain's home-grown challengers to American performers such as Bill Haley, Presley and Eddie Cochran, his chart single 'Move It' reaching number 2 in the NME chart in October 1958. Richard had been a regular performer on ATV's immensely popular 1958 television pop show *Oh Boy*, though his sleazy gyrations in the Presley mode led to some accusations of indecency in the press. This combination of provocative notoriety and evident commercial appeal to the teenage market led to him being shoehorned into a supporting role as Curley in Terence Young's film *Serious Charge* (1959), a part which had not existed in the original stage play. One of the four numbers sung by Richard, 'Living Doll', occupied the number one chart slot for six weeks in the summer of 1959. The film's rather sensationalist treatment of delinquent youth armed with flick knives and bicycle chains, together with a nude bathing scene and a plot involving accusations of homosexuality, ran into trouble with the BBFC; even after toning down objectionable scenes, the film was awarded an 'X' certificate, despite the censors despairing acceptance that 'the vulgarisation of motion pictures intended for older teenagers has proceeded so fast in the past three years that it does not seem anything out of the way now' (Aldgate 2003: 139).

The censor's misgivings about 'vulgarisation' seem justified in the opening scenes of *Expresso Bongo* with its sleazy Soho setting of striptease and prostitutes. Like Lionel Bart's 1959 stage musical *Fings Ain't Wot They Used T'Be*, the film seems to offer contemporary social comment on the recent 1957 Wolfenden Report, which examined contemporary attitudes towards homosexuality and prostitution, and the new Street Offences Act. Wolf Mankowitz's original stage play was designed to satirise the recent phenomenon of pop-star success, such as that enjoyed by Tommy Steele. This is why, in the film, the narrative focus is firmly on the antics of Johnny Jackson (Laurence Harvey), the shifty, aspiring show-business agent who manipulates Bongo Herbert's career. Mankowitz clearly understood the role of impresarios such as Larry Parnes and record producers such as Norrie Paramor in the construction of pop careers. In fact, through its plot reliance on the rising success of Bert Rudge, aka Bongo Herbert (Cliff Richard), the film manages to critique this shadier side of the entertainment industry, offering a narrative of reassurance through what the *Melody Maker* of 28 November 1959 termed the 'well-modulated tones and essentially quiet charm' of Richard (Caine 2001: 64).

The subsequent longevity of Cliff Richard's career has tended to skew critical readings of *Expresso Bongo*, which needs to be understood within that wider realist aesthetic which characterised much of British cinema of the late 1950s and early 1960s. The recurrent scenes of Soho strip shows and references to 'the vice squad', the gendered animosity between Johnny Jackson and Maisie (Sylvia Syms), the implicit sexual initiation that Bongo enjoys with the glamorous older woman Dixie Collins (played by Val Guest's wife Yolande Donlan), the almost obligatory cross-generational conflict played out in the Rudge household's front parlour (not least over Bert's 'bastardy'), Gilbert Harding and the BBC television's 'Cosmorama' documentary examination of youth culture and rebellion, the class differences evinced by Susan Hampshire's cut-glass-accented society debutante and her drunken 'officer and gentleman' companion, the alto-sax-dominated non-diegetic jazz score and, above all, the dubious ethical behaviour of Johnny Jackson and the show-business world he inhabits, all locate the film within that process of earnest social comment shared by British fiction films such as Tony Richardson's *Look Back In Anger* (1959) and documentaries such as *We Are The Lambeth Boys* (1959). It is after all, as Johnny Jackson says, 'a bastard world and I'm a fully paid-up member'.

Skilfully crafted by director Val Guest, *Expresso Bongo* is a high-energy, densely rich text that works well as a distinctly British musical film. Though some narrative and performance attention is focussed on Richard, the film contains a range of other songs, written mainly by Julian More, Robert Farnon, Val Guest and Norrie Paramor. Guest manages to exploit the teenage appeal of Cliff Richard (and to a lesser extent, The Shadows) in numbers such as 'Love', 'A Voice In The Wilderness' and the rather embarrassingly maudlin slow ballad number 'Shrine On The Second Floor'. Other more conventional songs – such as 'Nausea', amusingly critiquing new fashions in popular music, comparing 'this little bleeder with Aida', Maisie's introspective solo big-band-backed number 'Worry Go Lucky Me', expressing her frustration with her relationship with Johnny, and Dixie Collins' gentle simmering 'You Can Fool (Some Of the People)', a song full of wistful regret for her passing youth and fame – make a significant contribution to a balanced and structured blend of narrative and musical performance. Despite being given an 'X' certificate, the film did well at the box-office, boosted by Richard's presence, even if his acting is less assured than that of the rest of the cast. Equally, the film boosted Richard's already successful record career, with both the extended play (EP) 'Expresso Bongo' and the single 'A Voice In

The Wilderness' taken from the EP making a chart appearance in the early months of 1960.

In their different ways, both *The Tommy Steele Story* and *Expresso Bongo* are important and interesting films and certainly serve to indicate the social and cultural ruptures that characterised British society over the course of the 1950s, as well as the important demographic changes in the British cinema audience that had occurred during the decade. Both films cleverly acknowledge the newly constructed youth community and its role in the new taste culture emerging around popular music, then elide that specific community with a much wider, multi-generational community. In *Expresso Bongo*, this youth community is more marginalised, lost in the process whereby Bongo Herbert is groomed for mainstream show-business success; in *The Tommy Steele Story*, Steele's determination to avoid contact with his roots leads to a reiteration of the importance of the youth community, even if it is seen enjoying music which, it is implied, has universal appeal. Both films emphasise the growing importance of the metropolitan experience, though interestingly London seems ineluctably linked to other, more global, locations and experiences. Both films are remarkable in the sense that they successfully exploit the market appeal of 'rock'n'roll', but manage to contain its ideological and aesthetic excess within their realist narrative form. However, despite their commercial success, they are far from representing an uncontested triumph as the model for a successful pop musical. In the late 1950s, a musical film such as *Idle On Parade* (1959) in which rising stage star Anthony Newley played Jeep Jackson, a satirical comment on Presley's US army career, jostled for exhibition space alongside exploitation pop revue films such *Rock You Sinners* (1957) and *6.5 Special* (1958) and more traditional 'residual' musical films such as *Make Mine A Million* (1959) featuring Arthur Askey and pop balladeers Dicky Valentine and Dennis Lotus, or with the two Herbert Wilcox features starring Frankie Vaughan, *The Lady Is A Square* and *The Heart Of A Man* (both 1959).

Such diverse cinematic products offer a useful corrective to over-simplified and ahistorical accounts of British popular music in the late 1950s. They also serve to indicate the continuing variety of form and aesthetic that characterised the British musical film. Whilst the decade had witnessed a number of unsuccessful attempts to emulate aspects of the classical Hollywood musical, the continuing ability of the British musical film to resist narrow generic conventions and to draw upon indigenous talent, settings and social concerns produced a number of interesting films which made comment on the distinctive, if pluralistic, qualities of British culture. Capable of adjusting to the demands of fashionable cinematic realism, the British musical film continued to draw upon other aesthetic traditions. It retained the ability to be, at times, frivolous, silly, flippant and popular. It is true that those cultural traditions that had been so influential in British musical films of the 1930s and 1940s – music hall, live variety and the dance bands – were on the wane. In their place was the growing influence of the recording star and the grip of the Top Thirty charts, an influence that became pronounced in the films of the 1960s.

5

The 1960s: youth, home-grown talent and American money

The artificiality of trying to structure this book by decades, with its implication that one was somehow hermetically sealed from another, becomes pronounced as we slip from 1959 to 1960, ending the last chapter with the Cliff Richard vehicle *Expresso Bongo* and beginning this one with an examination of his three films made in the early 1960s, *The Young Ones* (1961), *Summer Holiday* (1962) and *Wonderful Life* (1964). Popular music as a cultural force with a distinct appeal to young people found a place in British cinema of the late 1950s and gained momentum in the films produced in the early and mid-1960s. As in previous decades, British musical films took a variety of forms. There were attempts to replicate the generic formulae of the Hollywood musical with numbers integrated within narrative developments, musical comedies in which the element of comedy vied for attention with musical performance, films which were essentially musical revues, and short films which featured one or a limited number of bands or artists.

There was continuity too in the on-going process of critical condemnation of British cinema. Just as British films of the 1950s were and continue to be subject to critical hostility, so too British cinema of the 1960s has not been short of its detractors. Given the enduring strength of that discourse of self-deprecation which surrounds British cinema, Alan Parker's late-1980s commentary on sixties British cinema should come as no surprise:

> Whatever the Swinging Sixties are going to be remembered for it won't be films. The moment you saw a red London bus go through the shot you knew you were in for a rotten time. (Murphy 1992: 1)

While Parker has the film-maker's eye for telling visual detail, it doesn't necessarily make for good, justified or balanced criticism, quite apart from the fact that a number of British films were still being shot in black and white during the early to mid-1960s. The reality is that British cinema of the 1960s was very distinct from that of the previous decade, even if some of the emerging trends in film-making and in shifting audience tastes begin in the late 1950s. If that cinema had begun to question the old attitudes and assumptions, then British cinema of the 1960s came up with some alternatives in a rich, heady welter of energetic and highly successful – critically and commercially – film-making. British society in the 1960s was radically different from what it had been in the previous decade, and marked a reaction away from the norms and mores that had held sway throughout much of the 1950s. In the words of one social historian, it was a decade in which 'the working class, women, provincials, young people, blacks, became visible as never before' (Marwick 2000: xii). British cinema of the 1960s reflected these pronounced shifts and signalled a flowering of creative film-making which came to be respected internationally.

The production context: new films for a declining audience

Much of this critical respect and international acclaim centred on what has become known as the 'kitchen sink' films of the British 'New Wave', films as different as *Room at the Top* (1959), *The Angry Silence* (1960), *Saturday Night and Sunday Morning* (1960), *Flame in the Streets* (1961), *A Taste of Honey* (1961), *The Loneliness of the Long-Distance Runner* (1962) and *This Sporting Life* (1963). Described by contemporary critic Isobel Quigly as the 'British sociological film' (Hill 1986: 206), these and other films shared a concern with aspects of contemporary British life articulated through a realist aesthetic, with its emphasis on location shooting, cinematography and editing which constructed a coherently credible British world, suffused with naturalistic acting which connected with cinema audience perceptions of 'ordinary people'. Signalling something of the important social and cultural changes underway in Britain in the late 1950s and early 1960s, they dealt with structural issues around class, race and gender in ways that asked audiences to question prevailing attitudes. Drawing upon documentary traditions, British New Wave films didn't just refocus attention on class and regionalism, but asserted newly defined problems around sexual politics driven by the availability of contraception and changing attitudes towards abortion, as sexuality became a more complex issue and women carried what Murphy calls greater 'emotional weight' within films (Murphy 1992: 33). Importantly, films such as *Victim* (1961) challenged assumptions that homosexuality was what a contemporary edition of *Time* magazine called 'a serious (but often curable) neurosis'. Other films focussed attention on aspects of peoples' working lives and attitudes to authority, examining new attitudes towards the work place and industrial relations, albeit sometimes in comic and confusing fashion as in *I'm All Right Jack* (1959). Many of the films, including *Saturday Night and Sunday Morning* and *Billy Liar*, were notable for their innovative use of music on the soundtrack, using composers as varied as John Barry, John Dankworth, Philip Green and Richard Rodney Bennett, often using modernist jazz-inflected under-scoring to heighten atmosphere, mood and emotion in ways which marked a rupture from much of 1950s British cinema.

Though not universally praised or appreciated by contemporary critics, British 'New Wave' films of the early 1960s have since gained a reputation as constituting one of the few periods of creative and significant British film-making. However, as Alan Parker's comments should serve to warn us, such critical acclaim tells only part of the story of British cinema of the 1960s. This is a point made by Jeffrey Richards who, whilst praising the New Wave films for 'tackling the lifestyle and aspirations of the young and working class in a fresh, unpatronising way' also argues that concentrating

> on these films at the expense of the many other cinematic products of the decade has also tended to distort the perceived picture of the age. (Richards 1997: 147–8)

Though hindsight regards the 'New Wave' films as crucial to an understanding of social and cultural shifts taking place in Britain in the early 1960s, it is important to place them within the wider context of sixties British cinema, as it struggled to compete with American product for screen space. It is salutary to remember that, for example, *Billy Liar* (1963) was promoted as 'the greatest escapist entertainment ever devised for a laugh' (sic) in its theatrical trailer, and that films such as *Doctor In Love* (1960), *Sink The Bismark!* (1960), *The Guns Of Navarone* (1961) as well as Cliff Richard's *The Young Ones* (1961) dominated the box-office. Though the 'New Wave' films remain significant, the discursive attention they have received and the emphasis on their realist aesthetic detract from other critical stories about sixties British cinema which need telling, not least developments in the British musical film which took place during the decade. Like other genres, such as the horror films coming out of Hammer, musicals throughout the decade offer an important corrective to assumptions that successful British films depended on a realist aesthetic.

British production figures appear relatively healthy for the early 1960s. In 1960, some 121 features were produced, in 1961 118, in 1962

143, and in 1963 120. Significantly, these figures include a number of films of around 60 minutes in length, films destined, at best, to appear as 'B' features on a double bill. However, this is not to deny the appeal and commercial success of many British features during these years, some of which went on to international success. In fact, the success of *Tom Jones* (1963), *Dr No* (1963) and *A Hard Day's Night* (1964) both in Britain and the United States triggered a flow of American investment into the British film industry; in 1966, 75 per cent of production finance came from American sources and a year later that figure had reached 90 per cent (Murphy 1992: 258). Though this investment enabled more big-budget productions, the actual number of features produced declined from 1964 onwards, 84 in that year, 81 in 1965, 71 in 1966, 90 in 1967, 81 in 1968 and 88 in 1969.

With the exception of films produced for the Children's Film Foundation, increasingly occasional 'naturist' films such as *The Reluctant Nudist* (1963) and *Peter Studies Form* (1964), and musical shorts, production of short and less-than-feature-length films declined as the decade unfolded. The musical shorts included an Anglo-Amalgamated series in 1961 featuring bands as diverse as Ted Heath, Hermanos Deniz Cuban Rhythm Band and the Tony Kinsey Quartet, as well as shorts such as *Four Hits And A Mister* (1962) featuring Acker Bilk and *Suddenly It's Jazz* (1963) with Dick Charlesworth and His City Gents that reflected the current popularity of traditional jazz. Others, such as United Artists' *Swinging UK* (1964) and *UK Swings Again* (1964), reflected the growing significance of radio disc-jockeys as they introduced pop bands such as Brian Poole and the Tremeloes, The Hollies and The Merseybeats. By the late 1960s, shorts such as AB-Pathé's *Go With Matt Monro* (1967) and Associated-London's *The Bee Gees* (1968) represented a seriously curtailed production trend.

The decline in production was matched by a decline in the British cinema audience. As domination over exhibition was concentrated in the Rank and ABC circuits, admissions continued to collapse throughout the decade, so that by 1970 they were down to 193 million spread amongst 1,492 cinemas. Cinema had ceased to be the prime entertainment activity and this decline in audience numbers continued beyond the sixties; by 1980, admissions had declined to 96 million at 942 cinemas, though the introduction of twinning and tripling which began during the 1970s kept the number of screens at 1,562. Much of the decline in attendance was due to the falling-away of the youth audience, though its importance in the first few years of the decade explains why musical films harnessing iconic chart talent were relatively numerous.

Musical film, the 'problem' of youth and its resolution

The concept of youth as a social problem – so evident in musical films such as *Serious Charge* (1959) as well as in films such as *Violent Playground* (1958), *The Boys* (1962) and *Spare The Rod* (1961) – was addressed in the pop musical, but largely failed to treat youth as a social threat that remained beyond adult control. This process of normative recuperation is evident in Clive Donner's *Some People* (1962), with Kenneth More and David Hemmings, in which the members of a pop group use the church hall to rehearse until they wreck it, but this is merely an excuse to illustrate how potential delinquents can be recuperated into society, in this case through the Duke of Edinburgh Award Scheme. Two years before, in the 'X'-rated *Beat Girl* (1960), a film that exploited the current chart success of Adam Faith ('What Do You Want' and 'Poor Me' reached the number one chart spot in late 1959 and early 1960), the daughter of comfortable middle-class parents flirts with the Soho world of striptease, prostitution and coffee bars. The physical proximity of the coffee bar and the strip club imply a proximity of immorality as Jennifer, having learnt something of her step-mother's dubious sexual past, mimics her behaviour in a drunken domestic striptease. This flirtation with what was called 'perverse sexuality' leads to accusations of much greater import, as Jennifer becomes embroiled in a murder charge, only to be rescued by patriarchy and the reassertion of the family unit.

Like *Serious Charge*, *Beat Girl* was essentially a 'B' feature melodrama that used the presence of a chart-topping, lip-synching singer to boost its marketing appeal, though the association of a pop-driven coffee-bar culture with the potential for sexual 'perversity' remains evident. Its narrative centre revolves around the 'problem' of female sexuality as the film attempts to engage with and mediate current moral preoccupations about gender roles and family structure. By contrast, ABPC's *The Young Ones* centres on Cliff Richard's increasingly wholesome star persona. A more conventional musical in its formal arrangement of the relationship between narrative and numbers, the film makes some effective use of non-realist fantasy sequences, but still manages in its way to connect with contemporary attitudes and debates about the 'youth problem'. Shot in CinemaScope, the film marked the successful transformation of Richard from 'rock'n'roll phenomenon' to 'all-round entertainer'. Kevin Donnelly is surely right in asserting that by 1960, following *Expresso Bongo* and *Tommy The Toreador*, British filmmakers had developed successful strategies for incorporating pop music into films (Donnelly 2001a: 6), though these strategies clearly drew upon successful precedents, including the use of American talent. In the case of *The Young Ones*, the model was very much that of the optimistic classical Hollywood musical, its narrative centring on the conventional backstage fantasy of 'putting on a show'. Canadian director Sidney Furie acknowledged that the film owed a debt to the Mickey Rooney and Judy Garland film *Babes In Arms* and was designed to appeal to a family audience that included the teenagers. The strategy paid dividends, as the film was second only to *Dr No* at the British box-office in 1962.

The colourful opening credits for *The Young Ones* – under-scored by Stanley Black's up-tempo, lavishly orchestrated instrumental medley of numbers from the film – take place against a background of a high-rise building plot, a reference not just to the optimism engendered by the early 1960s property development boom, but also to a plot that centres on the determination of affluent, socially conservative Hamilton Black (Robert Morley) to build yet another high-rise development in London, even if it means demolishing a rickety youth club attended by, amongst others, his son Nicky (Cliff Richard). In classic generic mode, the opening number 'Friday Night' serves to introduce the characters and to construct a sense of community. They are a community of youth despite the different jobs they do, their coded class differences, and the gendered identities they conform to: female shop workers, male building workers, male and female college students in their yellow jackets, female ballet students, Jimmy (Melvyn Hayes) the delivery boy on his bike, Barbara (Annette Robertson) the beatnik waitress, and Ernest (Richard O'Sullivan) who works in the city as a trainee solicitor, complete with bowler hat and umbrella. As the song passes from character to character, each reinforcing the anticipation of the freedom and fun that Friday night promises, the orchestral scoring encompasses musical inflections which, whilst reflecting class and gender differences, also serve to reinforce the experiences they share in common through the reassertion of the main melodic line. As night falls and they arrive at the youth club, a cut to a close shot of Hank Marvin's electric guitar (itself a key icon of pop culture of the period) leads to Cliff and Shadows performing the number 'Got A Funny Feeling', its lyrics referencing both the anticipation and centrality of (heterosexual) romance to the film.

Their pleasures are cut short and the narrative problem set in motion as Ernest reads a newspaper article about plans to build a new twenty-storey tower block on the site of the youth club. In a tangential acknowledgement of the 'youth problem' Chris, the film's token Teddy-Boy figure, proposes violent physical action to prevent the development, but this is rejected by all the others. Nicky seems the most amenable to finding an alternative to the existing wooden hut, understandably since, as we soon learn, he is Hamilton Black's son, a fact he keeps from everyone except girlfriend Toni (Carole Gray). Before she and, indeed, we know this, their duet 'Nothing Is Impossible', a number full of visual pyrotechnics which deny physical reality as they fly over and slip through railings and flowers suddenly appear in bloom, gives optimistic expression to the ability to overcome all obstacles. In this energetically choreographed number, the big-band orchestration plays around with jazz and blues inflections mixed with mainstream melodies and conventionally romantic waltz motifs.

Identities, – hidden, mistaken and misconceived – are central to the film. Just as Nicky's relationship to Hamilton Black remains hidden from his peers, so Black is unaware at the beginning of the film that his son belongs to the youth club whose members he imagines to be 'untidy adolescents, milling around in leather jackets, brandishing bicycle chains'. After Nicky has undertaken an 'impossible' voice masquerade, imitating his father over the telephone to find out about the loophole in the lease, Black makes an unrealistic monetary demand from the 'thugs', arranging a meeting on the assumption that they are not busy 'polishing their coshes'. From his opulent apartment, he imagines that all they need is a 'grubby little hut where they can take out their flick knives and carve their initials on the wall'. Though Nicky 'comes out' and tells Black that he is a member of the club, he later asks Toni to keep it secret from the others, citing the rare admission that his background, class and being the son of a millionaire would not go down well with the others. This awareness of the ability of class to divide and disrupt is immediately erased through the number 'The Young Ones' where, surrounded by pleasure seekers enjoying themselves and by a horde of children, Nicky reasserts the 'natural' importance of living life to the full while they are young, erasing all other distinctions as unimportant. This relationship, whereby the number serves as temporary resolution to a problem raised in the preceding narrative, positions *The Young Ones* firmly within those generic expectations usually associated with the classical Hollywood musical.

This is reinforced in the number 'One For All', which follows the group's decision to put on a show to raise the necessary money; lyrics and choreography emphasise community and togetherness, the importance of all 'sticking together'. Perhaps owing as much to *Sunday Night at the London Palladium* as to *West Side Story*, it is nonetheless a very effective number. Stanley Black's rich, energetic, but sensitive orchestration matches Herbert Ross's plethora of different choreographic moods, combining conventional 'show-business' motifs and scoring with jive, ballet, cool and comic effects, making good use of punctuating brass and a swinging sax section, without being afraid of utilising contemporary guitar-driven motifs, drum solos and sweet strings. Rooted in the solidity of common purpose, fantasy vies with material opposition from Hamilton Black. In classic 'putting-on-a-show' mode, we are treated to dialogue such as 'Barbara, you went to Drama School, but can you direct?' to which the answer is, of course, 'Sure!' The intrusion of recording star Dorinda Morrell (Sonya Cordeau) prompts the need for an appropriate song for her, as well as providing romantic conflict when the song 'First Lesson In Love', written by Nicky for Toni, is 'appropriated' by her. Toni's slow, introspective number 'No-One But Nicky', shot with a soft-focus frame, expresses her authentic and loyal love for Nicky, a love that competes with and survives his later success as the 'mystery singer'.

Frustrated by Hamilton Black's purchase of the theatre and its transformation into a bingo hall, they find another dilapidated, deserted venue. In an act of understated British youth rebelliousness, matched only by using the portable parking meter they carry with them, and aware that they have 'no stage, props, lights, costumes, make-up or script', they break into the theatre and into rehearsal, making imaginative use of the stage, lights, costumes and props they find lying around. Interestingly, though music is not included as an important structuring absence in this list of the things that they don't have, the rehearsal benefits from the non-diegetic musical accompaniment to their singing and dancing. The extended sequence that follows is as far from contemporary pop as it is possible to get. Ostensibly driven by the costume and props they find lying around, 'You've Got A Show' draws upon a gamut of British entertainment references including Victorian stage melodrama, Edwardian music hall, pantomime, pier-end concert parties, flickering silent films, the West End show and subsequent 1934 film musical *Chu Chin Chow*, as well as referencing the soft-shoe shuffle, Vernon and Irene Castle, Fred Astaire, and Arthur Murray's dancing schools. The number includes extended phrases from songs such as 'Where Did You Get That Hat' dating from 1888 and 'Josh-ua' from 1906, as well as clichéd ripostes from music-hall comedy such as 'watch our feet: they never leave our ankles' and 'shall we dance? It'll make a change!' It is as if the very physicality of the building serves to incorporate the youngsters into historical tradition and social continuity, as their impromptu performance connects them with an entertainment culture that they have clearly imbibed and inherited, despite the cultural specificity evinced by their awareness of the generation gap.

The need to promote the show leads to the illegal interruption of television programmes using a 'thirty-bob junk shop' radio transmitter which, in defiance of the realities of technology, just needs 'plugging in and turning on'. This publicity stunt, a strange pre-echo of the ways in which raves were organised in the late 1980s and early 1990s, motivates some privileged performance space for Cliff to sing 'Girl In Your Arms', a number written by American songwriters Sid Tepper and Roy Bennett, which is then broadcast across both commercial and BBC television. As rehearsals progress, including Ross's effectively choreographed number 'Just Dance' featuring Carole Gray and male dancers dressed as cross between city gents and Charlie Chaplin against a vivid red stage backcloth, Hamilton Black buys the theatre. The best efforts of the authorities to track down the illegal broadcast are frustrated by the youngster's constant inventiveness, the 'mystery singer's' song becomes a big hit and the show becomes a sell-out. Last-minute attempts by Hamilton Black to close the show are thwarted, father and son show solidarity against the violent Teddy-Boy element which has kidnapped Black, and all are finally reconciled in the show's finale, itself a strange mixture of the mainstream 'We've Got A Show', a snatch from the hit ballad 'Girl In Your Arms', and the rocking 'We Say Yeah' from Cliff, by this stage having clearly transmuted beyond his character Nicky as he performs in front of an audience of screaming female teenagers.

Though the 'youth problem' is acknowledged, the misconceptions held by Hamilton Black about young people are seen to be fallacious. Though there is a violent disruptive element, youngsters who 'are always looking for a punch-up', they are dismissed physically and ideologically. The fantasy of reconciliation is sealed when Hamilton Black proposes to build a brand-new youth club that will be surrounded by his new high-rise block; the young people are incorporated within capitalism, literally. The structural barriers that are part of the British social formation, class, gender, age and economics dissolve within the construction of imagined community, with Hamilton Black being made an honorary member of the club. This ideological erasure of difference is sealed in the very final number, 'What Do You Know, We've Got A Show', designed, as the lyrics say, to 'make the whole audience glow'. As I have argued elsewhere, *The Young Ones*

> comes closest of any British musical to the conventions of the classical Hollywood musical at its best. It has energy, optimism, romance and a sense of community, all the generic elements associated with the backstage musical, bound within a double-helix narrative which sees professional success matched by success in romance. (Mundy 1999: 169)

Very successful in Britain, the film failed to make an impact on the American market at a time when the musical was becoming increasingly unfashionable at the box-office there. Moreover, despite its close adherence to dominant generic conventions and the involvement of American creative talent, the film remains distinctly British, not least in its rather introspective narrative concerns and the accents of its leading characters.

Presumably Alan Parker's aversion to buses went into overdrive with Richard's next musical, *Summer Holiday*. Rather than simply passing through shots, a red London bus occupies centre stage, as it takes Cliff and friends on a quest through Europe. Trading on what was still at the time regarded as the exoticism and 'otherness' of the continent, the film exploited the voyeuristic pleasures of location in much the same way as the Bond films were to do and Jesse Matthews' musicals had done in a more limited way some thirty years earlier. With Herb Ross again responsible for the choreography, songs by Peter Myers and Ronald Cass together with additional songs variously credited to Cliff Richard and members of The Shadows, all under the musical direction of Stanley Black, *Summer Holiday* was clearly designed to repeat the success of *The Young Ones*. Director Peter Yates begins well, but the film does rather lose much of its narrative discipline so that, whilst it contains a great deal of effective dancing and four chart successes including the chart-topping title song, its pleasures are less well sustained, overwhelmed by its regressive sexual politics and rather xenophobic suspicion of what were still at the time seen as slightly threatening places.

If *The Young Ones* acknowledges the 'youth problem' only to dismiss it, then *Summer Holiday* does much the same for contemporary debates around sexual politics evinced in films such as *Saturday Night and Sunday Morning*, *A Taste of Honey*, *The Wild and the Willing* (1962) and *That Kind of Girl* (1963). Gendered identities are important within the paper-thin plot, as the four male mechanics first team up with Sally (Una Stubbs) and the two other girls of a singing trio on their way to Athens, and then take on board what they initially believe to be a fourteen-year-old boy, actually American singing star Barbara Winters (Lauri Peters) on the run from her show-business-obsessed mother. Though initially these female characters threaten to carry 'emotional weight' within the film with their ambitious, independent attempt to get to Athens in their battered old car, they rapidly succumb to the invitation, expressed in the complexly crafted (and, to contemporary ears, wonderfully ambiguous) song 'Let Us Take You For A Ride', to join forces with the four men on the bus. However, the extended itinerary they all undertake does nothing to destabilise conventional gender roles;

once on board, though their professional singing engagement in Athens provides plot motivation, the girls succumb to conventionally sub-servient and domestic roles.

After some rather cod-comic humour derived from Barbara's pretence to be male, as when she is asked to hand Don (Cliff Richard) a towel after his shower, the pair develop a tentative, begrudging romantic rela-tionship, despite Don's initial assertion in 'Bachelor Boy' that he is in no hurry for heterosexual liaisons. Given the growing sexual and moral permissiveness which came to mark the 1960s, Don's initial proposal to Barbara in the number 'A Swinging Affair', with its insistence that 'they play it cool', 'stay as free as the air', have a fling' and 'enjoy the magic but don't fall in love', appears initially permissive, if not promiscuous. However, these lyric sentiments are undercut by the choreography, as first Don and then Barbara dance flirtatiously with other people, and both become possessively jealous. By the time they reach the land of Strauss, *Die Fledermaus* and the waltz, Don admits his earlier senti-ments about 'swinging' were misplaced, as he sings the romantic ballad 'All At Once' and declares his love for her. As for Barbara, she tells Don that she has loved him 'ever since I was a little boy'. Though clearly not engaging with changing sexual attitudes in the manner of many 'New Wave' films, *Summer Holiday* reinforces Elizabeth Wilson's pertinent comment that 1960s 'sexuality was both to expand and flower in lib-erated fashion and to be organised within marriage' (Wilson 1980: 110).

In fact, the film almost seems to offer a deliberate riposte to the style and content of British New Wave cinema and its emphasis on social problems. The opening title sequence, shot in black and white, begins with a uniformed seaside brass band playing a version of 'Summer Holiday', though as the tide comes in and laps around their feet, thunder rolls and the rain comes down, they are forced to abandon their playing and run for shelter. As the number is taken up vocally by Cliff Richard, the lyrics extolling the virtues of a summer holiday, grainy actuality footage of a wet British summertime offers an ironic contrast, as holiday-makers shelter from the rain, walk along the rain-swept prom-enade, and a cricket match is abandoned. As Cyril (Melvyn Hayes) remarks, looking over the rain-soaked yard at the bus repair depot, 'there's nothing like a beautiful English summer's day, and this is cer-tainly nothing like one'. Worse, he calculates that, at best, they can afford a whole three hours on holiday in France. The gloom is dispelled by a transition to colour photography and some strident brass scoring, as Don arrives with a bus and a scheme to take it 'as a mobile hotel' through France. In a wonderful sequence that visually exploits the mechanical wizardry of the bus repair depot, Don leads the breezy up-tempo song 'Seven Days To A Holiday' as the mechanics get the bus ready. The factory, working for a living, and the gloomy black and white locations give way to the colour fantasy of carefree travel and the promise of romance in continental France.

This number works well, with clever lyrics, strong melodic lines and useful, energetic choreography making full use of the factory location. Unfortunately, other numbers are far less successful. 'Every Girl Is Beautiful' strays into the realm of the embarrassing, as stop-frame transitions turn old women and schoolgirls into scantily clad young women. The 'show' that Ron Moody and the cast put on to convince the French magistrate to let them go, with its slapstick routines and speeded-up motion, fails to convince. 'Really Waltzing' makes some good use of swirling camerawork, but the number fails to make the most of the underlying romantic concept. 'Dancing Shoes' has some witty lyrics based on well-known nursery rhymes and an effective syncopated beat, but the context in which the number occurs borders on the offensive; crossing into the former Yugoslavia and searching for food, they surround a peasant shepherdess and, whilst their intentions are clear to them, she is terrified by what she regards as their hostile behaviour. Matters get worse when she mistakenly believes that Don has proposed to her and the frenzied scene that follows is offensive in its clumsy caricature of the imagined exoticism of the villagers, who turn aggressive as the four men extricate themselves from the situation, their xenophobia confirmed by Cyril's comment 'I told you we should have gone to Blackpool'. The film's ending is partly redeemed by Cliff's two numbers 'The Next Time', a wistful solo shot against the background of the Parthenon, and 'Big News', as Don and Barbara announce their intention to marry and news comes through that London Transport have agreed to invest in Don's commercial project, the double-helix narrative of personal and professional success now fully realised. Far from rebels, the young people are supported by the benign influence of authority in the shape of the British Consulate in Greece, an indication that, faced with the inexplicable customs and hostility of 'foreigners', the British need to unite across any structural divides that might otherwise separate them. Stella, having tried her best to stop the bus throughout the film, seems reconciled to the promise of monetary success that Don now represents and begins to plan extending this to the United States, just as, in *Expresso Bongo*, imminent success for Bongo in the United States seems promised.

In fact, *Summer Holiday* failed to register in the United States, as did Richard's subsequent sixties films, *Wonderful Life* (1964), *Finders Keepers* (1966) and *Two A Penny* (1967). *Wonderful Life* has more than its share of eccentric silliness, not least a mild addiction to those speeded-up scenes that so bedevilled British popular cinema in the 1960s and 1970s. The plot could hardly be thinner, as Johnny (Cliff Richard), Jerry (Melvyn Hayes), Edward (Richard O'Sullivan) and the Shadows are sacked and blacklisted from serving on cruise ships. Landing in the Canary Islands, they become involved in the film being produced by aging, failing director Lloyd Davis (Walter Slezak) and starring Jenny Taylor (Susan Hampshire), whose lack of confidence in her abilities is obvious, unlike her relationship with Davis, who is actually her father. Johnny becomes romantically involved with her and, to boost her confidence, persuades the others to re-shoot Davis's scenes as a musical, where her talents (in combination with Richard's, of course) are better employed. Resolving problems put in their way through musical numbers, they almost manage to finish their clandestine musical, but Davis discovers what has been going on and puts a stop to it. After trading insults which mark their generational difference – Davis telling Johnny that he is 'sick and tired of people like you flourishing their youth at me like a passport', Johnny replying that he is equally 'sick and tired of people like you who condemn young people for being shiftless and without purpose' – the two are reconciled. Both have produced half-good films and decide to put the two good halves together to make one good film. At its premiere, with an audience that includes aged Chelsea Pensioners and young Boy Scouts and Girl Guides, Davis and his son-in-law sing 'Youth And Experience', a bright compelling number arguing for the need for young and old to 'march side by side', an ending redolent of the similar cross-generation reconciliation that marked the conclusion to *The Young Ones*.

Reconciliation, co-operation and community are key themes in the film, most clearly seen in the number 'All Kinds Of People' which, with its extended, hugely energetic and convincingly professional dance sequence (choreographed by Gillian Lynne), valorises the virtues of co-operation, as the number's lyrics announce that 'You may be French, Greek or Spanish, when you dance those frontiers vanish'. This sentiment sits rather uneasily with the early xenophobic nostalgia of 'Home', a variety-inspired number in which the three male protagonists, fantasising as they become lost in the Canary sand dunes, dance and sing on board a River Thames barge and pine for icons of 'Britishness' such as 'mods and rockers', 'fish and chips and racing tips' and the 'rain pouring down'. A distinct unevenness characterises both Sidney Furie's direction and the numbers in the film. Lyrics reach the depth of banality as in 'Wonderful Life', which exhort us to 'follow the sun / and you'll have lots of fun' and to 'go to the places that you've never been / see all the people that you've never seen' and lack the catchy minor-key driving melodic lines later played by The Shadows in 'On The Beach', with its phrase from The Beatles' 'Twist And Shout'. In the same way, early attempts to engage with the new mood of swinging sexuality in 'A Girl In Every Port' simply translates as chauvinist nonsense.

The film is interesting though for its self-reflexive qualities, not least in its referencing of film production and film history, often using big production numbers to do so. In 'A Little Imagination' where Johnny tries to bolster Jenny's self-esteem, a series of visual transitions take them, singing and dancing, away from the restaurant table to an ocean liner, an eighteenth-century ballroom, a 'wild west' corral, a 'Busby Berkeley' set, a beach picnic, a street of American cheerleaders and a Spanish flamenco set, the lyrics and melody forming an aural bridge across these transitions. In the romantic number 'In The Stars', a sort of *Sound Of Music* on sand, Johnny and Jenny serenade each other, with the lushest of 'impossible orchestrations' behind them. Though Davis acknowledges that he is not making 'some New Wave or avant-garde film', Johnny and the others draw their inspiration from film history as imagined and recounted by Richard O'Sullivan. 'We Love A Movie' triggers a semi-reverential but mostly ironic reprise of (mostly American) films, ranging from the antics of Chaplin and the Marx Brothers, by way of genres such as the western, the musical and the gangster, a wonderfully choreographed evocation of *West Side Story* and the 'youth problem' film, only here with drawn flick-knives being used to sharpen a pencil, through to replication of the James Bond films. Humbled by this rapid trip through films 'that will live in the annals of human existence' Jerry, in his usual mood of pessimistic defeat, remarks 'and we think we can make a film; that's the funniest joke of all'. It is a moment of genuine self-deprecation befitting the significant absence of British product in this canonical trot through film history, though one belied by their determination to complete their film, despite the borrowed, ramshackle equipment and the lack of corporate backing enjoyed by Davis for his rotten, outdated film. It is hard not to read this as some meta-textual comment on the British film industry and its relationship with its dominant American counterpart.

Wonderful Life deserves better critically than it has usually got. Though there is much in the film that roots it in 'Britishness', not least the accents and the running obsessive joke about tea, under Furie's direction it does have the structure, energy and optimism that is clearly designed to emulate the Hollywood musical. The numbers mostly work, enabling problems to be overcome, reinforcing the development of the romantic sub-plot, and delivering a range of pleasures designed to appeal to a wide audience demographic in ways which matched the overall development of Cliff Richard's career. By the time of *Two A Penny*, that appeal had begun to fragment, propelled in part by Richard's increasing self-proclaimed religiously inspired moral beliefs.

Two A Penny is a low-budget oddity, even though Richard gives a strong dramatic performance and considers it his best film. The most privileged performance space is given over to American evangelist Billy Graham at Earl's Court. A religious melodrama, Richard plays Jamie Hopkins, a cynical, manipulative, irresponsible and untrustworthy art student who dabbles in the world of drug dealing and whose sexual promiscuity is limited only by the conversion of his girlfriend Carol (Ann Holloway) to Christianity. With strong naturalist performances from Dora Bryan and Avril Angers, the film occupies the rather sordid underbelly of a London glamorised in Antonioni's *Blow-Up* (1967). The numbers are limited to the opening title song, an assertive, defiant expression of Jamie's sense of his individuality, the ambiguous romantic ballad 'I'll Love You Forever Today' sung non-diegetically, an energetic pub performance of 'Twist And Shout' sung to an audience who would prefer 'We'll Meet Again', and the passionate 'Questions' as Jamie wanders through a London park, on the cusp of conversion to Christianity. Denied a reasonable circuit release, the film plunged into obscurity, despite its curiosity value as a corrective to the dominant celebratory depiction of 'swinging London'.

'Trad jazz' and the pop musical

Though *The Young Ones*, *Summer Holiday* and *Wonderful Life* enjoyed considerably larger budgets, in the early years of the decade a number of other bands and performers made significant contributions to the pop musical. Often less polished than the Cliff Richard vehicles, with production values that included black and white photography, many of these films convey a greater sense of the excitement that surrounded the emergence of pop music in the early 1960s and its central importance in the construction of youth culture at that time. Norrie Paramor, a significant influence on Cliff Richard, was the musical director on Richard Lester's *It's Trad Dad!* (1962), a film that in part reflected the current popularity of British traditional jazz that had started with the chart success enjoyed by Chris Barber's 'Petite Fleur' in 1959. With appearances from Barber and his Band, Ottilie Patterson, Kenny Ball and his Jazzmen, Terry Lightfoot and the New Orleans Band, Acker Bilk and his Paramount Jazzband, and Bob Wallis and his Storeyville Jazz Men, together with American pop singers such as Chubby Checker, Del Shannon, Gene Vincent and Gary (US) Bonds, the film centred around attempts by two youngsters (British pop singers Helen Shapiro and Craig Douglas) to organise a jazz and pop music festival, despite the hostility of local figures of authority. In spite of this clichéd plot, the film's performances are shot with considerable verve by Lester who, two years later, was to break the mould with *A Hard Day's Night* (1964).

Audience familiarity with the traditions of New Orleans jazz had been developed in Britain during the 1950s on radio and on record by bands such as Humphrey Lyttelton and Ken Colyer. Given a distinctly British inflection by bands such as those of Acker Bilk, Kenny Ball and Terry Lightfoot, 'trad jazz' achieved popular commercial success in the early 1960s, with numbers such as Bilk's 'Buona Sera' and 'That's My Home', and Ball's 'Samantha' and 'Midnight In Moscow'. The parodic commercialism of The Temperance Seven – playing crisp, organised imitations of white 1920s jazz in numbers like 'You're Driving Me Crazy' not only in *It's Trad Dad!*, but in *Take Me Over* (1963) and *The Wrong Box* (1966) – and the huge commercial success of Bilk's 'Stranger On The Shore' in 1961 were far from the purists' concept of black New Orleans traditional jazz, but were hugely popular with sections of British youth, Significant sales of traditional jazz long-playing albums confirmed the vogue, as did the existence of dedicated divisions of record labels such as Pye-Jazz.

The growing importance of different forms of popular music to the British film industry in the early 1960s is reflected in the appearance of traditional jazz bands in musical films produced as 'B' features. Using stars who were not always the most conventionally photogenic and with a limited acting range, formats were developed which allowed their music to be privileged above all else. In the same year as *It's Trad Dad!*, Rank distributed *Band Of Thieves* (1962) starring Bilk and his Band at the centre of a comic heist narrative. Produced by Lance Comfort with music by Bilk and the increasingly ubiquitous Norrie Paramor, the film features a dozen instrumental numbers either in performance or strung across the soundtrack, beginning with a pre-credits number that leaves little doubt as to the point of this exploitation vehicle. From this opening concert in Gauntstone prison, we discover that the band are actually prisoners themselves, encouraged to play by one of those woolly, warm-hearted, ineffective liberal prison governors (Geoffrey Sumner) who punctuate British cinema. However, on their release, an engagement at the Thieves Kitchen, a club owned by the upper-class Honourable Derek Delaney (Jimmy Thompson) leads back into a life of crime, as he cracks safes while they play at nearby concerts. A contract with record executive Victor Henry (Norrie Paramor) of Jazz Records propels Acker and the boys to fame, a success charted in the popular music papers *Disc*, *Melody Maker* and *New Musical Express*. All goes well until Derek's girlfriend Anne (Jennifer Jayne) reveals herself as a police-woman. Back in prison, Acker is paroled to make a solo appearance on BBC Television playing Norrie Paramor's composition 'Lonely', a number that charted in September 1962.

None of this narrative matters, of course, since what the film is about is exposing as much of Bilk and his music as is possible. In this, the film is extremely successful. In addition to the vocal numbers 'Kissin' sung by Carol Deene (whose only other appearance was in the 1963 Tommy Steele vehicle *It's All Happening*) and Bilk's 'All I Want To Do Is Sing', the film is peppered with opportunities and excuses for the band to perform instrumental numbers, for their music to be heard diegetically (as on the prison governor's record player) or non-diegetically on the soundtrack. Though class is clearly inscribed through different characters such as the Duchess of Hartlepoole (Maudie Edwards) and Derek's friends whose riches are there for the picking, it makes no impact other than to provide mild satirical humour, not least in the Duchess's blind faith and optimism about recidivists such as Get Away (Arthur Mullard). Other comic pleasures come from the undermining of the stern authoritarian figure of the Chief Warder, the almost unquestioning acceptance of pervasive petty crime, and the easy use of contemporary terminology such as 'swinging', 'square' and 'crazy, man'. The film's exuberant celebration of popular British culture is heightened by constant references to films such as *The Leather Boys* and *The League Of Gentlemen*, to BBC Television's *Juke Box Jury* and BBC Radio's *Trad Tavern*. Get Away is told that, like the film *Cleopatra*, 'I expect you will both be released one day'. Shots of a recording session, Acker's appearance in a BBC Television studio, and of couples enjoying dancing at the Thieves Kitchen club, inscribe the film firmly within the self-reflexive world of entertainment, all of which serves to normalise the pleasures associated with the consumption of entertainment.

Bilk made subsequent appearances in shorts and 'B' films including *Four Hits And A Mister* (1962), *It's All Over Town* (1963) and *The Ghost Goes Gear* (1966), though 'trad jazz' waned in popularity fairly quickly. However, before it did, Kenny Ball followed up his appearance in *It's Trad Dad!* with *Live It Up!* (1963). Directed by Lance Comfort, it stars David Hemmings as pop-obsessed David Martin who dreams of becoming a pop star rather than, like his friends, working in London as a despatch rider for the GPO. Despite opposition from his father, who wants him to 'get a proper job', but with some encouragement from his mother who had a brief flirtation with the variety stage as a young girl, Dave and the other three members of the group manage to save enough to record a demo disc. Rejecting the initial name of 'The Maggots' (a clear reference to the early influence of The Beatles), the group call themselves 'The Smart Alecs' and set out to break into the seductive world of pop, film and television. They are not helped by a series of accidents and the loss of the demo tape. Old-time impresario Mike Moss offers them a gig in Glasgow which working for the GPO prevents them from doing, a promising appearance on live television gets cancelled, and the efforts appeared doomed until the demo tape turns up in a film studio, attracting the attention of American film producer Mark Watson, earning them a slot singing 'Don't You Understand' in a film that promises to be not unlike *Live It Up!*.

With eleven musical numbers including current chart hits from Heinz and two numbers from Kenny Ball and his Jazzmen, as well as an appearance from American rocker Gene Vincent, *Live It Up!* unashamedly privileges musical performance over plot and narrative. The search for a breakthrough into a pop-dominated entertainment business offers an opportunity for a youthful and star-struck David Hemmings to wander through the spaces of contemporary cultural production, where he and the film's audience witness the 'work' that goes into pop record production, live television shows and film production. The motivation for each of the numbers ranges from the non-existent to more integrated plot-driven demands, by way of music 'imagined' in a romantic fantasy sequence. These numbers are handled effectively, enabling them to achieve their impact 'on the basis of songs and singers, rather than on elaborate production' (McFarlane 1999: 155). There are also some pleasing interactions between young Dave and his father, whose aspirations for his son, based on an increasingly outdated and deferential work ethic, reveal something of the structural upheavals at work within British society and culture during the 'swinging 60s'. Like so many of these British 'B' feature programme-fillers, deficiencies in production values are countered by the appearance of 'real-life' characters from the world of British entertainment including, in the this case, television's Peter Haigh, film critic Peter Noble and *Daily Mirror* columnist Nancy Spain. Such appearances only serve to heighten the consistent blurring between the realm of constructed film diegesis and the 'real' that stems from the presence of 'known and knowable' pop music stars and the layering of identities which their screen presence involves.

Youth, gender, pop music and dreams of (male) success

This emphasis on mobility, as young people traverse class, sex, spatial and generational boundaries which had previously constrained them, is evident in Anglo-Amalgamated's *Play It Cool* (1962). Directed by Michael Winner, whose only previous experience had been directing a naturist documentary, the film featured Billy Fury, with Norrie Paramor as musical director. Though born in Liverpool, Fury's success pre-dated the so-called Mersey Sound that erupted with The Beatles. A genuinely talented rocker with the haircut to match, Fury achieved considerable chart success from early 1959, though by late 1961 was capable of producing bitter-sweet romantic ballads such as 'I'd Never Find Another You'. In the film, Billy Universe (Fury) and the Satellites seem to be on the verge of success with an appearance at the 'Golden Goblet' pop contest to be held in Brussels. At Gatwick Airport, they come across Anne (Anna Falk) and her wealthy father Sir Charles Bryant (Dennis Price) who is determined to stop her involvement with unsavoury pop singer Larry Grainger (Maurice Kaufmann) by sending her overseas. After the plane is delayed and they miss the contest (though not before Fury performs highly reverbed lip-synched versions of 'I Think You're Swell' and 'Once Upon A Dream' on board the plane and in the waiting lounge), the band persuade Anne to join them in night-time London and look for Grainger. Driving in their defiantly open-topped car, Fury sings 'Let's Paint The Town', declaring that 'the town is full of kids like us / raring to go'. What follows is a tour through London clubs where 'everybody is welcome' and where 'cool' dancers with cockney accents mix with poets and upper-crust academics asking whether 'the Twist has an inner meaning'. Crooners like Danny Williams singing 'Who Can Say' with violin accompaniment mix with the brash guitar and saxophone riffs of Shane Fenton's Twist number 'Like Magic' and dancer Lionel Blair's cabaret-style floor show. At the up-market Lotus Club, Helen Shapiro performs 'I Could Cry My Heart Out', an on-screen Norrie Paramor conducting the eight-piece band, and American star Bobby Vee is given similar privileged performance space for his all-too-obviously lip-synched version of 'At A Time Like This'. For all its concern with the pleasures of 'cool' London youth, this remains a steadfastly pluralistic musical mix, exploiting current chart favourites and dance fashions such as The Twist, whilst locating them in the commercial continuum that is the music industry.

It is these numbers that provide the appeal of the film, not the largely inconsequential narrative as Anne is prevented from marrying the heartless egotist Grainger, nor the execrable acting from Billy Fury. Though this and other films have young people at their centre, their quest for hedonistic pleasure is not seen as essentially disruptive or anti-social. If anything, the opposite is the case, as young people increasingly seem to occupy a moral centre-ground which, whilst driven by the pleasures of popular music and its increasingly sexualised culture, makes a stand against the oppressive, corrupt, hypocritical, often commercial or simply empty values of the older generation. By the mid-1960s, youthful pleasures are increasingly located cinematically in London, in what have been called the Swinging London films, often offering unprecedented narrative emphasis on female pleasure and sexual identity:

> Swinging London films pivot around single young women (and sometimes men), defying convention as they try to fulfil their ambitions and find romance in a modern and uniquely unconventional London. Many of the films are structured around the story of a single girl who arrives in London, a city that comes to represent a site of pleasure and autonomy. (Luckett 2000: 233)

Arguably, this shift towards London and the female is signalled at the climax of *Billy Liar* where, for all Billy's struggle for identity, his desire for liberation and autonomy, it is Liz (Julie Christie) who gets the train to London. Whilst this rejection of the masculine dominated (often regional) narratives of the New Wave and its replacement with narratives centred on issues around female sexuality and set in London is evident in films such as *Darling* (1965), *The Knack* (1965) and *Georgy Girl* (1966), it is far less evident in musical films of the mid-1960s which, whilst often acknowledging the growing significance of a new feminine perspective, continued to be driven by male protagonists. This shift away from the realist 'social problem' film of the early 1960s towards vehicles which were more accepting of the openly hedonistic pursuit of pleasure, towards what Murphy characterises as 'zany optimism' (Murphy 1993: 71), is evident in two films featuring cockney pop star Joe Brown, *What A Crazy World* (1963) and *Three Hats For Lisa* (1965).

Based on Alan Klein's stage musical, directed by Michael Carreras with musical direction from Stanley Black, ABPC's *What A Crazy World* features Joe Brown, Marty Wilde and Freddy and the Dreamers, all of whom were enjoying chart success at the time. Though set in London, this is still a *regionalised* London, its distinctly localised references and inhabitants a world away from the more cosmopolitan metropolis of the later 1960s. With a dual narrative focussing on the habitual social delinquency of Herbie (Marty Wilde) and his resistance to work, and the attempt by Alf (Joe Brown) to break free from his dysfunctional working-class family through his success in the pop music industry, the film successfully utilises music and dancing to both exclaim and interrogate the racist, sexist and homophobic discourse which seems to sit at the heart of this localised, problematic, London culture.

Like the New Wave films, *What A Crazy World* wrestles with a range of social issues that were seen by many to be at the heart of contemporary British society. One of the most important was the generation gap and the older generation's deep suspicion of young people. Articulated primarily through their apparent rejection of the work ethic and the drift into consumerism based on the growth of the leisure industries such as music, the bowling alley, the cinema, dance hall and amusement arcades, young people are the object of criticism by a generation which perceives itself as being profoundly different. As Sam (Harry H. Corbett), the irascible father, expresses it, when his generation wanted something, they worked hard to get it. Yet ironically, this older generation seems to be most at home with the leisure pursuits they value, dog-racing and bingo. Worse, the justification for their adherence to these forms of gambling and the easy money they promise are centred on the possibilities they provide to buy the very consumer items which young people are condemned for wanting. A crazy world, indeed. There is in this film, despite the overt criticism, actually a benign tolerance towards young people, expressed by The Common Man (Michael Ripper) in the often-repeated phrase 'bleeding kids', which forms a repeated coda at the end of many of the film's sequences and is said with an implied ambiguity.

Class, so central to British New Wave cinema, is here largely a given. With the exception of Fred, Doris's well-spoken boyfriend, this particular narrative universe is inhabited by the London working class. Alf (Joe Brown) and his family are crowded into their council flat and everything about their existence resonates with what are coded as working-class values and attitudes, from the physically overbearing patriarchial dominance of Sam, the willing resilience of Mum (Avis Bunnage) and her preferred domain of Bingo, the dynamics of sibling rivalry, through to the truancy and indifference of younger brother Joey (Michael Goodman). For such characters as Alf, the only escape from the dole or a mind-numbing job is through success in a glamour profession such as popular music.

Though the protagonists are male, issues of gender are far from ignored, not least in the number 'Brothers And Sisters', sung as Alf's sister Doris (Grazina Frame) orchestrates the domestic chores. The substance of the song revolves around perceived gender distinctions, Doris's supposed sexual activities coming in for criticism, the boys' anti-social attitudes posited as a matter of regret for the parents. *Supposed* may be wrong; as boyfriend Fred arrives at the flat, Doris spread out on the sofa, all short skirt and legs, says of Fred's dinner, 'I kept it hot for you Fred' – there is the suggestion that more is being referred to than the dinner.

There is a great deal of discursive material about work and the work ethic in the film. Youth unemployment seems not only endemic but is imbued with cultural respectability. When two members of the gang do get a job painting park railings, they keep it quiet from the rest. Even then, they are not the world's most dedicated workers, acutely conscious of their entitlement to lunch breaks. For much of the time and for most of the characters, their social structure revolves around the Employment Exchange and the 'thirty bob a week' they receive in social benefit. Though they rail against the limitations to their lives this involves, their commitment for much of the film is to the pursuit of leisure, not work. The fact that part of these limitations are overtly racist attitudes, rather cringingly expressed (aesthetically and ideologically) in the number 'Our Labour Exchange', with its Chinese and calypso musical inflection, seems not here to be an issue. For Alf, whom Mr Gold refers to as a 'budding Lionel Bart', success comes through the song he writes, but even then it is dependent on his willingness to ignore prevailing social and moral codes by switching tapes so that Mr Gold finally gets to hear his song, this despite protestations from the secretary (whose father 'has a business and a car' and is clearly coded as middle class) that Alf 'can't do that'. Intriguingly, though a montage sequence using headlines from the *New Musical Express* informs us that Alf's song is a huge success and makes number one in the hit parade, this neither excites Alf nor, more significantly, comes to the notice of his family. Despite seeing and hearing his hit being played on the family record player, Alf and the family seem as locked into the environment and its conflicts at the end of the film as they were at the beginning. Of course, as with all musicals, the extra-textual knowledge enjoyed by audiences is crucial in understanding the film's meanings; Joe Brown and this song are *in real life* a big hit, so a brief stare at the camera by Brown in the closing moments of the film is enough to take us beyond other readings the text offers us.

Herbie is even more firmly rooted in the lumpen proletariat. His entire family is either in gaol or is awaiting sentence, and he himself is awaiting the psychiatrist's report before his next court appearance. Crime is his line of work, something he pursues with habitual dedication throughout the film. Interesting, though the respectable working-class characters warn others away from Herbie and regard his propensity towards violence as dangerous, the film's narrational perspective fails to condemn him. This rebellious attitude is partly endorsed, measured not only by the screen time he enjoys, but also by the overshadowing physical presence that Wilde has over other characters.

The film ends with a reprise of the title song, passed around the characters as the end credits appear. Herbie's segment of this closing number tells us that he is going to gaol, but the song implicates him in the community despite this as he links hands with the rest of the cast in a cinematic curtain call. Shot on location in a London housing estate, with the sides of the tenement flats framing the cast in the foreground, these closing shots combine new-wave social realism with overt theatricality. In fact, the film is a peculiar hybrid, at one level sharing concerns of the kitchen-sink dramas which dominated much of British cinema in the late 1950s and early 1960s, whilst at the same time betraying the stage origins of Alan Klein's script, expressed most clearly through the theatrical aesthetic which characterises many of the numbers, from the opening number at the Employment Exchange with its rather wooden, stilted and clichéd choreography to the closing finale.

Rejecting the black and white photography and realist aesthetic which dominates a significant element of *What A Crazy World*, Anglo-Amalgamated's *Three Hats For Lisa* seems to have been imbued with that 'zany optimism' and hedonistic frivolity which marks the shift in sixties British cinema away from 'New Wave' towards 'Swinging London'. Though set in a London which remains partly rooted in work, with its urban-industrial dockland locations, the opening overhead panoramic shots and Joe Brown's vocal to 'This Is A Special Day' indicate an increasingly glamorous, attractive metropolis driven by the pursuit of leisure and entertainment. Johnny Howjego (Brown) is besotted with 'young, beautiful, single, famous, rich' Italian film star Lisa Milan (Sophie Hardy) who has a passion for collecting hats. Determined to meet her when she visits London, Johnny persuades girlfriend Flora (Una Stubbs) and Sammy (Dave Nelson) to join him in meeting her at London Airport. His euphoria at being kissed by Lisa is expressed in 'King Of The Castle', sung and danced on the airport rooftop, a transformational space which marks off internationalised, cosmopolitan London from Johnny's earthly working-class London roots.

Escaping from the attentions of her cynical press agent (Peter Bowles), Lisa takes up Johnny's offer to see London. What follows is a cinematic display of tourist London, with Brown singing 'London Town'. Though the lyrics and visuals have room for an element of self-deprecating deflation, declaring that London 'may not look as good as New York' and acknowledging that sunshine is far from ever-present, this is compensated for by shots of Hyde Park, the River Thames, St Pauls and Tower Bridge. However, Johnny is determined to show Lisa the 'real, rough-as-hell' London, centred on Bermondsey. Improbably, taxi-driver Sid (Sidney James) joins in the song, the lyrics extolling the 'happy smiling razor-slashed faces of the people I love' and other delights such as the school that was burnt down, the gas works, and relatives who are incarcerated in prison. However, this Bermondsey is characterised by an internationalist exoticism that serves to emphasise London as the 'capital of the world'. Much later in the film, the newly built Post Office Tower, a potent symbol of thrusting modernist London, is given prominence, though Johnny, Sid and the gang use its still unfinished restaurant space to cook some sausages in a frying pan. Though there are references to the fact that the tower restaurant will turn slowly round offering panoramic views of central London so that 'the rich people won't have to turn their necks', this is a London in which the connections between rich and poor, Hyde Park and Bermondsey, are unruptured, its diversity to be celebrated, not condemned.

The film's flimsy narrative quest is announced in 'Three Hats For Lisa', a number marked by some outstanding choreography from Gillian Lynne. The quest becomes problematic when Lisa announces that she wants to 'acquire' a bowler hat, a soldier's fur Busby and a policeman's helmet. Lisa's determination to steal the hats causes palpitations for her press agent, but also serves as an excuse for several numbers including 'Cockney Kids' and 'Covent Garden' with its 'Puccini and pomegranates' and dance codes that mingle barrow boy and ballet. Gillian Lynne's choreography consistently outshines Leslie Bricusse's music and lyrics, which in turn take Joe Brown a long way from his early pop music successes.

Much the same can be said about Billy Fury's career trajectory in *I've Gotta Horse* (1965). Though Jack Good had constructed Fury's mean and moody image in the late 1950s in ABC's television show *Oh Boy!*, this image began to dissipate in the early 1960s, largely through the influence of Larry Parnes, who is given co-writing credit for *I've Gotta Horse*. If *Play It Cool* had drawn its energy from his image as a rocker, *I've Gotta Horse* reflects Fury's growing self-indulgence and personal disenchantment with the popular music industry as much as the changes in the British film industry of the mid-1960s and the ways in which it was able to exploit popular music. As Storm Tempest, Fury was to give an ironic performance of his former self in *That'll Be The Day* (1973), but here, Fury plays an established pop star who is more interested in his animals than his career. On a whim, he buys a horse, gets involved in horse-racing and has to juggle these pleasures with the rigours of rehearsing and appearing in the seaside variety show run by Mr Bartholemew (Bill Fraser), much to the aggravation of manager Hymie Campbell (Michael Medwin). These provide ample opportunity for Fury to perform several numbers including 'Stand By Me' and the 'Soft Shoe'. In the latter, Ross Taylor's choreography tries to blossom as the number escapes its stage-bound diegesis out onto location, but only serves to place Fury firmly within mainstream entertainment tradition. Fury's number 'I Like Animals', sung in a pet-shop with some stage-school children, clearly references his real-life preference for animals over people, but represents a nadir in his performative talents. Numbers performed by The Gamblers and The Bachelors give the film its quota of contemporary pop sounds, but overall the film reflects a serious loss of direction, not just for Fury, but for the pop musical itself.

The film makes nodding use of conventional generic trappings with its backstage scenes and the uneasy romantic relationship between Billy and Jo (Amanda Barrie), the complications of gender politics expressed in her big production number 'Men'. However, the film's narrative centre consistently reverts to the scenes structured around horses, the attempts to conceal one in the theatre and, of course, the horse-racing. Fury's sentimental number 'Tell Me Why' laments the death of his horse, and Billy's career takes a dive, leading to manager Hymie's Yiddish-inspired number 'Problems'. This problem is resolved when Hymie buys another horse for Billy (actually Fury's own horse Anselmo), though the horse's appearance in the Derby coincides with Fury's own at the opening of the show. The film's affirmation of hedonism is glorified in the big production number 'You've Got To Look Right For The Part'. Asserting the power of costume and masquerade in contemporary fashion-conscious Britain, the number reinforces the notion of London as the centre of cosmopolitan internationalism. Costume serves to transcend class, as top-hatted Billy gets an invitation from Lord Bentley (Fred Emney) to join him in the owners' suite at Epsom. The opening of the show goes ahead on time, with Billy and the cast still wearing the top-hat and tails and expensive dresses they hired for Epsom, entertainment and pleasure flowing from race-course to seaside variety show in an attempt to suggest an effortless, irresistible flow of hedonistic energy.

Musical innovations: *A Hard Day's Night* (1964)

Though such films as *I've Gotta Horse* served a purpose in exploiting pop talent and widening its appeal, as well as helping to ensure the presence of British product in British cinemas, the reluctance of seasoned film-makers to undertake such projects is understandable. This was certainly the case in what became the best-known and most written-about British musical film of the 1960s, *A Hard Day's Night*, directed by Richard Lester and starring The Beatles. Associate producer Denis O'Dell has recounted his reluctance to be involved in the project when first approached, only being persuaded by his children who were already fans of The Beatles. At least one pop insider has considered that without American intervention in the shape of producer Walter Shenson, United Artist's UK chief Bud Ornstein and transplanted American director Richard Lester, 'British movie-makers would [not] have been capable of "getting" the Beatles' (Oldham 2001: 11).

The ultimate exploitation film, *A Hard Day's Night* was part of a three-picture deal signed by United Artists, who were keen to access album rights before the appeal of The Beatles melted away. In fact, sales of the long-playing album of the same name meant that the film, which cost £190,000, was 'to become the first-ever movie in history to go into profit while it was still before the cameras' (Carr 1996: 29). What gave the film its unlooked-for distinctive qualities were the songs (under the musical direction of George Martin), Alun Owen's script, the refreshing almost meta-textual performances from the Beatles and, perhaps above all, Richard Lester's direction. With his experience of working with BBC radio's *Goon Show* stars Peter Sellers and Spike Milligan – firstly in the television series *Idiot Weekly* and *A Show Called Fred* and subsequently in the short film *The Running, Jumping and Standing Still Film* (1959) – Lester's surrealist sensibility perfectly matched the irreverent off-hand cynicism which was an early hallmark of The Beatles. Collectively determined to avoid what was already becoming seen as the conventional pop musical format evident in Cliff Richard's films, director, scriptwriter and cast nonetheless produced a film that is, at one level, a version of the backstage musical, its 'one day in the life of' narrative culminating in the climactic television variety show in which The Beatles perform three numbers to a screaming audience. More than one critic has seen the film as 'remaining faithful to the traditions of the backstage musical' (Agajanian 2000: 96). However, the film refuses to implicate The Beatles within that wider entertainment tradition in ways that most pop musicals had done and were to continue to do. The difference is evident in the treatment of Lionel Blair and his dancers in *Play It Cool* and *A Hard Day's Night*. In the former, Blair and his dancers are given privileged performance space and the applause and appreciation they receive from the on-screen club audience positions the film audience into the same unquestioning acceptance. In *A Hard Day's Night*, Blair and his dancers occupy a more marginal filmic space, and it is Lennon's cynical cavortings and his ironic declamation 'Hey kids, why don't we do the show right here' which construct our own sense that we are watching something rebelliously refreshing.

Though there were some contemporary reservations about the film, the *Monthly Film Bulletin* considering the four lead characters 'too inexperienced' to make the best of the script, most reviews were favourable and recognised the distinctive qualities of the performances as well as Lester's direction. In America, though some struggled with the 'quaint dialect and slang expressions', Andrew Sarris called the film

> the *Citizen Kane* of jukebox musicals, a brilliant crystallisation of such diverse cultural particles as the pop movie, rock'n'roll, cinema verite, the nouvelle vague, free cinema, the affectedly hand-held camera, frenzied cutting, the cult of the sexless adolescent, the semi-documentary and studied spontaneity. (Yule 1994: 17)

With its hand-held black and white cinematography, *A Hard Day's Night* certainly resonates with the realist aesthetic of the New Wave films made earlier in the decade, though its more insular celebration of pop music hedonism and exuberant surrealism looks forward to that 'zany' quality associated with later sixties British cinema. However, although the film stood up well on its recent 2004 re-release, it is difficult to make a case for its enduring influence on the British musical. Indeed, one recent critic considered that

> *A Hard Day's Night* was actually the high point of a genre that has almost fizzled out . . . It may be that what The Beatles, Owen and Lester created was the template not for a sustainable movie genre, but rather for the pop video. (Edwards 2001: 14)

Their next film, *Help!* (1965), goes some way towards confirming this view since, with its heavily contrived plot, the main pleasures of the film reside in the musical sequences, many of which (such as 'Another Girl' and 'Ticket To Ride') resemble embryonic music videos. With the commercial success of *A Hard Day's Night* and the even more phenomenal success of the Beatles' records in Britain, the United States and globally, it was inevitable that their next picture, known as 'Beatles 2' until the title *Help!* was settled upon, attracted a much bigger £500,000 budget. Though the film was even more successful at the box-office and the album had pre-release orders of over one million copies in the US alone, the film is retrospectively regarded as much weaker than *A Hard Day's Night*. Complaints from Lennon that he felt like an extra in his own film and comments from McCartney that the film was a 'fun romp' indicated that all was not well. Despite the strength of the songs and an able cast that included Eleanor Bron, Leo McKern and Victor Spinetti, *Help!* somehow loses the engaged performances from The Beatles that had marked the previous film. Much of this stems from United Artists' concern to maximise the global commercial potential of The Beatles, as they moved away from being a localised 'Mersey Beat' and British pop phenomenon to the world's biggest-selling band. This transition is signalled at the beginning of the film as John, George, Paul and Ringo enter what appear to be the doors of their separate terrace houses, only for the interior shot to reveal that they lead to one giant spacious shared living space, full of quirky, contemporary gadgets. The villains' attempts to steal Ringo's ring seem to epitomise the demands that were now being placed on the group, demands that rapidly led to Lennon's view that the band had turned into a 'money-making machine' (Carr 1996: 53).

Lester's unabated zest for the surreal remains evident, confident enough to include the visual non-sequitor of an 'intermission'. Marc Behm and Charles Wood's script delivers a stream of comically inconsequential dialogue, as when Roy Kinnear's incompetent British laboratory scientist, asked what his electricity bill is like, answers that it's 'a long counterfoil'. Laboratory boss Professor Foot (Victor Spinetti) is out to 'rule the world – if he can get a government grant' and, in the meantime, remains obsessed with British incompetence and inferiority, as he uses a succession of futuristic but unreliable gadgets in his attempt to snatch the ring and rule the world. A Scotland Yard chief (Patrick Cargill) asks The Beatles, self-referentially, 'so how long do you think you will last?' More than one commentator has seen in these and other characters, such as the oriental high priest Clang (Leo McKern), a playful pastiche of the immensely successful cycle of Bond films *Dr No* (1962), *From Russia With Love* (1963) and *Goldfinger* (1964), a reference compounded by the use of the Bahamas and Switzerland for location shooting. The film also reveals Lester's reverence for the black comic humour associated with Peter Sellers, Spike Milligan and Harry Secombe; the one-dimensional oriental villains lead by Clang spring from those Goon-influenced negotiations with images from Britain's imperial past, an influence that is equally evident in the discordant soundtrack to the film's closing credits. Importantly, Lester's innovative and sympathetic filming of the numbers such as 'You've Got To Hide Your Love Away', 'Ticket To Ride', 'Another Girl' and 'I Need You' rescues the film from the inanities of the plot and some incipient racism. Lester's creative approach to visualising musical performance, already evident in *It's Trad Dad!* and *A Hard Day's Night*, is developed further in *Help!*: as Neaverson argues, 'The "Ticket To Ride" sequence is arguably the first time that the full potential of editing for pace and rhythm was prioritised above choreography in a pop film' (Neaverson 1997: 39).

Though Alexander Walker considered that the film 'hangs together remarkably well', he also recognised that The Beatles 'were trapped, physically and metaphorically, in their fame' (Walker 1974: 267) and that this impacted upon their performances. Neither The Beatles nor United Artists' Bud Ornstein were happy with the film and even Lester was of the opinion that critics and audiences would 'find nothing new about *Help!* There's not one bit of insight into a social phenomenon of our times' (Carr 1996: 73). In this, of course, he was mistaken, since the band themselves were a social phenomenon and the film reveals the shift away from identities and allegiances which were distinctly British towards what was to become the global appropriation of The Beatles. The film also seemed to confirm the sound economic sense of American financial investment in the British film industry, at a time when British popular music, its culture and style, 'made British society suddenly exciting, charismatic and fashionable' (Murphy 1992: 257).

Ultimately, what made *A Hard Day's Night* and *Help!* distinctive, what marks them off from other British pop musicals of the early and mid-1960s, is the music. Though it is possible to place the two films in that larger frame which saw the move away from representations of a Britain struggling to understand itself towards the energetic celebration of more superficial social pleasures, in some respects they represent a dead end. The global success of The Beatles was instrumental in helping forge the ubiquitous presence of pop music within cinema, but the cynical vacuity that haunts *Help!* somehow marks a final drift away from the authentic excitement which surrounded the early pop exploitation films. Significantly, John Boorman's *Catch Us If You Can* (1965) eschews performance and uses the music from the Dave Clark Five on the non-diegetic soundtrack for what is essentially an episodic fantasy on the escape from work and social responsibility into a world of glamour and fashion. Other films produced in 1965 still made use of an appetite for pop performance, such as *Gonks Go Beat* with its musical war between 'Beatland' and 'Balladisle', and *Pop Gear* in which radio DJ Jimmy Saville comperes a number of bands including The Animals, Herman's Hermits, The Spencer Davis Group and Billy J. Kramer and the Dakotas, making use of clips recycled from musical shorts such as *Swinging UK* (1964). However, though Clive Donner's *Here We Go Round the Mulberry Bush* (1967) with Traffic and The Spencer Davis Group, and *Mrs Brown, You've Got a Lovely Daughter* (1968) featuring Herman's Hermits, kept the pop musical alive as a distinctive genre, increasingly pop music was incorporated non-diegetically within cinema soundtracks. For some, the conclusion draw from this transmutation is that the pop film had 'by and large . . . faded into obscurity' (Stokes 1999: 122). Actually, far from fading away, the pop aesthetic seeped into other, and often more traditional, elements of British film-making in the late 1960s and beyond.

The impact of American investment on the British film musical: from *Half a Sixpence* to *Performance*

The appeal of Britain – and more specifically of London – as the centre of young, fashionable, pop-music-dominated culture where, in one of the key phrases of the time 'it's all happening', together with the international success of the British film industry with *Dr No* (1962), *Tom Jones* (1963) and *Billy Liar* (1963), attracted foreign film-makers and, more significantly, American money. Directors as distinct as Polanski, Truffaut and Antonioni chose London to shoot *Repulsion* (1965), *Farenheit 451* (1966) and *Blow Up* (1966). In differing ways, the intersection between directorial sensibilities and the London 'scene' make for interesting films, though the attraction of working within Britain was short-lived. Of more importance was the influx of American investment in British film-making, which became pronounced in 1965. A report from the National Film Finance Corporation calculated that it had been able to supply financial assistance to 17 per cent of the films produced in Britain in 1965, but that 64 per cent had been financed wholly or in part by American investment. With the success of British films such as *Goldfinger* at the American box-office, Universal, United Artists, MGM and the other US majors became convinced that 'to make a film in Britain was somehow to acquire a touchstone for success everywhere it was shown, especially in the American market' (Walker 1974: 288). At a pragmatic level, American investment was welcomed in many quarters, not least by those earning a living within the British film industry. However, others voiced concern about the effect on what they regarded as the distinctive qualities of British film; writing in 1969, Michael Balcon expressed his concerns about possible dilution: 'My most heartfelt hope for British films is that domination by American finance will not destroy all sense of consistent or distinctive style in pictures made in British studios' (Balcon 1969: 210).

As historical precedent might have suggested, this flow of American money into the British film industry was both significant and short-lived. Of the 76 feature films produced in Britain in 1967, 60 made use of American money. Budgets for individual films far exceeded those that the British industry was used to, as the American companies brought their blockbuster mentality with them. Such budgets only made sense if the films produced in Britain were successful at the American box-office and this eventually proved a problem, despite often using American directors such as Jack Smight, Franklin Schaffner and Robert Parrish. The unquestioning assumption that films based on 'happening' British culture would inevitably appeal to American audiences was sorely tested with films such as *Charlie Bubbles* (1968), *Three Into Two Won't Go* (1968) and *Isadora* (1968), especially at a time when American cinema was rediscovering its vernacular feet with films such as *The Graduate* (1967) and *Easy Rider* (1969). MGM's lamentable 'youth epic' *Alfred The Great* (1970) was final confirmation that Americanised visions of British culture were not guaranteed box-office.

Though these follies were played out across a range of genres, the musical film played its part, not least in the attempt to create big-budget musicals in the classical generic mould. Just as in the 1940s *London Town* had attempted an assault on the American market, so in the late 1960s American financed blockbuster musicals such as *Half a Sixpence* (1967) and *Goodbye, Mr Chips* (1969) were thought likely to have international appeal. However, American investment was not confined to mainstream products and supported some projects that signally failed to appeal to American audiences. Peter Watkins, having made a name with documentaries such as *Culloden* (1964) and *The War Game* (1965), was financed by Universal with a budget of $700,000 to direct his first feature film *Privilege* (1967). The film was considered 'offensive' by Rank executives, given limited distribution in Britain, and proved incomprehensible to American audiences. The story of a young pop star Steven Shorter (Paul Jones) who is cynically manipulated by the music industry (in the form of veteran Max Bacon), politicians and the church, the film offers some dazzling set pieces shot in rich colour, though the songs, from Jones and the George Bean Group, disappoint. This vision of pop music's subversive power that is all-too-easily manipulated seemed unattractive to both the adherents and the critics of pop culture at a time when youthful rebellion was becoming increasingly politicised, especially in the United States. In some ways ahead of its time, *Privilege* anticipated later films such as *Tommy* (1975) and *Pink Floyd The Wall* (1982) in realising the relationship between politics, society and popular music.

No such problems could have been anticipated when Paramount financed *Half a Sixpence* (1967). Based on the H.G. Wells novel *Kipps: The Story of a Simple Soul*, the stage musical had been written for Tommy Steele and enjoyed lengthy runs at the Cambridge Theatre in London in 1963 and at the Broadhurst Theater in New York in 1965.

This combination of a return to 'established' English literature and a proven Broadway run, together with the services of American director George Sidney, whose Hollywood musical credits included *Anchors Aweigh* (1945), *Show Boat* (1951) and *Pal Joey* (1957), must have allayed Paramount's aversion to risk. With an initial budget of $2,500,000, *Half a Sixpence* was 'meant to be an invigorating return to the engine-roaring musicals with big set-pieces' prompted by the huge commercial success of *The Sound of Music* (1965) (Walker 1974: 394). Unfortunately, and despite *The Sound of Music*, many of the musicals being produced in Hollywood in the late 1960s were destined for commercial failure and *Half a Sixpence* shared the neglect of *Doctor Doolittle* (1967), *Star!* (1968) and *Sweet Charity* (1968).

This and subsequent neglect is far from justified, since *Half a Sixpence* rebuffs that earlier 1950s criticism that Britain simply doesn't possess singing and dancing talent. The film's narrative centres on Arthur Kipps (Tommy Steele), who works as an impoverished draper's assistant at autocratic Mr Shalford's Edwardian clothing emporium. Arthur pledges his romantic allegiance to childhood sweetheart Ann (Julia Foster), each keeping half a sixpenny coin as a token of their love. After some energetic contact with actor Harry Chitterlow (Cyril Richard) and other theatre folk, Kipps learns that he has inherited huge wealth. He attracts the attention of the haughty upper-class Mrs Walsingham (Pamela Brown), her daughter Helen (Penelope Horner) and stuffy arrogant son Hubert (James Villiers). Despite their constant criticism of his manners and speech, Kipps is persuaded to become engaged to Helen, much to the disgust of Ann, who throws her half of the coin away. Gradually driven away by the gulf that separates him from the Walsinghams and their world, Kipps realises that he has always loved Ann and they get married. In the midst of planning his eleven-bedroomed house, Kipps learns that Hubert Walsingham, acting as his financial adviser, has fraudulently squandered his inheritance. Reduced to near poverty, Kipps and Ann find strength in their relationship, only to discover that the money Kipps previously invested in Chitterlow's play has paid dividends as it proves a smash stage success.

Although the film deflects much of Wells' early-twentieth-century socialist zeal, it engages with the British class divide. True, the opening number 'All In The Cause Of Economy' does offer an economic critique of Shalford's capitalist regime of 'buying things low and upping the price' and his harsh enforcement of shop discipline which will have 'none of that socialist muck in my emporium'. Shalford bullies Kipps into attending night school, but this is soon forgotten in the romance between Ann and Kipps and the fantasy of his unexpected inheritance.

Director Sidney works hard to foreground Kipps' working-class environment, the rigours of shop work (economically depicted through a series of still photographs), the intense pleasures of limited time off, as well as the shy, innocent clumsiness of the blossoming relationship between Kipps and Ann, only overcome in the number ''Alf A Sixpence' which allows the couple some physical intimacy through their dancing and song duet.

Kipps' contact with Chitterlow, his exuberant theatre world and its charged sexuality leads to the first intimation that he has come into money. Here, the world of entertainment is the mechanism that destabilises class position, in much the way that pop music and its culture was doing in the late 1960s. In the number 'Money To Burn', added for the Broadway version of the stage show and given considerable prominence in the film, Kipps' limited horizons are expressed in his desire to own and play a banjo, above everything else. In the fantasy space offered by the theatre stage, Gillian Lynne's energetic choreography perfectly expresses the emotional and physical release which Kipps experiences. Lynne's choreography is outstanding in what is perhaps the best number in the film, 'Flash, Bang, Wallop' as Kipps and Ann get married, and is consistently interesting in the other numbers. Sidney's direction, aided by Geoffrey Unsworth's crisp cinematography, is equally at home in the location sequences, most notably the rowing race at Henley, which he invests with real drama, the visuals and editing pace matched by the increased tempo of the soundtrack song. The issue of Kipps' class betrayal as he rows for the Walsingham set against his former shop colleagues is acknowledged as they call him a 'traitor', but remains secondary to the visual and aural excitement that permeates this sequence. David Heneker's music and lyrics produce some memorable songs, not least 'If The Rain's Got To Fall' (matched by Lynne's inventive, intelligent choreography for this sequence shot by the Thames) and the fetchingly expressive 'I Know What I Am' sung by Ann in her moment of crisis as she reaffirms her working-class roots and identity. Tommy Steele, now firmly ensconced in mainstream entertainment and hardly off-screen, gives a consistently strong performance and gets support from an equally strong cast of British actors. Steele himself had made sufficient impact to appear in the American musicals *The Happiest Millionaire* (1967) and *Finian's Rainbow* (1968) before returning to a career in British stage musicals such as *Scrooge* that has continued into the new century.

There are some irritating things, such as Sidney's insistence of soft-focus shots whenever an infatuated Kipps sees Helen Walsingham, but *Half a Sixpence* is a much better film than its reception and reputation suggests. It's perhaps easy to understand why, for American audiences, the harsh and unfeeling mannerisms of the upper class and their disdain for Kipps and his working-class world loses something of the impact that it had on British audiences. Hubert Walsingham's taut comment that 'you people are such prudes' is as important as Kipps' inability to cope with upper-class dinner etiquette in his decision to walk out on Helen and her friends. Moreover, the clear implication that wealth and happiness do not invariably co-exist represents a distinctly British sensibility, far from the optimism that so often surrounds the celebration of material acquisition in much of American cinema. Whilst Kipps' inheritance reveals the imperviousness of privilege based on material wealth, the class structure of Edwardian Britain remains firmly in place, each class hermetically sealed off from the other. However, in treating Mrs Walsingham and her brood wholly unsympathetically and placing Kipps at the film's narrative and moral centre, *Half A Sixpence* reflects contemporary convictions that class was becoming increasingly irrelevant in British society.

Though less convincing, the 1969 musical remake of *Goodbye, Mr Chips*, based on James Hilton's 1934 novel about a quintessentially British schoolmaster, must have seemed an equally bankable proposition for MGM. Directed by American Herbert Ross, the film starred Peter O'Toole, enjoying considerable adulation since his appearance in David Lean's *Lawrence Of Arabia* (1963), Petula Clark, who had enjoyed American chart success with 'Downtown' and other songs since 1964, and Michael Redgrave. Though Terence Rattigan's screenplay pushes the story forward so that it covers the Second World War and endures into the 1960s, *Goodbye, Mr Chips* is set in an England that seems far removed from 'swinging' Britain of the 1960s. Arthur Chipping (Peter O'Toole) is a rather staid, stern middle-class schoolmaster at Brookfield boys' public school, a stickler for discipline and decorum. An unwilling spectator at a music hall, he witnesses the exuberant Katherine Bridges (Petula Clark) in the number 'Flossie From Fulham'. They accidentally meet again on a European holiday and, despite their class differences and background, decide to marry. Despite hostility based on class prejudice that mars Chips' career, the couple remain happy until she is killed in an air raid, a startling point-of-view shot seen from the bomb itself. Unable to share the news of his long-awaited promotion with his wife, Chips settles back into devoted service as headmaster at Brookfield.

Ross tries hard to introduce a number of visual pyrotechnics into the film and Peter O'Toole gives a convincing performance, visibly aging across the years. However, neither Nora Kaye's choreography nor the songs from Leslie Bricusse impress. The *New York Times* review of the film on 6 November 1969 was of the opinion that 'the twelve songs haven't been so much integrated into the book as folded into it. Like unbeaten egg whites in a soufflé, they do nothing for the cause of levitation.' With the exception of Clark's music-hall number and the big show-business number staged at the boys' school, the numbers remain rather empty and emotionless. Given Bricusse's other triumphs with songs such as 'What Kind Of Fool Am I?' and the title theme to *Goldfinger*, the songs in *Goodbye, Mr Chips* disappoint.

Before the economic stringencies besetting the American majors hit home in 1970, American investment produced two outstanding, if very different, musical films. Both films offered a distinctive take on British, particularly English, identity, constructed through very different coded representations of London life. Both were successful in distinctly different ways and reflected not just the pluralistic discourses that influenced debates about national identity, but also the diversity that has been a consistent feature of British film-making. One film drew its energies from that long-established relationship British cinema had with British literary and theatrical heritage and with songwriters working within an essentially mainstream show-business tradition, the other engaged with the challenges posed by what were perceived as the more radical components of the new youth-orientated popular music and its emergent sub-culture. Both financed by American majors, their distribution and reception by audiences and critics were radically different. Carol Reed's *Oliver* (1968) won six Academy Awards: Best Picture, Best Director, Best Musical Score, Best Art Direction, and Best Sound, together with a special award for Onna White's choreography. By contrast, Donald Cammell and Nicholas Roeg's *Performance*, a dark and disturbing take on contemporary British culture and described by one critic as 'the greatest British film ever made' (MacCabe 1998: 24), so alarmed Warner Bros that its release was delayed for two years until 1970. In their very different ways, both films offer evidence of British cinema's ability to produce significant musical films that engage with the specific, though complex, inflections of British national culture.

Though both Paramount and MGM were disappointed with *Half a Sixpence* and *Goodbye, Mr Chips*, Columbia had every right to be optimistic over their agreement to finance John Woolf's Romulus Films' production of *Oliver!*, based on Lionel Bart's stage musical. With its record-breaking 2,618 West End performances and its sixteen songs (not all of them used in the film), four of which entered the British Top Twenty and one of which, 'As Long As He Needs Me', gave Shirley

Bassey a continuous chart hit for six months from August 1960 to January 1961, it was the sort of apparently risk-free vehicle that merited the blockbuster treatment. As so often with big-budget British musicals in the past, the film drew upon transatlantic talent including American musical director John Green and Canadian choreographer Onna White, as well as an array of British technicians, including cinematographer Oswald Morris. The film was directed by Carol Reed, who made his directorial debut in 1935 with *Mr Midshipman Easy* and had become a leading figure in the British industry. Reed had achieved international recognition with films such as *Odd Man Out* (1946), and *The Third Man* (1949) and a reputation for being particularly skilled at literary and stage adaptations. John Box, the production designer, had worked on *Lawrence Of Arabia* (1962), *Dr Zhivago* (1965) and *A Man For All Seasons* (1966). Above all, the film was enlivened by Lionel Bart's music and lyrics that managed to give a pronounced contemporary cockney inflection to Charles Dickens' 1838 novel whilst deflecting the element of menace that had been a feature of David Lean's non-musical version of *Oliver Twist* (1948).

The power of the music and the sweeping scale of the numbers rather dwarf the character of Oliver (Mark Lester) himself, who in this version is as much an anonymised 'item of mortality' as he is at the beginning of Dicken's novel. In fact, Oliver and Lester (his voice dubbed by the musical director's daughter Kathy Green) is handed the weakest, least effective numbers or parts of numbers such as 'Where Is Love?'. This fails to matter, given the exuberant staging and performance of ensemble numbers such as 'I'll Do Anything', 'Pick A Pocket Or Two', and 'Be Back Soon'. The film is rightly remembered for big production numbers such as 'Food Glorious Food' in which, at the beginning of the film, the desire for some decent food of the kind enjoyed by Bumble (Harry Secombe) and the workhouse governors prompts Oliver's ejection from this dystopian world into one in which there is underlying structure and order, though Oliver has to make a long and often painful voyage to discover his place within it. Along the way, he comes into contact with the subterranean criminal world of juvenile pickpockets and thieves lead by Fagin (Ron Moody), the altogether more menacing world of Bill Sykes (Oliver Reed) and the more benign upper-middle-class genteel world of Mr Brownlow (James O'Conor). Of course, in that web of coincidences which drives Dickens' novels, Oliver is Brownlow's blood-relation, but in the film this has less importance than the implication that, with the exception of the truly wicked, Oliver is part of a much wider organic London community which, whatever distinctions may superficially separate them, has a place for everyone. This sense of community is constructed in the extravaganza 'Consider Yourself', where 'nobody tries to be la-di-da or uppity / there's a cup of tea / for all'. Meat porters, washer women, street orphans, chimney sweeps, road menders, newsboys, street entertainers, middle-class gentlemen, policemen and a host of others including the Artful Dodger (Jack Wild) and his fraternity of minor criminals co-exist in mutually inter-dependent harmony.

When the spatial locus shifts to Brownlow's Georgian terrace in Bloomsbury, it includes a similar mix of people, professions and classes, from the serving girls with their street cries, window cleaners, smartly dressed schoolchildren and marching soldiers. In another big production number, Onna White's busy choreography to 'Who Will Buy?' conveys a strong sense of a community essentially at one with itself. Class distinctions are not erased, but they serve as parts of a much greater organic whole, though one driven by the necessity of commodity exchange. Morris's swooping panoramic camerawork, Box's clean vibrant set and costume colours, and Green's carefully nuanced and euphorically paced orchestration construct what Stanley Green calls a 'sentimentalised and sanitised view of colourful, picturesque London in 1830' (Green 1988: 212), its utopian harmonies interrupted only by the presence of Bill Sykes at the end of the number.

Though the combined handling of these big production numbers is extremely effective, Bart's numbers also provide important moments of character introspection, such as 'As Long As He Needs Me' sung by the loyal Nancy (Shani Wallis) or Fagin's comically inflected 'Reviewing The Situation' which serves to make him a loveable rogue driven by a perfectly reasonable sense of self-preservation rather than an irredeemable villain like Sykes. Equally, Harry Secombe's perfectly pitched delivery renders 'Boy For Sale' a deeply moving, wistful lament for the harsh cruelties of the Victorian workhouse system, as he trudges through the snow with Oliver, looking for somewhere to off-load the boy. Though the film is not without an element of social criticism, compounded in Hugh Griffith's drink-besotted magistrate's confirmation of the asinine qualities of the British legal system, Bart's music and Reed's direction mitigate against serious engagement with it, valorising instead the visual and sonic pleasures involved in this celebration of a late-1960s view of the increasing meaningless of the British class system. Though it exploits literary heritage, the film negates those elements of social criticism which are invariably inscribed within the Victorian novel, defusing its recognition of the structural imperatives which created juvenile crime and turning Fagin and his gang into lovable rogues, a comic parenthesis in an otherwise vibrant and robust community/nation.

The success of *Oliver!* was not enough to sustain the big budget musical, either in Britain or the United States, though Ronald Neame's *Scrooge* (1970) starring Albert Finney and Alec Guiness enjoyed some success. Ironically, even prior to its success on screen, Bart had suffered a serious decline in fortune; his 1965 stage musical *Twang!!!* was booed by audiences and only ran for eight performances in London (Staveacre 1980: 38). Whilst the successes of Tim Rice and Andrew Lloyd Webber were in the future, it appeared in the late 1960s that the 'Tin Pan Alley' tradition which Bart's music seemed to represent was being rendered increasingly obsolete by the emergence of rock music, performed by bands such as The Rolling Stones and Led Zeppelin in live concert and on long-playing albums.

The American majors were as aware of this emerging trend and as keen to exploit it as United Artists had been to exploit The Beatles earlier in the decade. Given the group's popularity, the commercial potential of starring The Rolling Stone's Mick Jagger in a film must have seemed attractive. *Performance* is far from being a conventional musical, to the point where one otherwise incisive analysis of the film barely mentions the music, regarding it as 'the finest British gangster film ever made' (MacCabe 1998: 8). Yet, as Donnelly has argued, it 'is the key film concerned with late 1960s British pop music culture and its embracing of counterculture and the underground' (Donnelly 2001b: 152). A former Rolling Stones' manager has referred to the film as being 'symptomatic of late-60s ennui. Part of its sinister appeal is that it is an ode to excess, drugs, sloth and an inability to produce' (Oldham 2001: 11). The film is, at one level, very much a product of its time, but it also marked the beginning of a process whereby popular music both interrogated and informed the politics of identity constructed around class, gender and nation, and when the distinctive qualities of late-twentieth-century hedonism and their attendant politics of pleasure sanctioned liberating and often rebellious rejection of established structures, attitudes and values. For all their corporate myopia, it may be that the unease felt by Warner Bros about *Performance* indicated some glimmering awareness of the seismic shifts that were under way.

Initially, however, they were convinced that they were financing a vehicle that would exploit not just Jagger's growingly iconic status, but the interest in popular music which had gathered such momentum by the late 1960s. McCabe argues that Warner Bros were blasé about the production on the basis that they had a vehicle combining two 'hot mini-genres', the pop star vehicle and the 'swinging London' film, and committed a large budget with virtually no oversight, 'with no representative of the studio to ensure that they would produce an acceptable movie' (MacCabe 1998: 49). Straddling the two worlds of the trendy Chelsea set, with its mix of the British metropolitan upper-class and pop stars, and the working-class world of London's gangland, exploring what happens when these worlds collide, *Performance* questions the stability of identity which is under threat from a variety of directions. Having become an irritant to the 'firm', gangster Chas Devlin (James Fox) ends up hiding in the house of reclusive rock star Turner (Mick Jagger), a house which he shares with Pherber (Anita Pallenberg) and Lucy (Michele Breton), along with drugs and sex. Though the plot centres on Chas's attempts to escape to America, the film is actually concerned with the disintegration of identity as Chas engages in sexual and hallucinogenic games with Turner, Pherber and Lucy, to the point where at the film's climax Chas and Turner appear to merge identity. In the process, sexual, class and national identity undergo a process of total destabilisation.

Importantly, the journey that Chas undertakes from homophobic, racist class-bound bigot to an acceptance of 'otherness' is underscored by the varieties of world and pop music in the film. Though there is only one performance number from Jagger, 'Memo From Turner' which comes as part of the film's climactic sequence, the soundtrack calls upon a heterogeneity of musical styles and influences to suggest Chas's journey. Written mainly by Jack Nitzche and performed by artists including Buffy Saint-Marie and Randy Newman, the songs serve a structuring function within an often rather fragmented diegesis and suggest the powerful potential that popular music has for contemporary film, given the extent to which popular music and questions of identity have become intertwined. Like *Oliver!* the film makes much of the fractured class worlds which have traditionally characterised British society. Like *Oliver!* it also suggests, though in a very different way, that a nation based on stabilities of class division is no longer sustainable. *Performance* captured the sense in which, in Britain of the late 1960s and early 1970s, the growing power of popular music was able to render barriers of class, money and their attendant privileges irrelevant. The democratising pleasures of popular music made new ways of understanding the politics of identity possible and, though issues of race, ethnicity, gender and class were still contested sites throughout the late twentieth century, British culture was more diverse and heterogeneous as a result. Inevitably, the commodification of popular music and its appeal to a youth market whose upper age limit seemed increasingly elastic was not lost on the British film industry, even if by the end of the decade it could no longer rely on American investment.

One of the last films to benefit from this wave of American investment was Richard Attenborough's *Oh! What A Lovely War* (1969), a big-budget musical based on plays by Charles Chilton and Joan Littlewood, satirising those follies of First World War commanders such as Sir Douglas Haig which resulted in such enormous and needless loss of life. By implication, the film was critical of the British class system and reflected the meritocratic aspirations for a classless society that characterised British society in the 1960s. With a cast that was a veritable 'who's who' of British acting talent, and with a central conceit based on an end-of-the-pier show on Brighton Pier, the film enjoyed considerable success.

Though big-budget, generically conventional British musicals such as *Oliver!* and *Oh! What a Lovely War* were to become increasingly rare, popular music became an increasingly staple element of British film from the 1970s onwards. A number of British musical films, from *That'll Be the Day* (1973), *Give my Regards to Broad Street* (1984) to *Spice World the Movie* (1997) continued to make use of screen performances by established pop and rock stars in narrative and performance roles, often exploiting plots that can be located within the 'backstage musical' tradition. Though such films share a lineage with British musical films since the 1920s, it became increasingly common for non-musical films to exploit pop and rock music as non-diegetic soundtrack, to the point where sales of soundtrack albums from a film such as Danny Boyle's *Trainspotting* (1995) have become of real significance to the music industry. To the regret of many who bemoan the passing of the conventional film score, the pop music soundtrack has become increasingly ubiquitous in commercial cinema, so that by the end of the century 'pop music had become an object fully integrated with films as a seemingly essential part of the soundtrack' (Donnelly 2001a: 153). This is as true of British cinema as it is of American commercial cinema and represents the continuing vitality and commercial appeal of British popular music and its performers.

6

The 1970s and beyond: signs of success

The withdrawal of American investment from British film production in the late 1960s, combined with the continuing decline in cinema attendances, necessarily entailed a shift in production strategy. In 1970 there were 193 million cinema admissions, but these nose-dived to just 101 million in 1980 and decreased throughout the 1980s, until a revival began in the mid-1990s. Ironically, though cinemas continued to struggle to stay open, film-goers were often faced with greater choice, especially in towns with competing ABCs and Odeons: as a result,

> [c]inema-goers became increasingly selective, partly because admission prices were no longer cheap. Only the main feature mattered now, so double bills, shorts and supporting features vanished: a single feature, and advertising, was shown with separate performances replacing the time-honoured continuous show. (Eyles 2001: 167)

As always, most of the films that audiences chose to see were American and domestic productions had to fight hard to get distribution and exhibition. Just as previous periods of ambitious British film-making in 1933–37 and 1944–49 had given way to retrenchment and greater concentration on films designed for the domestic market, British film production of the 1970s seemed dominated by smaller-budget genre films, particularly comedies, crime, risqué sex films and horror which, if not always great cinema, at least said something about British culture, not least the democratic 'trickling down' of 1960s permissiveness to wider social groups. Though finance on a more modest scale often came from the American-dominated corporates including MGM-EMI, Fox-Rank and Columbia-Warner, production initiatives came from independent companies. By the 1980s, a total of 342 production companies were involved in production throughout the decade, though 250 of these only produced one film (Hill 1999: 49). The number of musical films declined and there was certainly no one production company that took a specialist interest in musical films in the way that Hammer did with horror.

However, in their very different ways, Ken Russell, Alan Parker and Julien Temple were three British directors who explored possibilities the genre still offered and, whilst the overall number declined, some innovative, startling yet commercially successful British musical films were produced.

Faced with competition for audiences from television, then enjoying what has retrospectively been regarded as its 'golden age', British film production was increasingly inseparable from the burgeoning television industry and responded in part by producing big-screen versions of television comedy shows such as *Mutiny on the Buses* (1972), *The Alf Garnett Saga* (1972) and *Nearest and Dearest* (1973), as well as exploiting cinema's laxer censorship regime by bringing out product which relied on greater or lesser sexual titillation and innuendo, from the *Carry On* series through to films such as *The Love Box* (1972), *Escort Girls* (1974) and *The Great British Striptease* (1980). Though capable of producing some outstanding films such as Nicolas Roeg's *Don't Look Now* (1973), Robin Hardy's *The Wicker Man* (1974), Hugh Hudson's *Chariots Of Fire* (1981) and Roland Joffe's *The Killing Fields* (1984), British film production in the seventies and eighties concentrated on relatively inexpensive product aimed squarely at the domestic market, much of which attracted critical opprobrium.

Pop music, hallucinations, and fractured self-importance

Within a context of declining audiences, continuing strong competition from American films and scarcity of production finance, the industry produced a number of musical films that attempted to exploit the apparently exponential interest in popular music which, during most of the 1970s and with the exception of shows such as *Top Of The Pops* and *The Old Grey Whistle Test*, was not well served by television programming. This remained the case until the commercial development of music video and the introduction of MTV in Britain in the 1980s. Though the failure of big-budget American musicals had rendered generically conventional big-budget musicals an endangered species, the demand to see pop performers was met in part by a series of shorts, films based on rock concerts, and lengthier documentaries based on specific bands or rock tours. Though their distribution was limited and often erratic, these films made an important contribution to the visual economy of popular music until they were supplanted by the development of dedicated music video television channels and direct-sale DVDs.

Though paltry in comparison with production of musical films in previous decades, British musical films were still characterised by variety of form and content. This is evident when looking at production output in just one year, 1970. There was *Scrooge*, a conventional feature-length musical starring Albert Finney and Alec Guinness and using songs by Leslie Bricusse; Olivia Newton John appeared in the feature *Toomorrow*, written and directed by veteran Val Guest, about a pop group who attract the attention of aliens; and The Beatles stumbled through the production of the faux-documentary *Let It Be*. In addition, there were two shorts, *Enigma Variations* and *The Nutcracker Suite*, based on the music of Elgar and Tchaikowsky respectively, a rather old-fashioned revue from Butchers, *Under The Table You Must Go*, featuring old-stagers such as Tommy Trinder and Richard Murdoch as well as newcomers Jonathan King and BBC Radio One DJ Stuart Henry, a 33-minute concert film featuring bands *Colosseum and Juicy Lucy* in performance, as well as Horace Ove's documentary *Reggae*, shot at the Wembley Reggae Festival of 1970.

As we have seen and despite its erasure from most film histories, the musical short, privileging the performance of a band or a singer, had been a staple item in British film production from the early days of sound cinema. However, the decline of the mixed cinema programme through the 1970s and 1980s meant that the tradition of the musical short was difficult to sustain. Some promotional films remained relatively short, such as *Status Quo at Wembley* (1975), *Queen at the Rainbow* (1976), *Natural High: The Commodores on Tour* (1978), *Dire Straits Presents Making Movies* (1981) and *The Perfect Kiss* (1985) featuring New Order. However, in keeping with the self-regard that surrounded much of the British music industry at this time, reinforced by unprecedented attention in quality newspapers such as *The Guardian* and *The Times*, many concert or tour films tended to inflate in length and pretentiousness. Whilst many films attempted to recreate and simulate the concert experience, others tried to give expression to some underlying concept, often using special effects to enhance what would otherwise be a straightforward record of a performance. Emerson, Lake and Palmer's 95-minute *Pictures at an Exhibition* (1972), referencing Mussorgsky's work of the same title, the 91-minute *Glastonbury Fayre* (1973), *The Song Remains the Same* (1975) featuring Led Zeppelin, *Bob Marley and the Wailers Live* (1978) and *Elton John in Central Park* (1981) were part of this tendency. To argue that many of these films were 'made at great speed, with little money, often by people with no real film-making experience or understanding of the music' (Wootton 1995: 101) is harsh. Before the ready accessibility of video and DVD, these films played an important role in providing fans opportunities of seeing favoured bands on screen in exactly the same way that they had done since the coming of synchronised sound.

Whilst the variety of British musical film production in the 1970s might be seen as a healthy antidote to increasingly formulaic cinematic fare, it could equally be seen as a serious lack of direction in an industry that was increasingly unsure about its relationship with a declining audience. It was possible for Cliff Richard to reprise his earlier 1960s format in *Take Me High* (1973) just a year after Pinewood had given studio space to Tony Palmer and Frank Zappa's *200 Motels* (1972). In their very different ways, both films were commercial disasters. In *Take Me High*, Richard plays Tim Matthews, a merchant banker who teams up with Sarah (Debbie Watling) to launch the Brumburger, Birmingham's very own hamburger. Though the film has twelve songs, not one of them produced a chart hit for Richard. Producer Kenneth Harper wanted to prove that it was possible to make a musical without dances, but failed. It proved a curiously old-fashioned film, as if nothing had changed since Richard had his earlier film successes. As Richard's biographer remarks, '[t]here was the same attempt at innocent joviality and coy flirtatiousness but cinema audiences no longer found the immaturity believable' (Turner 1994: 263). 'Take Me High' might have been a more appropriate title for Frank Zappa's hallucinogenic, narrative-defying *200 Motels*, a stunningly uncommercial melange of concert performance, fantasy sequences, and animation. The first film to be shot on video then transferred to film, it makes excessive and undisciplined use of current state-of-the-art video effects. Performances from Zappa and The Mothers of Invention mingle with musical passages from the Royal Philharmonic Orchestra, who at times look on bemusedly at events taking place around them. Ringo Starr and Keith Moon (drummers respectively with The Beatles and The Who) make a series of spasmodic appearances to little effect. Gillian Lynne's choreography produces some inspired moments, though the obsession with video effects detracts from their impact. As a document of a moment of cultural specificity, capturing the drug-induced hallucinatory 'happenings' that were part of The Mothers Of Invention package, the film has its interest, though its confused intimations of the power of masquerade and its interrogation of gender roles remain undeveloped. There are some moments of interesting self-reflexivity, as when a member of the Mothers declares 'I tried to get a hit single. It drove me to drink', and asks when he is going to get paid for doing the film. The film makes frequent use of direct address to camera, as in the closing sequence when Rance Muhammitz (Theodore Bikel) asks the 'Lord to have mercy' on the English for the terrible food they have to eat. Zappa himself announces 'Touring can make you crazy. That is precisely what *200 Motels* is about.' This is a world that was later explored on video by

American bands Devo and The Residents, but clearly had little or no appeal to British cinema audiences.

The turn to nostalgia: *That'll Be the Day* (1973) and *Stardust* (1974)

Essentially a politically conservative decade, the social and economic tensions that led to racial hostility, conflict around union power, power cuts and restrictions on television viewing sat alongside savage debates about 'permissiveness', especially female sexuality. Female liberation co-existed with homophobic legislation and the soft-pornography sex-ploitation films that kept the British film industry going through the 1970s. Arguably, 'Britain had, indeed, never been more (sometimes violently) fragmented – by nationalism, regionalism, class conflict, race, gender and sexuality' (Hunt 1998: 18). Whilst these structural tensions may in themselves explain what some have seen as a 'cult of nostalgia' in the 1970s, perhaps the wilder shores of early 1970s progressive rock help to explain the turn to nostalgia that was evident in two of the more commercially successful musical films of the 1970s, *That'll Be the Day* (1973) and *Stardust* (1975), both starring David Essex as Jim Maclaine, who journeys from disillusioned schoolboy to famous but equally dis-illusioned rock star. *That'll Be the Day* is set in 1959 against a back-ground soundtrack of chart hits from (more or less) that year. Initially, the film appears rooted in British social realism, as director Claude Whatham creates a series of atmospheric sequences in which, as a young boy, Jim and his mother are deserted by his father. The role of memory and the loss of a father is something that attains significance in a number of British films of the 1970s and 1980s. Here, however, there is also a suggestion that Jim's subsequent rejection of his grammar school edu-cation is as much the result of the corrupting influence of rock'n'roll. Preferring to listen to records on coffee-bar jukeboxes and his bedroom record player than study, Jim goes to the cinema, queuing next to a poster advertising the Tommy Steele film *The Duke Wore Jeans*. His involvement in the basement of the entertainment industry enables his discovery of sex and he is soon exploiting a succession of women through his openly promiscuous behaviour. Jim's rejection of normative social and moral values offers a sharp contrast to his friend Terry (Robert Lindsay), who goes on to university and, by implication, a good job. Returning home to run his mother's corner shop, Jim marries Terry's sister Jeanette, his mother-in-law assuming that Jeanette is preg-nant. His return to domesticity is deceptive; he sleeps with Terry's girl-friend on the evening of his wedding and finally deserts Jeanette and their young son much as his own father had deserted him. The attraction is rock'n'roll, an attraction strengthened when he bumps into two former school friends who are forging a career as a band. In the closing shot of the film, Jim buys a guitar and, in response to the music shop-keeper's query 'sure you'll be able to handle it', replies 'Yeah, I'll be all right', in the film's defiant rejection of narrative closure and resolution.

Aided by the presence of Ringo Starr, Billy Fury and Keith Moon, *That'll Be The Day* can be considered a proto-musical. Like George Lucas's *American Graffiti* (1973), it offers a nostalgic wallpaper sound-track, though unlike the American film, it implicates its protagonist within the world of rock music entertainment. What limited perfor-mance sequences there are, including the one featuring Storm Tempest (Billy Fury), serve to indicate Jim's growing desire to get involved rather than offer privileged space for the performance itself. This is very dif-ferent in the sequel *Stardust*, again based on Ray Connolly's script. Directed by Michael Apted and with a bigger budget, *Stardust* features more on-screen numbers (performed on the soundtrack by Dave Edmunds), as Jim Maclaine and his group the Stray Cats enjoy huge commercial success. Ringo Starr, who gave a credible performance in *That'll Be the Day*, is replaced by another British pop icon, Adam Faith, playing Jim's initially reluctant manager Mike. Though the Stray Cats enjoy huge commercial success, touring America and giving TV inter-views, the internal dissension within the band and its remorseless exploitation by managers and agents sour the experience. The inability to keep his mother's funeral as a private occasion, the break-up of the band and experiments with drugs turn Jim into a recluse. The decision to return to performing, based on the realisation that his money is running out, proves disastrous and Jim takes a drug overdose. Whilst Jim achieves his desire, it is at huge personal cost, as he plunges into an increasingly dystopian world. Like Bob Fosse's *All That Jazz* (1979), *Stardust* offers an extremely cynical take on showbusiness, far from the euphoric triumphalism that marked musical films of earlier decades.

Ken Russell, visual excess and visions of dystopia

The suggestion that the utopian fantasies constructed by musical films were no longer credible by the 1970s is reinforced in the extensive, complex and often visually stunning work of Ken Russell. Like so many other directors working in the British film industry in the last decades of the twentieth century, Russell served an apprenticeship in television, where he developed a reputation for programmes such as *Elgar* (1962), *Bartok* (1964) and *The Debussy Film* (1965) based on the lives of clas-sical composers. Translated onto the cinema screen, this penchant caused controversy when *The Music Lovers* (1969) concentrated as much on Tchaikovsky's sex life as it did his music. Following controversy over what many regarded as the sexual and religious sensationalism of *The Devils* (1971), Russell turned to a more innocuous vehicle, *The Boy Friend* (1971). Sandy Wilson's 1954 stage musical, a pastiche of 1920s musical revue, originally starred Julie Andrews and ran for a total of 2,084 West End performances. Russell's screenplay makes some significant alterations to Wilson's original, creating greater opportunity for visually excessive fantasy sequences which both reference and pastiche Busby Berkeley routines in American musical such as *42nd Street* (1933). The American film director looking for talent for his 'all-talking, all-dancing, all-singing' movie extravaganza is Cecil B. DeThrill (played by Vladek Sheybal), who stumbles across understudy Polly Browne (Twiggy) as she steps in at the last minute. A pastiche of classical Hollywood musical utopian fantasies about success, Polly's love for leading man Tony (Christopher Gable) motivates a number of fantasy sequences that Russell directs with visual gusto. Some of these numbers, such as 'Nicer In Nice' and 'I Could Be Happy With You' work well, not least in their refusal to be taken seriously, but the film as a whole suffers from an unevenness in tone and direction. However, *The Boy Friend* received Oscar nominations for Best Music and Best Original Song Score, the performance from Twiggy justified her Golden Globe awards in 1972 for Best Actress in comedy and musical and Most Promising Newcomer, and the film was one of a number of influences on Baz Luhrmann's *Moulin Rouge* (2000).

Significantly, though it can be argued that much of Russell's films of the 1980s worked *within* genres, *The Boy Friend* serves to illustrate the extent to which it was no longer possible to do this with the musical. The film

> employs camp as a double-edged sword that simultaneously mocks and celebrates the classical Hollywood musical, although ultimately the film attacks the genre that inspired it by contextualising the mounting of the show as a battle among individual egos rather than as a harmonious group effort. (Grant 1993: 191)

The Boy Friend, for all its ostensible nostalgia, is clearly a long way from either version of *The Good Companions*. The double pastiche at work in *The Boy Friend* (Wilson's 1950s take on 1920s entertainment, Russell's 1970s take on Wilson's 1950s sensibilities) and its ironic distancing from ideologies that had been central to musical films in earlier decades reflects those complex conditions of cultural refusal central to what became known as postmodern culture. Yet the playfulness of *The*

Boy Friend or of Alan Parker's *Bugsy Malone* (1976) should not detract from the seriousness that surrounded the consumption of contemporary rock music or the centrality of that music as a source of pleasure and in constructing personal and social identities. If the symbiotic relationship between the film and the popular music industries was established with the coming of synchronised sound, this relationship became increasingly complex during the 1970s and beyond. Though film had always exploited popular music talent for its own commercial ends and, in the process, had served to boost sales of sheet music and records as well as performers' careers, the increased importance of long-playing albums meant that it became increasingly common for films such as *Tommy* (1975) and *Pink Floyd The Wall* (1982) to be based on a pre-existing concept album. Significantly, developments in music recording that enabled increasingly complicated mixes of complex stereo sound on albums were being matched by developments in cinema sound.

All of these trends and developments were evident in *Tommy*, the film that Pete Townsend of The Who 'gifted' to Ken Russell. The conceptual origins of Townsend's project began as early as 1968 when, in an article in *Rolling Stone* on 14 September that year, Townsend described his idea for a concept album in rock opera format:

> The package I hope is going to be called 'Deaf, Dumb and Blind Boy' It's a story about a kid that's born deaf, dumb and blind and what happens to him throughout his life . . . the boy is . . . seeing things basically as vibrations which we translate to music. (Barnes and Townsend 1977: 6)

Influenced both by Townsend's odyssey with hallucinogenic drugs and by the spiritualist teachings of Meher Baba, this concept became an album, a rock opera performed at 'opera houses all round the world' (Barnes and Townsend 1977: 31), an arrangement utilising a full symphonic orchestration, and finally a film. Though working with an already successful entity, Russell brought a visual flair to the music, such as the 'Acid Queen' sequence, and a screenplay with some additional and rewritten material, including strengthening the motivation for Tommy's traumatisation by seeing his father, the returning RAF hero Captain Walker (Robert Powell), killed by 'Uncle' Frank (Oliver Reed). Producer Robert Stigwood was able to cast Ann-Margaret, Reed and Jack Nicholson despite Townsend's initial objections. In addition to The Who's singer Roger Daltry as Tommy, Elton John, Tina Turner, Eric Clapton and the Who's drummer Keith Moon were also cast, though the proposed involvement of Stevie Wonder, Mick Jagger, David Bowie and David Essex failed to materialise.

If nothing else, *Tommy* is an extremely innovative film, though its rock opera format militates against the need to provide narrative back-story, so that the first twenty minutes of the film are perhaps the least successful. Though the film is clearly influenced by Townsend's contact with Baba and new-age spiritualism that was closely liked with the rise of the drug culture, it is clearly critical of all forms of idolatry. This is clear in the 'Eyesight To The Blind' sequence where the conflation of religion and celebrity in the form of Marilyn Monroe is revealed as empty and hollow, as well as in the finale where Tommy's extreme behaviour is designed to force his followers back to their own lives, away from their commercial exploitation by his mother Nora, Frank and Uncle Ernie (Keith Moon). Ultimately, the pleasures of *Tommy* are less to do with its success or otherwise in capturing contemporary cultural sensibilities, and more to do with Russell's high-impact visual excess and the electrifying impact of the music and its performance. Even Clapton's apparently reluctant and certainly rather visually stiff rendition of the only non-Who number, Sonny Boy Williamson's 1951 'Eyesight To The Blind', is to be treasured. Tina Turner's performance of 'Acid Queen' is simply stunning, described by Jonathan Rosenbaum in his *Monthly Film Bulletin* review as a 'mini-masterpiece of visual inventiveness and dramatic cohesion' (Rosenbaum 1975: 89). Equally startling is 'Pinball Wizard' where an outrageously costumed Elton John competes against Tommy at the pinball championship.

The dramatic cohesion evident in individual scenes is not apparent throughout the film as a whole. Equally, though much of the film is set in the 1950s, including the sequence at Bernie's Holiday Camp, there is little attempt to exploit any nostalgic potential. Arguably, the naivety of this holiday camp when compared with the overt commercialism of Tommy's cult holiday camp reinforces commentary on the increasingly thin divide between the divine and the commercial, but this is not a film that wants to operate at the level of social critique. If anything, the film remains rather confused about what it is saying, though its significance today remains with the music and with Russell's exploration of the imaginative possibilities of picturing musical performance. Very much a film of its time, it represented for Townsend a pinnacle in the 'gesture toward musical and verbal freedom':

> It is the prime example of Rock and Roll throwing off its three chord musical structure, discarding its attachment to the three minute single, openly taking on the unfashionable questions about spirituality and religion and yet hanging grimly on to the old ways at the same time. (Barnes and Townsend 1977: 129)

Given the film's origin, it was not surprising that the decision was made to confront existing technical limitations in sound recording. The result was a soundtrack that used what was known as Quintaphonic Sound, which provided surround sound using five phase-encoded multiple tracks. In those cinemas equipped to deliver it, the sound quality and the volume came close to that which many young people were experiencing at live rock concerts. Given the growing ubiquity of pop music soundtracks across a range of non-musical British films, these advancements in soundtrack quality were increasingly of commercial interest to the film industry, culminating in the development of the Dolby sound system. In fact, Russell's next film *Lisztomania* (1975), again starring Roger Daltry, was the first film with a Dolby stereo optical soundtrack to go on general release (Hayward 2004: 20–2).

Despite the productive relationship between The Who and Ken Russell whilst working on *Tommy*, the band's next film project *Quadrophenia* (1979) was directed by Franc Roddam, with all four members of The Who credited as Executive Producers and Roger Daltrey, John Entwhistle and Pete Townsend as Musical Directors. Based on The Who album of the same name released in 1973, *Quadrophenia* is an altogether more conventional film, a retrospective account of the youth movement, particularly the conflict between so-called Mods and Rockers, during 1964, an 'almost immaculate realist reconstruction of a mid-Sixties cultural movement' (Taylor 1979: 199). Even within the catholic definition of musical film used within this book, *Quadrophenia* clearly operates at the margins, at least in formal terms. Yet rarely has a British film managed to convey the absolute centrality of popular music to the lives of young people and ways in which they use it to construct their identities. As well as some performance numbers and tracks from the album heard non-diegetically at key dramatic moments, much of the music is heard diegetically, on bedroom and party record players, at coffee bars and dance clubs and on television, an ongoing daily soundtrack dripping into to the lives of these young people. Significantly, music appears to have been internalised, as Jimmy and other characters belt out their own renditions of hit numbers. Music is used to code identity and allegiance, as when Jimmy (Phil Daniels) and his old school friend Kev (Ray Winstone), now a rocker and hence one of the 'enemy', sing their different songs in the public bath-house; naked, they are clothed with differing identities by the music. Just as difference is marked through music, so the leathers and Parkas serve to indicate identity and allegiance, forging enmity that 'naturally' doesn't exist.

On the original album, Jimmy's four identities, the double-schizophrenia of the title, are the hooks that prompt the music. In the film, though the issue of Jimmy's identity and breakdown remains central, it is less complex, less intimately tied in with the music and cedes narrative ground to wider social issues. His adherence to the Mod lifestyle, its music, Lambretta scooters and 'blues' drug culture gives him a precarious identity, as he declares that 'he doesn't want to be like everyone else, that's why I'm a Mod', a position whose irony eludes him. His search for a settled identity articulated through Mod culture brings him into conflict with a range of authority figures. Taking part in the Bank Holiday riots in Brighton, he is arrested and fined. His parents finally lose patience and throw him out of the house, and he loses his job as a post-boy after being reprimanded by the boss of the advertising company. Happiest when with the crowd, cruising on his scooter and getting high on drugs and drink at parties, Jimmy is nevertheless looking for more than the other weekend Mods appear to be. Jimmy occupies a confusing world of unsettled and often conflicting identities. Though his main source of drugs is his black friend, he is happy to make racist comments along with the rest of the group. Sexual identity is rendered problematic, as when a group of rockers who surround a Mod couple demand to know which one of them is the girl. Jimmy finds relationships with women difficult especially when, though Steph (Lesley Ash) has casual sex with him during the height of the Brighton riot, she rejects Jimmy's desire for a steady relationship. His growing disillusion at the limits of what Mod culture can deliver is sealed when he discovers that his hero Ace (Sting) works as a hotel bellboy, his demeaning costume mocking the faith that Jimmy has invested in his own Mod uniform and fashionable suits. For the majority of the group, the tribal mindset is something they discard during the week, when work in hotels, scrap yards and supermarkets takes over. Unable to accept this, Jimmy disintegrates, the scooter he has stolen plunging over the cliff and smashing on the rocks below. As the lyrics to the soundtrack number 'Love Reigns Over Me' announce an end to pill-taking and any interest in fashion, the ambiguous suggestion is that Jimmy may have gone the same way.

Focussed on the importance of popular music in the lives of ordinary young working-class people, drawing upon the long-standing tradition of British cinematic realism, *Quadrophenia*'s strong narrative drive reduces the impact of The Who's music. The film lacks the big performance numbers that were so important in *Tommy*, yet succeeds in placing popular music at the centre of youth culture in ways that, when the film was reissued in the mid-1990s, propelled it to cult status amongst adherents of 'Britpop'. Lacking the element of spectacle so evident in *Tommy*, *Quadrophenia* remains perhaps a more typically British product, in content and form.

Alan Parker: American money and innovation

The rock opera format remained unusual, though Alan Parker was to refine and extend it two decades later with *Evita* (1996). Before then, Parker was to innovate in profoundly different ways with his film *Bugsy Malone* (1976), a musical pastiche of the 1930s gangster genre, using child actors. *Bugsy Malone* was Parker's first feature film, following experience in television and with commercials, including a notable series of adverts for Bird's Eye beefburgers featuring child actors. The central, improbable, conceit in the film of having children inhabit an adult world of crime, entertainment and boxing is maintained throughout, from the use of pedal-powered cars, brightly coloured non-alcoholic drinks, through to the use of the splurge guns firing custard pies. With finance from Rank and the National Film Finance Consortium dependent on a US distribution deal, producer David Puttnam (who had produced *That'll Be the Day* and *Stardust*) managed to persuade Paramount to back the film. With the exception of Jodie Foster playing Tallulah, Parker assembled a cast of young unknowns and coaxed some enduring performances from them. With the exception of the 'Down and Out' sequence that was filmed at a disused Huntley and Palmer biscuit factory, the film was shot in the studio at Pinewood, the sets and costumes contributing much in overcoming the potential pitfalls of using child actors. Gillian Gregory, who had choreographed *Tommy* and *The Boy Friend*, produced some wonderful mock-1930s-musical chorus routines, as well as some highly effective dancing from the young gangsters.

Searching for a composer and lyricist who could deliver 'a 1920s sound but with a modern feel to it to make it a little more palatable to an audience more in tune with Alvin Stardust than Rogers and Hart' (Parker 2002: 6), Puttnam was able to deliver American Paul Williams, whose songs had been recorded by Sinatra, Streisand and The Carpenters. The ten numbers in the film vary from the energetic 'So You Wanna Be A Boxer' to Foster's torch song 'My Name Is Tallulah', Blousey Brown's introspective regret at apparently being let down by Bugsy in 'Ordinary Fool', to Busy's moving number 'Tomorrow' where expressions of ambition and frustration are movingly inscribed with intimations of racial discrimination. Though this is, as Parker acknowledged, a musical world far removed from contemporary taste, the numbers work to give a resonance to the narrative, both serving to construct the rich, sustained pastiche. Though at one level the film elevates conventional generic concerns as primary material for the narrative, such as the on/off romance between Bugsy and Blousey and the turf war between the rival organisations led by Fat Sam and Dandy Dan, any potential ideological weight such concerns may once have had are here completely dissipated by the film's style.

The reception and commercial success of *Bugsy Malone*, 'a captivating adult film for children made with much wit, much originality and no patronising sentiment' (Brown 1976: 146), contrasted with earlier attempts to attract finance for his screenplays, which were rejected as being too English and parochial. His subsequent films were made with American finance and often shot in America. Having directed the drama *Midnight Express* (1978), he returned to the musical with *Fame* (1980), essentially a rather conventional generic musical made in the United States, and *Pink Floyd The Wall* (1982). Stemming from the growing disillusion experienced by Roger Waters of Pink Floyd about rock concerts and the band's relationship with their audiences, Waters and the other members of Pink Floyd produced *The Wall*, a double album released in 1978. Using the album as a basis, Parker undertook what he described as an experiment in form, with virtually no dialogue scenes except those few that are heavily muted and virtually inaudible. However, the link between the lyrics of the Pink Floyd numbers and Parker's visualisation are far from literal, as he vividly realises the journey into memory and madness of exhausted rock star Pink (Bob Geldof). True, 'Comfortably Numb' fits perfectly with the attempts to revive a comatose Pink from his drug-induced overdose, whilst his memory flashes back to his childhood attempts to revive an injured rat, the cross-cutting between the scenes of the adult Pink in the Los Angeles hotel and the young Pink in his mother's house and its neighbourhood carrying its implications about Pink's behaviour and character.

Waters is on record as regarding *The Wall* as symbolising growing alienation in contemporary society. As a concept, it has possibilities, but in the film it gets confused with a number of other targets for criticism, not least the institution of schooling, which is seen as processing children as fodder, literally so in Parker's sinister sequence where the children are fed into a giant meat grinder. Pink's harsh treatment at the hands of a sadistic schoolmaster who mocks his creative attempts at poetry, and the literal and metaphorical barriers that school places in front of young people, eventually leads to rebellion, focussed around the number 'Another Brick In The Wall (We Don't Need No Education)', which had been a number-one single in late 1979. Despite his celebrity status as a rock star and consequent access to drugs, promiscuous sex and pampered high life, Pink is increasingly isolated from a world he leaves behind, spiralling into despair, drugs, self-mutilation and the attractions of fascist power which are shown as not unlike the mesmeric attractions associated with rock concerts. Pink's behaviour is 'explained' in a number of ways. Much is made of the loss of his father during the war, depicted in gruesome scenes rivalling those in *Saving Private Ryan* (2002). Parker makes brilliant use of wonderfully evocative period sets, as the young Pink discovers and tries on his father's army uniform. At the same time, his treatment at school and the mockery of any pretensions to creativity and feeling are seen as formative aspects of his life. However, a more disturbing cause is the blame that is placed on his mother and other female characters in the film, including his wife. In both the lyrics to 'Mother' and Parker's visualisation, Pink's mother is revealed as a deeply unsympathetic character. His wife, whom he neglects and abuses, is criticised when she seeks comfort and approval through an affair. This virulent anti-female stance is replicated in the animated sequences produced by Gerald Scarfe, most uncomfortably in the male and female flower sequence and again in the animated trial sequence at the end of the film where Pink's wife takes on the shape of a scorpion. Women are also depicted unfavourably through the behaviour of the five groupies, seen to be willing to hand out gratuitous sexual favours in order to gain backstage access to the concert.

Though concerned with the personal journey through memory, loss and recovery of the protagonist, *Pink Floyd The Wall* clearly comments on perceived dangers in contemporary British society. At the fascist rally, Pink singles out 'queers', Jews, 'coons' and drugtakers for violent punishment as gangs of uniformed skinheads smash their way into houses and shops owned by Black and Asian British families. This seems direct comment on the activities of the National Front who, at this period, were fomenting racial hatred in a number of major British cities. Yet the weakened narrative resolution, as a group of young children try literally to pick up the shattered debris of street violence, seems tentative at best. Just as with *Tommy*, it may be confirmation that film is not necessarily the best medium to explore complex issues, though it also remains the case that the concepts behind the film are confused and ambiguous, rooted as they are essentially in a rock musician's personal disillusion with the realities of celebrity status and the work it involves. Like Jim Maclaine in *Stardust*, Pink discovers that the pleasures of success in the music business carry a heavy price; *Pink Floyd The Wall* is a long way from those utopian representations of fame, success and heterosexual happiness that characterised musical films of earlier decades. The film attracted its share of critical hostility, one influential contemporary review regarding it as 'a vacuous, bombastic and humourless piece of self-indulgence' (Jenkins 1982: 173). It remains, however, a significant, innovative film, a tribute to a British director who continues to be consistently unappreciated, this despite later successes including *The Commitments* (1991) and *Evita* (1996).

Tradition revived and challenged: punk and the musical film

Though rock and 'serious' pop dominated musicals as well as an increasing number of non-musical film soundtracks, the 1970s and beyond did see some attempts at producing more traditional mainstream musicals using more middle-of-the-road songs. Part financed by Readers Digest Films, Anthony Newley wrote the music and starred in *Mister Quilp* (1975), based on Dickens' *The Old Curiosity Shop*. Even with stalwarts David Hemmings, David Warner and Michael Hordern and some fine photography by Christopher Challis, the film failed to make an impact. Bryan Forbes had more success with *The Slipper and The Rose* (1976), an updating of the Cinderella story starring Richard Chamberlain and Gemma Craven, enough to be reissued in a slightly shortened version in 1980. This attempt to revive the previously successful formula of basing a film on the literary canon was severely at odds with music sensibilities that were much more interested in feature-length concert films such as Led Zeppelin's *The Song Remains the Same* (1976) and The Who's *The Kids Are Alright* (1979). Even when iconic figures such as post-Beatles Paul McCartney attempted a more conventional musical, *Give my Regards to Broad Street* (1984), with a showbiz narrative based around the theft of some master tapes, commercial success proved elusive.

If established rock musicians such as Roger Waters were disillusioned with the commercial music business, so too, in very different ways, were a number of other aspiring young musicians and style entrepreneurs who wanted to revive the oppositional potential associated with popular music briefly in the late 1950s, to breathe new life in what had become, for many, a comatose nation:

> England wasn't free and easy: it was repressed and horrible . . . Consider the music of the time – then called 'Rock' in a bid for respectability. What a pompous, middle-class facsimile of the anarchy that was fifties Rock'n'Roll. The music industry was now in control and conning everyone: how could that industry's 'Rock' retain any trace of Rock'n'Roll's original teenage revolt? (Savage 1991: 9)

The emergence of British punk rock around 1976 challenged the dominance of commercial popular music and, in the process, opened up debates about cultural significance that have intensified since. As Simon Frith has argued, we need to beware any simplistic elision between what sells and what is popular. The fact that punk records sold less well than Elton John albums does nothing to lessen the significance that punk rock had upon the British music scene and British culture in the late 1970s (Frith 1998: 15–6). Yet, given the different technological and economic regimes that characterise music and film production, it proved difficult to reflect the impact of punk within cinema. Derek Jarman succeeded with *Jubilee* (1978), which included music by, amongst others, Siouxie and the Banshees and Adam Ant. However, Don Letts' *The Punk Rock Movie* (1978) achieved only limited distribution. Those films that were made appeared as the influence of punk was waning and many groups, notably the Sex Pistols, had disbanded. Jack Hazan and David Mingay's *Rude Boy* (1980), a semi-fictional account centred on The Clash, took two years to shoot. Brian Gibson's *Breaking Glass* (1980) employed a more conventional showbiz narrative trajectory, with punk rock manager Daniel Price (Phil Daniels) driving singer Kate Crawley (Hazel O'Connor) to stardom and a breakdown in a contemporary London in which the National Front loom significantly. Racism and racial conflict occupied the heart of Franco Rosso's *Babylon* (1980) as Aswad's Brinsley Forde reacts to the smashing of his reggae sound system by white thugs. One of the most significant punk films, if only because it centred on the Sex Pistols, was Julien Temple's *The Great Rock 'n' Roll Swindle* (1980).

Temple, whose subsequent career has straddled both feature film and music video, made a number of film shorts including *Where Is Your Love* (1979) and *Punk Can Take It* (1979). The latter, a parody of Jennings' wartime documentary *London Can Take It*, reveals Temple's strong interest in the cultural condition of England. Though not actually an easy film to watch and certainly not one with much commercial appeal, *The Great Rock 'n' Roll Swindle* is a complex, multilayered text. Purporting to tell the story of the Sex Pistols and how they 'swindled' major corporations into lucrative deals, it was shot between 1976 and 1978 and reached the screen after Sid Vicious was dead and the band effectively defunct. Structured around the 'Ten Lessons', a litany of amoral business advice including the exhortation to 'steal as much money from the record company of your choice', the film offers an interrogation, not just into the history and management of the Sex Pistols, but of wider questions of manipulation, opportunism and authenticity, with Malcolm McLaren in the role of 'The Embezzler'. Temple attempts to shape and structure the film to reflect punk itself, so that he

> mixes and matches film genres in much the same fashion as punk clothing, cobbling together burlesqued elements from the classical film musical with documentary footage, animation and ribald comedy. Yet the film is still a musical. (Donnelly 2000: 174)

This assemblage of punk aesthetics is reflected in the range of music in the film, which ranges from Sex Pistols classics 'Pretty Vacant', 'Anarchy In The UK', and 'God Save The Queen', burlesqued spoofs of classics such as 'Rock Around The Clock', Chuck Berry's 'Johnny B Goode', Sinatra's 'My Way', McLaren singing a version of Max Bygraves' 'You Need Hands' and an accordion version of 'Anarchy' sung in French. In announcing the end of the conventional musical, *The Great Rock'n'Roll Swindle* finds itself in company with other British musical films of the 1970s and 1980s. But in announcing the end of punk, declaring that it amounted to little more than a cynical media construction, the film attempted to close off a moment of British cultural history.

That moment was reopened temporarily with Alex Cox's *Sid & Nancy* (1986), a biopic of former Sex Pistols bass player Sid Vicious (Gary Oldman) and his girlfriend Nancy Spungen (Chloe Webb). Though its claim as a musical is greater than earlier vehicles such as the Robin Askwith film *Confessions Of A Pop Performer* (1975), *Sid & Nancy* certainly challenges the formal integrity of the genre, as the distinction between a musical film and a film with a pop-music-saturated soundtrack becomes increasingly blurred. Produced by Zenith, a subsidiary of Central Television, the film focuses on the love between its eponymous anti-heroes and what director Cox regarded as their betrayal of the punk revolution. Though this necessarily entailed showing the break-up of the Sex Pistols, this is secondary to Sid and Nancy's descent into drug-fuelled oblivion and death. Originally entitled *Love Kills*, a title to which Zenith objected, the film erects a disturbing vision of contemporary romance, far from the utopian visions of earlier decades, but a love affair for all that. As one commentator has put it, 'take away the drugs and the vomit and you are left with a very convincing love story' (Davies 2000: 29).

Unable to use the Sex Pistols' original recordings, Drew Schofield did his own vocals playing Johnny Rotten, aided on different numbers by Glen Matlock, Steve Jones and Paul Cook. Gary Oldman sang 'My Way', 'Somethin' Else' and 'I Wanna Be Your Dog'. Performance numbers are used skilfully to reveal the initial appeal of the Sex Pistols, chart their downward spiral, and show the growing audience disaffection with their on-stage antics. Other numbers appear non-diegetically, with additional incidental music played by Joe Strummer of The Clash, The Pogues and Pray For Rain. Ultimately, given the narrative focus of the film, *Sid & Nancy* degrades the cultural significance of punk, its vision of graffiti-scarred, burnt-out urban landscapes and the horrors of heroin dependency only partly redeemed by the film's awkwardly romantic fantasy ending where, as Vicious dances along with some

Black American children, their ghetto-blasters promoting the new Black Philadelphia sound, he seems reunited with Nancy as they ride off in a yellow cab. Given that over half the film is set in America, Cox's film says little about Britain other than some over-hyped scenes that suggest that it remains a society essentially conservative and repressed, unimpressed with the brief cultural eruption that was punk.

Julien Temple's concern with the condition of England and its representation in film continued beyond *The Great Rock'n'Roll Swindle* and was to find expression in another musical film, *Absolute Beginners* (1986). British cinema of the 1980s attempted to make sense of shifting British identities through imagining the past, largely though the heritage film, but also through revisiting the 1950s, a period that evoked both 'stability and contentment' as well as 'repression and privation' (Hill 1999: 125). Temple was particularly critical of British heritage films, not least the jingoistic 'rubbish' of the Oscar-winning *Chariots Of Fire* (1981). Arguing that 'we don't have to make imperial romps and flashback images of Oxford and Cambridge and so on', Temple wanted to make what he saw as 'different kinds of British films', of which his planned *Absolute Beginners* would be one,

> designed totally to be a hit and shake things up. It's a very optimistic, anti-racist film. It's about looking at the choices that were made in the 1950s, and reinterpreting them, because a lot of those choices have determined the way that people live now. (Jenkins 1984: 231)

Whilst this impulse of reinterpreting actions and choices made in the past in order to make sense of the present was something that Temple shared with other film-makers of the 1980s, the decision to turn Colin MacInnes' novel into a musical was not. Citing the pleasures that musicals such as *An American in Paris* (1951) and *The Band Wagon* (1953) had given him and regretting the form's neglect, Temple clearly saw the potential for his musical to be 'fantastic entertainment'.

Rooted in one of the most significant events of 1958, the Notting Hill race riots, *Absolute Beginners* transcends any notion that such important events demand treatment through a realist aesthetic. References to Hollywood musicals abound, not least *West Side Story* (1961), with Colin (Eddie O'Connell) and Crepe Suzette (Patsy Kensit) in the role of Tony and Maria, only here crossing both race and class divides. The party held by gossip columnist Dido Lament (Anita Morris) references Bob Fosse's *Sweet Charity* in its allusion to social spaces where difference is apparently but not really abolished. Temple provides numerous touches that carry authenticity, the hula-hoop, the TV aerial that needs positioning, a television producer reading D.H. Lawrence's *Lady*

Chatterley's Lover, but this remains an evocation of London in 1958 rather than realist depiction. This is, as Colin's voice-over declares at the beginning of the film, a post-war England in which 'life broke out in warm colours again', in which every class and race 'mix on equal terms', an assertion reinforced by the varieties of music on screen and on the soundtrack. His utopian declaration is rapidly undercut, however, by scenes of the run-down multiracial area where Colin lives, by harassment from slum landlord Saltzsman (Johnny Shannon) and by the slide into politically orchestrated race riots. Colin's naivety about teenagers (tellingly, his surname is Young) and his love for Crepe Suzette are also challenged by the dystopian realities of contemporary Britain. Suzette, having declared her ambitions in the number 'Having It All', is seduced by the wealthy upper-class Henley of Mayfair (James Fox) and Colin also temporarily 'sells out', persuaded by the seductive fantasies put before him by Vendice Partners (David Bowie) in the highly effective 'That's Motivation' number to become a 'professional teenager'. As Partners tells him, 'we don't sell things, we sell dreams'. In fact, Temple's target seems to be as much the commodification of youth culture and its corruption by hard-bitten 'professionals' such as Harold Charms (Lionel Blair), his fourteen-year-old singing 'discovery' Baby Boom (Chris Pitt) and the cynical disc jockey Call Me Cobber (Alan Freeman), as it is white right-wing racists like Flikker (Bruce Payne) and The Fanatic (Steven Berkoff).

The personal and the political merge, as it is revealed that Henley, in company with Vendice Partners, is the driving force behind White City Developments, a front for the fascist white supremacist group who incite racial violence. Suzette leaves Henley and his sumptuous upper-class lifestyle to return to Colin, whilst he sees through Partners and the inauthenticities of commodified youth, 'the new economic class', and returns to the optimistic affinities declared in his opening voice-over. Temple is unable to avoid an element of melodrama, chiefly in the climatic fight between Flikker and Mr Cool (Tony Hippolyte) and reasserts the supremacy of romantic love as Colin and Suzette make love at the end of the film, revelling in being the 'Absolute Beginners' which Bowie reprises on the soundtrack. Though many scenes work well and the elaborate choreography (by David Toguri) involved in the race fights holds up, the film never really surmounts the weak casting of its two protagonists, O'Connell being particularly unconvincing. Sade's performance of 'Killer Blow' is both pleasurable and effective, reinforcing narrative developments as Colin, smoking dope, learns of Suzette's marriage and storms off on a stolen Vesta scooter, the deep notes of the string bass an indication of the shock to his system. Equally moving is the scene shot to The Style Council's 'Have You Ever Had It Blue', as Colin and Suzette begin to drift apart. Temple's experience in shooting promos is evident in the fantasy number between Bowie and O'Connell, extolling the power of advertising, the huge single record titled, like the song, 'That's Motivation' not only referencing Vance Packard's *The Hidden Persuaders* but also conflating the power of advertising with music-industry promotion. However, 'Quiet Life', performed by The Kinks Ray Davies, is neither effective nor necessary, serving only to muddy narrative waters.

Though *Absolute Beginners* deserved better than the critical and commercial failure it experienced on release, and contains a number of intriguing cameos beyond the evident importance of attempting to express serious social issues in ways that people would attend to because they found them entertainingly expressed, it's hard not to agree with the view that the film

> dissipates its youthful energies between the desire to make a film about the realities and fantasies of the past and the need to make a commercial product for the teenage audiences of the present. (Newman 1986: 103)

Two decades later and stripped of this latter requirement, the film still attracts some harsh criticism, Alexander Walker considering it 'dazzling but confused, with the restlessness of an extended Pop video, not the rhythm of a movie musical' (Walker 2003: 52). Yet *Absolute Beginners* remains testimony of the power of the musical film not just to entertain (however unevenly), but to offer incisive comment on questions of identity and social meaning in ways which ought not to be lost.

Given the hopes riding on this joint production from Goldcrest, Palace and Virgin, the three most enthusiastic British independent companies of the period, the commercial failure of *Absolute Beginners* both in the UK and in America did nothing to make it easier for other filmmakers to explore the possibilities of the musical film form in the late 1980s and into the 1990s. In fact, Virgin Films ceased film financing shortly after. By 1987 Goldcrest, taken over by Brent Walker, had become primarily a sales and distribution company, and Palace Pictures collapsed in 1992. Though other independent companies such as Working Title stumbled on, the crisis in production deepened, increasingly dependent on the involvement of television: the BBC, Channel 4, and ITV companies such as Granada, Central and London Weekend Television. Though arguments raged about the effect of this on the 'cinematic' quality of British films, it seems clear that growing reliance on television companies was not helpful to the musical film, still an expensive genre. Though some interesting television musicals were produced, most notably Dennis Potter's BBC series *The Singing Detective* (1986) and BBC Scotland's *Tutti Frutti* (1987), cinema musicals struggled to survive at a time when, ironically, pop music soundtracks were becoming a ubiquitous element in British feature films.

Commercial synergies and the exploitation of pop music stars

The mutually productive relationship between the film and music industries became increasingly pronounced at the end of the 1980s and into the 1990s, with a number of companies such as EMI having interests across both sectors. It was now commonplace to include a number of pop songs on film soundtracks, a strategy that clearly enhanced the commercial appeal of the film as well as providing opportunities to promote soundtrack albums on CDs with their enhanced digital sound quality. The introduction of this new digital format opened up enormous potential for back-catalogue sales, as the buying public replaced music on vinyl with new CD versions. This was a commercial opportunity that film producers were alert to, and the nostalgic potential of pop music was exploited both in American cinema and, somewhat less commercially aggressively, in British cinema throughout the 1990s. The integrity of the different media was acknowledged, so that the CD package of songs didn't always simply replicate the film soundtrack. A film might contain just a few bars of a song, but the full version would appear on the soundtrack album. Hollywood developed the commercial possibilities of this symbiotic relationship to the point where a song such as Bryan Adam's 'Everything I Do (I Do It For You)' spent fifteen weeks at number one in the British single charts, marketed as being 'from' the Kevin Costner film *Robin Hood – Prince of Thieves* (1991), even though the song only played over the film's closing credits. Warners' *Batman* (1989) had two soundtrack albums, one featuring the songs in the film sung by Prince, the other featuring Danny Elfman's orchestral score. *Dick Tracy* (1990) went one better with three albums.

In Britain, this commercial synergy was most evident in *Four Weddings and a Funeral* (1994), which produced a number one single hit for Wet Wet Wet's version of 'Love Is All Around' and in the soundtrack album from Danny Boyle's *Trainspotting* (1995), but few British films of the 1990s, whatever their generic affiliations, failed to capitalise on the continuing marketability of British pop music. Comedies such as *Nuns On The Run* (1990) and *Bean* (1997), gangster heist films such as *Face* (1997) and *Lock, Stock and Two Smoking Barrels* (1998), melodramas such as *Truly Madly Deeply* (1990) and *When Saturday Comes* (1995) and generic hybrids such *The Full Monty* (1997) and *Human Traffic* (1999) all made extensive use of pop songs on their soundtracks.

A number of films featured rock and pop stars, sometimes constructed around the public persona of a singer or band constructed partly through their musical image, sometimes in more conventional dramatic roles that allowed the music in through the backdoor, as in David Green's *Buster* (1988) starring ex-Genesis drummer Phil Collins as train robber Buster Edwards. In addition to songs from British groups such as The Hollies and Gerry and the Pacemakers and American groups such as The Four Tops and the Everley Brothers, which helped locate the film in its contemporary 1963 setting, the film included two songs from Collins, 'Two Hearts One Mind' and 'Groovy Kind Of Love', both of which were chart hits.

It Couldn't Happen Here (1987) featured Neil Tennant and Chris Lowe, the Pet Shop Boys, in a picaresque, episodic series of loosely connected scenes overlaid with the non-diegetic soundtrack of their hits. Starting with scenes set in a British seaside resort, the duo undertake an increasingly surreal spatial and temporal journey through England, as the late 80s 'cool' represented by the Pet Shop Boys is contrasted with the perceived awfulness of traditional British culture, its seaside guest houses, saucy comic postcard attitude to sex, shady used-car salesmen, racist thugs, and ambivalence about religion and morality. Both cinematography and soundtrack privilege what is promoted as the poetic and intellectual qualities of the Pet Shop Boys numbers, which contrast with the plethora of clichés that are seen to inhabit much of British culture. Quality actors such as Barbara Windsor and Joss Ackland are largely wasted in a film that is unsure whether style or substance is more important. The film owes much to the aesthetics evident in the Pet Shop Boys' music videos, but *It Couldn't Happen Here* offers an interesting visual, aural and choreographic commentary on British cultural heterogeneity.

Both *Buster* and *It Couldn't Happen Here* reveal ways in which British film was exploring the dramatic and aesthetic potential of popular music in ways that went beyond mere commercial exploitation of contemporary or nostalgic soundtracks. This understanding that popular music had become an essential element in contemporary cinema aesthetics, both as a formal device in narrative and dramatic construction and as an attraction in its own right, was increasingly evident in British films of the 1990s. For a generation that had grown up with rock'n'roll and the Sixties pop revolution and that had refused to let go of its interest in popular music, as well as for a new generation whose identification with music and musical trends was at least as strong, the formal and aesthetic importance of the film soundtrack could only become more pronounced, even if their interest in the musical genre (however broadly defined) was in decline.

In a decade in which it became harder to categorise British films in conventional generic terms this decline is understandable. Moreover, whilst those traditional obstacles to a vibrant British film industry and film culture remain – the tension between depending on American money for films which have high production values and hence international marketing appeal and the ways in which such dependency compromises the articulation of (an increasingly complex) 'Britishness'; the scarcity of British stars who can both guarantee international sales and resist the lure of Hollywood; the weak tradition of original screenwriting and support for script development; the problems of getting British films into distribution and the continuing preference of the domestic market for American product – it has also become more difficult to define what is British about British cinema. Whether it is right to think in terms of a post-national British cinema, or to see those contemporary British films which acknowledge multiculturalism, devolution and difference as being merely the inheritors of a national cinema that has always attempted to reflect debates about nation, culture and identity, the fact is that British culture is ineluctably regarded as more diverse, heterogeneous and pluralistic than ever before. This is not to eradicate the struggles for identity that have sat at the heart of all British cinema throughout the decades, merely to state that perceptions of difference inform our debates in more powerful ways than ever before, forming the starting point of those debates rather than requiring decoding and unravelling.

The contemporary British musical film

Given the central role of music in contributing to this growing cultural diversity and plurality, as well as the sheer abundance of music video on satellite, cable and digital television, it seems surprising that the musical film has been an increasing rarity during the 1990s and the early part of the new century. Yet, if musical film has been in decline, that decline is far from terminal, as a number of contemporary films testify. Some of them seem strangely old-fashioned, attempting to defend and resurrect those ideologies and pleasures which traditionally adhere to the genre, others attempt to understand the present through their interpolation of the recent past, whilst yet others engage directly with the multifarious elements of contemporary British culture. More than one film has attempted to perpetuate that distinctive ability of the musical film to deliver those simultaneously intimate and spectacular pleasures of popular song and music and harness them to issues that are – or perhaps ought be – worthy of serious intellectual interrogation.

Although the dependence of British talent on American investment was nothing new, it became especially pronounced in the 1990s, making it more difficult than ever to delineate 'British' musical films. Not strictly speaking a British film, the Paramount-financed Canadian production *Stepping Out* (1991) merits mention because of British director Lewis Gilbert and the looming comic presence of Julie Waters. A curiously old-fashioned musical that has some resonance with Judy Garland's *A Star Is Born* (1954), Garland's daughter Liza Minnelli plays a fading singer and choreographer who 'got to touch Bob Fosse's sleeve once'. She runs an amateur dance class attended by a group of misfits and loners, beset with myriad social and personal problems. Overcoming ethnic and gender differences, they pull together to star in a charity show and, in the process, develop and bloom as individuals. A 'romantic' sub-plot has Minnelli painfully disengaging from her unsuitable and cynical rock-band boyfriend despite being pregnant, but the narrative focuses firmly on the hard work involved in reaching the 'professional' standards expected for the show. Along the way, there is space to exhibit Minnelli's dancing and acting talents, complete with non-diegetic big-band accompaniment, in a film that unashamedly promotes its utopian resolution to all the social and personal problems on display. Perhaps more than anything else, this optimism, so much at odds with contemporary Britain, discounts the film as British and helps to explain its neglect at the British box-office.

Confirming his reliance on American investment to finance the films he wanted to make, Alan Parker's return to the musical with *The Commitments* (1991) proved an outstanding triumph. For Robert Murphy, *The Commitments* is a

> key film, not only for its box-office success when the fortunes of British cinema were at a low ebb, but for its genuinely populist appeal and the example it set (particularly in its audition sequence) to films as different as *Shallow Grave* and *The Full Monty*. (Murphy 2000: 13)

Based on the book by vogue novelist Roddy Doyle with a script by British writers Dick Clement and Ian La Frenais, the film recounts the formation, rise and subsequent break-up of a group of Dublin youngsters who form a soul band. Casting the film from unknown actors and musicians, Parker's film achieves an authentic raw edge demanded by the story and its setting. In the process, Parker manages to situate the film within that broad tradition of British social realism, make an incisive comment about the influence of Afro-American traditions on popular music, and deliver a great deal of pleasurable excitement through the music, a sharply observed script, crisp direction and brilliantly realised performances.

Agreeing to take on the management of no-hope North Dublin band And And And, aspiring impresario Jimmy Rabbitte (Robert Arkins), ditches their lead singer and demands that they play soul music. In the same way that Don Lockwood's voice-over in *Singin' in the Rain* (1952) inflates his early career, only to be undercut by the visuals, Jimmy's credentials in the music business are less than impressive, as we see him trying to sell cassettes to local market stall-holders and kids on the train. In the opening scenes at a wedding and on the decrepit council estate, we are plunged into a working-class world of dereliction, unemployment, chaotic family life and foul language, a world that, as Jimmy argues, can only be represented by 'Dublin soul' music. In a wonderful sequence where people audition in response to Jimmy's newspaper advert, the rich plurality of other musical influences, including the 'blasphemous' suggestion that 'Elvis was a Cajun', are on display, but are rejected by Jimmy. Amidst this plethora of musical references, Jimmy puts the band together and plays them video footage of James Brown, countering objections that the band are 'a little too white' to imitate soul music with the view that 'The Irish are the blacks of Europe, Dubliners are the blacks of Ireland, and north-side Dubliners are the blacks of Dublin'. Having recruited the raw vocal talent of Deco Cuffe (Andrew Strong), his plans are boosted by the mysterious arrival of Joey 'The Lips' Fagin (Johnny Murphy), who claims to have played with the likes of B.B. King, Sam Cooke, Otis Redding and Martha Reeves. The band is completed by the feisty female vocal trio and, against an infectious non-diegetic soundtrack of soul music, sets about rehearsing its numbers using equipment supplied by a local fence and drug-dealer. This is conventional territory, as the narrative expends energy detailing the hard work involved in putting the music together, though considerable friction between the band members and a crying baby distinguishes this from other, more utopian versions of the road to success.

Under the guise of being part of an anti-heroin campaign, the band persuades the local Catholic priest to let them play their first gig at the church hall. Deco's inflated ego and exhibitionism proves almost as disruptive as the electrical equipment that blows up, but the band clearly exhibits promise. Despite having to replace their drummer, the band plays more gigs, though sexual jealousy and their increasing professionalism creates further problems and group dissension. Joe leads them to believe that Wilson Pickett, on a European tour that includes Ireland, will be able to jam with them at their next gig. Superb performances of soul classics such as 'Try A Little Tenderness' and Pickett's 'Midnight Hour' are given privileged performance space and serve to assuage audience anger at the soul star's non-appearance. However, Jimmy walks away as violence breaks out between the band members. As he does so, Wilson Pickett's limousine stops him to ask directions to the gig, too late to seal the band's potential success. Joe assures him that success would have been too predictable and that the important thing is what being in the band has done for each individual; this way, he tells Jimmy, is poetry. The film's postscript details what happened to each band member, though Jimmy fails to find any meaning in the whole experience.

Despite its displacement to Dublin, *The Commitments* marks a return to those themes and ideas in those early, rejected, angry British working-class Parker scripts. Comparing north Dublin to his own working-class upbringing in north London, Parker recognised that music offered dreams of escape from working-class poverty, unemployment and dead-end jobs. As Dean tells Jimmy, 'it feels better to be an unemployed musician than an unemployed pipe-fitter'. For Jimmy, the whole point of soul music is that is it working-class music, music produced by people who were at the bottom of the heap. Selling his views to the band on a late-night train, Jimmy argues that 'soul is the rhythm of sex and the factory too, the working man's rhythm'. The message gets across, as the non-diegetic soundtrack song is picked up and sung diegetically by the group. The fact that they are white should not, for Jimmy, preclude identification with black Americans, expressed through the music. Importantly, the music doesn't act as a force for community integration, since there appear to be no black people in Dublin to integrate with. Rather, the music allows a reorientation of identity, leading the band to a recognition of their place but enabling them to take pride in it, to give the system a kick. Though Parker doesn't flinch from the realities and avoids the fantasy of easy success, *The Commitments* marks an important acknowledgement of the power of popular music, internalised and appropriated, to construct identity. It is at the very least, as Bernie says, when surrounded by crying babies and piles of ironing, 'something to look forward to'.

For Jimmy, soul music is more effective than those other opiates, drugs and religion. The band's strapline, the 'Saviours of Soul', clearly makes reference to that other claimant to be a saviour of souls, the Catholic Church. Religious images ripple through the film but, unlike the band's concerts, the churches are empty. The church organ is used to play Procul Harum's 'Whiter Shade Of Pale', the candles simply make a mess that need clearing up, and confession doesn't deliver any more than the church delivers for the working class of north Dublin. In marked contrast with *Sid & Nancy*, drugs play no part in the band's existence and Duffy, the *unterwelt* drugs dealer, gets short narrative shrift. In the end and despite the abundance of energy that the music delivers, success eludes most of the band and the film avoids over-romanticised excess. The camaraderie that they briefly experience is blown apart by the bickering, the sexual jealousy and some inflated egos, but for a period they all experience a sense of purpose. The totalising influence of class reasserts itself, with 'nice boy' piano-playing Steven becoming a doctor, Derek and Outspan busking in Dublin's Grafton Street.

Though album sales from the film exceeded twelve million, Parker does more with the music than use it simply as a promotional tool. *The Commitments* remains an outstanding example, not just of the rich possibilities that contemporary musical films can offer, but of ways in which music can become a central element of the dramatic and aesthetic meaning and form of film, delivering pleasures in complex, multilayered ways. This was something that Parker would return to with *Evita* (1996).

In a very different way, *Backbeat* (1993), Iain Softley's film about The Beatles, also successfully exploits music as an essential component of its dramatic landscape. Set between 1960 and 1962, *Backbeat* examines the early career of The Beatles, with particular emphasis on the role of Stuart Sutcliffe and his death in April 1962. The first production from Scala, the new independent company company founded by former Palace Pictures producers Steve Woolley and Nik Powell, the film was partly reliant on money invested by Channel Four Films and made use of the time-honoured strategy of including some American film actors in an attempt to boost appeal in the States. Much of the film is set in Hamburg and deals with the considerable influence exercised by Astrid Kircherr (Sheryl Lee) and her boyfriend artist Klaus Voormann (Kai Wiesinger) over Sutcliffe (Stephen Dorff). He is more interested in his painting than he is in the band and his attitude and indifferent commitment cause dissent within the group. Though he is initially defended by John Lennon (Ian Hart), who shares Sutcliffe's interest in art, a fight between the two of them leads to Sutcliffe leaving the band to concentrate on his painting. Shortly after, Sutcliffe dies from a massive brain haemorrhage, the result, the film suggests, of a beating-up that occurs in the opening sequence. Though the film was marketed as 'the story of the Fifth Beatle', director Softley declared that the film was 'about the origins of Pop Art' (Yates 1994: 35).

Earlier attempts to detail The Beatles' story, Richard Marquand's *Birth Of The Beatles* (1979: released 1982) and Christopher Munch's

The Hours And Times (1992), had met with indifferent success. However, *Backbeat* was released during a major Beatles revival, coinciding with the thirty-year anniversary of the the group's storming of America and the re-release of *A Hard Day's Night*. The opening credit titles with their nostalgic black-and-white footage of the late 1950s and early 1960s suggest that the film intends to cash in on nostalgic appeal, wanting 'its cake of nostalgia frosted over with the icing of tragedy' (Rich 1994: 11), but this is undercut by the successful re-versioning of the music. Avoiding early recordings by the Beatles themselves, the soundtrack features new recordings from the so-called Backbeat Band, featuring American musicians from bands including Nirvana, REM, Sonic Youth and Gumball, with the on-screen actors lip-synching in performance. Abundant screen space is given to these numbers 'performed' at the Hamburg strip-club, before Astrid arrives and tries to expand the band's horizons by taking them to Bar Enfer, the centre of Hamburg's intellectual, artistic and homosexual scene. Lennon explodes at what he regards as the hypocrisy of these intellectual posers and, from then on, the narrative revolves around the struggle for Sutcliffe, between Lennon and Astrid, between music, the band and painting, between Lennon's determined avowal of his Liverpool working-class anti-intellectual credentials and its vision of English insularity, and Astrid's mind-expanding voyage through the arts, painting, photography, art-house cinema and readings from Rimbaud, between haircuts and everything they entailed. This struggle is foregrounded when Sutcliffe's painting teacher in Liverpool tells him to paint rather than play, and by Lennon's earlier comment, as the two have sex with female groupies, that Sutcliffe had 'made the right choice'. Significantly, Lennon denies any suggestion that he is homosexual, jealously guarding his unquestioned masculinity in the face of the gay activity he sees in Hamburg.

   Sutcliffe's choice to follow painting is, at one level, the wrong one, given the subsequent success of The Beatles. Yet Lennon's perception of the choices facing them both proved equally wrong-headed. Just as their 1950s American-inspired quiffs give way to Astrid's mop-cuts, so Lennon's residual hold on anti-intellectual English insularity gives way to broader horizons that include Europe and subsequently the globe. He reveals more knowledge than he pretends to have when, driving with Sutcliffe and Astrid, he is the one who identifies Edith Piaf singing on the car radio. This view contradicts one reviewer who regards the film as

> unapologetically reconstructive, It is nostalgic rather than imaginary, resting solidly on memories imported from the past. In so doing, it leads the audience by hand back to the poignant days of 1960. (Rich 1994: 8)

This misreads a film that opens up and reflects on issues and shifts which were simply not visible in 1960, as the British began to 'discover' continental Europe and its energising cultures, a discovery that continues to change what being British means. In fact, *Backbeat* does try hard to resist the conventional histories of The Beatles and of popular music, despite Ian Hart's strong performance as Lennon delivering all the best lines in the film. The decision to re-record The Beatles' music renders it not simply part of patchwork pop history, but a music which remains of relevance to contemporary audiences of all ages, as the successful sales of re-issued Beatles compilation albums in 1995 and 1996 testified.

If proof were needed of the British film industry's dependence on the hegemonic power of its American counterpart, at least in its ability to produce big-budget features designed to appeal to global markets, then Alan Parker's *Evita* (1996) provides it. Taking on the role of chairman of the British Film Institute in 1997, Parker declared that he 'never thought of himself as part of the American film industry' (James 1997), but was aware of the constraints attached to British production which failed to attract American finance. *Evita* was financed in part by (the now defunct) Cinergi Pictures, and was assured global distribution. Starring Madonna as Eva Peron in what is undoubtedly her most successful screen appearance, the film benefits from a strong supporting cast that includes Antonio Banderas, Jonathan Pryce and Jimmy Nail. Based on the stage musical by Andrew Lloyd Webber and Tim Rice, the film adopts a rock opera format to recount the rise and early death of Eva Peron and her iconic status within Argentina. Though at least one reviewer regarded it as a weakness, Parker links the personal with the political: Eva's trajectory from orphan waif to president's wife is used to track and comment on the political traumas experienced by Argentina and its people in the 1940s and early 1950s. These events are commented on by Che (Banderos), a kind of Greek chorus figure who, through frequent direct address to camera and songs, expresses his scepticism about Eva's professed love of the masses. Though Banderos's singing cannot match Madonna's superb performance, he offers an earthy antidote to the increasingly glamorous political world that Eva invades and comes to dominate, a world increasingly detached from the real political needs of the people. At the same time, Madonna's numbers, including 'Another Suitcase In Another Hall' and 'I'd Be Surprisingly Good For You' serve to link personal fragility with political ambition. Strong performances are matched by superb set and costume design, convincing location shooting (much of it in Hungary), rich deep photography and, of course, the numbers which range from the declamatory 'High Flying Adored', the anthemic 'Don't Cry For Me Argentina', to the touchingly introspective and frail 'You Must Love Me'.

The film appeared to polarise critical opinion. For some, the traditional pleasures of the musical genre, enshrined in the emotional pleasures of singing and dancing, the representation of imagined and sustainable utopias, were in short supply. For the film to work, the review in *Sight and Sound* argued,

> the film-makers would have had to reinvent the musical as a film genre, or at least to re-inflect it in the way that *Cabaret* or even *Tommy* did. But since the rise of MTV . . . the video-clip has so ransacked the genre it now seems aesthetically exhausted and commercially successful only when animated and aimed at children. (Arroyo 1997: 40)

Though the undoubted influence of the music video aesthetic is rightly acknowledged, this is to miss the extent to which *Evita* not only comes to terms with that influence, but appropriates it (not least through using one of its most iconic performers) in ways that remain profoundly cinematic, recounting a narrative – albeit in innovative form – which maintains coherence for over two hours. Moreover, far from being an exercise in obscure nostalgia, *Evita* cunningly exploits the complex extra-textual resonance enjoyed by Madonna within those complex discourses surrounding gender politics to reinforce the assertion that the personal is political. Though *Evita* no more re-invents the genre than does Baz Luhrmann's *Moulin Rouge*, both films reassert its relevance within a culture where affective sensibilities demand attention.

If Alan Parker represents that tradition of British film-makers who willingly made successful accommodations with American finance in the effort to produce films with British talent but with international appeal, by the late 1990s it seemed increasingly difficult to avoid American support even for those films that were likely to appeal primarily to the domestic audience. Mark Herman had attracted considerable attention with *Brassed Off* (1996), a political drama that made effective use of brass band music to detail attempts to keep a threatened mining community together. A year later, Scala producers Nik Powell and Stephen Woolley turned to Miramax Films to finance Herman's *Little Voice* (1997), the story of shy, talented, Judy-Garland-obsessed 'Little Voice' Laura Hoff (Jane Horrocks) who is 'discovered' by seedy impresario Ray Say (Michael Caine). She resists his attempts to exploit her talents, other than to make one public appearance. *Little Voice* is rooted firmly within that tradition of British film-making that details the lives of ordinary working-class, in this case northern, characters, whilst offering a distinctly British self-deprecating take on the business of show business. Ray boasts to Little Voice ('LV') that he once met 'Monro'; she is impressed until he tells her he means Matt Monro, the British ex-bus-driver singer from the 1960s, not Marilyn. Caine delivers a strong, convincing performance, ably supported by Jim Broadbent, Ewan McGregor and Brenda Blethyn, in a film that marks out that gulf between conventional American optimism found in the film musical and its downbeat, inhibited, British equivalent. Not that LV is without talent. On the contrary, her one performance, especially her version of Garland's 'Get Happy' attracts the attention of bigger showbiz impresarios and, with its on-screen big-band accompaniment, takes the film – briefly – into a different dimension. In the end, the show does go on, with Take Fat, 'five burly men from Barnsley', Brenda Bailey and Her Farmyard Frolics, but not Little Voice. Ray Say sings, discordantly, 'you won't be seeing rainbows anymore / it's over', as his career disintegrates and the Hoff house burns down. Though an element of normality is restored following scenes of desolation and bitterness, the film's use of Ethel Merman's 'There's No Business Like Show Business' over the closing credits can only be read ironically.

Mike Leigh's *Topsy-Turvy* (1999) continued British cinema's irregular but persistent interest in the work of Gilbert and Sullivan. Leigh's production company Thin Man Films sought the help of Los-Angeles-based Newmarket Capital Group to finance the film, which achieved international distribution and several awards, including Academy Awards for costume design and make-up. Andy Medhurst is surely right in detecting Topsy-Turvy's 'attention to the anxious underbelly of Victorian culture' (Medhurst 2000: 37), its understated examination of imperialist, racist and homophobic attitudes saving the film from accusations of 'heritage mongering'. At the centre of the film is the tension between Gilbert and Sullivan, Gilbert glorying in the success that formulaic librettos consistently deliver, Sullivan haunted by fears that his musical integrity and ambitions are being consistently undermined. Leigh's respect and liking for the music is evident, but he also uses it to expose the inability of the leading characters to articulate their feelings, most painfully where Gilbert is completely incapable of responding to his wife's emotional fears for their marriage at the film's climax. The strictures of Victorian formality are sublimated through alcoholism, sexual promiscuity and drug taking, though as these are located within the film's overall concern with representational authenticity, they are treated in ways that are totally devoid of sensationalism. Musically, the film centres on the creation and subsequent success of *The Mikado*, following the relative failure of *Princess Ida* in the summer heat of 1884. Generic conventions are self-evident in the backstage bickering and arguments that take place between Gilbert and Sullivan and in the rehearsals for the new production but, despite the extensive footage devoted to the music, these conventions are subservient to Leigh's determination to expose the effects of complex social forces on individual lives. Visually stunning though the film is, this is not something that was ever likely to appeal to a broad audience, though it is perhaps the most satisfying of all British films dealing with Gilbert and Sullivan.

In their very different ways, *Evita*, *Topsy-Turvy* and *Little Voice* are musical films whose realms of concern extend beyond the provision of 'mere entertainment'. However formally different or innovative they are, the fantasies and excesses they hint at seem restrained by that rich shaft of social concern that runs through so much of British cinema. Even a film like *Billy Elliot* (2000), ostensibly a film that offers a utopian celebration of success, relies for its dramatic and emotional weight on young Billy's ability to transcend the constraints of class, region and gender, though significantly the cost of that process are elided and obscured by the film's narrative climax. Yet at the same time, far from being exhausted, the British variant of the musical film has continued to produce vehicles of engaging silliness, exploiting and celebrating the success of contemporary pop music icons as it has done across the decades. Bob Spiers' *Spice World* (1997) built upon the phenomenal global success of the five-girl group the Spice Girls in a film which, as a contemporary noted was 'far too straightforwardly funny and bouncily colourful to be a flop or a cult' (Sinker 1998: 49).

More cult television show *The Monkees* than *A Hard Day's Night*, *Spice World* utilised musical film's capacity for self-reflexivity to play around with the phenomenon of the Spice Girls' success and its dependency on the media discourses surrounding their music and image. A narrative ostensibly built around the group's anxieties about their first 'live' appearance at London's Albert Hall (an acknowledgement of contemporary media speculation about whether the girls could 'really' sing) is augmented by media attention in the shape of a proposal for a Hollywood film, a pretentious but incompetent documentary film crew, and the machinations of tabloid newspaper editor Kevin McMaxford (Barry Humphries). Fantasy scenes within the film serve to reference a range of film and television genres including science-fiction aliens, horror-haunted houses, and female action shows such as *Charlies' Angels* and *Wonder Woman*. Appearances by a plethora of 'real-life' celebrities such as Jonathan Ross, Jools Holland, Elvis Costello, Bob Geldof and Elton John are supplemented by a succession of cameo roles delivered by the likes of Meatloaf, Stephen Fry, Richard Briers, Hugh Laurie and Roger Moore, the latter invoking a comically inverted world of James Bond. The resulting sense of displacement, refusing us unalloyed belief in the diegetic world constructed by the narrative, per-petuates a tactic that has been central to the musical film since its incep-tion. In *Spice World*, this is cleverly reinforced by the intelligent comic play around the girls' apparent discontent with their own media images, a game which continues right through to the closing credits which serve to compound the complex line between filmic construction and its ref-erents which are, themselves, essentially media constructs.

The real point of the film, of course, other than those traditional plea-sures of *seeing* popular music performers, is to discount any anxieties that anyone may have about the Spice Girls and the reasons for their success. The film uses every opportunity to feature their music, from the opening images of an appearance on BBC's *Top of the Pops*, in rehearsal scenes, as the soundtrack in dance-clubs, as well as their final appear-ance at the Albert Hall. Whilst the film acknowledges the status of the group as a 'well-oiled global machine' who, as their road manager Clifford (Richard E. Grant) tells them, have 'schedules, not lives', it also employs British cinema's capacity for self-deprecation, not least in the scene where high-court judge Stephen Fry forces them to ponder poten-tial failure and a future of 'twenty years of cheesy chat shows on tele-vision in Taiwan' or where the camp military dance-master (Michael Barrymore) criticises the dancing in Spice Girls' videos. Ultimately, the film revels in the constructed ordinariness of the five girls whilst paying homage to the extraordinary impact they have had upon contemporary popular culture. As such, and for all its limitations, *Spice World* sug-gests that the musical film retains that long-standing capacity to trans-mute and articulate contemporary popular music pleasures onto the cinema screen.

Whilst such tried and tested formats appear adaptable to contempo-rary audience demands, Michael Winterbottom's *24 Hour Party People* (2002) suggests that the British musical film is capable of being re-energised in ways that appeal to contemporary audiences. A version of events surrounding Tony Wilson and his management of Manchester's Hacienda club and bands including Joy Division and the Happy Mondays from the late 1970s into the 1990s, the film skilfully blends its mix of actuality footage and dramatic reconstruction with enormous energy and to good effect. Trapped in his daytime job with Granada TV, reporting on local trivia such as a sheep-herding goose, Wilson (Steve Coogan) narrates what he clearly regards as the more momentous events of post-punk Manchester and the rise of club culture. Part fictionalised autobiography, part dramatic reconstruction, this backstage narrative is dominated by the figure of Wilson as imagined by Wilson, despite his declaration that he is only 'a minor character in my own story'. The edgy, fragmented narrative is disrupted by frequent address to camera, declarations that events just shown or described by Wilson did not really happen, and the presence of real-life characters from the Manchester scene of the period, as the film busily and consistently deconstructs what it has just asserted. What matters, declares Wilson in a voice-over, is to 'print the legend', a legend which the film erects as being of central importance in the recent history of youth culture.

Though the obsession with Manchester is both a strength and a weakness, Winterbottom's film is a timely reminder that, along with those other structural issues that British cinema needs to engage with, regionalism remains important. The city is ever-present, both in physical form and Wilson's emotional attachment to it, but is never sentimentalised, not least in the clear acknowledgement of the drugs and guns culture that was part of a 'Madchester' scene that threatens to take Wilson out of his depth. Neither are the bands, particularly the drug-induced depravities committed by Shaun Ryder and the Happy Mondays, whose lack of professionalism finally exposes the gulf between them and 'Cambridge graduate' Wilson, leading to the demise of Factory, his successful independent record label. The fact that the film is so partial and selective in its account of Manchester's contribution to contemporary youth culture, erasing, for example, the significance of bands such as The Smiths and the Stone Roses, only serves to reinforce the centrality of Wilson's self-regarding egotism which sits at the centre of the film, to heighten the creative friction between narrator and the film's subject matter. At the climax of the film when he witnesses a drug-induced comic-book vision of God telling him that, despite all that has happened, he was right, Wilson remarks that God looked just like him. He is gracious and intelligent enough to concede, however, that if Shaun Ryder had seen God, he would look just like Ryder. The film manages to incorporate the music in ways that reflect not just Wilson's passion, but solidifies its cultural significance. Never lingering too long on diegetic performance, the numbers do enough to suggest the tortured sensitivity of Ian Curtis, the disintegration of the Happy Mondays and the often fraught rehearsal and recording sessions. Archive footage and snatches on the soundtrack serve to construct a sense of the rich density of the music scene in Manchester during the period. *24 Hour Party People* engages not just with its subject matter and expectations of contemporary film style, but also with its audience in ways that suggest that, far from being exhausted, the British musical film has a distinct future in its ability to address both the rich heritage of British popular music and its contemporary significance.

Postscript

In *Icons in the Fire*, written in the year he died, Alexander Walker recounts the role of the Chinese butterfly in what is often termed chaos theory, where the difference between the butterfly flapping its wings once or twice can have the most enormous consequences. Walker concludes that 'tiny changes . . . can have huge results. Prediction is thus rendered foolish, indeed impossible' (Walker 2003: xxi). With these words in mind, this postscript gives brief consideration to the future of the British film musical.

The commercial success of Baz Luhrmann's *Moulin Rouge* (2000) and Rob Marshall's *Chicago* (2002) would suggest that the musical as a genre is far from dead, despite earlier predictions that the 'market for film musicals . . . provides no evidence that a resurgence is either imminent or desired' (Fehr and Vogel 1993: 260). Hollywood, of course, has the infrastructure and resources to make whatever films promise commercial success. In Britain, the future of the musical, no less than any other film, remains dependent on the vagaries of British film production and its traditional roller-coaster pattern of boom and bust. At a time of growing uncertainty within the television industry, the support that television has given to British film production cannot be taken for granted. European co-productions continue to be problematic and do not have a good track record of supporting musicals. American finance has a much better record of supporting British talent in musical films, as the career of Alan Parker proves, though experience suggests that the extent of that support and its consistency cannot be taken for granted. Finance provided through the Lottery Fund has become significant, but poses some issues around the types of films likely to be supported; as young film-maker John Maybury has argued, 'the language spoken by young people in this country is not the language of the government and the lottery' (James 1998: 15). After a flurry of activity and considerable commercial and critical success in the mid- and late 1990s, British film production appears to have slowed down. True, film-makers such as

Michael Winterbottom seem able to finance their films although, despite the success of *24 Hour Party People*, he shows no particular dedication to the musical, no matter how broadly defined.

If the difficulties of raising finance are not enough, British films continue to struggle to find distribution and exhibition space. Throughout the 1990s, 'dozens of feature films made in Britain . . . have simply been left to gather dust' (Macnab 2000: 138). Julian Henriques' *Babymother* (1998) fared better than that, obtaining a commercial release, albeit a short one. This 'reggae musical' was 50 per cent funded by Channel 4, the other 50 per cent provided by the lottery fund. One of the few British films where all the protagonists are black, *Babymother* centres on black British youth culture, based around the dance hall and gender politics. Though the film has some problems over structure and style, it vibrates with energy and its musical sequences are 'beautifully choreographed' (McGrath 1998: 39). However, if the film was seen as 'one of the first of the new cinematic wave to test the treacherous waters of British film distribution' (Hall 1998: 25), the results were disappointing as it failed to reach a general British audience.

Despite all this, however, there is room to be optimistic about the British musical film and its future. In the first place, the interest in and consumption of popular music in Britain continues to increase. The synergies forged between the music and film industries mean that British films are likely to continue to make extensive use of music on their soundtracks, whatever the genre. In the United States, there are already instances of the sound/vision hierarchy being reversed, with film narratives being structured around a director's choice of popular music, as in Cameron Crowe's *Elizabethtown* (2005). Such trends render the notion of 'the musical genre' increasingly problematic, though, as I have argued throughout this book, the British musical film has always defied that limited generic categorisation usually associated with the Hollywood musical. Given the importance of popular music in contemporary British culture, it is not being unduly optimistic to expect to see that importance translating into something we would want to call musical film.

Babymother suggests another reason why optimism about the future of the British musical film might be justified. If British society and culture has become less homogeneous, more heterogeneous, and contemporary British cinema articulates a much more ambivalent image of this changing Britain, the effects of these changes are also happening within British popular music. For Stuart Hall, *Babymother* was 'wired directly into the motor of assertive energy which is powering so-called multi-cultural Britain' an energy expressed through street fashion, sexuality, dance and music (Hall 1998: 26). Drawing upon Afro-Caribbean musical traditions and influences, the film reflects the extent to which these and other black musical influences such as rap and hip-hop are becoming part of mainstream popular music culture in Britain. Though lagging behind, musical influences from the Asian subcontinent are beginning to make an impact on mainstream musical culture. Though Bollywood cinema has been increasingly significant in Britain, British Asian audiences have traditionally watched imported material. Significantly, in the late 1990s the Bombay-based industry began taking a keener interest in the working of the UK distribution of their films, and have even used some British locations for their films. It is not unreasonable to hope that, in the near future, British Asians and perhaps a wider audience will want films that reflect the British Asian experience and which draw upon Bollywood's musical traditions. As Heather Tyrell argues,

> Bollywood adds another area of creative potential to the UK cinema scene, one that sits well with the Hammer and *Carry On* traditions that remain the best examples of a truly popular British cinema (Tyrell 1998: 22).

To date, British Asian film directors such as Gurinda Chanda have produced films that work within some of the best traditions of British film comedy. The possibilities for musical films that reflect the British Asian experience, make use of Asian musical traditions transmuted into pop formats, and that appeal to multi-ethnic British audiences are self-evident.

The point is that while the film musical clearly promotes pop music, it does so much more than that. In harnessing the creative potential of spectacle, fantasy and exuberance, the musical can offer audiences experiences that are different from other cinematic experiences. The ability of the British musical film to temper utopian optimism with cultural sensibilities that are specifically British – no matter how defined – suggests that it has a future. To suggest that it *ought* to have seems neither unduly utopian nor optimistic, even for British film.

Bibliography

Agajanian, Rowana, 'Nothing Like Any Previous Musical, British or American: The Beatles' film *A Hard Day's Night*' in Anthony Aldgate, James Chapman and Arthur Marwick (eds), *Windows On The Sixties: Exploring Key Texts of Media and Culture*, London, I. B. Taurus, 2000.

Aldgate, Tony, 'Comedy, Class and Containment: The British Domestic Cinema of the 1930s' in James Curran and Vincent Porter (eds), *British Cinema History*, London, Weidenfeld and Nicholson, 1983.

Aldgate, Tony, '*Women of Twilight, Cosh Boy* and the Advent of the "X" Certificate', *Journal of Popular British Cinema*, Vol. 3 (2000), pp. 59–68.

Aldgate, Tony, 'From Script to Screen: Serious Charge and Film Censorship' in MacKillop and Sinyard (eds), *British Cinema of the 1950s: A Celebration*, Manchester, Manchester University Press, 2003.

Aldgate, Anthony and Richards, Jeffrey, *Britain Can Take It: The British Cinema in the Second World War*, Oxford, Basil Blackwell, 1986.

Allen, Michael, 'In The Mix: How Electrical Reproducers Facilitated the Transition to Sound in British Cinemas' in K.J. Donnelly (ed.), *Film Music: Critical Approaches*, Edinburgh, Edinburgh University Press, 2001.

Altman, Rick, *The American Film Musical*, Bloomington, Indiana University Press, 1989.

Anon., 'The Tales of Hoffmann', *Picturegoer*, 24 November 1951, p. 5.

Arroyo, Jose, 'Evita', *Sight and Sound*, Vol. 7, No. 2 (February 1997), pp. 40–1.

Askey, Arthur, *Before Your Very Eyes: An Autobiography*, London, The Woburn Press, 1975.

Babington, Bruce (ed.), *British Stars and Stardom*, Manchester, Manchester University Press, 2001.

Babington, Bruce, *Launder and Gilliat*, Manchester, Manchester University Press, 2002.

Bailey, Peter (ed.), *Music Hall: The Business of Pleasure*, Milton Keynes, Open University Press, 1986.

Balcon, Michael, 'The British Film During the War' in R.K. Neilson Baxter, Roger Manvell and H.H. Wollenberg (eds), *The Penguin Film Review*, London, Penguin Books, 1946.

Balcon, Michael, *Michael Balcon Presents . . . A Lifetime of Films*, London, Hutchinson, 1969.

Bamford, Kenton, *Distorted Images: British National Identity and Film in the 1920s*, London, I. B. Taurus, 1999.

Banks, Jack, *Monopoly Television: MTV's quest to control the music*, Oxford, Westview, 1996.

Barnes, John, *The Beginnings of Cinema in England*, Newton Abbot, David & Charles, 1976.

Barnes, Richard and Townsend, Pete, *The Story Of Tommy*, Twickenham, Eel Pie Publishing, 1977.

Barr, Charles, *Ealing Studios*, New York, The Overlook Press, 1980.

Barr, Charles, 'Desperate Yearnings: Victor Saville and Gainsborough' in Pam Cook (ed.), *Gainsborough Pictures*, London, Cassell, 1997.

Barr, Charles, *English Hitchcock*, Moffat, Cameron and Hollis, 1999.

BBC, *The BBC Year Book 1932*, London, BBC, 1932.

BBC, *The BBC Year Book 1943*, London, BBC, 1943.

Bergfelder, Tim, 'The Production Designer and the Gesamtkunstwerk: German Film Technicians in the British Film Industry of the 1930s' in Andrew Higson (ed.), *Dissolving Views: Key Writings on British Cinema*, London, Cassell, 1996.

Bergfelder, Tim, 'Surface and Distraction: Style and Genre at Gainsborough in the Late 1920s and 1930s' in P. Cook (ed.), *Gainsborough Pictures*, London, Cassell, 1997.

Bourdieu, Pierre, *Distinction: A Social Critique of the Judgement of Taste*, translated by Richard Nice, London, Routledge & Kegan Paul, 1984.

Brand, Neil, 'Distant Trumpets: The Score to *The Flag Lieutenant* and Music of the British Silent Cinema' in A. Higson (ed.), *Young and Innocent? The Cinema in Britain 1896–1930*, Exeter, University of Exeter Press, 2002.

Bret, David, *Gracie Fields: The Authorized Biography*, London, Robson Books, 1995.

Bret, David, *George Formby: A Troubled Genius*, London, Robson Books, 2001.

Briggs, Asa, *The History of Broadcasting in the United Kingdom, Volume I: The Birth of Broadcasting*, London, Oxford University Press, 1961.

Brown, Geoff, 'Bugsy Malone', *Monthly Film Bulletin*, Vol. 43, No. 510 (July 1976), pp. 145–6.

Brown, Geoff, *Launder and Gilliat*, London, British Film Institute, 1977.

Brunel, Adrian, *Nice Work: Thirty Years In British Films*, London, Forbes Robertson, 1949.

Caine, Andrew, ' "The Best Teenage Romp Ever": Cliff Richard and the Construction of a British Teenage Identity, 1959–63', *Journal of Popular British Cinema*, Vol. 4 (2001), pp. 58–71.

Carr, Roy, *Beatles At The Movies*, London, Harper Collins, 1996.

Chapman, James, *The British At War: Cinema, State and Propaganda 1939–1945*, London, I. B. Taurus, 1998.

Chibnall, Steve, *J. Lee Thompson*, British Film Makers Series, Manchester, Manchester University Press, 2000.

Christie, Ian (ed.), *Powell, Pressburger And Others*, London, British Film Institute, 1978.

Christie, Ian, *Arrows Of Desire: The Films of Michael Powell and Emeric Pressburger*, London, Waterstone, 1985.

Cohan, Steven (ed.), *Hollywood Musicals: The Film Reader*, London, Routledge, 2002.

Cook, Pam, *Fashioning The Nation: Costume and Identity in British Cinema*, London, BFI Publishing, 1996.

Cook, Pam (ed.), *Gainsborough Pictures*, London, Cassell, 1997.

Crafton, Donald, *The Talkies: American Cinema's Transition to Sound 1926–1931*, Berkeley, University of California Press, 1999.

Crangle, Richard, ' "Next Slide Please": The Lantern Lecture In Britain 1890–1910' in Richard Abel and Rick Altman (eds), *The Sounds Of Early Cinema*, Bloomington, Indiana University Press, 2001.

Davies, Steven Paul, *Love Kills: The Making of Sid & Nancy*, Eye, Suffolk, ScreenPress Books, 2000.

Dixon, Wheeler Winston (ed.), *Re-Viewing British Cinema 1900–1992; Essays and Interviews*, Albany, State University of New York Press, 1994.

Donnelly, Kevin, 'Wicked Sounds and Magic Melodies: Music in 1940s Gainsborough Melodrama' in Pam Cook (ed.), *Gainsborough Pictures*, London, Cassell, 1997.

Donnelly, Kevin, 'Entertainment and Dystopia: the Punk Anti-Musical' in Bill Marshall and Robyn Stillwell (eds), *Musicals: Hollywood and Beyond*, Exeter, Intellect Books, 2000.

Donnelly, Kevin, *Pop Music in British Cinema: A Chronicle*, London, BFI Publishing, 2001a.

Donnelly, Kevin, '*Performance* and the Composite Film Score' in Kevin Donnelly (ed.), *Film Music: Critical Approaches*, Edinburgh, Edinburgh University Press, 2001b.

Dyer, Richard, *Only Entertainment*, London, Routledge, 1992.

Earl, John, 'Building the Halls' in Peter Bailey (ed.), *Music Hall: The Business of Pleasure*, Milton Keynes, Open University Press, 1986.

Edwards, Mark, 'Say You Want a Revolution', *The Sunday Times*, Culture Section, 8 April 2001.

Ehrlich, Cyril, *The Music Profession in Britain Since The Eighteenth Century: A Social History*, Oxford, Clarendon Press, 1985.

Ellis, John, 'British Cinema as Performance Art: *Brief Encounter*, *Radio Parade of 1935* and the Circumstances of Film Exhibition' in Justine Ashby and Andrew Higson (eds), *British Cinema, Past and Present*, London, Routledge, 2000.

Elsaesser, Thomas, 'The Tales of Hoffmann' in Ian Christie (ed.), *Powell, Pressburger and Others*, London, British Film Institute, 1978.

Everett, Wendy, *Terence Davies*, Manchester, Manchester University Press, 2004.

Eyles, Allen, 'Exhibition and the Cinema-going Experience' in Robert Murphy (ed.), *The British Cinema Book*, 2nd edn, 2001.

Fehr, Richard and Vogel, Frederick, *Lullabies of Hollywood: Movie Music and the Movie Musical 1915–1992*, Jefferson, NC, McFarland & Co., 1993.

Fields, Gracie, *Sing as we Go: Her Autobiography*, London, Frederick Muller Limited, 1960.

Frith, Simon, 'The Making of the British Record Industry 1920–64' in J. Curran, A. Smith and P. Wingate (eds), *Impacts and Influences: Essays on Media and Power in the Twentieth Century*, London, Methuen, 1987.

Frith, Simon, *Performing Rites: Evaluating Popular Music*, Oxford, Oxford University Press, 1998.

Geraghty, Christine, *British Cinema in the Fifties: Gender, Genre and the 'New Look'*, London, Routledge, 2000.

Gifford, Denis, *The British Film Catalogue 1895–1985: A Reference Guide*, Newton Abbot, David and Charles, 1986.

Gifford, Denis, *Entertainers in British Films: A Century of Showbiz in the Cinema*, Trowbridge, Flicks Books, 1998.

Gledhill, Christine, '"An Abundance of Understatement": Documentary, Melodrama and Romance' in C. Gledhill and G. Swanson (eds), *Nationalising Femininity: Culture, Sexuality and British Cinema in the Second World War*, Manchester, Manchester University Press, 1996.

Gledhill, Christine, *Reframing British Cinema 1918–1928: Between Restraint and Passion*, London, British Film Institute, 2003.

Grant, Barry Keith, 'The Body Politic: Ken Russell in the 1980s' in Lester Friedman (ed.), *British Cinema and Thatcherism: Fires Were Started*, London, UCL Press, 1993.

Green, Hughie, *Opportunity Knocked*, London, Frederick Muller Limited, 1965.

Green, Stanley, *Encyclopaedia of The Musical Film*, New York, Oxford University Press, 1988.

Greenfield, Amy, 'The Tales of Hoffmann', *Film Comment*, Vol. 31, No. 2 (March 1995), pp. 27–38.

Guy, Stephen, 'Calling All Stars: Musical Films in a Musical Decade' in J. Richards (ed.), *The Unknown 1930s: An Alternative History of the British Cinema 1929–1939*, London, I. B. Taurus, 1998.

Hall Stuart, 'A Rage in Harlesden', *Sight and Sound*, Vol. 8, No. 9 (September 1998), pp. 25–6.

Harper, Sue, *Picturing The Past: The Rise and Fall of the British Costume Film*, London, British Film Institute, 1994.

Harper, Sue, 'From Wholesome Girls to Difficult Dowagers: Actresses in 1930s British Cinema' in Justine Ashby and Andrew Higson (eds), *British Cinema: Past and Present*, London, Routledge, 2000.

Harper, Sue and Porter, Vincent, *British Cinema of the 1950s: The Decline of Deference*, Oxford, University of Oxford Press, 2003.

Hayward, Philip, 'Sci Fidelity – Music, Sound and Genre History' in Philip Hayward (ed.), *Off the Planet: Music, Sound and Science Fiction Cinema*, Eastleigh, John Libbey/Perfect Beat Publications, 2004.

Henry, Mark, '*It's Great to Be Young*', *ABC Film Review*, August 1956, pp. 66–7.

Hepworth, Cecil, *Came The Dawn: Memoirs of a Film Pioneer*, London, Phoenix House, 1951.

Higson, Andrew, *Waving The Flag: Constructing a National Cinema in Britain*, Oxford, Clarendon Press, 1995.

Higson, Andrew, 'A Film League of Nations: Gainsborough, Gaumont-British and Film Europe' in Pam Cook (ed.), *Gainsborough Pictures*, London, Cassell, 1997.

Higson, Andrew (ed.), *Young and Innocent? The Cinema in Britain 1896–1930*, Exeter, University of Exeter Press, 2002.

Hiley, Nicholas, 'At the Picture Palace': The British Cinema Audience, 1895–1920' in John Fullerton (ed.), *Celebrating 1895: The Centenary of Cinema*, London, John Libbey, 1998.

Hiley, Nicholas, 'Let's Go To The Pictures: The British Cinema Audience in the 1920s and 1930s', *Journal of Popular British Cinema*, Vol. 2, 1999, pp. 39–53.

Hiley, Nicholas, ' "Nothing More than a Craze": Cinema Building in Britain from 1909 to 1914' in Andrew Higson (ed.), *Young and Innocent? The Cinema in Britain 1896–1930*, Exeter, University of Exeter Press, 2002.

Hill, John, *British Cinema in the 1980s*, Oxford, Clarendon Press, 1999.

Hulbert, Jack, *The Little Woman's Always Right*, London, W. H. Allen, 1975.

Hunt, Leon, *British Low Culture: From Safari Suits to Sexploitation*, London, Routledge, 1998.

Huntley, John, *British Film Music*, London, Skelton Robinson, 1947.

Irving, Ernest, *Cue For Music*, London, Dennis Dobson, 1959.

James, Nick, 'The Thoughts of Chairman Alan', *Sight and Sound*, Vol. 7, No. 11 (November 1997), pp. 10–12.

James, Nick, 'Medium Cool', *Sight and Sound*, Vol. 8, No. 8 (August 1998), pp. 12–15.

Jenkins, Glyn, 'Oh . . . Rosalinda!!', *ABC Film Review*, December 1955, p. 30.

Jenkins, Glyn, 'Oh . . . Rosalinda!!', *ABC Film Review*, January 1956, p. 16.

Jenkins, Steve, '*Pink Floyd The Wall*', *Monthly Film Bulletin*, Vol. 49, No. 583 (August 1982), pp. 172–3.

Jenkins, Steve, 'Absolute Beginners', *Monthly Film Bulletin*, Vol. 51, No. 607 (August 1984), pp. 230–1.

Jones, Stephen K., *The British Labour Movement and Film 1918–1939*, London, Routledge & Kegan Paul, 1987.

Jones, S.G., *Workers at Play: A Social and Economic History of Leisure 1918–1939*, London, Routledge & Kegan Paul, 1986.

de Jonge, Jon, *Tune Up The Hoover! Cinema Musicians tell Their Story*, Blackpool, Jon de Jonge, 1994.

Kilgarriff, Michael, *Sing us One of the Old Songs: A Guide to Popular Songs 1860–1920*, Oxford, Oxford University Press, 1998.

Lacey, Joanne, 'Seeing Through Happiness: Hollywood Musicals and the construction of the American Dream in Liverpool in the 1950s', *Journal of Popular British Cinema*, Vol. 2 (1999), pp. 54–65.

Lack, Russell, *Twenty Four Frames Under: A Buried History of Film Music*, London, Quartet Books, 1997.

Landy, Marcia, *British Genres: Cinema and Society 1930–1960*, Princeton NJ, Princeton University Press, 1991.

Landy, Marcia, 'The Extraordinary Ordinariness of Gracie Fields: The Anatomy of a British Star' in Bruce Babbington (ed.), *British Stars and Stardom*, Manchester, Manchester University Press, 2001.

Leader, Raymond, 'British Musicals', *ABC Film Review*, October 1951, pp. 10–11.

Leader, Raymond, 'Welcome Back to a Great Team', *ABC Film Review*, March 1955, pp. 10–11.

Levy, Louis, *Music For The Movies*, London, Sampson Low, Marston & Co., 1948.

Lewis, Jon, *The Road To Romance and Ruin: Teen Films and Youth Culture*, New York, Routledge, 1992.

Low, Rachael, *The History of British Film 1918–1929*, London, Routledge, 1997.

Low, Rachael, *The History of the British Film 1929–1939: Film Making in 1930s Britain*, London, Routledge, 1997.

Low, Rachael and Manvell, Roger, *The History of the British Film 1896–1906*, London, George Allen and Unwin, 1948.

Luckett, Moya, 'Travel and Mobility: Femininity and National Identity in Swinging London Films' in Justine Ashby and Andrew Higson (eds), *British Cinema, Past and Present*, London, Routledge, 2000.

Lynn, Vera, *Vocal Refrain: An Autobiography*, London, W. H. Allen, 1975.

MacCabe, Colin, *Performance*, London, BFI Film Classics, 1998.

Mackillop, Ian and Sinyard, Neil (eds), *British Cinema of the 1950s: A Celebration*, Manchester, Manchester University Press, 2003.

Macnab, Geoffrey, *J. Arthur Rank and the British Film Industry*, London, Routledge, 1994.

Macnab, Geoffrey, *Searching For Stars: Stardom and Screen Acting in the British Cinema*, London, Cassell, 2000a.

Macnab, Geoffrey, 'Unseen British Cinema' in Robert Murphy (ed.), *British Cinema of the 90s*, London, BFI Publishing, 2000b.

McFarlane, Brian, *Lance Comfort*, Manchester, Manchester University Press, 1999.

McGrath, Melanie, 'Babymother', *Sight and Sound*, Vol. 8, No. 9 (September 1998), pp. 38–9.

McIlroy, Brian, 'British Filmmaking in the 1930s and 1940s: The Example of Brian Desmond Hurst' in Wheeler Winston Dixon (ed.), *Re-Viewing British*

Cinema 1900–1992; Essays and Interviews, Albany, State University of New York Press, 1994.

Majumdar, Neepa, 'The Embodied Voice: Song Sequences and Stardom in Popular Hindi Cinema' in Pamela Robertson Wojcik and Arthur Knight (eds), *Soundtrack Available: Essays on Film and Popular Music*, Durham NC, Duke University Press, 2001.

Manvell, Roger (ed.), *The Cinema 1951*, Harmondsworth, Penguin Books, 1951.

Marovitz, Charles, Milne, Tom and Hale, Owen (eds), *The Encore Reader: A Chronicle of the New Drama*, London, Methuen, 1965.

Martland, Peter, *Since Records Began: EMI The First Hundred Years*, London, Batsford, 1997.

Marwick, Arthur, 'Introduction' in Anthony Aldgate, James Chapman and Arthur Marwick (eds), *Windows on the Sixties: Exploring Key Texts of Media and Culture*, London, I. B. Taurus, 2000.

Mathieson, Muir, 'Developments in Film Music' in R.K. Neilson Baxter, Roger Manvell and H. H. Wollenberg (eds), *The Penguin Film Review 4*, London, Penguin Books, 1947.

Matthews, Jesse, *Over my Shoulder: An Autobiography*, London, W. H. Allen, 1975.

Medhurst, Andy, 'Music Hall and British Cinema' in Charles Barr (ed.), *All Our Yesterdays: 90 Years of British Cinema*, London, BFI Publishing, 1986.

Medhurst, Andy, 'It sort of Happened Here; the Strange, Brief Life of the British Pop Film' in Jonathan Romney and Adrian Wootton (eds), *Celluloid Jukebox: Popular Music and the Movies since the 50s'*, London, British Film Institute, 1995.

Medhurst, Andy, 'The Mike-ado', *Sight and Sound*, Vol. 10, No. 3 (March 2000), pp. 36–7.

Merz, Caroline, 'The Tension of Genre: Wendy Toye and Muriel Box' in Wheeler Winston Dixon (ed.), *Re-Viewing British Cinema 1900–1992: Essays and Interviews*, Albany, State University of New York Press, 1994.

Miller, Maud M., 'Filming *The Tales Of Hoffmann*', *Photoplay: The Film Monthly*, London, March 1951.

Mordden, Ethan, *Beautiful Morning: The Broadway Musical in the 1940s*, New York, Oxford University Press, 1999.

Mundy, John, *Popular Music On Screen: From Hollywood Musical to Music Video*, Manchester, Manchester University Press, 1999.

Murphy, Robert, 'Rank's Attempt on the American Market 1944–49' in James Curran and Vincent Porter (eds), *British Cinema History*, London, Weidenfeld and Nicholson, 1983.

Murphy, Robert, *Realism And Tinsel: Cinema and Society in Britain, 1939–49*, London, Routledge, 1989.

Murphy, Robert, *Sixties British Cinema*, London, BFI Publishing, 1992.

Murphy, Robert (ed.), *British Cinema of the 90s*, London, British Film Institute, 2000.

Murphy, Robert (ed.), *The British Cinema Book*, 2nd edn, London, British Film Institute, 2001.

Napper, Lawrence, 'A Despicable Tradition? Quota-quickies in the 1930s' in Robert Murphy (ed.), *The British Cinema Book*, 2nd edn, London, British Film Institute, 2001.

Neaverson, Bob, *The Beatles Movies*, London, Cassell, 1997.

Newman, Kim, 'Absolute Beginners', *Monthly Film Bulletin*, Vol. 53, No. 627 (April 1986), pp. 102–3.

Noble, Peter, *Ivor Novello: Man of the Theatre*, London, The Non-Fiction Book Club, 1952.

Nott, James J., *Music For The People: Popular Music and Dance in Interwar Britain*, Oxford, Oxford University Press, 2002.

Oldham, Andrew Loog, 'A Day in the Life', *The Guardian*, 6 April 2001, pp. 10–11.

Parker, Alan, 'The Making Of *Bugsy Malone*', DVD notes, London, Carlton Visual Entertainment, 2002.

Pearsall, Ronald, *Edwardian Popular Music*, Newton Abbot, David & Charles, 1975.

Pearson, George, *Flashback: An Autobiography of a British Film Maker*, London, George Allen & Unwin, 1957.

Pearson, Roberta E. and Simpson, Philip, *A Critical Dictionary of Film and Television Theory*, London, Routledge, 2001.

Peet, Stephen, 'George Pearson and his Two Minutes Silence' in Alan Burton and Lorraine Porter (eds), *The Showman, The Spectacle and the Two Minute Silence: Performing British Cinema Before 1930*, Trowbridge, Flicks Books, 2001.

Poole, Julian, 'British Cinema Audiences in Wartime: Audience Preference at the Majestic Macclesfield 1938–1948', *Historical Journal of Film Radio and Television*, Vol. 7 (1987), pp. 15–34.

Porter, Vincent, 'Methodism versus the Market Place: The Rank Organisation and British Cinema' in Robert Murphy (ed.), *The British Cinema Book*, 2nd edn, London, British Film Institute, 2001.

Powell, Michael, *A Life In Movies: An Autobiography*, London, William Heinemann, 1986.

Powell, Michael, *Million-Dollar Movie*, London, Heinemann Mandarin, 1993.

Rees, Dafydd, Lazell, Barry and Osborne, Peter (eds), *Forty Years of NME Charts*, London, Boxtree, 1992.

Rich, B. Ruby, ' "Still the Same as they Were Before they Were": *Backbeat* and the Story of the Beatles', *Sight and Sound*, Vol. 4, No. 4 (April 1994), pp. 88–11.

Richards, Jeffrey, *The Age of the Dream Palace: Cinema and Society in Britain 1930–1939*, London, Routledge and Kegan Paul, 1984.

Richards, Jeffrey, 'Cinemagoing in Worktown: Regional Film Audiences in 1930s Britain', *Historical Journal of Film Radio and Television*, Vol. 14, No. 2 (1994a), pp. 147–66.

Richards, Jeffrey, *Stars In Our Eyes: Lancashire Stars of Stage, Screen and Radio*, Preston, Lancashire County Books, 1994b.

Richards, Jeffrey, *Film and National Identity: From Dickens to Dad's Army*, Manchester, Manchester University Press, 1997.

Richards, Jeffrey, *The Unknown 1930s: An Alternative History of the British Cinema 1929–1939*, London, I. B. Taurus, 1998.

Richards, Jeffrey and Sheridan, Dorothy (eds), *Mass Observation at the Movies*, London, Routledge & Kegan Paul, 1987.

Roberts, E. M., *Working Class Barrow and Lancaster 1890–1930*, Lancaster, University of Lancaster Occasional Paper No. 2, 1976, p. 54.

Rosenbaum, Jonathan, *Monthly Film Bulletin*, Vol. 42, No. 495 (April 1975), pp. 88–9.

Ross, Steven J., 'The Revolt of the Audience: Reconsidering Audiences and Reception During the Silent Era' in Melvyn Stokes and Richard Maltby (eds), *American Movie Audiences: From the Turn of the Century to the Early Sound Era*, London, British Film Institute, 1999.

Rowson, Simon, 'A Statistical Survey of the Cinema Industry in Great Britain in 1934', *Journal of the Royal Statistical Society*, Vol. 99 (1936), pp. 67–118.

Rubin, Martin, *Showstoppers: Busby Berkeley and the Tradition of Spectacle*, New York, Columbia University Press, 1993.

Ryall, Tom, *Britain and the American Cinema*, London, Sage, 2001.

Sanders, Lise Shapiro, 'Indecent Incentives to Vice: Regulating Films and Audience Behaviour from the 1890s to the 1910s' in Andrew Higson (ed.), *Young and Innocent? The Cinema In Britain 1896–1930*, Exeter, University of Exeter Press, 2002.

Savage, Jon, *England's Dreaming: Sex Pistols and Punk Rock*, London, Faber and Faber, 1991.

Sedgwick, John, 'Cinema-going Preferences in Britain in the 1930s' in J. Richards (ed.), *The Unknown 1930s: An Alternative History of the British Cinema 1929–1939*, London, I. B. Taurus, 1998a.

Sedgwick, John, 'Film "Hits" and "Misses" in mid-1930s Britain', *Historical Journal of Film Radio and Television*, Vol. 18, No. 3 (1998b), pp. 333–51.

Sedgwick, John, *Popular Filmgoing in 1930s Britain: A Choice of Pleasures*, Exeter, University of Exeter Press, 2000.

Sinker, Mark, 'Spice World', *Sight and Sound*, Vol. 8, No. 2 (February 1998), p. 49.

Stafford, Roy, 'What's Showing at the Gaumont?: Rethinking the Study of British Cinema in the 1950s', *Journal of Popular British Cinema*, Vol. 4 (2001), pp. 95–111.

Stanfield, Peter, ' "From the Vulgar to the Refined": American Vernacular and Blackface Minstrelsy in Showboat' in Bill Marshall and Robynn Stilwell (eds), *Musicals: Hollywood and Beyond*, Exeter, Intellect Books, 2000.

Staveacre, Tony, *The Songwriters*, London, BBC, 1980.

Stead, Peter, *Film and the Working Class: The Feature Film in Britain and American Society*, London, Routledge, 1989.

Stokes, Jane, *On Screen Rivals: Cinema and Television in the United States and Britain*, London, Macmillan, 1999.

Stokes, Jane, 'Arthur Askey and the Construction of Popular Entertainment in *Band Waggon* and *Make Mine A Million*' in Justine Ashby and Andrew Higson (eds), *British Cinema, Past and Present*, London, Routledge, 2000.

Sutton, David, *A Chorus Of Raspberries: British Film Comedy 1929–1939*, Exeter, Exeter University Press, 2000.

Swynnoe, Jan G., *The Best Years Of British Film Music, 1936–1958*, Woodbridge, The Boydell Press, 2002.

Taylor, Paul, 'Quadrophenia', *Monthly Film Bulletin*, Vol. 46, No. 548 (September 1979), pp. 198–9.

Thornton, Michael, *Jesse Matthews: A Biography*, London, Hart-Davis, MacGibbbon, 1974.

Turner, Steve, *Cliff Richard: The Biography*, Oxford, Lion Publishing, 1994.

Tyrrell, Heather, 'Bollywood in Britain', *Sight and Sound*, Vol. 8, No. 8 (August 1998), pp. 20–2.

Vincendeau, Ginette, 'Hollywood Babel', *Screen*, Vol. 29, No. 2 (spring 1988).

Vorse, Mary Heaton, 'Some Picture Show Audiences' in Gregory A. Waller (ed.), *Moviegoing In America*, Oxford, Blackwell, 2002.

Walker, Alexander, *Hollywood England: The British Film Industry in the Sixties*, London, Michael Joseph, 1974.

Walker, Alexander, *Icons in the Fire: The Rise and Fall of Practically Everyone in the British Film Industry, 1984–2000*, London, Orion Books, 2003.

Warren, Patricia, *Elstree: The British Hollywood*, London, Elm Tree Books, 1993.

Warren, Patricia, *British Film Studios: An Illustrated History*, London, Batsford, 1995.

Weiss, A. 'A Queer Feeling when I Look at You' in C. Gledhill (ed.), *Stardom: Industry of Desire*, London, Routledge, 1991.

Wilcox, Herbert, *Twenty-Five Thousand Sunsets: The Autobiography of Herbert Wilcox*, London, The Bodley Head, 1967.

Wilson, Elizabeth, *Only Halfway to Paradise: Women in Postwar Britain 1945–1968*, London, Tavistock, 1980.

Wood, Leslie, *The Romance of the Movies*, London, William Heinemann, 1937.

Wood, Linda, 'Low Budget British Films in the 1930s' in Robert Murphy (ed.), *The British Cinema Book*, 2nd edn, London, British Film Institute, 2001.

Wootton, Adrian, 'The Do's and Don'ts of Rock Documentaries' in Jonathan Romney and Adrian Wootton (eds), *Celluloid Jukebox: Popular Music and the Movies since the 1950s*, London, British Film Institute, 1995.

Yates, Robert, 'Backbeat', review in *Sight and Sound*, Vol. 4, No. 4 (April 1994).

Bibliography

Young, Cynthia, 'Revision to Reproduction: Myth and its Author in *The Red Shoes*' in Wheeler Winston Dixon (ed.), *Re-Viewing British Cinema 1900–1992, Essays and Interviews*, Albany, State University of New York Press, 1994.

Yule, Andrew, *The Man Who 'Framed' The Beatles: A Biography of Richard Lester*, New York, Donald I. Fine, 1994.

Index

200 Motels (1972) 224
24 Hour Party People (2002) 253–4, 256
6.5 Special (1958) 149, 172, 179

Absolute Beginners (1986) 238–40
Addinsell, Richard 107–8
Addison, John 168
Alfredo and his Gypsy Orchestra 43, 72, 133
All That Jazz (1979) 226
Alwyn, William 1, 107
American Society of Composers, Authors and Publishers 29
Anglo-Amalgamated 172, 176, 184, 199, 203
Armistice (1929) 44
Ashton, Sir Frederick 155
Askey, Arthur 88, 89, 90–3, 111, 136, 137, 179
Associated British Picture Corporation 40, 42, 117, 151, 200
Associated Sound Film Industries 7
Associated Talking Pictures
   see Dean, Basil
Atwell, Winifred 165, 166
Auld Lang Syne (1928) 26, 30
Aunt Sally (1933) 46

'B' features 4, 42, 147, 197
Babylon (1980) 236
Babymother (1998) 256, 257
Bachelors, The 205

Backbeat (1993) 247, 248–9
Balcon, Michael 44, 45, 59, 65–6, 84, 94, 107, 115, 210
ballet 110, 126
Ball, Kenny 195, 196, 197, 198
Bamforth, James 13
Banderos, Antonio 249
Band Of Thieves (1962) 196–7
Band Waggon (1940) 90
Banks, Monty 42, 57, 59
Bart, Lionel 174, 176, 177, 202, 215, 217, 218
Barry, John 183
Bassey, Shirley 215–16
Bath, Hubert 107–8
Battle For Music (1943) 87
Baxter, John 48, 88, 94
Beat Girl (1960) 185
Beatles, The 199, 206, 207, 208, 209, 223, 224, 235, 247
Beecham, Sir Thomas 155
Beggar's Opera, The (1953) 149, 158, 160–3
Berners, Lord 95
Bilk, Acker 184, 195, 196
Billy Elliot (2000) 252
Billy Liar (1963) 183, 200, 210
Birth Of The Beatles (1979) 247
Blackmail (1929) 31
Blackpool 54–6, 105–6
Black, Stanley 187, 200
Blades, James 15
Blair, Lionel 199, 206, 239
Bliss, Sir Arthur 107, 160, 162

Blossom Time (1934) 43
Blue Danube (1932) 46
Bollywood 3, 257
Boorman, John 209
Born Lucky (1932) 125
Boult, Sir Adrian 109
Bowie, David 239
Boy Friend, The (1971) 227–8, 232
Brassed Off (1996) 250
Breaking Glass (1980) 236
Bricusse, Leslie 204, 215, 223
Brief Encounter (1945) 110
British and Dominion Film
    Corporation
  see Wilcox, Herbert
British Board of Film Censors 21,
    173, 177
British Broadcasting Corporation
    (BBC)
  growth in radio broadcasting
    25–6, 74, 77
  radio dance bands 8, 38, 42, 65,
    77, 109
British film production
  in 1920s 12
  in 1930s 33, 39–42, 48
  in 1940s 84–5
  in 1950s 146, 147–8
  in 1960s 182–4, 210–11
  in 1970s 221–2
  in 1980s and 1990s 240, 255
  American finance and involvement
    4–5, 23–4, 29, 41, 45–6, 57,
    64–5, 66, 85–6, 126, 147, 148,
    151, 206, 209, 210–11, 215,
    221, 232, 243, 249, 250, 255
British International Pictures 29, 31,
    40, 42–3, 65, 74, 108
British Lion 31, 36, 40, 48, 82–3,
    89, 97, 162
British Lion Varieties (1936) 82, 97
British School of Cinema Organists
    22
British Sound Films 27, 28
Brook, Peter 161, 162

Brown, Joe 200, 202, 203, 204
Brunel, Adrian 30–1
Buchanan, Jack 41, 46–7, 64, 68,
    172
Bugsy Malone (1976) 228, 232–3
Bulldog Jack (1935) 45–6
Burke, Johnny 116
Buster (1988) 242
Butchers 28, 29, 74, 88, 115, 154,
    223
Bygraves, Max 149, 165

Caine, Michael 250, 251
Calling All Stars (1937) 48, 74
Calvert, Eddie 165
calypso 175, 202
Catch Us If You Can (1965) 209
Champagne Charlie (1944) 94–6,
    103, 117
Carousel (1956) 2
Chanda, Gurinda 257
Channel Four Films 247, 256
Charlesworth, Dick and his City
    Gents 184
Charley Moon (1956) 149
Chicago (2002) 255
cinema audiences 4, 14–17, 20,
    25, 85, 146–7, 172–3, 184–5,
    221
cinemas
  early 15–17, 22–3
cinema sound
  mechanisation of 21–3
  synchronisation of 23–30, 31–2
Cinematograph Exhibitors
    Association 12
Cinematograph Films Act 1927 11,
    33
Cinematograph Films Act 1938 84
Clapton, Eric 228, 229
Clark, Petula 115, 214
class
  as theme in musicals 8, 51–2,
    60–1, 67, 87, 104, 117, 120–1,
    159, 201, 212–14, 219, 220

classical music 18, 21, 87, 107–8, 109, 110, 112–13, 122, 168, 223, 224, 226
Cliffe, Fred E. 39
Clue Of The New Pin, The (1929) 31
Cogan, Alma 165
Colosseum and Juicy Lucy (1970) 223
Come Dance With Me (1950) 145
Coming Through The Rye (1923) 18
Commitments, The (1992) 6, 244–7
co-productions
   European 7, 40–1, 45, 68
Cottage On Dartmoor, A (1929) 28
Courtneys of Curzon Street, The (1947) 85, 122–4
Courtneidge, Cecily 40, 45, 46, 89
Crazy Gang, The 35, 80–2

Dall, Evelyn 91, 93, 136
dance bands
   popularity of in 1930s 38–9, 76–9, 82
Dance Hall (1950) 148, 150–1
Dancing Years, The (1950) 145
Dankworth, John 183
Date With A Dream, A (1948) 115
Dave Clark Five, The 209
Davies, Terence 7
Dean, Basil 39, 40, 47, 49, 59, 62
Dene, Terry 166, 172
Distant Voices, Still Lives (1988) 7
Dolby sound 230
Donner, Clive 209
Down Melody Lane (1943) 104
D'Oyly Carte Company 158
Dr No (1962) 186, 208, 210
Duke Wore Jeans, The (1958) 71, 144, 172, 176, 225
dystopia 127, 226

Easdale, Brian 126
Electrocord 28, 29
Elizabethtown (2005) 256

Elstree Calling (1930) 24, 31–2, 35, 42
Essex, David 225, 228
Evergreen (1934) 1, 34, 39–40, 55, 66–7
Eve's Fall (1930) 42
Everything Is Rhythm (1936) 48, 76, 78–9, 140
Evita (1996) 232, 247, 249–50, 252
Expresso Bongo (1959) 146, 176, 177–9, 181, 185

Faith, Adam 185, 226
Fame (1980) 233
Famous Music Melodies (1925) 27
Farnon, Robert 178
Feather Your Nest (1937) 7, 62
Fields, Gracie 7, 20, 33, 47, 48–58, 88, 166
Fields, Sid 115–16
First A Girl (1935) 1, 67–8
Flag Lieutenant, The (1926) 19
Flanagan and Allen 80, 88, 97, 138
   see also Crazy Gang, The
Flynn, Errol 142, 149, 164
Foreman Went To France, The (1941) 94
Formby, George 7, 33, 47, 59–64, 88, 89, 115, 166
Four Weddings and a Funeral (1994) 241
Frankel, Cyril 154, 167
Furie, Sidney 193, 194
Fury, Billy 199, 204

Gainsborough 30, 40, 42, 44, 46, 65, 74, 88, 90, 108
Gainsborough Gems (1930) 44
Gallone, Carmine 7, 126
Gangway (1938) 70
Gaumont-British 22, 39–40, 44, 45, 66, 70, 72, 108
Gay, John 160, 161, 163
Gay, Noel 39, 81, 89, 95, 128, 137
Geldof, Bob 233

Genevieve (1953) 149
Geraldo and his Orchestra 38, 88,
    98, 99, 151
Gert and Daisy Clean Up (1942)
    104
Gilbert and Sullivan
    see *Story of Gilbert and Sullivan,*
    The; Topsy-Turvy
Gilliat, Sidney 158, 159, 160
Give my Regards to Broad Street
    (1984) 220, 235
Glamorous Nights (1937) 43, 117,
    121
Golden Disc, The (1958) 172, 176
Gonks Go Beat (1965) 209
Good Companions, The (1933) 65,
    66, 227
Good Companions, The (1957) 149,
    171, 227
Goodbye Mr Chips (1969) 211,
    214–15
Good Night, Vienna (1932) 46–7, 72
Goon Show 206, 208
gramophones 8, 23, 37
Great Mr Handel, The (1942)
    111–14, 159
Great Rock'n'Roll Swindle, The
    (1980) 236–7, 238
Green, Hughie 88
Gregory Gillian 232
Guest, Val 91, 93, 103, 106, 151,
    152, 178, 223
Gypsy Blood (1931) 72
'gypsy' music 71–2

Hacienda 253
Hale, Sonny 40, 64, 65, 67, 70, 71,
    117
Half A Sixpence (1967) 176, 211–14
Hall, Henry 35, 38, 39, 76
Handley, Tommy 35
Happy-Go-Lovely (1951) 148,
    151–4
Happy Ever After (1932) 40, 130,
    130, 131

Hard Day's Night, A (1964) 184,
    196, 205–7, 208, 248, 252
Harvey, Laurence 177
Harvey, Lilian 40, 130
Hay, Will 34, 74
Heart's Desire (1935) 43, 71–3
Heath, Ted 151, 165, 166, 184
Heckroth, Hein 126, 155, 160
Help! (1965) 207–9
Hemmings, David 197
Henderson, Dick 27
Henson, Leslie 7, 35, 46, 79–80
Hepworth, Cecil 5–6, 13, 18, 22
Here We Go Round The Mulberry
    Bush (1967) 209
Herman, Mark 250
His Lordship (1932) 125
His Master's Voice (HMV) 26, 45,
    49, 54
Hollies, The 184
Holloway, Stanley 56, 94, 160, 161,
    163
Hollywood musical
    comparison with British musical
    film 2–5, 6–7, 58, 63–4, 66–7,
    148, 176, 179–80, 181, 186,
    227
    popularity of 2–3, 42, 115, 148,
    238
Holst, Gustav 107
Horrocks, Jane 250
Hours And Times, The (1992) 248
Hudis, Norman 175, 176
Hulbert, Jack 35, 40, 44–6, 89, 131
Huntley, John 1–2, 6, 103
Hurst, Brian Desmond 117, 121
Hylton, Jack 86, 87, 90

Ideal Cinemagazine 82
I'll Be Your Sweetheart (1945) 6,
    103–6
In A Monastery Garden (1929) 30
Irving, Ernest 1, 63, 95, 107, 112
It Couldn't Happen Here (1987)
    242

It's Great To Be Young (1956) 166–71
It's In The Air (1938) 59, 63
It's Love Again (1936) 68–70
It's Trad Dad! (1962) 195–6, 208
I've Gotta Horse (1965) 204–5

Jack's The Boy (1932) 45
Jailhouse Rock (1957) 176
Jazz Singer, The (1927) 23, 28
Jazz Time (1929) 42
Jennings, Humphrey 87, 110, 114, 236
John, Elton 223, 228, 229, 252
Jubilee (1978) 236
Just For A Song (1930) 44

Keep Your Seats Please (1936) 62
Kendall, Kay 116
Kent, Jean 92, 117, 121
Kids Are Alright, The (1979) 235
Kiepura, Jan 7, 34, 72
King's Rhapsody (1956) 142, 149, 163–5
Kitty (1929) 30
Klangfilm-Tobis 24, 28, 29
Korda, Alexander 45, 108, 111

Lambeth Walk, The 89–90, 117
Lauder, Harry 26, 27, 30, 42
Launder, Frank 31, 158, 160
Lean, David 110
Led Zeppelin 218, 223, 235
Leigh, Mike 159, 160, 251, 252
Lester, Richard 195, 206, 208
Let It Be (1970) 223
Let's Be Happy (1957) 153–4
Let's Make A Night Of It (1937) 43
Levy, Louis 1, 13, 17–18, 63, 68, 103, 107, 108, 151
Leybourne, George 94
Lilacs In The Spring (1954) 149
Lisztomania (1975) 230
Little Voice (1997) 250–1, 252
Live It Up! (1963) 197–8

Lockwood, Margaret 47, 105, 108
London Philharmonic Orchestra 87, 110
London Schools Symphony Orchestra 168
London Town (1946) 85, 114–17, 211
Long Day Closes, The (1992) 7
Loss, Joe and his Band 38, 43, 97
Lotus, Denis 165, 166, 172, 179
Love Story (1944) 108
Loving You (1957) 176
Lubin, Sigmund 22
Lupino, Stanley 35, 43, 128
Lynn, Vera 82, 85, 88, 96–103, 111, 134, 135, 166
Lynne, Gillian 193, 204, 213, 224
Lyttleton, Humphrey 168, 170, 196

Mackey, Percival 17–18, 88, 89, 115
Madonna 249, 250
magic-lantern shows 12–13
Magic Bow, The (1946) 108–9
Mancunian Films 59, 74, 85, 88–9, 108
Man Of Mayfair (1931) 41
Mantovani 166, 172
Mathieson, Muir 1, 107, 108, 160, 162
Matthews, Jessie 1, 7, 33–4, 39–40, 43, 64–71, 88, 141
Mayerl, Billy 27, 95, 138, 154
Maytime In Mayfair (1949) 122, 124–5
Meet The Navy (1946) 115
Melody Maker 177
Merseybeats, The 184
Merson, Billy 27
Mikado, The (1939) 159
Milestone Melodies (1925) 27
Mills, John 46, 166, 167, 170
Ministry of Information 87
Miss London Ltd (1943) 90–3, 136
Mister Quilp (1975) 235
Mollinson, Clifford 43, 74–6

Moody, Ron 192, 216
More, Kenneth 145, 185
Moulin Rouge (2000) 227, 250, 255
Moyne Committee (1936) 84
*Mrs Brown You've Got A Lovely
    Daughter* (1968)
Murray, Ruby 166, 167, 170
musical comedies 35–6, 50–64,
    79–81
musical shorts 25–6, 27, 36, 42,
    82–3, 86–7, 154, 184, 223
music hall 8, 27, 28, 43, 47, 50, 59,
    74, 88, 94, 95, 103, 104, 118
Music Hall Parade (1939) 88
Music Hath Charms (1935) 76–8
Musicians Union 19, 22, 23
Music Lovers, The (1969) 227
music video 222, 240, 250

National Film Finance Corporation
    146, 154, 161, 210, 232
Neagle, Anna 46, 47, 122, 123, 142,
    149, 164
Newell, Norman 165, 166
Newley, Anthony 149, 179, 235
New Musical Express 165, 174,
    177, 202
'New Wave' films 9, 145, 149,
    182–3, 200, 201, 203, 207
Niven, David 151, 152
Noble, Ray 39
No Limit (1935) 59–62
Novello, Ivor 39, 43, 44, 150, 163,
    172, 176

Oh Daddy (1935) 46, 79–80
Oh . . . Rosalinda!! (1955) 143, 149,
    154, 156–7, 158
Oh! What A Lovely War (1969)
    219–20
O-Kay For Sound (1937) 7, 46, 79,
    80–2, 88, 158
Oklahoma (1955) 2
Oliver! (1968) 1, 10, 215–18, 219
Olivier, Laurence 160, 161

One Exciting Night (1944) 103
operetta 34, 43, 71–3
Ostrer, Maurice 90
O'Toole, Peter 214
Out Of The Blue (1931) 65
Ove, Horace 223
Owen, Alun 206, 207

Palace Pictures 247
'parade' films 36, 43, 74
Paramor, Norrie 172, 177, 178, 196,
    197, 199
Parker, Alan 181, 183, 190, 222,
    228, 232, 234, 244, 246, 247,
    249, 250, 255
Parker, Cecil 167, 170
Parr-Davies, Harry 39
Passport To Pimlico (1949) 158
Pathé 35, 36, 72, 82, 86, 133
Payne, Jack 35, 38, 39, 42, 44, 47,
    139
Pearson, George 13–14, 26–7, 30,
    42, 47–8
Peers, Donald 149
Performance (1970) 215, 218–19
Pet Shop Boys 242
Phonofilm, 24–5, 26–8
Pictures at an Exhibition (1972) 223
Pink Floyd The Wall (1982) 211,
    228, 233–5
Play It Cool (1962) 199, 206
Poole, Brian and the Tremeloes 184
Pop Gear (1965) 209
Popular Music and Dancing Weekly
    139, 140
popular music, influence of
    American 2, 29, 39, 66
    British 8, 13, 27, 32, 33–4, 37–9,
        42–3, 44, 88, 94
    European 46, 71, 72–3
    record sales 37, 97
Potter, Denis 37, 240
Powell, Michael 48, 117, 125, 126
    Pressburger and 1, 125, 143, 149,
        154–8

Presley, Elvis 66, 176, 177
Privilege (1967) 211
propaganda 87, 89–90, 104
punk rock 235–6
Punk Rock Movie, The (1978) 236
Puttnam, David 232

Quadrophenia (1979) 230–1
Quintaphonic Sound 230
quota quickies 41–2

Radio Parade (1933) 36
Radio Parade of 1935 (1934) 24,
     43, 73–6
Rank, J. Arthur 80, 85, 111, 115,
     125, 127, 150, 160, 166, 232
Red Shoes, The (1948) 1, 115, 117,
     125–7, 155, 156
Reed, Carol 1, 71, 215, 216
Reggae (1970) 223
Rennie, Michael 105, 106
Reveille (1924) 13
Rhythm Serenade (1943) 98, 101–3,
     135
Rice, Tim 218, 249
Richard, Cliff 166, 176–8, 181, 183,
     185, 206, 224
rock opera 232
Rolling Stones, The 218
Romulus Films 215
Room At The Top (1958) 173, 182
Ross, Herbert 187, 214
Roy, Harry 39, 48, 76, 78–9, 140
Rude Boy (1980) 236
Ruggles, Wesley 115, 116
Ruritanian musicals 43, 46, 48,
     71–2, 78, 117, 149, 163, 165,
     176
Russell, Ken 162, 222, 226, 228,
     229, 230

Sailors Three (1940) 94
Sally In Our Alley (1931) 49–53
Saturday Night and Sunday Morning
     (1960) 149, 182, 190

Saville, Victor 30, 44, 66
Scarfe, Gerald 234
Scrooge (1970) 213, 218, 223
Secombe, Harry 217
Serious Charge (1959) 145, 177,
     185
Seventh Veil, The (1945) 108
Sex Pistols 236–7
Shadows, The 186
Shearer, Moira 126, 127, 155
sheet music 19, 29, 228
Shelton, Anne 91–2, 136
Shepherd, Horace 86, 154
Sherwin, Manning 103
Sid & Nancy (1986) 237–8, 247
Sidney, George 212
Sing As We Go (1934) 39–40, 54–6
silent cinema musicians 13, 15–16,
     17–22, 26
Sing Along With Me (1952) 149
skiffle 172, 175
Sleepless Nights (1932) 43, 128
Slipper and the Rose, The (1976)
     235
Softley, Ian 247
Some People (1962) 185
Sound Of Music, The (1965) 212
soundtrack albums 241
South Pacific (1958) 2
Spice World the Movie (1997) 220,
     252–3
Spring In Park Lane (1948) 122,
     123–4
Stardust (1975) 225, 232, 234
Steele, Tommy 71, 144, 166, 174,
     177, 179, 211, 213, 225
Stepping Out (1991) 244
Storm, The (1901) 13
Story of Gilbert and Sullivan, The
     (1953) 149, 158–60
Summer Holiday (1962) 181, 190–2
Sunshine Susie (1931) 44
Sweet Charity (1968) 212, 238
'Swinging London' films 200, 203,
     210

Take Me High (1973) 224
Tales of Hoffman, The (1951) 149, 154–6
Tauber, Richard 34, 43, 72–3, 82, 115
television 24, 31, 76, 147, 177, 178, 189, 197, 198, 204, 206, 222, 240, 241, 253, 256
Television Follies, The (1933) 36
Temple, Julian 222, 236, 238
That'll Be The Day (1973) 204, 220, 225–6, 232
There Goes The Bride (1932) 65–6
'thermionics' 23
This'll Make You Whistle (1936) 47
Thompson, J. Lee 171
Three Hats For Lisa (1965) 200
Tommy (1975) 162, 211, 228, 229–30, 231, 232, 234
Tommy Steele Story, The (1957) 172, 174–6, 179
Tommy The Toreador (1959) 176, 185
Toomorrow (1970) 223
Top Of The Pops 222, 253
Topsy-Turvy (1999) 159, 160, 251–2
Toye, Wendy 104
'trad' jazz 195–7
Train, Jack 91
Trainspotting (1995) 220, 241
Trinder, Tommy 88, 90, 94–6, 111, 223
Trottie True (1949) 114, 117–21
Trouble Brewing (1939) 59, 63
Turner, Tina 229
Tutin, Dorothy 160, 161
Two A Penny (1967) 192, 195

Under New Management (1946) 115
Under The Greenwood Tree (1929) 31, 42, 108
United Artists 206, 209

Valentine, Dickie 165, 179
Vance, Alfred 94
Van Heusen, Jimmy 116
Variety Jubilee (1943) 104
Vaughan Williams, Ralph 1, 107
Vaughn, Frankie 149, 179
Vera-Ellen 149, 151, 152, 153

Walker, Norman 111, 112
Walton, William 1, 107, 110
Waltzes From Vienna (1934) 46, 66
Watkins, Peter 211
Webber, Andrew Lloyd 218, 249
We'll Meet Again (1942) 98–101, 102, 103, 134
We'll Smile Again (1943) 138
Western Electric 24, 29
What A Crazy World (1963) 200
When Knights Were Bold (1936) 47
Who, The 224, 228, 230, 231, 235
White, Onna 215, 216, 217
Whitfield, David 165
Wilcox, Herbert 7, 30, 43, 44, 46–7, 71, 85, 110, 115, 122, 142, 149, 160, 161, 163–5, 179
Wilde, Marty 200
Wilding, Michael 122
Williams, Paul 232
Wilson, Anthony 253, 254
Wilson, Sandy 227
Winner, Michael 199
Winterbottom, Michael 253
Wisdom, Norman 8, 149, 166
Wolfenden Report 177
Woods, Harry 39, 68
Wonderful Life (1964) 181, 192–5

Young Ones, The (1962) 6, 181, 183, 185, 186–90

Zappa, Frank 224